The Tourist City

EDITED BY

DENNIS R. JUDD AND SUSAN S. FAINSTEIN

Yale University Press   New Haven and London

Published with assistance from the Louis Stern Memorial Fund.

Designed by James J. Johnson and set in Aster Roman type by Running Feet Books, Morrisville, North Carolina.
Printed in the United States of America.

Credits: P. 5: Reprinted, with permission, James C. Stevenson, © 1965 from the New Yorker Collection. All rights reserved. / Pp. 8, 15, 29, 32, 48, 57, 84, 97, 132, 148, 149, 172, 209, 217, 236, 251, 265: Corel Photo Studio. These images are protected by the copyright laws of the U.S., Canada and elsewhere. Used under license. / Pp. 112, 118: Las Vegas News Bureau / Pp. 130, 162: Tammy Kim / Title page and pp. 164, 168: Bruce Ehrlich / P. 191: Lily J. Hoffman / P. 203: M. Aharoni, Pantomap Ltd., Jerusalem

Library of Congress Cataloging-in-Publication Data

The tourist city / edited by Dennis R. Judd and Susan S. Fainstein.
        p.   cm.
    Includes bibliographical references and index.
    ISBN 0-300-07405-0 (cloth : alk. paper).—
ISBN 0-300-07846-3 (paper)

    1. Tourist trade. 2. Tourist trade and city planning. 3. City promotion. I. Judd, Dennis R. II. Fainstein, Susan S.
G155.A1P538   1999
338.4'791—dc21   98-42139

A catalogue record for this book is available from the British Library.

The paper in this book meets the guidelines for permanence and durability of the Committee on Production Guidelines for Book Longevity of the Council on Library Resources.

10 9 8 7 6 5 4 3 2 1

The Tourist City

Contents

Part III. Converting Cities into Tourist Sites

Part IV. Tourism Strategies

SUSAN S. FAINSTEIN AND

DENNIS R. JUDD

Global Forces, Local Strategies, and Urban Tourism

Travel is as old as humanity, but mass tourism has a much more recent vintage, originating in the railroad excursions and Cook's Tours of the mid-nineteenth century. At the time Thomas Cook, the founder of the travel agency bearing his name, began offering "packages" of organized visits to shops and historical places; eventually he had led more than a million people on trips to cities and sights all over Europe.[1] During subsequent years new transportation technologies made travel ever cheaper and more flexible. After the railroad had greatly broadened the market, the automobile further revolutionized travel by giving tourists the ability to choose destinations virtually at will. Later, jet planes allowed middle-income people to move long distances in remarkably brief periods of time. Even more recently, computerized reservation systems have permitted the efficient management of hundreds of millions of journeys. At the end of the twentieth century, travel to distant places has become an ordinary experience, taken for granted as a routine part of life. In this way, tourism has shrunk the globe as much as the revolutions in telecommunications and computers.

What transformed mere travelers into tourists was the rise of an industry that defined, organized, and commodified "tourist" experiences. Mass tourism involves more than just the movement of large numbers of people. It encompasses, first, the consumption of a complex array of tangible goods, including souvenirs, food and drink, rental cars and jets, plus physical facilities in the form of lodges, hotels, and convention centers. The industry also is made possible by and sustains a large number of occupations, such as waiter, reservations clerk, tour guide, and booking agent. Finally, tourists consume advertising and experience; in this sense travel involves desire and culture as much as it does products and services.[2] Without hotel and restaurant chains, travel agencies, steamship lines, officially designated historical sites, and numerous, recognizable attractions, modern tourism could not possibly exist. Madame Tussaud's Wax Museum, an exhibition of lifelike figures that opened in London in 1835, pioneered the development of wholly manufactured tourism venues.

Over the past half-century tourism has become one of the world's most important economic sectors. Since World War II rising affluence and the growth of a middle class with leisure time produced a vastly expanded market for travel. Advertising, public relations, and television made tourism into as important a component of the good life as cars, clothes, and household appliances. Between 1950 and 1992 international tourism, measured in number of arrivals, expanded at an annual rate of 7.2 percent.[3] In the decade 1980–90 international tourism receipts grew at an annual rate of 9.6 percent, considerably exceeding the rate of growth of world trade as a whole. In 1990 only petroleum, petroleum products, and motor vehicles and parts comprised a higher proportion of the value of world exports.[4] The economies of many countries are more dependent on tourism than even these numbers might suggest: according to the World Tourism Organization, in 1995 the world's overall volume of domestic tourist movements exceeded international tourist arrivals by a factor of ten to one.[5]

Within the United States and Western Europe, the century-long decline in agricultural employment and the more recent and sometimes sudden loss of industrial jobs have forced cities and towns into a desperate struggle for survival. Because tourism is an industry with few barriers to entry and the potential for large returns to investment, even the most unlikely of places are tempted to turn themselves into tourist magnets. The competition among cities has become more frenetic with every passing year. City governments sponsor advertising campaigns, sales missions, and special events, join with property developers in public-private partnerships to build hotels and retail malls, and finance convention centers, arts venues, and sports arenas. Once cities prospered as places of industrial production, and in the industrial era they were engines of growth and prosperity. On the eve of the twenty-first century, they are becoming spaces for consumption in a global economy where services provide the impetus for expansion.

Why Tourism Has Grown

The remarkable boom in tourism results from both the increase in demand and the efforts of suppliers. Tourists travel out of a variety of motives—for pleasure, of course, but also for business or to attend a meeting. Because the reasons for visiting a place intermingle, and the same visitor may combine several different activities—seeing a relative, going to the theater, conducting a business transaction—we do not limit our description of the sector to pleasure travel alone. It is the element of distance from home rather than the visitor's purpose in traveling that establishes tourism as a regional and national export industry. Consequently, we adopt the World Tourism Organization's definition of the tourist, which includes, simply, any person who stays away from home overnight.[6] Because most of the commodities and services purchased by tourists are available to nontourists as well, the boundaries of the supply network are extremely blurred.[7]

Travel and commerce always have been inextricably entwined; thus it can come as no surprise that recent dramatic increases in business travel constitute an important component of modern tourism. The business trip, of course, has a lengthy history, starting with the advent of long-distance trading and colonization.[8] In the first part of the twentieth century, changes in the organization of industry, including the clustering of wholesale and retail trade at a distance from manufacturing locations and the rise of the branch plant, heightened the need for travel by executives and sales representatives. Recently, as firms have decentralized, downsized, and contracted out production, different parts of the same corporation and networks of suppliers are scattered across the globe. Customers likewise are dispersed worldwide.

Coordination of production, supervision of local managers, design of new facilities, meetings with consultants, purchasing of supplies, product servicing, and marketing—all require visits from company officials, technicians, or sales personnel. Within large corporations, meetings are often held outside company walls so that employees who work in different localities can come together for training, strategic planning, and motivational development. These meetings are usually held in cities. A consultant's report explains: "You can pay less having a meeting at a resort than at a downtown hotel, but you don't do it because of the perception [that employees are having too good a time]."[9] Telecommunications, rather than making travel superfluous, has enabled people to carry on their jobs away from their workplaces. Although business travelers do not constitute a majority of tourists, their spending power, backed by company expense accounts, has enormously broadened the market for travel services. Moreover, business travel, because of the concentration of offices in metropolitan areas and, still to a great degree, within city centers, contributes especially to urban tourism.

The thickening of linkages among people around the world through shared publications, the Internet, immigration, the prevalence of English as a second language, and a common discourse around interests that transcend local, and even national, boundaries has intensified, rather than diminished, the desire for face-to-face contact. Conventions and conferences bring together individuals sharing an astonishing variety of avocational, business, and professional interests, ranging from science fiction and stamp collecting enthusiasts, to auto and home-furnishings merchants, to Apple computer users, cardiologists, and political scientists. Participants in these events often, like business travelers, enjoy the benefits of expense accounts. Such meetings take place outside as well as within cities, but cities offer unrivaled groupings of amenities, accommodations, economic and cultural activities, and meeting venues.

Place marketing has added to the allure of tourism. Places constitute the essence of the tourist experience, and they are therefore the basic products of the industry. It is rarely self-evident that a location must be visited; thus, some significance must be assigned to it that invests it with importance: "Many attractions are unrecognizable as such except for one crucial element—the markers: these are any information or representation that labels a site as a sight."[10]

Cities are sold just like any other consumer product. They have adopted image advertising, a development that can hardly escape any traveler who opens an airline magazine and reads its formulaic articles on the alleged culinary and cultural delights of Dallas, Frankfurt, or Auckland. Each city tries to project itself as a uniquely wonderful place to visit, where an unceasing flow of events constantly unfolds, a process Holcomb describes in this volume. The product must plausibly resemble the representation, and thus cities often remake themselves in conformity with their advertised image. If an infrastructure that will attract and nurture the needs of tourists does not already exist, it must be constructed.[11] Since this cannot be left to chance, governments are inevitably involved in coordinating, subsidizing, and financing the transformation of the urban environment.

"The town <u>has</u> no history, Signore. It was built from scratch three years ago, entirely for the tourist trade."

The Ecology of Urban Tourism

The three elements of urban tourism—the tourist, the tourism industry, and cities—interact to produce a complex ecological system. The tastes and desires of tourists are fickle; just like car buyers, they will yearn for next year's model even before it appears. With the entry of transnational corporations, plus the globalization of credit, media, and electronic communications, the tourist industry is in the midst of a revolution in which images, information, and money are transmitted at lightning speed. The object of the chase, the tourist, is a moving target. To appeal to tourists, cities must be consciously molded to create a physical landscape that tourists wish to inhabit. No city can afford to stand still for a moment, no matter how much it has recently done or how much money it has spent doing it. The constant transformation of the urban landscape to accommodate tourists has become a permanent feature of the political economy of cities.

The Tourist

Some years back, the author of a book called *The Tourist* noted, in a laconic, scholarly tone, that "it is intellectually chic nowadays to deride tourists."[12] It would probably be safe to say that it has *always* been chic to deride tourists. The adventure and travel literature is an especially rich source of derogatory comments. For example, Paul Theroux's *The Pillars of Hercules,* an account of his modern-day Grand Tour around the shores of the Mediterranean, begins: "People here in Western Civilization say that tourists are no different from apes, but on the Rock of Gibraltar, one of the Pillars of Hercules, I saw both tourists and apes together, and learned to tell them apart. . . . The apes are better mannered than the tourists, and while the tourists brutalized and screamed at their kids, the apes were tender towards their young. . . . The tourist yakked and giggled, the apes were quiet and thoughtful. The tourists teased the apes, the apes never teased the tourists."[13] Seen through the lens of such invective, we would naturally expect the author to find that tourists despoil everything they touch. On this score Theroux does not disappoint. In his travels around the Mediterranean he discovers two principal kinds of pollution: industrial and touristic. He finds the coastline of Spain marred by vacation condominiums and seedy tourist villages. So notorious are the crowds on the French Riviera that Theroux skips it altogether, acknowledging it merely with a snide comment.

The relationship between visitor and visited, however, is both more ambiguous and more positive than such typical critiques suggest.[14] In fact, as Daniel Hiernaux-Nicolas notes in this volume, the developers of Cancún perceived tourism as an instrument for improving relations among nations. Nonetheless, one does not have to adopt Theroux's view to recognize that tourists do change the places they visit, often negatively.[15]

Tourists seek distraction from the ordinary experiences of everyday life. Escape may take the form of contrived diversion and amusement, so families visit Disney World,[16] Disneyland Paris, and their lesser ilk, go to the Mall of America, or seek specialized diversions like Planet Hollywood. As described by Parker in this volume, Las Vegas explicitly advertises itself as a fake neon city, and hundreds of thousands of people flock

there every year precisely because it delivers on its promise. But tourists
do not always want to be humored or amused. Instead, they often seek
immersion in the daily, ordinary, *authentic* life of a culture or place that
is not their own.[17] Thus, the tourism industry is preoccupied with shaping and responding to the desire for carnival-like diversion, on the one
hand, and a yearning for extraordinary, but "real," experience on the
other.

Tourism is divided up into well-defined circuits. Even when not traveling, people know the places they might visit and the sights at which
they might look. The habit of visiting the familiar sites that define the
tourism circuits gave rise to the expression "Been there, done that." The
experiences and places marking these established routes are constructed through signs and signifiers that name and enshrine particular places as sacred objects of the tourist ritual.[18] In this way the tourist
is taught how to "gaze" upon the object or place being visited. People
are, in effect, coached on how to become a tourist: "Such gazes cannot
be left to chance. People have to learn how, when and where to 'gaze.'
Clear markers have to be provided, and in some cases the object of the
gaze is merely the marker that indicates some event or experience which
previously happened at that spot."[19] The media and electronic communication have, in effect, made the entire globe into a potential object of
the tourist gaze.

A city that tries to build an economy based on tourism must project
itself as "a dreamscape of visual consumption."[20] People expect to experience the heritage, architecture, and culture that make up a city's essence. A construction of any version of a city's heritage requires large
doses of "mythology, folk memory, and popular fantasy."[21] Within cities,
spaces or monuments like the Eiffel Tower, Tower Bridge, or the Vatican,
to name just a few, become identified as official tourist attractions.[22]
Such places are "famous for being famous"; the "sacred objects" that
make up a circuit of urban tourism, a circuit so well fixed in the popular mind that "most people living in the west would hope to see some of
these objects during their lifetime."[23]

The icons of the urban tourism circuit take a variety of forms. In resort cities like Cancún or Las Vegas, which lack a marketable historic
past, a tourism infrastructure is constructed out of whole cloth. In those
cities, themed environments have emerged that owe more to Disneyland
and Disney World than to urban history or culture. By contrast, in older
cities heritage and an architecture signifying the past provide the prin-

Night view beneath the Eiffel Tower, Paris

Erected for the Paris Exposition of 1889, the Eiffel Tower is one of tourism's most widely recognized icons.

cipal motifs for place marketing. These tourist-historic cities possess a huge advantage in heritage marketing; indeed, such cities as Jerusalem and Prague—both of which are described in this book—or Athens, Paris, and Beijing occupy an exclusive urban tourism circuit, and no amount of advertising or reconstruction can place a new city on it.

The port and industrial cities that slid into an economic decline some years ago have formed another, quite specialized circuit that trades on images of a prosperous past. Portions of the history and architecture left over from the commercial and industrial glory days have become converted into vehicles for nostalgic versions of a bygone era. "Industrial archeology" now exceeds manufacturing in economic importance within Great Britain, and no doubt in some other places as well.[24] One author's description of the "Rye [England] Town Model" captures the sometimes ludicrous quality of this transformation: "The Rye Town Model showed how you could turn almost anything that didn't work into a museum piece. Its most startling application came up during the miners' strike of 1984, in a parliamentary debate on pit closures. One Conservative member saw no problem: it was easy, he said—just close the unproductive pits and reopen them as museums. Redundant miners could be retrained as tour guides and conduct coach parties down the shafts, through the tunnels and round the exhausted coalfaces. It struck me as a weird vision. The miners, presumably, would have their faces artfully blacked with greasepaint, wear Davy lamps and carry canaries around in cages."[25]

In areas fortunate enough to have escaped the urban renewal bulldozer, historic districts have evolved from renovated waterfronts, railway stations, factory and loft buildings, and residential neighborhoods. Where large port and industrial cities that have experienced massive decline cannot be wholly reclaimed, carefully bounded districts have been set aside as "tourist bubbles" (as Judd calls them in Chapter 3) isolated from surrounding areas of decay. Within these districts, historic and architecturally significant structures are integrated with a new generation of tourist facilities that, instead of evoking images of an urban golden age, are quite contemporary. The new urban tourism typically superimposes onto the template of old streets and buildings various combinations of festival markets and shopping districts, arcades and atriums, sports stadiums, pedestrian malls, and, in some cases, gaming casinos.

What these variations of the tourist city have in common is that they try to anticipate the tourist's desire for the extraordinary and the unusual. Tourist spaces are designed to produce "liminal moments" that lift the tourist above ordinary, everyday experience. This is as true for shoppers experiencing the "depthless consumption" offered by the West Edmonton Mall as it is for the people staring in wonder at the Mona Lisa in the Louvre.[26] Both are "sites of carefully contrived consumption and excitement, often involving controlled relaxation of normal social behaviour."[27]

The Industry

A vast network of institutions has evolved to supply products, services, and experiences to travelers and tourists. The industry's major institutions include, among others, airline companies, city governments, hotel operators, auto rental companies, and banks offering specialized financial services. Within cities, the supply system is made up of a complex matrix of international chains and local businesses—restaurants, bars, music clubs, sports stadiums, souvenir shops. Between these suppliers and the traveling public a group of intermediaries—principally package-tour operators, travel agents, and meetings managers—act as go-betweens, supplying the grease to keep the tourist system running smoothly.

Except for tour operators and the businesses that provide holiday and tour packages, few tourism entrepreneurs distinguish among tourists on the basis of their motivation. Regardless of whether their purpose is to take a vacation, conduct business, attend conferences, or see relatives, different kinds of visitors are likely to use the same facilities and exert similar effects on the local economy. As Hoffman and Musil point out in their essay on Prague, much of the boost to that city's tourism industry resulted from visits by business travelers exploring new opportunities in Eastern Europe. In their essay, Ehrlich and Dreier make similar assertions about Boston.

The tourism industry is rapidly becoming better organized. Multinational conglomerates shape the industry and wholly dominate parts of it. Airlines, which are the largest suppliers of tourist services, have gone through a global consolidation.[28] Increasingly, they have established their own package-tour bureaus, which coordinate ground transportation and rental cars, hotel and resort stays, and tourist events. Hotel companies, travel agencies, and tour operators have either been brought under the umbrella of transnational corporations or are plugged into integrated electronic booking systems that favor large firms. Consolidators act as wholesalers of vacation packages to travel agents, and a few large travel agencies like American Express and Thomas Cook play dominant roles in identifying places to visit and ways of getting there. Planners of conventions and meetings constitute an organized group and put pressure on cities to underbid each other in order to attract trade shows and conferences.

Cities

Local boosters realize that they must do more than merely shape the images that tourism entrepreneurs sell. The must also "adapt the 'product' . . . to be more desirable to the 'market.'"[29] Some cities possess qualities that make them an easy sell, while others must undergo not only a change of image but a facelift if they are to be competitive.

Cities vary significantly in their capacity to absorb tourists. The great cities of the world evolved as places of commerce and trade and also as centers of religious, military, cultural, and political power. Today, the signs and signifiers of urban power and culture in these historically dominant places have become commodified as the tourist attractions that make up what might be labeled the "empire city" circuit. European cities of this type were the main itineraries on the Grand Tour of the seventeenth and eighteenth centuries, with Rome as the most sacred site of all. If a locale is invested with enough historical and cultural significance, tourists will bear considerable inconvenience to get there, and advertising is not even necessary. The Parthenon is overrun not only with tourists but with surly guards and aggressive hustlers. Rome is a beautiful city filled with the treasures of antiquity; but its streets are dirty, traffic is perpetually snarled, and crime is a constant worry. In Jerusalem the visitor runs the risk of being caught within the crossfire of civil war. The examples multiply; the point is that these cities do not need to achieve a Disneyland-like sense of cleanliness and order to attract tourists. They possess a sort of "place luck" in the same way that cities with deep harbors became trading centers in the era of seaborne commerce.

Cities that lie outside this orbit must take steps to transform themselves into tourist sites. Virtually all the second-tier cities of the industrial age possess interesting architecture and a marketable past, but much of the built environment that signifies their past was abandoned and left to dereliction or renewed into oblivion decades ago. These cities have been forced to construct a new narrative of regeneration and a physical infrastructure that evokes that narrative.

In the 1980s some cities managed to make a smooth transition from industrial wasteland to tourist mecca. Magazines and Sunday supplements regularly featured positive stories about the revitalization of these "livable cities"—in 1989, for example, *Newsweek* identified the "hot" cities that combined renovated neighborhoods, culture, a downtown renaissance, good jobs, and other amenities.[30] Yet, despite the emergence of this "good news" genre of reporting, sustaining a narrative of regeneration has not been easy, and there continue to be serious setbacks. The portrayal of regeneration stands in contradiction to an older, well-established discourse of urban decline that has been given renewed life in recent decades. Since the presidential race of 1964, Republican candidates have employed a code language that equates liberal ideology with negative images of cities: terms such as *ghetto, welfare, the underclass, crime,* and *inner city* have been utilized to play upon the racial fears and resentments of suburbanites and Sunbelt Republicans.[31] Americans have become accustomed to thinking in dichotomies—city/suburban, black/white, poor/affluent, crime/safety—that cast cities in a dismal light.[32] In the face of a nightly local news report that feeds upon lurid stories of murder, mayhem, and drugs in the inner city, it is not easy for tourism entrepreneurs to project an image of central cities as places of leisure and play.

The construction of tourist enclaves, which is the typical method of allaying the sense of threat, creates a sharply segmented urban space in the places that have been converted from sites of production to sites of consumption. The urban landscape comes to consist of fragments of development, each offering a scenic view or a set-piece tableau meant to evoke a romanticized version of urban life or the past; the resulting patchwork "reduces a city to a map of tourist attractions."[33] In developing countries, the differences between affluent tourists and local residents is extreme, and it is highlighted by the "opulent and highly capitalized" nature of the resort developments.[34] Within the older cities of wealthy nations, the juxtaposition can seem almost as sharp, and the result of all these efforts at transforming the city for the purpose of tourism promotion can be a numbing sameness.

Standardization

The globalization of mass tourism leads to an odd paradox: whereas the appeal of tourism is the opportunity to see something different, cities that are remade to attract tourists seem more and more alike. The multinational firms that supply the convention hotels, chain restaurants, and retail establishments follow a corporate model, resulting in the seemingly endless proliferation of atrium lobbies, formulaic restaurants, and chrome-and-glass boutiques selling identical merchandise. The wholesale procurers of tourism services (tour packagers and meetings organizers) also are a force for standardization. In spite of the growth of ecotourism and more individualized vacations, the pressure of handling large numbers of people and the efficiencies that can be achieved by selling a uniform product motivate suppliers to provide standardized services and facilities. Consequently, all over the world high-end tourist facilities share a remarkable similarity: the Oberoi in Katmandu, the Taj in Delhi, the Ramada in Amsterdam, the Hyatt in Washington, are virtually indistinguishable, as are the historic structures converted to festive malls. Even Bohemian milieus seem imitative of one another—the Left Bank in Paris, New York's East Village, London's Camden Locks—all boast similar cafés, galleries, and street vendors. Cities seemingly would gain by distinguishing themselves from their competitors, but their civic leaders and their tourism entrepreneurs either fear to break the mold that resulted in apparent success elsewhere or cannot envision anything different.

The imprint of tourism development does not, of course, constitute the only force shaping the contemporary city. History, culture, and social division all leave their imprint. Nevertheless, the impact of tourism on most cities is instantly recognizable and is probably more widespread than that of other industries. The great size of the industry and the fact that hardly a place has failed to enter the tourism sweepstakes means that it differs from, say, heavy manufacturing or finance in the extent of its influence (although these sectors, where they do exist, probably surpass tourism as a force for imposing likeness among places). Cities like San Antonio, Texas, or Brisbane, Australia, which never had much manufacturing and lack an extensive financial industry, can successfully compete with much larger and more complex metropolises for tourist spending. Consequently, they boast the same Hyatts and Marriotts as Dallas or Sydney and come to have an economic base that is largely tourism-dependent. Their ability to attract vacationers and conventioneers, however, has not crowded older cities with more diverse economies out of the market.

As well as deploying a similar set of spatial arrangements, cities have adopted a relatively small number of marketing strategies. They rely on contrived promotional events associated with their status as the European "city of culture" for a year or the host of the Olympics, the World Student Games, the World Cup, or the Superbowl. Cities sponsor music or culinary festivals and blockbuster art exhibits. Vertical banners advertise these big events, and there are the inevitable tie-ins with restaurants and shops, the marketing of T-shirts and coffee mugs—anything to entice the tourist not just to visit but to buy.

For, quintessentially, the tourist is a consumer away from home. Tourism depends on the commodification of leisure. The viewing of a harbor or a walk through downtown is insufficient as a tourist experience. Rather, satisfaction for the visitor and profit for the investor require that place become transformed into an object. The tourist's gaze composes the urban landscape into a collage of frozen images. Photography is a perfect expression of this process: "To photograph is in some way to appropriate the object being photographed. . . . To have visual knowledge of an object is in part to have power, even if only momentarily, over it."[35]

Similarly, the act of buying a souvenir condenses a city into a thing now possessed and owned. Just as snapping a picture captures a fleeting moment, buying something transcends the transient act of shopping and promises the prolongation of pleasure. Each time a person sees the buyer in a T-shirt proclaiming "Planet Hollywood—Sydney" and exclaims, "Oh! Were you there?" or admires the tasteful Balinese sculpture displayed in the traveler's living room, the experience can be relived. Even when the commodity is a dress or a scarf that does not proclaim the place it was acquired, it retains its original associations in the memory of the wearer. If given as a gift, the object becomes the vehicle for sharing the pleasure of travel, the assurance that the recipient, though out of sight, was not out of mind. From the point of view of city governments, local retailers and product manufacturers, this form of objectification is far more valuable than a thousand photographs of their beloved city, for unlike a paper image, it offers that much vaunted economic multiplier that is the raison d'être of city marketing.

Tourists consume both standard products and unique creations. At its most vulgar, marketing to travelers occurs in the "tourist trap," purveying mass-produced cedar boxes embossed with place names, emblematic statuary, and souvenir key chains; in its more refined manifestations, it gives rise to the specialty boutiques of the festive malls,

The House of Parliament and Big Ben, London

Heritage, architecture, and symbol combine in this famous neo-Gothic attraction (built between 1840 and 1860) on the tourist circuit.

artisans, and museum stores. The limits of tourism consumption seem unreachable. The best example of the extraordinary elasticity of demand for souvenirs is the Disney empire. Despite the existence of Disney stores in shopping centers everywhere, visitors to the parks, where every theme component but the actual rides is really a store, queue up to buy the same articles they can buy right at home—Mickey Mouse watches, ties, socks, and shorts, Daffy Duck fountain pens. The remembered fact of acquisition at the hallowed site invests the purchase with singularity despite its commonplace character.

This process is a fundamental feature of all tourist venues. Outside Cairns, Australia, a quaint scenic railroad transports tourists up a mountain to an "authentic aborigine village" called Kuranda. In the village, shoppers wander among several markets, where they can purchase sweaters, jewelry, food, leather goods, and home furnishings. Most of the products are mass-produced in China, Malaysia, or other low-wage countries, and even the few handmade objects are crude. When not shopping, the tourists can buy a ticket to a butterfly museum or watch native dancers put on a music hall–type show. The sum of their interaction with aboriginal culture is the act of purchase, which, possibly, might assist in preserving native communities.

Travel seems to remove the constraints that normally prompt people to restrict their consumption. Tourists often buy diamond rings and expensive sweaters at full list price in the duty-free malls that have taken over the terminals of international airports. They procure handwoven shawls and socks with iconic pictures knit into them. They add the hundredth T-shirt to their collection. The drive to acquire roars on, propelled by the desire to make the fleeting experiences of tourism real and material.

Sameness and Diversity

Despite the rise of mass tourism and the globalization of the tourism industry, local characteristics do persist. Even as they seem to be becoming more alike, cities remain differentiated. Tourist locales are occupied by real people leading their daily lives. As such, they retain a subjectivity that cannot be reduced, in the end, only to objects of the tourist gaze or products of the tourist industry. As a consequence of the intermixture of the global and the local, any attempt to capture the essence of urban tourism is difficult. The structure of the industry and the types of tourism can be described in broad terms. The standardization of the tourist product likewise allows generalization. But the variation in the impacts of tourism and its multiple meanings, depending on type of tourist and context, call for an examination of individual cases. In this volume we seek to combine the large picture and the close view by including essays that describe the nature of urban tourism in general as well as essays that capture the nuances of individual cities. In our concluding essay we address some key questions that arise from the chapters considered as a whole. These include:

- What are the spatial components of the tourist city? How much variation is there?

- How should we evaluate the effects of urban tourism on local populations? Do citizens benefit from tourist amenities, and is there equitable access to facilities? Does tourism maintain or undermine the local culture? Do tourist and indigenous uses support one another and intermix, or does the tourist bubble constitute an isolated, secured fortress for outsiders? Is the relationship between residents and visitors respectful, or does it demean the providers?

This last group of questions about the local impacts of urban tourism is of special concern. The same answers will not fit all tourist cities. As the studies that make up this volume reveal, tourism assumes various guises when filtered through the lens of local culture and context. In this way global forces are reduced to human scale.

Part I

The Political Economy of Tourism

SUSAN S. FAINSTEIN AND

DAVID GLADSTONE

Evaluating Urban Tourism

It is said that novels have only two plots: a stranger comes to town, or someone goes on a journey. Each of these story lines revolves around travel and resonates with the possibilities of change and the unknown. Though perhaps overly facile when applied to literature, the witticism points to a particularly consequential characteristic of the tourism industry—its function as a vehicle for fantasy and personal growth. Of course, tourism promoters are not unique in offering transformation to those who partake of its offerings—the marketers of cosmetics, movies, even home furnishings, promise their consumers the consummation of a vision of an idealized life. More than these other industries, however, tourism has a genuine potential to deliver on its promises: travel can change the spiritual as well as the physical existence of both visitor and host. Even the packaged tour, the business trip, and the stay in a standard hotel represent a break from routine and the possibility for new experience. Consequently, evaluations of tourism's urban consequences must explore its symbolic aspects.

At the same time, analyses restricted to just the symbolic domain of tourism evade economic issues. Far more than art or literature, which, of course, also constitute industries, tourism is a significant component of the economic base of cities; in fact, in places like Las Vegas and Cancún it may be the chief element. Capitalists within the tourism industry, in combination with public officials, are the primary creators and reproducers of tourist attractions. As part of the development and marketing process, a locale must convey something seemingly out of the ordinary to fulfill its economic purpose of drawing people to it; at the same time tourists need to be reassured that they will feel safe and comfortable in a given location. The result is the paradoxical creation of the tourist space, in which visitors experience simultaneously novelty and familiarity, excitement and security.[1] The outcome of this effort determines the fate of large numbers of workers employed in the tourist industry and related services. In addition, its molding of urban space affects peripheral industries, whose access to the city and to work opportunities is channeled by tourism investment.

Tourism is therefore a cultural commodity that contains both material and nonmaterial dimensions. The former comprise both direct (job and revenue creation) and indirect outcomes (social structure, opportunities foregone, access to the city). Symbolic consequences include the creation and promotion of urban tourist sights and the significance these hold for the consciousness of visitor and visited alike. In this chapter, we show how the symbolic and material aspects of tourism interact and are in tension, with consequences that make any unqualified assertion concerning tourism's value extremely problematic.

Regeneration through Tourism

Despite the fanfare associated with festival retailing throughout the United States and "heritage" creation in Britain, tourist-related development remains a contested area of central-city regeneration efforts. Proponents argue that jobs in tourism are relatively cheap to create and that the industry spurs economic development through strong multiplier effects, improves a city's aesthetic and built environment, and enhances leisure facilities for residents.[2] In addition, advocates point to the lack of alternatives in developing a sound urban economic base: unless cities compete for tourist dollars (tourism is, allegedly, the world's fastest-growing industry), they stand a good chance of losing out in an increasingly competitive global environment.[3]

Opponents of tourism development contend that its potential as an engine of growth falls far short of the claims that have been made. They point out that imitations of widely publicized festival marketplaces in Boston or Baltimore do not necessarily work in other cities.[4] For example, imitative central-city retail markets in Toledo, Ohio, Richmond, Virginia, and St. Louis, Missouri, failed to meet projected visitor flows and incurred substantial losses.[5] Likewise the impact of convention centers has frequently fallen short of projections; even so, increased competition means that cities must continually expand their convention facilities simply to maintain their position.[6] Even when tourism facilities do produce a positive cash flow, many of the gains are plowed back into further support of the industry.

Tourism has significant impact on urban form. The spatial organization of tourist-destination cities differs from the older industrial cities that have specialized historically in producer services, distribution, and manufactured goods. Whereas warehousing and goods production activities were clustered around the ports of old industrial centers, luxury hotels and high-end residential buildings usually line the waterfronts of contemporary tourist cities. Their core tends to be dominated by retail and entertainment facilities rather than office uses, and centrally located working-class residential districts are a rarity. Consequently the city center belongs to affluent visitors rather than to residents, resulting in the exclusion of working-class residents from the core. Although tourist areas are heavily patrolled against "undesirables," other parts of the city are often allowed to deteriorate and become centers of criminal activity, anomic, and physical decay.[7]

Ironically, many of the components of tourism-related restructuring of cities have occurred as a response to earlier attacks on large-scale bulldozer renewal.[8] In the 1960s urban social movements mobilized to stop the destruction of housing and to demand support for cultural facilities and conservation of historic neighborhoods. At the same time intellectuals like Jane Jacobs were calling for a sensitivity to small-scale, textured urban environments. The combination of street protests and the formulation of a coherent rationale for preservationism resulted in a number of victories that safeguarded areas that subsequently became magnets for tourism.[9] Local activists in New York, for example, fought to protect the cast-iron factory buildings in New York's SoHo district from demolition to make room for a highway, and their counterparts in San Francisco struggled to keep the city's Victorian homes from being replaced with modern multifamily housing.[10] Their successes, however, did not preserve the industries and communities that had occupied these buildings.

In tandem with providing new facilities for conventioneers and sports fans, city governments promoted arts districts and historic areas as well as retail malls that simultaneously evoked and sanitized the variety of the old downtowns. Once formerly disparaged structures revealed their potential for commodification, as articulated in spiraling property values and the displacement of marginal businesses and low-income occupants, major developers began to see the promise of historic preservation, arts-related development, and adaptive reuse. They used artists as stalking horses for gentrifiers and exploited ethnic neighborhoods for the local color that large-scale, modernist developments so glaringly lacked.[11] The resultant mixture constituted the new tourist zone and drew a new chorus of disapprobation from some of the same forces that previously had tried to block wholesale redevelopment.

Tourism Urbanization

Our discussion until now has indicated the effects of tourism—namely the distribution of jobs, income, and control of space—on existing populations with a defined class structure. In specialized tourist locations like Venice or Cancún, however, its effects are formative. Rather than distributing costs and benefits among existing groups, it is the prime determinant of the social structure. Mullins, in a pioneering examination of Australia's Gold Coast, investigated the class structure of an urban area devoted mainly to tourism. Surprisingly, rather than finding a shrinking middle class and domination by large corporations, he discovered a growing petit bourgeoisie.[12] His study lends weight to a view that tourism urbanization, because of ease of entry by small suppliers, can contribute to an expanding middle class.

The Australian Gold Coast, however, is probably not typical of tourism urbanization. Certainly it differs in its development from the vast leisure complexes of Las Vegas and Orlando, which are dominated by large hotel and gaming corporations. Control of the casino industry in Las Vegas, for instance, has shifted since the 1960s from individual families and organized crime to corporate capital.[13] In Disney World, the Disney Corporation has total control of all aspects of development.[14] Moreover, even in the Australian Gold Coast, despite its more egalitarian ownership structure, wage workers in the tourism industry are disproportionately drawn from immigrant and other low-income groups.[15]

Judging the Outcomes

Tourism represents one of a relatively small number of economic development strategies available to urban regimes. Moreover, ordinary residents have often benefited from tourism-related investment, both financially and through improved amenities.[16] It is therefore simplistic to argue that investment in tourism is a waste of government funds or that it necessarily reinforces social inequity. The distributional outcomes of tourism development in any particular place are, in fact, indeterminate. Whether tourism produces good jobs or bad is not an inherent characteristic of the industry but rather a consequence of how it is structured in a specific location. A given structure depends not just on public policy but also on the mobilization of workers in the industry. The key to the maintenance of labor standards is the development of trade unionism among tourism workers and the creation of benefits pools for employees in seasonal or part-time jobs. The organization of labor thus becomes part of the analysis when investigating the impacts of tourism.[17]

When evaluating public-sector tourism policy from the perspective of social justice, the issues boil down to government's role in fostering fair labor practices, the kind of deal the public sector makes with developers and service providers, and the extent to which policy fosters equitable distribution of the proceeds. Examination of virtually any public policy adopted within a capitalist framework generally finds that the better-off obtained the lion's share of the benefits. Rather than dismissing tourism for producing negative outcomes, its critics would do better to insist that subsidies for tourism promotion be balanced by provisions for higher minimum wages, local participation in the supply of services, and job placement and training programs.

Tourism and Urban Culture

Cultural analysts stress the effects of the tourist industry on spatial form and symbolic referents. Because the commodity it purveys is the quality of the city itself, its connection to urban culture is profound. It is formative in what David Harvey terms the "intimate connection between aesthetic and cultural movement and the changing nature of the urban experience."[18]

The special nature of tourism has made it a significant focus within cultural studies. The intangibility of this particular product means that the tourist experience is largely perceptual. As a result, tourist sites are writ large with signifiers, where the representation (and hence the anticipation) of the experience is at least as important as its actuality.[19] In their famous discussion of the symbolic messages of architectural forms,

Venturi et al. comment on the persuasive functions of tourist-oriented development at the time when the traveler is in motion: "The commercial persuasion of roadside eclecticism provokes bold impact in the vast and complex setting of a new landscape of big spaces, high speeds, and complex programs. Styles and signs make connections among many elements, far apart and seen fast. The message is basely commercial; the context is basically new."[20] Similarly, the ersatz castle of Disney World and even the real Eiffel Tower, that most venerable of tourist icons, convey in shorthand the vast amount of sensations available to be consumed, usually at a price, within the referenced space. The tourist landscape heightens reality, so that, according to Debord, each activity "is supposed to offer a dramatic shortcut to the long-awaited promised land of total consumption."[21]

Cultural analysis broadens the range of indicators by which to assess tourism's impact, causing sign value, however subjective as a consideration, to become central to evaluation: "Commodification is the process by which objects and activities come to be evaluated *primarily* in terms of their *exchange value* in the context of trade, in addition to any *use-value* that such commodities might have. . . . But . . . when one conceptualizes tourism as commodity, this meaning has to be extended to include at least one other value as well: sign-value."[22] Sign, rather than constituting simply an epiphenomenal consequence of material transactions and economic relations, itself becomes a source of value.

If we take seriously the importance of sign value, then certain aspects of the interaction between tourism development and urban structure come to the fore. These can be summarized under two headings: first, the creation of the fortified city, its cultural meaning, and its social effects; and, second, commodification, the fabrication of a false authenticity, and consciousness.

The Fortified City

Tourism promoters have reacted to the geographic proximity of tourist districts and impoverished, high-crime areas by constructing defensible spaces.[23] Rather than being woven into the existing urban fabric, hotel and convention facilities, sports stadiums, restaurant districts, and downtown shopping malls are cordoned off and designed to cosset the affluent visitor while simultaneously warding off the threatening native. Private police, video surveillance, and architectural design all work to keep undesirables out of touristic "compounds" and "reserves." This militarization and privatization of urban space has reached its extreme in the United States, Brazil, and many poor countries. It is less obvious—and less needed—in nations with greater income equality. It culminates in real estate developments like the Renaissance Center in downtown Detroit and the exclusive resort hotels of the Caribbean. These physical structures are closed off from working-class neighborhoods by freeway moats (and even literal moats), walls, and open spaces.

Virtually all the analyses of the partition of urban space conclude implicitly or explicitly that it is a bad thing. And, without question, when cultural critics deconstruct the physiognomy of the contemporary U.S. city, discerning beneath its lineaments intolerance and domination, their interpretations reveal considerable unpleasant truths about American society.[24] Spatial segregation does contradict values of diversity and equality. But it also serves to maintain the peace in situations where the underlying social structure could make conflict inevitable. Thus, unless one takes the position that proximity will breed tolerance, one cannot easily call for the elimination of these *cordons sanitaires* without an amelioration of the underlying structural bases of social division. Spatial separation may perpetuate social hostility; depending on the situation, however, it can also mitigate the intensity of that antagonism. Critiques that simply call attention to the function of exclusionism in maintaining an unsatisfactory status quo are generally intended as exposés of systems of domination and subjugation. But a greater integration of space would not attack root causes, though it would, most likely, increase conflict and scare away potential visitors.

Commodification, Authenticity, and Consciousness

According to its critics, the commodification of tourism inhibits an understanding of difference and the self-realization that flows from such a relational insight.[25] Since the tourist experience is contrived, staged authenticity replaces the genuine. At their most extreme, tourist destinations become wholly disattached from their social context, creating a sort of virtual reality in which they constitute reproductions of themselves, as the following description of a street scene in Manhattan illustrates: "People waiting outside the 57th Street Hard Rock Cafe wear clothing purchased from Hard Rock Houston, Atlanta, Cancún, London, Miami, Orlando, or any of the 41 locations worldwide. Their T-shirts and leather jackets are coveted by those standing before and behind them. 'You were at the Hard Rock Maui! What was it like?'"[26]

Ideally, tourism would genuinely enlarge the mind of the traveler by bringing him or her into contact with an authentic "other." Instead, however, tourist locales simply become products to be exchanged within the confines of advanced capitalism; the resulting process inevitably means that "tourism is the chance to go and see what has been made trite."[27] As products, moreover, tourist attractions share a peculiar characteristic with theatrical production: tourism, like the theater, objectifies those who attract the tourist's interest, falsifying their customs and producing within them conflicting attitudes of dependence and resentment.[28] For place is not constituted only by the physical objects that define the environment; the occupants of the tourist space, whether employees or residents, are, in Disney's phrase, "cast members" who provide local color and ambiance. The impact on their lives may be minimal, as residents become the objects of amused glances, or they may be transformative, as when those who have fished for a living turn into tour-boat guides and young girls are sold into prostitution to satisfy the demands of sex tourists.

For most commentators, *inauthentic* is a damning word. Boorstin regards the typical tourist experience as superficial, reflecting the unwillingness of consumers to immerse themselves in other cultures.[29] The image prevails over reality, the historical tableau over actual history, the fake over the original—a phenomenon taken to its extreme in Disneyland and other theme parks.[30] Watson and Kopachevsky argue that mass tourism, by standardizing the experience of travelers, destroys individual thought, choice, and action. The producers of the tourism commodity dominate the relationship with workers and consumers, causing the perversion of local culture, the alienation of the tourist, and a strained social relation between hosts and guests. They conclude that "the often unrecognized consequence of all this is a form of internalized domination that preserves capitalism and its overriding aim: commodification for the maximization of private profit."[31]

Assessing Commodification

The concept of commodification therefore provides a link between cultural analysis, based on an inquiry into patterns of consumption and the diffusion of symbols, and political economy, rooted in an examination of the relation between structures of production and social domination.

South Street Seaport, on the waterfront of the Lower East Side of Manhattan

This themed festival market was constructed in the environs of the Fulton Fish Market.

Commodification refers to the transformation of a good or service into an exchange relationship. The person producing the good or service loses control of his or her work; the purchaser pays for it according to its market value regardless of its use value. Alienation is the outcome of the process. The concept hearkens back to the early Marx, but Marx's focus was on the situation of the worker; in contrast, critiques of tourism dwell on the manipulation of the consumer and of the residents of the place visited. Because the causes of commodification spring from the capitalist drive for profit, they are to be understood through analysis of the political economy; the outcomes of tourism's commodification, however—in particular the degradation of experience arising from inauthenticity and the packaging of leisure—lie at the core of the cultural analysis of tourism.

Commodification is a powerful analysis, but incomplete, since it does not explicitly examine assumptions concerning the production of culture and its connection to social relations in space. Underlying this critique of tourism is an unspecified utopia of unmediated experience controlled by the visitor and visited and a corresponding devaluation of those who achieve pleasure from trips to Disney World or the many Hard Rock Cafes. A thread of moral Puritanism runs through the analysis: real enjoyment should not involve escapism, and self-created entertainment is better than that which is simply purchased and consumed.[32]

Yet, what is the harm? Are the groups herded onto the tourist buses merely exploited victims? Would they be happier, better off, more fulfilled, on their own, dealing with their mislaid luggage and insecurities at negotiating foreign tongues and customs? In a rather odd inversion of conventional morality, the bland and superficial become more highly demonized than the uncomfortable or even the sadistic. Like the Greek tragedians, many cultural critics believe in learning through suffering.

In contrast, however, some theorists (Robert Venturi and Denise Scott Brown are prominent examples) celebrate the meretriciousness of the tourist landscape and accuse its derogators of snobbery. For them the contrived spectacle serves important psychological and social functions; it needs to be understood, not dismissed. Lash and Urry, while not precisely endorsing the tourist scene, seemingly approve of its contemporary evolution. They assert that as economies have moved from the stage of organized to disorganized capitalism, tourism has similarly advanced from the highly organized forms of mass tourism characterizing the postwar period to a more fragmented phase.[33] Building on Giddens's interpretation of "reflexive modernity," they argue that travel and tourism are central elements in the formation of a reflexive consciousness within contemporary North Atlantic rim societies. Tourism involves a "manufactured diversity" corresponding to broad economic changes involving niche marketing and flexible specialization.[34] This pluralistic world requires that individuals constantly respond to and interpret the multitude of signs and images bombarding them. For Lash and Urry, contemporary travelers are more "ironic and cool, self-conscious and role-distanced" than their predecessors.[35] Tourists are not simply manipulated by the purveyors of symbols but choose among them and control their own interpretations. Lash and Urry thus break with earlier critics like MacCannell, who consider the tourist as a deluded consumer chasing a chimerical authenticity.[36] Commodification, by framing and assimilating experience, allows the individual to shape his or her consciousness through choice. Despite the standardization imposed by commodification, it contributes to reflexive modernity precisely because of the distancing it produces between the subject and the object of his or her gaze. In contrast to the authentic or unalienated experience, the touristic production allows the visitor to be both participant and voyeur, engaged and critical, thus preeminently reflexive.[37]

Portrayals of tourism outside the lens of social science point to its paradoxical nature and highlight the difficulty of any simple assessment of its effects. Mary McCarthy's brilliant analysis of Venice captures why the relationship between visitor and visited escapes easy characterization and can be subjected to sharply varying interpretations:

> No stones are so trite as those of Venice, that is, precisely so well worn. It has been part museum, part amusement park, living off the entrance fees of tourists, ever since the early eighteenth century, when its former sources of revenue ran dry. The carnival that lasted half a year was not just a spontaneous expression of Venetian license; it was a calculated tourist attraction. Francesco Guardi's early "views" were the postcards of that period. . . . The Venetian crafts have become sideshows—glass-blowing, bead-stringing, lace-making; you watch the product made, like pink spun sugar at a circus, and bring a sample home, as a souvenir. . . . And there is no use pretending that the tourist Venice is not the real Venice. . . . The tourist Venice *is* Venice: the gondolas, the sunsets, the changing light, Florian's, Quadri's, Torcello, Harry's Bar, Murano, Burano, the pigeons, the glass beads, the vaporetto. Venice is a folding picture-post-card of itself."[38]

McCarthy goes on to ask how Venice transcends its clichés. Ironically her answer is precisely that of commodification—one might say without irony, of an authentic commodification: "But why should it be beautiful at all? why should Venice, aside from its situation, be a place of enchantment? One appears to be confronted with a paradox. A commercial people who lived solely for gain—how could they create a city of fantasy, lovely as a dream or a fairy-tale? This is the central puzzle of Venice, the stumbling-block that one keeps coming up against."[39] She observes that "a wholly materialist city is nothing but a dream incarnate. Venice is the world's unconscious: a miser's glittering hoard, guarded by a beast whose eyes are made of white agate, and by a saint who is really a prince who has just slain a dragon."[40] McCarthy simply ignores the hoary sociological distinction between use and exchange values and accepts that the latter can produce the former, that the human drive for wealth and its symbols is deeply embedded within the subconscious.

The Rialto Bridge (constructed between 1588 and 1591) over the Grand Canal

"The tourist Venice *is* Venice," Mary McCarthy observed. Commodification of the urban environment has nurtured the fantasies of tourists for centuries.

Appropriate Criteria for Judging Tourism

Measurement of the effect of tourism on equity can be achieved in a reasonably objective fashion. Appropriate indicators include the number of jobs directly and indirectly produced; the overall number of jobs going to local people, especially low-income and minorities; the proportion of jobs that lead to advancement; wage levels; and tax revenues contributed to the general fund. Also of importance is the organization of the industry and the ease of entry into it. Are employees represented by unions, and are casual workers able to participate in benefit pools? Does local small business share in the proceeds? Is there a framework for cooperative endeavors so that associations of local businesses can market their products widely, as is done by groups of bed-and-breakfast establishments in various locations? Where multinational corporations dominate management and marketing of enterprises, are franchise opportunities and needed credit available to local entrepreneurs?

Enumerating criteria for judging economic consequences is relatively easy. In contrast, reaching conclusions about the desirability of tourism as it affects culture ultimately boils down to a highly subjective hierarchy of values. In their quick dismissal of mass taste, many cultural critics succumb to snobbism without analyzing whether there is sufficient cause for their disdain. Still, their judgments do raise pertinent and extremely difficult problems. Perhaps the hardest issue lies in how to provide democratic access to extraordinary experience. Inevitably the mass production of touristic phenomena results in the fabrication of ersatz locations ranging from roadside attractions to themed restaurants to urban tourist zones; retaining authenticity requires limiting visits or pricing attractions out of the means of most people. Just as mass-production processes in industry produced the family automobile, they have also generated the standard vacation. Without this widespread availability of a uniform product, most people would be unable to travel at all. Yet, this standardization means that the typical consumer does not experience the exceptional and is led by marketing strategies to falsely believe that he or she is getting all there is to get. The still unspoiled places and the spontaneous interactions with people from other cultures remain reserved for cultural and economic elites.

Although capitalism generates the form of most tourist facilities in the contemporary world, some of the contradictions involved in tourism would also arise under a more egalitarian form of economic organization. Any democratic system, whether capitalist or socialist, would be in danger of overwhelming unique places when attempting to provide exceptional experiences on a large scale. A recent article on Florence reveals the difficulty:

> There is a consensus that something must be done if this small Tuscan city—for centuries an obligatory stop on any respectable Grand Tour of Europe—is to survive the smothering embrace of modern mass tourism. . . . Florentines, whose numbers have dwindled 20 percent over the last decade to 372,000, are finding that they are unevenly matched in any face-off with tourists. Last year, the city welcomed 2.8 million visitors—more than seven tourists for each inhabitant—and that is without counting the millions of day trippers who manage to "do" Florence in the space of a few hours en route, say from Rome to Venice.

"We have a very narrow path we have to tread," Mr. Roggi [a consultant to the city] said. "On one hand, we want to be hospitable: It is our duty to the rest of the world to let people visit the birthplace of modern society. But we also have to keep in mind the needs of Florentines. . . .

"You can't increase supply to meet increased demand," Mr. Roggi said.[41]

Basically, the total of places with genuine historic interest or aesthetic merit is limited, while the numbers intending to see them, particularly during the summer months, are escalating rapidly. The very presence of droves of similarly motivated individuals precludes the sense of discovery that presumably constitutes the goal of every visitor.

Another perplexing question that arises independent of the economic context in which tourism functions has to do with the demystification of fantasy. Tourism depends on exoticism to fulfill the desires of the traveler, but exoticism is almost necessarily fake. The reality of life for the people being visited is just as humdrum as the daily grind from which the tourist is escaping. Tourists, however, receive few benefits from finding that out, and indeed their trips are more enjoyable if they see Paris as populated by lovers or Istanbul as the site of a thousand and one nights of imagined pleasures. To ask that every trip be an anthropological expedition aimed at forming a valid picture of the lives of the natives denies the importance of fantasy for psychic satisfaction. Nevertheless, representing the populations of tourism sites as conforming to the stereotypes of tourists reproduces prejudice, corrupts social life, and robs indigenous groups of their autonomy. Consequently tourism is almost always two-edged; it both enlightens and demeans. Commodification refers to the particular form that tourism takes under capitalism, but the cultural outcomes of standardization and stereotyping associated with it would remain even if capitalism were transcended. In evaluating the effects of tourism we must recognize that some compromise of values is inescapable and that it is necessary to assess each instance situationally.

Because tourism remains one of the few growing industries that can assimilate unskilled labor, it is important to discover those circumstances where, despite the presence of global forces prompting homogenization, equitable paths have been followed. And if one retains the Enlightenment faith that knowing more about the experience of others can, in fact, allow one to transcend the limits of one's personal situation, then one must value tourism as a mode of entertainment that also instructs.

DENNIS R. JUDD

Constructing the Tourist Bubble

Since the early 1980s, cities in the United States have been engaged in a competitive struggle that parallels the railroad wars of more than a century ago, when cities all over the country bid up the price of railroad stocks in an effort to secure connections to an emerging national transportation system. The latest round of competition was ignited when it became clear to central-city mayors that the federal government would no longer help them cope with the economic and fiscal problems brought on by suburbanization and deindustrialization. Upon assuming office in 1981, the Reagan administration moved rapidly to reduce or eliminate all urban policies aimed at helping distressed cities. To make up for the loss of federal funds, President Reagan's first National Urban Policy Report observed, "State and local governments will find it is in their best interests to concentrate on increasing their attractiveness to potential investors, residents, and visitors."[1] After only a brief pause to lobby the federal government to reconsider its withdrawal, local officials began doing what their predecessors had so often done before: they threw themselves into the fray by initiating a major round of local public investment.

The promotion of culture and tourism quickly became a principal component of the new economic development strategy. In assessing their prospects, mayors knew that the central cities would never regain their dominance in manufacturing. They accepted as well the pointlessness of trying to compete head-to-head with suburbs for certain kinds of wholesaling and retailing. In city after city, they therefore aimed at a mix that combined financial, administrative, and professional services—increasingly clustered into a downtown office complex—and a more or less well-defined space composed of facilities and amenities devoted to leisure activities and the tourist trade.[2] Between 1976 and 1986, in the service of the new downtown development strategy, 250 convention centers, sports arenas, community centers, and performing arts facilities were constructed or started, at a cost of more than $10 billion, and over the next decade, the competition continued unabated.[3] This remaking of the physical infrastructure of the urban core has approached, in scale, the restructuring of downtown economies and land use wrought by the massive urban renewal clearance projects of the 1950s and 1960s.[4]

The Tourist Bubble

Cities have been reshaped in fundamental ways. Tourist and entertainment facilities coexist in a symbiotic relationship with downtown corporate towers, often with a substantial spatial overlap: shopping malls, restaurants, and bars cater to tourists as well as to daytime professionals who work downtown and weekend suburban commuters. In many cities, however, a well-defined perimeter separates the tourist space from the rest of the city. Where crime, poverty, and urban decay make parts of a city inhospitable to visitors, specialized areas are established as virtual tourist reservations. These become the public parts of town, leaving visitors shielded from and unaware of the private spaces where people live and work.[5] Baltimore provides an excellent example of a pure tourist space carved out of urban decay. The miles of abandoned, derelict buildings that crowded its harbor as late as the 1970s have given way to the Harborplace development, with its broad marble and stone plazas, fountains, restaurants and bars, aquarium, and the two-block-long translucent pavilions developed by the Rouse Corporation. The 30 million visitors who visit Harborplace each year are conveniently protected from seeing the Baltimore beyond the tourist enclave, the other half of what has been labeled "the two Baltimores."[6] Likewise, Greektown, a two-block-square renovated district in downtown Detroit anchored by an enclosed mall, is an island in a sea of decay.[7] Such areas constitute, in effect, tourist "bubbles"[8] that "envelop the traveler so that he/she only moves inside secured, protected and normalized environments."[9]

Because the centers of most European cities are still vibrant, tourism blends into and becomes a permanent, even mundane feature of everyday life. This is particularly true for the so-called international big league of cities—Paris, London, Rome, Madrid, Athens, Vienna, Munich, Amsterdam, Brussels, Copenhagen, and a few others—all of which offer extraordinary cultural opportunities.[10] Some cities in the United States—notably San Francisco, New York, and Boston—also absorb tourists seamlessly. But where urban decay or social problems cause tourists to regard a city as dangerous or inhospitable, the city government, in partnership with tourism entrepreneurs, constructs places where visitors can find suitable facilities and amenities, in a safe and convenient environment.

For a tourist space to function, the image and the material product must complement each other; the city as a whole is made attractive to the tourist and accessible to the imagination through processes of reduction and simplification."[11] The positive images projected by civic boosters and the advertising firms they hire amount to a coaching process: advertisements and tourist articles (such as those found in trade journals and airline magazines) interpret a city's essence, its history and culture, and tell the tourist what to do, even what to feel.[12] Tourist images invariably invoke a romanticized, nostalgic sense of history and culture. Such impressions are conveyed by photographic or stylized cityscapes composed of famous or architecturally significant mansions, public landmarks, museums, symphony halls, and the like, all set (depending on the geography) within a tableau of scenic vistas, harbors, parks, promenades, oceans, rivers, or distant mountains. Such images trade on a sense of nostalgia for what cities allegedly have been or ought to be. In Britain, the "Great English Cities Promotion" of the late 1980s undertook a successful conversional marketing campaign that capitalized on, rather than ignored, the industrial past. The English Tourist Board promoted thirteen "industrial 'coketowns', with negative, tourist-repellent, images," and repackaged them as places that represented an interesting industrial past.[13] The textile mills of Bradford, Leeds, and Manchester, for instance, were renovated into tourist sites; the pottery ovens of Stoke were refurbished as markets for their goods. In the United States, Lowell, Massachusetts, is the most famous example of this strategy.

For most U.S. cities, the strategy of converting heritage directly into tourist venues involves an intimate flirtation with a problematic past. Although tourist venues are often constructed on sites once devoted to gritty, primary production, such locales are normally rebuilt to project an overtly nostalgic and idealized version of city life. They are intended to summon an unthreatening past evoked by "authentic reproductions" of a working harbor, Main Street, frontier town, or colonial village—not unlike parts of Disney World, with its Fantasyland, Tomorrowland, and Frontierland.[14] The examples abound: South Street Seaport in New York, Liverpool's Albert Docks, Fisherman's Wharf and Ghirardelli Square in San Francisco, and the ubiquitous renovated Union Stations (the actual train stations having been relegated to a shed well out of sight and sound).

Marketing images frequently are built around a mélange of stylized urban tableaux.[15] Cities characterized by memorable cityscapes find it easy to project an alluring image, though even these attributes are not self-defining; they are necessarily represented through photographs and art as caricatures. Thus, New York City enters the mind's eye through decontextualized images of Times Square, Wall Street, and the Empire State Building, San Francisco through the Golden Gate Bridge and the Transamerica Tower, and St. Louis through the Gateway Arch. The Eiffel Tower is doubtless the best-known city symbol in the world. Roland Barthes has observed that it is impossible to be in or to imagine Paris without confronting its image: "The Tower is present to the entire world. First of all as the universal symbol of Paris, it is everywhere on the globe where Paris is stated as an image; from the Midwest to Australia, there is no journey to France which isn't made, somehow, in the Tower's name, no school book, poster, or film about France which fails to propose it as the major sign of a people and of a place."[16] According to Barthes, the tower succeeds because it stands as a symbol of so many things, evoking images of "modernity, of communication, of science or of the nineteenth century, rocket, stem, derrick, phallus, lightning rod or insect." By provoking such a kaleidoscope of associations, the tower "makes the city into a kind of nature; it constitutes the swarming of men into a landscape, it adds to the frequently grim urban myth a romantic dimension, a harmony, a mitigation."[17]

Cities that lack powerful symbols or historical and architectural signifiers must devise them, whereas cities that have them risk becoming subsumed by them. Thus, Baltimore is now known for Harborplace, and San Antonio for Riverwalk. Even Boston, which seamlessly absorbs visitors much like European cities do (as noted by Ehrlich and Dreier in this volume), owes much of its current image to the Cheers bar, featured in a popular television sitcom, and to Faneuil Hall Marketplace, which houses a Rouse Corporation mall within a collection of three 150-year-old restored buildings. Ironically, as the tourist spaces become more and more alike from city to city, it becomes easier for cities that otherwise have no outstanding tourist attractions to remake themselves into tourism sites. This happens when the tourist space, not the historic city, becomes the principal signifier of a locality.

The Components of the Bubble

The tourist bubble is like a theme park, in that it provides "entertainment and excitement, with reassuringly clean and attractive surroundings."[18] The term *Fordism* has been used to refer to the mass production of manufactured goods for mass consumption. It is, however, equally apt when applied to certain kinds of tourism development. The standardized venues of the tourist bubble seem mass-produced, almost as if they are made in a tourism infrastructure factory (say, south of Indianapolis). Because cities compete so vigorously with one another, it may be said that they are entangled within a system of coerced production: the status quo is not an option; they have to run just to keep up.[19] As a result, urban leaders feel that they have little choice but to invest in all the components that make up the tourist enclave.

There is, to be sure, some variation among cities in how tourist and visitor spaces are constructed. Indianapolis has built a critical mass of sports facilities equipped with Olympic-regulation swimming pools, tennis courts, weight rooms, and the like. As a result, the city has become home to a multitude of sports events and to a sports training and medical industry. A unique tourist space also exists in New Orleans, whose French Quarter, Mardi Gras, and sin industry have never been successfully mimicked. With few exceptions, however, the tourist strategy has become an extraordinarily standardized phenomenon in the United States. Bernard Frieden and Lynn Sagalyn referred to the requisite set of physical components as a mayor's "trophy collection": typically, they said, the set contained an atrium hotel, festival mall, convention center, restored historical neighborhood, domed stadium, aquarium, new office towers, and redeveloped waterfront.[20] If they had published their book in the mid-1990s rather than a decade earlier, they might have added a casino gambling facility to their list. In the remainder of this chapter, I comment on the character of the various components making up the standard central-city tourist bubble.

Convention Centers

Tourism has not always been the primary focus of local boosters. Until the 1930s, town halls generally doubled as assembly facilities, if needed. In the 1920s some cities helped construct the first generation of sports stadiums, arenas, and exhibition halls; later, during the Great Depression, the federal Public Works Administration financed a flurry of more ambitious structures. This generation of halls often contained one or more auditoriums as well as exhibition space under one roof; many cities did not replace these buildings until the 1980s or 1990s. These all-purpose facilities were expensive to operate and virtually always lost money, but they had the effect of attracting and even helping to create an array of traveling shows and exhibitions. The benefits to the local economy were quickly comprehended by civic boosters and entrepreneurs, who then pushed for public subsidies. Beginning in the 1950s, larger cities began constructing a second generation of meeting halls in the form of convention centers designed specifically to attract meetings and exhibitions.

Nevertheless, before 1960 only a few big cities actively sought to attract the convention business, and competition did not really heat up until the mid-1970s. Cities have entered the race because much is at stake. In the United States, more than 25,000 associations spent $32 billion for meetings in 1992, and corporations spent an additional $29 billion on meetings and conventions held outside company venues.[21] Although only 4 or 5 percent of these meetings are held in convention centers, the scale of the meetings, and of convention business in general, has prompted hundreds of cities to build or expand their existing centers.[22] Between 1970 and 1985 more than 100 convention centers were constructed in the United States; in 1970 the nation had available 6.7 million square feet of convention space, but by 1990 this area had almost tripled, to 18 million square feet.[23] In the 1980s cities began a virtual arms race for the convention trade, with even small localities joining the competition. From 1980 to 1987 the number of convention centers increased by 37 percent, but the square footage of exhibition space rose even faster, by 60 percent.[24] By the end of the 1980s, 331 convention centers were operating, which constituted a 50 percent increase in only a decade. At least 434 centers were on line by 1995.[25]

The convention business is extraordinarily competitive. In 1981 New York and Chicago easily led the nation as magnets for meetings with ex-

Table 1   Convention Trade, U.S. Cities, 1981

Top 33 Cities Hosting Meetings with Exhibits	Percentage of National Attendance
1. New York	10.6
2. Chicago	6.7
3. Atlanta	4.4
4. Las Vegas	3.8
5. Dallas	3.8
6. Los Angeles	3.7
7. Anaheim	3.5
8. San Francisco	2.9
9. New Orleans	2.6
10. Boston	2.3
11. Detroit	2.0
12. Kansas City	2.0
13. Philadelphia	1.7
14. Indianapolis	1.7
15. Houston	1.5
16. St. Louis	1.4
17. Atlantic City	1.3
18. Columbus	1.2
19. Minneapolis	1.2
20. San Antonio	1.1
21. Louisville	1.1
22. Miami Beach	1.1
23. Seattle	1.1
24. San Diego	1.0
25. Denver	1.0
26. Cleveland	.8
27. Orlando	.8
28. Phoenix	.6
29. Cincinnati	.6
30. Oklahoma City	.6
31. Memphis	.5
32. Pittsburgh	.5
33. Tulsa	.3

Source: Successful Meetings 1983.

hibits, claiming more than 17 percent of the trade between them (see table 1). The next thirty-one cities fought for very small individual shares, with the top ten cities dividing up 44 percent of the nation's convention attendance and the remaining twenty-three cities sharing 25 percent. Those cities outside the top thirty-three received about 31 percent of the nation's convention business in 1981.

As the number of cities vying for conventions increases, it becomes

Table 2   Top U.S. Convention Cities, 1990–92

City	1992 Rank	1991 Rank	1990 Rank*
Chicago	1	1	1
Orlando	2	5	2
Dallas	3	2	3
Atlanta	4	3	6
Los Angeles	5	4	5
San Diego	5	7	9
New York	7	8	6
Boston	8	9	8
New Orleans	9	14	14
Phoenix	10	12	13
San Francisco	10	6	4
Houston	12	10	10
Las Vegas	13	13	10
Washington, D.C.	14	11	18
Nashville	15	—	—
Denver	16	16	18
Philadelphia	17	20	15
Anaheim	18	14	31
Miami	18	—	—
St. Louis	18	—	—

Source: Successful Meetings 1993, 62.
*Duplicate rankings indicate ties.

difficult for a particular city to increase significantly its share of the country's convention business. Nevertheless, there has been considerable volatility in the rankings (see table 2). By 1992 New York City had fallen from first to seventh place, and Anaheim had dropped from seventh to eighteenth. Orlando, however, had shot up from twenty-seventh in 1981 to second place in 1990 but slipped to fifth in 1991, then rebounded to second in 1992.

Conventions, exhibitions, and conferences are also an important component of tourism outside the United States. As host to 61 percent of the world's international conferences in 1990, Europe far surpassed North America, which hosted 14.3 percent. The world's leading international conference cities in 1990 were, respectively, Paris, London, Brussels, Geneva, Vienna, Berlin, Madrid, Singapore, and Rome. It is clear that the cultural and political positions of these cities—that is, their status as general tourist destinations and the presence of many international organizations within them—account for their importance as meeting locations.[26] Because they clearly dominate as meeting destinations in their respective countries, the construction of convention centers does not appear to be as widely distributed outside the United States. In Germany and Britain, exhibition halls are constructed with central government assistance; few towns and cities build large facilities without such external aid.[27] London and Birmingham account for two-thirds of the meetings and conventions held in Britain. Within their countries, Paris, Vienna, Rome, and Geneva are at least as dominant as London in this regard.

As the European situation illustrates, the construction of a convention facility may provide a foundation, but a lot of other factors also determine a city's ability to successfully compete for meetings. Convention centers do not exist in isolation from the cities in which they are located. Large cities, with their multitude of entertainment, cultural, and commercial attractions, remain the primary drawing cards for national and international conventions. Certain essential components must be available: hotel space, cultural and entertainment opportunities, sightseeing, restaurants, and other amenities.[28] The one major attraction of smaller cities is lower cost, though this advantage is insufficient in itself.[29] According to a meetings planner, "If we're going to use a second-tier city and promote it as an attraction, then we have to make it an attraction. We bill it as a tourist destination and give that equal billing with the technical [meeting] program."[30]

As a consequence, cities expend considerable effort to establish good relations with the people and institutions making up the meetings and convention industry. Two-thirds of convention and trade shows and a large proportion of other meetings are coordinated by professional planners.[31] City promoters have had to professionalize their efforts to deal with these intermediaries, and by the 1980s virtually every major city in the United States had established a convention and visitors' bureau.[32] Like textbook publishers who know that their books must be marketed to professors before they can be sold to students, convention and tourism bureaus realize that they must appeal to the gatekeepers of the tourist industry. They construct lists of associations that regularly sponsor or organize conventions, send them promotional literature, attend the meetings of these organizations, where they sometimes stage rather elaborate promotional presentations, and even convene meetings of their own to which they invite association representatives. Professional meetings planners, whose job it is to secure the best deal possible for their groups, have, however, learned the art of playing cities off against one another.

All convention centers require yearly subsidies for the payment of construction bonds and for operating expenses; even so, escalating construction, maintenance, and promotion costs have not deterred cities from investing in larger and more elaborate facilities. From the point of view of local boosters, the competition for tourism requires them to be aggressive just to stay even. According to Jim Hutchinson, of the Kansas City Convention and Visitors Bureau, "It's even more important to be aggressive when competition is up and the economy of the industry down. This industry is just like any other industry. To be competitive, you have to continue to improve the business."[33] The precarious position in which cities find themselves has not escaped the attention of the groups that use convention facilities. The biggest associations generally assume that they can persuade cities to give them convention space rent-free—and their bargaining position is certain to improve over time. In 1993 the Future Farmers of America, a youth organization that has traditionally met in Kansas City, demanded that the city give it cash subsidies, lower hotel rates, and other incentives to continue meeting there. Because their annual convention brought 28,000 visitors to the city, the chair of the Convention and Visitors Bureau thought it worthwhile to spend "whatever it takes" to keep the group from going elsewhere.[34] Kansas City's effort ultimately failed, providing ample comment on the poor bargaining position facing every city.

Professional Sports Franchises

As pointed out by Charles Euchner elsewhere in this volume, the movement of sports teams from city to city is a uniquely North American phenomenon. In the United States, professional sports became an object of interurban competition about a half-century ago, and over the last decade the battle for franchises has become increasingly intense. Sports teams have long been central to the civic and cultural life of American cities. Oddly, the current mobility of teams has not eroded the notion that a team expresses a city's essence, spirit, and sense of community. Civic boosters consider professional sports franchises pivotal to the economic revitalization of central cities, and it is doubtful that arguments showing the limited economic contributions of sports to local economies will do much to deter their often desperate efforts to get or keep professional teams. Stadiums and sports arenas are some of the most expensive components of the tourism and recreational complex being subsidized by cities, but boosters consider them to be an essential signifier of "big league" status. Sports teams carry a substantial emotional charge, so that their worth is rarely, if ever, calculated in simple economic terms. Through the national and international publicity accompanying network broadcasts of games and playoffs, professional sports teams are a powerful vehicle for conveying a city's image.

For local boosters, the big-business aspect of sports in America is undoubtedly part of its allure. In 1992 there were 102 North American franchises in four major sports, worth almost $9.5 billion (two new National Football League franchises have been awarded since then). In the same year, major-league baseball franchises were valued from $75 million for the Montreal Expos to $200 million for the New York Yankees. National Football League teams ranged in value from $103 million for the New England Patriots to $150 million for the Miami Dolphins and the New York Giants. Some National Basketball Association franchises could be bought for smaller sums; the Indiana Pacers, for example, would have cost only $43 million. The Detroit Pistons, however, were valued at $120 million, and the Los Angeles Lakers, the most valuable professional basketball team, at $150 million. Professional hockey teams went for less, their values ranging from $30 million for the Winnipeg Jets to $70 million for the Detroit Red Wings.[35]

Cities are willing to go to extraordinary lengths to get and keep a professional sports team. Teams are increasingly mobile, and owners realize that public subsidies are theirs for the asking. From 1953 to 1986, sixty-seven of the ninety-four stadiums used by professional sports teams were publicly owned.[36] For the last several years the two most important new revenue sources for sports teams have been network broadcasting and local and state subsidies.[37] By the end of the 1980s, it could be safely assumed that no owner in any of the professional sports would ever agree to build a stadium with private dollars. Owners have come to expect other subsidies as well, in the form of guaranteed attendance minimums, the construction of luxury boxes, and control of stadium merchandising.

As teams become more and more footloose, cities find themselves in a poor bargaining position. Stadiums require generous subsidies because almost all of them lose money. Annual operating deficits are generally considerable: the New Orleans Superdome lost about $3 million a year during the 1980s, for example, compared to the annual $1 million loss for the Silverdome, in Pontiac, Michigan. In its first year, the Florida

Suncoast Dome lost $1.3 million, plus $7.7 million in debt payments.[38] Domed stadiums cost so much to build that it is impossible to schedule enough events or charge high enough rents to avoid large operating deficits. Toronto ended up paying $400 million for its domed stadium in the early 1990s, while Baltimore spent $200 million for its new open-air stadium. St. Louis's domed stadium, completed in 1995, cost $301 million.[39] In 1998 the estimated cost of a proposed Yankee Stadium on Manhattan's West Side was over $1 billion.

Do stadiums justify their enormous costs by bringing gobs of money into local economies? A review of studies on the economic effects of stadiums concludes that they may have an extremely limited economic impact—and that some may even have a negative effect by replacing spending that stays within local enterprises with spending that quickly leaves the local economy.[40] Claims that investing in sports stadiums will have a multiplier effect by introducing a stream of new economic activity into a local economy are, therefore, suspect. Civic boosters who argue that the most important benefits of a major sports franchise are intangible and cannot be measured solely in economic terms are unquestionably correct. As teams become more mobile and owners more insatiable, however, such arguments may eventually wear thin.

Festival Malls

Cities have come to use enclosed malls as a principal weapon in the competition for recreational shopping and tourism. These self-contained areas are important not only because they can help reverse the long-term decline of downtown retailing but also because they are a means of creating defended space even in the midst of urban crime and decay. Malls built by the developers John Portman and James Rouse and their imitators have become such common features of American downtowns that one forgets how recently they have been constructed. These social and physical complexes increasingly engulf and centralize activities that were formerly spread through the urban community at large. Criticized as "fortified cells of affluence,"[41] they are nonetheless extremely successful as locations for tourism and recreation. In 1992, for example, Atlanta ranked fourth among cities in the United States for convention business—without doubt because of Portman's Peachtree Center.

The Peachtree complex dates back to the original cylindrical towers that distinguished Portman's first atrium hotel, which opened in downtown Atlanta in 1967. It was an instant hit with architectural critics, the media, and the public. By the late 1980s Peachtree Plaza had swallowed up Atlanta's historic downtown. Sixteen buildings clustered around the aluminum cylinder that housed the Marriott Hotel, encompassing a constantly expanding, enclosed downtown business district. Atlanta has moved indoors, and the city streets have been almost deserted by pedestrian traffic. Shops, hotels and their lobbies, offices, food courts, and atriums are connected by a maze of escalators, skytubes, and arcades. The glassed-in skyways of Peachtree Center isolate its inhabitants from the streets below. A similar isolation characterizes Portman's other developments as well—the Renaissance Center in Detroit, the Hyatt at Embarcadero Center in San Francisco, the Bonaventure Hotel in Los Angeles, and the Marriott Marquis in Manhattan's Times Square.

Like Peachtree Center, many of the enclosed malls began modestly and then, over many years, accreted block by block, connected by tubes and skyways. In Minneapolis, a sprawling mall complex has grown by eating away the interiors of the downtown buildings, leaving their historic facades intact. In Kansas City, the Crown Center has inexorably spread from its beginnings as a luxury hotel; by the mid-1990s it occupied several city blocks. In Montreal and Dallas, veritable underground cities have been formed through a maze of molelike tunnels.

Amid much skepticism about its viability, Rouse opened his first mall on August 26, 1976, in Boston, adjacent to the old Faneuil Hall.[42] Few people were convinced that a retail mall of any kind could make it in the middle of an older city. The skeptics could hardly have been more wrong. In its second year of operation the market complex drew 12 million visitors—more than Disneyland that year. What made Rouse's development so unique, and newsworthy, was its artful combination of play and shopping. Rouse's formula was to create a carnival-like atmosphere, accomplished through a mixture of specialty shops, clothing stores, restaurants, and food stands and by the presence of musicians, jugglers, acrobats, and mimes for the entertainment of shoppers. There soon were Rouse or Rouse-like malls at the Gallery of Market Street East in Philadelphia, Grand Avenue in Milwaukee, Horton Plaza in San Diego, Trolley Square in Salt Lake City, Union Station in St. Louis, Harborplace in Baltimore, South Street Seaport in New York, and on and on.

Typically, cities have heavily subsidized the construction of downtown malls. To support mall development they drew on funds from federal Community Development Block Grants and Urban Development Ac-

At sea inside the West Edmonton Mall, Alberta, Canada, the largest shopping center in the world

Described by one of the project's developers as the "eighth wonder of the world," the 121-acre supermall covers 5.2 million square feet of developed space, which includes 800 shops, a hotel, and a huge indoor amusement park.

tion Grants, floated bonds to finance site acquisition and loans to developers, offered property tax abatements, created tax increment districts, built utility tunnels, constructed sewer lines and water mains, and rerouted and repaved streets. The melding of public subsidies and private dollars took place through new public-private entities established specifically to receive both public subsidies and private investment funds. Such agencies took on a wide variety of projects, but in the case of sports stadiums and malls, private-public authorities were usually created specifically for the purpose of building and managing a single facility. As detailed by Ehrlich and Dreier in this volume, Boston set an example by taking a profit-sharing position in development projects.

The new downtown malls generally do not revitalize retailing in the urban core overall. They are targeted at recreational shoppers rather than at a resident population seeking mundane necessities. Their mix of gift and souvenir shops, specialty food stores, bars, and fast-food or franchise restaurants mimics tourist villages such as Jackson Hole, Wyoming, and Estes Park, Colorado. They rely on a style of shopping that is most effectively promoted within a controlled environment, one totally planned for shopping and entertainment. The combination of shopping and relaxing in this way encourages a "shop 'til you drop" approach to buying, a kind of depthless consumption, a "calculating hedonism."[43]

Malls and themed shopping-leisure environments are making downtowns into places of specialized consumption segregated from the rest of the city. In these environments, out-of-town visitors do mingle with local residents, but both groups are prompted to act as if they are, in effect, in a dreamscape far removed from the city that surrounds them. The similarity between Disneyland and Disney World and these environments is not accidental—thirteen years before he opened Faneuil Hall Marketplace, James Rouse commented on how influential Walt Disney was as an urban planner. The playful, fantastical character of his malls reflects Disney's impact. Probably more than any other component of the standardized tourism space, malls establish the atmosphere and the context of a "utopian visual consumption" that potentially makes every city, whatever its past function or present condition, a tourist attraction.[44]

Casino Gambling

Until the 1980s there were few casinos in the world's major cities, but in the space of less than two decades casino gambling has spread rapidly.

Since the mid-1980s casino gambling has become established as a component of tourism promotion in cities in Australia, Canada, New Zealand, and the Netherlands, as well as in several cities on the Mediterranean, including Athens, Istanbul, and Cairo.[45] In the United States, Atlantic City, New Jersey, broke Nevada's monopoly in 1978, and in 1992 New Orleans opened the first casino (now in bankruptcy) in a major U.S. city. Within a year Kansas City and St. Louis, Missouri, joined the list, and Chicago's mayor announced his intention to seek state legislative approval for the construction of casinos there.

As with other components of the tourist infrastructure, urban leaders feel that the logic of competition forces them to seek gaming. The commission recommending that four casinos be opened in Chicago reasoned that it would "prevent other cities from using the attraction of casinos to siphon off visitors from Chicago."[46] In making his pitch for casinos in his city, the mayor of Philadelphia predicted that by the end of the decade "almost every urban area will have some form of gambling. . . . If people are going to gamble away their paychecks, better they do it here than in Atlantic City."[47] As expressed by the general counsel of the St. Louis Redevelopment Corporation, casino gaming was the latest essential feature of the city's tourist infrastructure: "In a city that has recently built a new convention center, dome[d] stadium, indoor sports arena and light rail system, gaming was the element needed to provide the necessary critical mass to draw visitors to St. Louis and enhance the city experience for residents."[48] Driven by such logic, most mayors will try to add land-based casinos or riverboat gaming to their trophy collection, but given a very uncertain and sometimes hostile political atmosphere, only some will succeed, as pointed out by Deitrick, Beauregard, and Kerchis in this volume.

Although concerns about the social and moral effects of gambling once were invoked mainly by religious groups, now a diverse array of people sound the alarm. Opponents of casino gambling usually raise three issues. First, substantial research has demonstrated that teenagers have about twice the rate of addiction to gambling as do adults.[49] Perhaps as part of a public relations effort, the industry has acknowledged that some individuals do indeed become addicted to gambling, and it has begun to finance research on the problem (supporting, for example, the National Council on Problem Gambling). Second, many question the economic effects of casino gambling on local communities. There is substantial fear that casinos cannibalize other businesses by locating restaurants, bars, and shops on their premises, thereby taking business away from local enterprises. Research is also accumulating that demonstrates a spending substitution effect, whereby gamblers spend less on goods and services to make up for what they lose on the lotteries and in the casinos.[50] A third oft-expressed concern is that the gambling industry brings with it organized crime, opportunistic crime, and political corruption. Virtually all efforts to legalize casino gambling are accompanied by well-publicized reports of political corruption. For instance, just weeks before the April 1994 vote in Missouri, the governor asked the members of the St. Louis Election Board to resign, because all of them had financial ties to gambling companies. The governor's action followed weeks of newspaper stories detailing how politicians had become investors in the companies competing for gambling franchises.

Industry projections of the potential contributions of gaming to local treasuries often make it appear that the pastime would constitute a magic elixir for ailing central-city economies. Despite this promise, casino gambling is likely to spread somewhat more slowly than was anticipated only a few years ago. In 1996 ten state legislatures refused to pass laws that would legalize casinos or slot machines,[51] and on March 5, 1996, Congress passed legislation to initiate a two-year study of gaming. A slowdown will occur, above all, if state and local officials begin to doubt the contributions that gaming can make to public treasuries. In May 1996, *Governing*, a magazine published for state and local public officials, spoke of the gambling "glut" and predicted that casino gaming would spread slowly over the next few years.[52] In their unremitting search for ways to regenerate central-city economies, however, mayors will do their best to prove that prediction wrong.

The Effects of Tourist Bubbles

In the United States, the competition for tourists has brought about large-scale changes in land use in central cities. Critics often note that sports stadiums, convention centers, and other components of the recreation and tourist infrastructure rarely pay for themselves. Public officials and civic boosters do not, on the whole, care much if they do. This apparently cavalier attitude toward taxpayers' money can be explained by noting the general irrelevance—to city officials and civic boosters—of cost-benefit analyses of tourism infrastructure. The attitude of public officials toward development projects has "little do with the . . . profitability . . . of a project" and far more to do with the vision officials share concerning the overall direction a city is taking.[53] Such a stance often means that civic elites become driven by a vision of regeneration not entirely of their own invention. The manner in which interurban competition in the United States is conducted dictates that cities compete, that they be as generous as their competitors in providing subsidies, and that they try to adopt every new variation on a theme that comes along.

Civic leaders tempted to proceed on blind faith alone should keep in mind that total, abject, even humiliating failure is possible. In the 1970s Flint, Michigan, tried to turn itself into a tourist city. Rather than projecting a positive image, its sad and sometimes pathetic efforts gained it fame in the low-budget but popular movie *Roger and Me*.[54] After the closing of its General Motors plant had devastated the local economy, public officials in Flint launched an effort at regeneration through the motto "Our New Spark Will Surprise You." The city committed $13 million in subsidies to the construction of a luxury hotel, the Hyatt Regency. Within a year it closed its doors. Approximately $100 million in public money was used to build AutoWorld, a museum that contained, among other items, the "world's largest car engine" and a scale model that portrayed downtown Flint in its more prosperous days. AutoWorld closed within six months. Still more public subsidies were committed to the construction of the Water Street Pavilion, a theme park–festival market. Most of its shops closed within the first year. Commenting on Flint's failure to become a magnet for tourism, the former director of AutoWorld said, "You can't make Palm Beach out of the Bowery. If you want to make Palm Beach, you have to go to Palm Beach."

The lesson for Flint, however, may be that it just did not try hard enough to become a Palm Beach. Disney World and the West Edmonton Mall point the way to a strategy of creating a sense of placeness out of whole cloth, with no reference to the surrounding context at all. This, in effect, is the strategy used by cities that lack built-in advantages as tourist destinations. Although quite a few cities are located in or near scenic spots, a great many U.S. municipalities cannot lay claim to a local culture or an urban landscape that tourists will find compelling. Consequently, if these cities want to claim a share of the fastest-growing sector of the world economy, they are obliged to create spaces that tourists might want to inhabit.

How will tourist bubbles affect the cities that build them? Because tourist enclaves are frequently the locations for communitywide celebrations (or, more accurately, corporate-sponsored events that are advertised as such), one must consider the possibility that they help foster community solidarity and spirit. Communal celebrations often brought a measure of social cohesion to medieval societies: "In otherwise stratified and faction-ridden communities, men and women put their differences aside long enough to share communal meals, engage in neighborhood games, and march through the streets shoulder to shoulder in processional demonstrations of fraternity."[55]

In today's cities, the closest equivalents to the medieval festivals may be July Fourth fireworks and St. Patrick's Day parades or even, to some degree, the mingling of diverse people attending sporting events, garden and auto shows, and the like. Is it likely that the tourist bubble contributes in this way to maintaining the cohesion of local community? Possibly. But it is equally likely that the opposite occurs. Tourist bubbles create islands of affluence that are sharply differentiated and segregated from the surrounding urban landscape. Within American cities they may not seem as alien to their surrounding environments as, say, the beach-front hotels of Acapulco, Mexico, or the Club Med in Jamaica, but the comparison is apt: like those venues, they are places of pure consumption for people who are more affluent than those living in the surrounding community. Once in such enclaves, tourists are "placed at the centre of a strictly circumscribed world."[56] When this is the case, tourist bubbles are more likely to contribute to racial, ethnic, and class tensions than to an impulse toward local community. It should be pointed out that medieval celebrations often had the effect of fomenting discord rather than harmony, as when fraternal organizations organized celebrations meant to reaffirm their status within local social and political structures. Such gatherings "could be insidiously divisive, drawing attention to the lines separating different social groups within the community."[57] Tourism can also have this effect, especially if tourist reservations are constructed as artificial, segregated environments devoted to consumption and play, while substantial areas of the city outside the tourist bubble fester with physical decay, crime, and poverty.

BRIAVEL HOLCOMB

Marketing Cities for Tourism

"Is the city a product to be sold on the tourism market and/or a location in which to invest money? Or is a city a place to live, where people can express themselves, even if it is in terms of resistance to, rather than rejoicing in, the dominant culture?"[1] As tourism has become an ever more vital strategy for urban regeneration, governments and the tourist industry have invested greater amounts of resources on campaigns to "sell" the city to potential "consumers." This increasingly is how cities are marketed. The growing professionalism of place marketing has made this a multibillion-dollar industry, even though its efficacy is, at the very least, debatable. Public funds are spent on marketing campaigns, and the city "product" is both redesigned and reimaged for visitors rather than for residents. Cities compete with one another regionally, nationally, and internationally to attract free-spending tourists to fill their hotels, convention centers, stadiums, and museums, just as earlier they competed for footloose industries. Their competitive advantage, however, lies not in labor, lax regulation, or tax incentives but in their perceived appeal as places for play.

In tourism consumption, it is the consumer, not the product, that moves. Because the product is usually sold before the consumer sees it, the marketing of tourism is intrinsically more significant than in the conventional case where the product can be seen, tested, and compared to similar products in situ. It means that the representation of place, the images created for marketing, the vivid videos and persuasive prose of advertising texts, can be as selective and as creative as the marketer can make them—a reality check comes only after arrival. This is not to imply that people selling cities are less scrupulous than those selling cars, or that false advertising prevails in either case, but simply that marketing plays a particularly important role in urban tourism. One can have a great city, but unless that is recognized by potential buyers, the number of visitors will be limited.

The City as Product

It is undeniable that brand names are important in urban marketing. Some cities are either fortunate enough, or have campaigned hard enough, to have names strongly associated in the public mind with romance (Paris and San Francisco), culture (Venice and Kyoto), night life (Rio de Janeiro and Las Vegas), or sports (Sydney and Indianapolis). A few have global reputations as business meeting venues (New York, Paris, London, Tokyo). But who would have thought that Glasgow would be known not for the Gorbals (slums) of my youth but for culture; that the old Yorkshire woolen industry city of Bradford would attract both East Asian residents and thousands of tourists; that Pittsburgh, once a steel capital, would become the "most livable" city in the United States and attract visitors to an amusement park built on the site of a former steel mill? So just as the reputation of firms like Marks and Spencer, Benneton, Nestlé, and Ford may rise and fall with the quality of their products and the effectiveness of their marketing, so too a city's reputation will fluctuate according to local conditions (such as infrastructure, services, and crime rates) and the effectiveness of the city's marketing efforts.

The marketing industry makes a clear distinction between marketing and mere selling. It is said that selling is an attempt to persuade the consumer to buy what one has available, whereas marketing is the production of what the consumer wants. In marketing, the product is custom made to suit the consumer's needs and preferences. The role of the marketer is to identify, anticipate, and satisfy the consumer's requirements profitably.[2] Selling, on the other hand, is persuading the customer to buy your product. Although virtually all the academic, professional, and industry literature refers to the *marketing* of places for tourism, one can argue that selling is what is really meant, because the seller has limited control over the character and quality of the product: "The tourism marketer can never research the market and develop a product from scratch. The climate, geography, topography, history, culture and traditions are all inherited. The product can be modified and appropriate new infrastructure developed. But even here the . . . marketer can only identify opportunities and encourage developments. Rarely is he given the opportunity of bringing the development about. He can present the destination in an appealing way, he can make it easier to buy and he can provide the cooperative marketing base . . . [but he] has little control over the product . . . [or] price."[3]

The malleability of the product, the power of the tourist industry to modify it for marketing purposes, and the ethics of doing so are all debatable. Nevertheless, in the case of city marketing, efforts are made to enhance the product for tourist consumption, which may or may not be in the interests of city residents. As other authors in this volume show, cities are being remodeled, environments redesigned, and even their inhabitants' behaviors modified to create a more appealing product.

Image Creation

In marketing parlance, parity marketing refers to the task of selling a product that is essentially indistinguishable from its competitors. Detergents, yogurts, or life insurance schemes differ little from one another except, perhaps, in packaging design, but the particular brand one buys must be perceived to wash whiter, be creamier, or provide greater future stability than its competitors. Although every city is unique in numerous other ways, many of the qualities that attract tourists (e.g., "heritage," the range of accommodations, facilities such as sports stadiums or museums, night life, and culinary offerings) are frequently similar among competing cities. There are, for example, sufficient four-star restaurants in New York, San Francisco, Dallas, and a dozen other U.S. cities to satisfy any gourmet's palate for two weeks. Although New Orleans is the birthplace of jazz, aficionados of that genre may indulge their taste at least as easily in Chicago or New York (to say nothing of Paris or London). Florence and St. Petersburg have great art museums, but hundreds of cities have galleries worth visiting. Chartres, Maduri, and Bangkok boast world-famous religious architecture, but many cities have a notable cathedral, temple, or mosque. How, then, does the generic city, one with a range of suitable but not extraordinary attractions, market itself to compete with other similar cities?

Although selling cities is especially hard because they can rarely count on customer loyalty, several strategies have been used, with vary-

The Space Needle, Seattle, Washington

Constructed for the 1962 World's Fair, the Space Needle became an instant landmark on tourists' mental map.

ing success. One is to construct, sometimes intentionally, a landmark that will put the city on the tourist's mental map. In the 1970s Melbourne held a competition, with a large cash prize, to design a landmark that, like Sydney's Opera House, would imprint an image of the city on the world's consciousness. (Whatever the outcome of the competition, it appears not to have worked, as the city today has no such world-class marker.) But many cities have succeeded in establishing, through a specific structure, a symbolic shorthand for their identities—Seattle's Space Needle, St. Louis's Gateway Arch, and the Eiffel Tower are obvious examples. Other buildings, though not necessarily constructed for the purpose, may also serve the function: the Empire State Building, the Tower of Pisa, Santa Sophia in Istanbul. And a few city symbols are physical features—Rio de Janeiro's exfoliation dome topped by a statue of Christ, Edinburgh's volcanic plug, and Cape Town's Table Mountain. Building a landmark doesn't always work, however. A huge phallic skyscraper superimposed on a three-story townscape in Penang is more than just an aesthetic and financial disaster: how many readers, for example, even know it exists (or could accurately locate Penang)? Indeed, perhaps once the landmark has served its purpose of mental location, it may even be taken for granted. In a short story by Graham Greene, a man temporarily steals the Eiffel Tower and takes it for a spell of country air. If anyone noticed its absence, "no one in Paris could admit that the tower was absent for five days unnoticed—any more than a lover could admit to himself he had failed to notice the absence of his mistress."[4] Although such landmarks are sometimes visited by a significant portion of incoming tourists, others (e.g., Sydney's Opera House) may be more valuable as symbols than as actual attractions.

Another strategy for putting a city on the map is the staging of events, an approach that may incorporate landmark construction. Perhaps the first such hallmark event was the Great Exhibition held in London in 1851, at which a kaleidoscope of products from many parts of the British Empire was displayed in the Crystal Palace. Similar glass houses continue to draw many visitors 150 years later, and some subsequent World's Fairs (e.g., those in Chicago and New York, Expo 1988 in Brisbane, and Expo 1986 in Vancouver) were successful in attracting many visitors and leaving a legacy in the built environment. The Knoxville World's Fair of 1983, however, is an example of the futility of using such an event in an unsupportive context. There is a growing literature in this area and considerable controversy concerning the relative costs and benefits of hosting mega-events. Most policy makers believe that landing the Olympic Games or a World's Fair is a key to global recognition. As C.M. Hall has noted, "Hallmark events are the image builders of modern tourism. . . . [The] promotion of an event is not just concerned with the event but to convey images of the destination and region within which the event is located."[5] Nevertheless, it may be that World's Fairs and expositions are more successful in keeping a well-known city famous than in establishing a new destination.

The Olympic Games represent the biggest prize for cities seeking mega-events. Held every four years, the competition to host the Olympics is fierce and indicates the value in both revenue and image that cities expect to gain. Significant investments are required even to enter the competition. Atlanta's bid for the 1996 Games began more than five years earlier. Backed by local politicians and financed by donations from businesses with local headquarters, the campaign produced glossy bid books, appropriate supporting events, and generous hospitality for selection-committee members. Most important, plans and promises of financial support for facilities and infrastructure were in place. Atlanta's winning bid surpassed those of Athens, Manchester, Sydney, Toronto, and Belgrade. Although the cost of the Atlanta Games was estimated to be $1.7 billion (including $550 million for construction), much of the money came from the private sector, television revenues, and ticket sales, resulting in little expense to the taxpayer other than for security.

As a direct result of the Games, Atlanta attracted an estimated six million visitors and took in $4–$5 billion.[6] Furthermore, the city benefited from $500 million worth of building projects available for local use after the Games. These include Centennial Park (laid out in a previously blighted downtown area), the eighty-five-thousand-seat Olympic Stadium (which became the home of baseball's Atlanta Braves), as well as an aquatic center, eight new dormitories for Georgia Tech, and a basketball arena for Morehouse College.

But perhaps the biggest anticipated gain was the consolidation of Atlanta's image as the capital of the New South and, as an entry in the competition for a new slogan suggested, "the World's Next Great City." (Rejections included "Atlanta: The City Too Stupid to Be Ashamed," "Atlanta: Not Bad for Georgia," and "Atlanta: A Southern city of great hospitality where the weather is generally fair, the business climate is positive, a number of large buildings exist and you can have fun at Underground.")[7] Atlantans hoped that their city would emerge as a model of racial harmony, southern hospitality, and corporate-government collaboration. After the Games were over, city leaders concluded that despite a pipe-bomb explosion and some critical international press coverage, the overall improvement in Atlanta's image was substantial.[8] Critics, however, noted that five thousand units housing low-income residents were demolished to build Olympic venues and lamented the highly conspicuous commercial profile: "The corporate footprint will be on everything from drug testing to building the Olympic stadium to providing ambiance to deciding the start of the men's marathon. A 92-foot Swatch Watch will adorn a local building, McDonald's will place six restaurants in the athletes' village, an eight-acre Coca-Cola Olympic City will feature interactive games, and Daimler-Benz, the German automaker, has pledged to restore the crumbled house where Margaret Mitchell, author of 'Gone With the Wind,' was born."[9]

Staging the Olympics is a financial gamble for a city. Montreal is still paying off debts incurred in 1976, and although the Los Angeles (1984) and Seoul (1988) Games were debt free, Barcelona (1992) spent $6.1 billion of public money, resulting in a $1.4 billion public debt.[10] Nonetheless, by the bidding deadline of January 1996 for the 2004 Games, eleven cities (Athens, Buenos Aires, Cape Town, Istanbul, Lille, Rio de Janeiro, Rome, San Juan, Seville, Stockholm, and St. Petersburg) had submitted proposals. Indeed some would argue that even if the hallmark event is not a financial success in the short run, the remaking of a city's image, and its place on the international mental map, while impossible to quantify, can eventually more than compensate. The mayor of Edmonton remarked that highly visible "international events provide a value well beyond the monetary-cost overruns, and deficits must be compared against the positive world image you create for a city through such events."[11] As Law notes, a serious bid, especially if it gains national support, can bring rewards even if the city is not ultimately selected. Both public and private investments are attracted to support the city's bid, but perhaps "of greatest importance is the element of unity which the bid engenders. Politicians of different parties, leaders of the private sector and voluntary groups are able to come together around a bid and perhaps agree not only on the proposal itself, but also on the general direction in which the city should be moving. Almost certainly included in this will be a role for the tourist industry in the city, how it should be developed, and how the city should be marketed."[12] The bidding alone is so successful a form of destination promotion that the Sydney Olympic Games Review Committee declared: "In terms of international marketing the cost of bidding is regarded as a highly cost-effective method of promoting Sydney and Australia."[13]

Less conspicuous, but more frequent, activities such as garden and flower shows, cultural and ethnic festivals, religious feast-day celebrations, and sports events are effective both in attracting temporary visitors and in gaining media attention for the locale. Historical anniversaries, too, can provide useful promotional foci for cities: the visit of the "Tall Ships" to New York harbor in 1976 to mark the bicentennial of American independence and the 1992 festivals to mark Montreal's 350th birthday attracted visitors and publicity.[14] But again, success is far from guaranteed. To celebrate the quincentennial of Christopher Columbus's arrival in America, Santo Domingo spent more than $70 million to construct a lighthouse tomb for what are reputed to be the explorer's mortal remains. The hoped-for visits of the Pope and the king of Spain failed to materialize, as did the equally anticipated tourist hordes. Instead, several thousand local residents were displaced, and the illumination of the laser lighthouse always results in a brownout in adjacent city neighborhoods.

Promotional Strategies

Cities are marketed for tourism using a mix of strategies applicable at other geographic scales and to other products. As in most marketing efforts, promotion consumes the largest part of the budget. Most cities produce guides, maps that show the locations of hotels, restaurants, transit facilities, and local attractions, and promotional materials that are distributed to travel agencies and visitors' centers and through the mail. Because urban marketing commonly involves governmental participation, it involves a greater emphasis on planning than do strictly commercial marketing campaigns.[15] Although individual cities are usually too small to have the resources and personnel to carry out a full-blown and continuous marketing program, many are able to adopt several strategies through the use of in-house staff, a marketing firm, or both.

There is, however, little published research on the efficacy of these promotional efforts, and indeed, the impact on actual travel behavior is difficult to measure.[16] One of the earliest such campaigns did seem to demonstrate the efficacy of professional efforts: in 1977 New York State increased its tourism budget from $200,000 to $4.3 million so as to fund the "I Love New York" advertising campaign. This promotion stimulated an 11.8 percent increase in travel receipts over those of the previous year, producing $4 million in tax revenue for each $1 spent on the campaign. Theater revenues alone increased by 20 percent in one year—and the slogan has been replicated ad nauseam!

Some cities advertise in print and on television. A particularly striking campaign by New Orleans, presumably aimed at upscale markets and appearing in such quality magazines as *Harper's* and the *New Yorker*, used quotations from well-known individuals that were potentially applicable to New Orleans: "Life is something to be spent, not to be saved" (D. H. Lawrence); "A beautiful lady is an accident. A beautiful old lady is a work of art" (Louis Nizer); "If music be the food of love, play on" (William Shakespeare). More typical advertisements feature happy, beautiful people enjoying the city's leading attractions, while the copy extols the city's excitement, amenities, and (usually) uniqueness. As I and others have noted elsewhere, not surprisingly the choice of people and places depicted in urban promotional materials is highly selective.[17] Deteriorating neighborhoods, industrial districts, racial minorities, and environmentally polluted areas are not represented. And even though high crime levels are major deterrents to tourist arrivals, safety is seldom mentioned, presumably because to do so would be to reveal the need for such concerns.

Other promotional strategies include familiarization tours (especially for travel agents) and press photo shoots, during which media personnel are offered hospitality and, in return, disseminate favorable images of the city. Miami used this strategy with considerable success. In a period of three years, about five thousand travel agents and tour operators and two thousand journalists were lured to the city. Subsequent press coverage described Miami as a city of the future, one that is "outward looking, open hearted . . . and aggressively international."[18] In the "Great Miami Shootout," the city provided a dozen top photojournalists from leading magazines with hospitality and a car. Although television images of the city on "Miami Vice" were regarded with ambivalence by the Greater Miami Convention and Visitors Bureau because the program was rife with bloodbaths, cocaine cowboys, and marijuana millionaires, it nevertheless established Miami as the "new Casablanca," a vibrant city with an edge, and placed it firmly on the cognitive map of television viewers.[19]

Many cities operate tourist offices or visitor centers that furnish information, arrange accommodations, provide personal guides, sell tickets to events, and generally assist tourists to orient themselves. The range of services, operating hours, and specialization naturally varies considerably, but large centers, such as the one in New York, offer such amenities as electronic searches for specialized attractions. City tourism organizations send representatives to trade shows and may constitute all or part of a city's official public relations operation. Many cities now maintain web sites delivering information about and images of their attractions.

Cities also seek out niche markets. One such market that has recently attained prominence is gay tourism, exemplified by the Gay Games held in New York in 1995. Gay tourist destinations in both the United States and Europe are few and relatively specialized.[20] For fairly obvious reasons, gay men have tended to select destinations with significant resident gay populations (e.g., Provincetown, Mass., and San Francisco). Nevertheless, some places, for example, Miami Beach, have set out to woo gay and lesbian tourists, recognizing their relative affluence, their high level of spending on travel, and their tendency for repeat business. Perhaps predictably, not all local people support this welcoming policy, and some argue that a conspicuous gay presence may deter other tourists.[21] But for a city with the size and reputation of New York, such considerations are irrelevant. New York won the Gay Games IV in competition with other cities, including Birmingham, U.K. The New York Gay and Lesbian Visitor Center was influential in the negotiations that led to the site choice. The Games attracted thousands of domestic and international visitors and generated as much economic impact as did the World Cup soccer games held simultaneously in the city. The festive atmosphere of the city, draped with rainbow banners and crowded with affectionate strollers and Apollonian roller bladers, was contagious; many of those who experienced it are likely to return to New York.

Cultural, Arts, and Heritage Tourism

Compared to tourists seeking outdoor recreation, urban visitors are disproportionately drawn by cultural, historical, architectural, and ethnic attractions. Over a decade ago, Tighe emphasized the importance in the United States of this type of tourism, which has long been a staple in European cities. Cultural tourists consume not only art, opera, and *son et lumière* in historical settings but also gourmet food and locally produced crafts. Typically well educated, affluent, and broadly traveled, they generally represent a highly desirable type of upscale visitor. In the United States, New York has long been established as the leading arts destination, and the contribution of arts tourism to the city's economy is well recognized. In 1992 an estimated 43 million people visited the metropolitan region, generating $20.7 billion in revenue and nearly 268,000 jobs. A survey of domestic leisure visitors ranked the region's performing arts as the top attraction, and more than 40 percent of overseas tourists visited a museum or gallery.[22]

The arts provide numerous promotional opportunities. In 1994, the exhibition "The Age of Rubens" attracted 234,000 visitors to Toledo, Ohio, more than half of whom were from out of state. A 1995 show of pre-Raphaelite art in Wilmington, Delaware, increased attendance at its museum by 434 percent over the previous summer and drew an audience from throughout the mid-Atlantic states.[23] In San Antonio, Texas, the "Splendors of Mexico" exhibition generated nearly $8 million in state and local taxes. A cultural tourism consultant is reported as claiming that the cultural tourist is "better educated, spends more time at a destination, and is more likely to stay in a hotel than with family or friends. . . . For cities, this is a new way of marketing themselves, and for arts organizations, this is a way to diversify revenues."[24]

The arts are important in the creation of a city image, projecting an aura of high quality, civility, creativity, and sophistication and consequently conferring status on its visitors. "Even a city which does not attract large numbers of tourists coming specifically for an arts event, can still draw or retain additional tourists by 'spicing up' its attractiveness with arts activities."[25] Certainly, the prestige of Glasgow improved dramatically after its 1990 designation as Europe's City of Culture (even if its slogan, "Glasgow's Miles Better," was countered by a competitive "Edinburgh: Slightly Superior"!). The yearly competition to be named the City of Culture by the European Union is so intense that for the year 2000 the union decided that nine cities should share the honor (and the money). A number of towns and cities have established regular cultural festivals, including Baltimore and Seattle (which celebrate Wagner); Portland, Oregon (Strauss); Ashland, Oregon, and Stratford, Ontario (Shakespeare); Aspen (music, ballet, and theater); Durham, North Carolina (dance); and Charleston, South Carolina (the Spoleto Festival of Performing Arts).

Heritage tourism has been one of the most traditional motivations for leisure travel; for centuries people have visited sites of special historic interest—the Grand Tour being an exemplar of the genre. Perhaps nowhere is the past better exploited than in Britain, where every city has a cathedral, birthplace, grave, castle, or setting of note, some of world-class standing (Coventry Cathedral, the Shakespeare theater in Stratford-upon-Avon, Marx's grave in Hampstead, Harlech Castle). In a few cases, entire towns (e.g., Ironbridge and Shropshire) are essentially heritage museums. York is now better known for its Jorvik Viking Center than for its cathedral, while the docks in Liverpool, once busy with shipping, currently house a maritime museum and the Tate Gallery North. Even when the principal attraction is outside of town, cities benefit from proximity to leading historical landmarks (e.g., Beijing's to the Great Wall, Cairo's to the pyramids, etc.) Industrial heritage has become an increasingly important draw. One of the more successful examples is Bradford, whose industrial past centered on woolen textiles. The former hub of that trade—the Wool Exchange—has been converted into a thriving retail center and, somewhat ironically, the graves of the city's nineteenth-century wool barons were restored with public money.[26] Other examples include Bristol's dockland and Leeds's Industrial Museum. Newcastle, on the other hand, is building a reputation on a different aspect of tradition. "The town best known for its now almost extinct shipyards has reinvented itself as a party destination able to rival Amsterdam, northern Europe's established good time city. In fact, the town's growing popularity was unexpectedly confirmed when in 1995 a Texas travel firm listed Newcastle as one of the world's top ten fun spots, joining more obvious choices like Rio de Janeiro and Las Vegas."[27] The main ingredient in Newcastle's success is its highly developed pub culture, a reputation enhanced by a recent incident in which armed police laid siege to a pub where three bank robbers took refuge—and the regular clientele stayed inside for a nine-hour booze-up!

Obviously, history sells and heritage is hyped. Despite critics who argue that the nostalgia industry distorts and commodifies the past, allusions to art and hints of heritage are vital colors in the urban marketer's palette. There is probably no city that does not include references to its glorious past in its tourist brochures, even if for much of its history its citizens have toiled in mills and mines and never gone on holiday in their lives.

Who Markets Cities? Public and Private Roles

As in other forms of economic development marketing, the promotion and marketing of cities to tourists are both carried out by and serve the interests of public- and private-sector stakeholders. In North America the tradition of promoting a place to attract potential settlers extends to early explorers who "usually stressed the economic plenitude of the new settlement, the excellence of its climate, the healthiness of its situation, and the gentleness of its natives"—claims not dissimilar to those found in some contemporary tourist-luring copy.[28] Marketing strategies in frontier America included political and financial inducements, pamphlets and brochures, postcards and highway signs and, perhaps most important, the press.[29] Burd has observed that "newspaper editors were salesmen for the South and West long before irrigation and air-conditioning made the deserts and swamps palatable, and long before television, country-western singers and advertising made the Sunbelt popular."[30] Today newspapers remain among those locally dependent businesses that, because they are relatively immobile, are reliant on the health of the local economy for circulation and advertising. At the same time, they shape the perceptions of an area, resulting in a tension between their roles as local booster and local critic.

In many cities public-private partnerships have been formed to plan and implement promotional campaigns, and indeed it may be in this arena that conventional distinctions between public and private sectors are most blurred. Local government frequently acts entrepreneurially ("investing" in tourist services and facilities and "selling" tourist products), while businesses may open services and facilities to the public or fund the upgrading of public infrastructure. Tourism is an industry composed of a few large businesses and a large number of small, independent ones. Both small and large businesses want to see cities marketed to attract visitors, and in many cases a local chamber of commerce or visitors' and convention bureau will be supported by member firms for this purpose. The earliest chambers of commerce in America were established in southern cities (including Raleigh, Atlanta, Macon, New Orleans, Houston, and San Antonio, all of which established associations in the 1880s), with the aim of improving municipal services.[31] In smaller cities today, the chamber of commerce often includes tourism in its purview; in larger cities, a public-private partnership such as a visitors' and convention bureau or tourist board is more common.

Still, efforts at city marketing suffer from a free-rider problem. The Organization for Economic Cooperation and Development (OECD) notes that, at the national level, it is "not in the commercial interests of any single group of firms to invest in promoting the generic image of the country, because returns from such promotion would be widely and uncertainly spread among direct competitors and other sectors."[32] The same is true of the local level. Although all hotel owners might wish to maximize the number of visitors to their city, their particular objective is to maximize their share of those visitors. Their marketing strategies are therefore most likely to target people who have already arrived in the city or have already decided to visit. Moreover, since many tourist businesses are small, their individual marketing budgets are proportionately limited, as is the geographical range of their promotional messages. As a result, city governments have increasingly assumed at least a coordinating role in fostering cooperative city-marketing schemes.

The mix of public- and private-sector participants in urban marketing organizations varies over time and space. In the United Kingdom urban tourism marketing is usually carried out by local departments (such as those responsible for museums, heritage sites, and the like), a visitor and conference bureau (commonly a public-private partnership), or a tourism association (whether composed entirely of private-sector firms or of private and public partners). Several of these organizations may exist in a single city. In addition, the national English Tourist Board plays a role in some localities, having set up Tourism Development Action Programmes to encourage local authorities to join forces with the private sector to create jobs in tourism.[33] In the United States, too, local governments frequently play an important role in city tourism marketing, with departments of economic development, transportation, cultural affairs, and mayors' offices participating. The increase in state-level promotions in recent years has also benefited cities. A recent study of the role of the arts in tourism within the New York metropolitan region lists fifty-eight sponsors and participating organizations: thirteen departments of local government, the Port Authority of New York and New Jersey, fourteen nonprofit organizations (including the New York Convention and Visitors Bureau and the New Jersey Sports and Exposition Authority), eight private-sector corporations, and twenty-three arts organizations.

The financing of urban tourism marketing is derived from various sources, both public and private. Although some funding comes directly from general tax revenues, governmental financial contributions are commonly derived from dedicated sources such as hotel or guest-room taxes, commissions from conference or booking services, and sales from tourist information centers. Sources of private-sector funding are also often linked to user fees and charges rather than being directly taken from profits. The proportion of funding contributed by the private sector can range from 0 to a 100 percent public share. In the United Kingdom, for example, 64 percent of the 1991–92 budget for the Birmingham tourist bureau was publicly funded, and only 5 percent came from private subscriptions. In Manchester, however, the contribution of the local authority was 44 percent in 1992–93, and in Sheffield the equivalent figure was 60 percent.[34] The Munich City Tourist Office's budget in 1989 was DM 23.3 million, 40 percent of which was supplied by the city council. Tourism Auckland (New Zealand), a regional nonprofit organization, received half of its 1990–91 budget of NZ $40,000 from the public sector. The level of spending on marketing is much higher for American cities. Page cites annual promotional budgets of $81 million for Las Vegas, $9 million for San Francisco, $8 million for Atlanta, and $6 million for San Diego, the public share largely raised by room taxes, membership fees for visitors' organizations, and advertising revenue in promotional literature.[35]

Local governments are increasingly allocating scarce resources for tourism promotion, but "questions need to be asked about the manner in which the provision of resources for tourism-related development and promotion may represent a switch from more traditional welfare functions."[36] According to Hall, the effect of tourism promotion is to "strengthen dominant ideology and further individual interests, legitimize hegemonic relationships and change the meaning and structure of place."[37] Whether or not this is a conscious purpose, Hall and others can present numerous examples of such consequences. They argue that the local state in Western Europe and North America is experiencing crises of both legitimacy (as public resources are channeled from the social and economic needs of disadvantaged groups) and finance (as the central state privatizes functions and reduces social expenditure). Tourism is important to local elites because it can lead to a reimaging of the city, a reorientation of local priorities, consolidation of power by elites and, as Mommass and Van der Poel have argued, to a new "social and spatial segregation and new private and public cultures."[38] Tourism strategies, however, may sometimes backfire. Roche's analysis of the relatively unsuccessful World Student Games held in Sheffield in 1991 reveals that they had the effect of reducing electoral support for the Labor Party in local council elections.[39] Similarly, the cost of attracting the Northern Ballet to Halifax caused a large swing against the incumbent party (Labor), and in Birmingham, Labor party councillors resigned in objection to the costs of creating "white elephants" to attract tourists.[40]

Selling the City to Tourists: A Faustian Bargain?

Packaging and promoting the city to tourists can destroy its soul. The city is commodified, its form and spirit remade to conform to market demand, not residents' dreams. The local state and business elites collude to remake a city in which their special interests are paramount; meanwhile, resources are diverted from needy neighborhoods and social services. Equally, intercity competition for tourists can become the same zero-sum game as that for footloose industries and mobile capital. True, tourism is a growing industry, but there are limits to the elasticity of demand for it. Fickleness and fluctuations in visitor numbers are hazards of all tourist destinations. Although urban residents might enjoy the use of comparatively empty "circuses" (convention centers, shopping malls, stadiums) when the supply of tourists dries up, they still need the bread that tourist revenues provided. But in a sense city marketers, like Faust, are damned if they do and damned if they don't. If the marketing is poor and the tourists few, the local economy loses.

A high official in the tourist industry remarked, "I can think of no industry other than tourism where the interests of the public and private sectors so closely converge."[41] This observation, however, rings truest when *public* means government leaders (rather than community) and *private* means business (not the private citizen). The criteria for evaluating the impact of tourism and the relative costs and benefits of public investment in tourism versus other industries are uncertain and contested, as Fainstein and Gladstone note in their chapter.

From the viewpoint of public policy, one of the problems of public investment in tourism marketing is the inexactness of its science. It has been said that tourism is one of the last industries to experience a change from a seller's to a buyer's market, with the result that marketing techniques are less advanced than in the brand goods industry.[42] Certainly there is agreement that measurement of the impact of city marketing campaigns is infrequent and imprecise. Nevertheless, for the foreseeable future, cities in many countries will continue to market themselves for tourism. Within that context, the goals of progressive policy should be to minimize public spending on promotion that primarily benefits private interests, to ensure that the images projected are inclusive of community sectors and accurate in their representation, and to more equitably distribute the costs and benefits of tourism within the city.

JOHN URRY

Sensing the City

People encounter the city through the senses. In particular, there is a fascination with the sense of sight as the apparent mirror of the world, and more generally with the "hegemony of vision" that has characterized Western social thought and culture over the past few centuries.[1] Such a dominance of the eye—what Bermingham calls "optical truth" and its ambiguous consequences—is part of the process by which subjects have come to be understood in the past two centuries in the West, a process I began to capture with regard to tourism in *The Tourist Gaze*.[2] That book presents a fairly sustained effort to demonstrate the role of the visual sense in a variety of tourist developments and to analyze the consequences for those who are gazed upon within such sites. I particularly distinguish between the romantic and the collective tourist gaze.[3] In this chapter, however, I suggest that there are more types of gaze than this relatively simple pairing. (I propose five modes of visual consumption.) Also, I suggest that more senses than just vision are involved in the consumption of urban place. The various human senses make their respective contributions to how people bodily confront environments. What are the senses involved in the perception, interpretation, appreciation, and denigration of different built environments? How do people sense what other environments are like? How do senses operate across space? Are there hierarchies of value among the senses?

In answering these questions I try to develop further what Rodaway terms a "sensuous geography," in which he brings together the analyses of body, sense, and place.[4] He argues that all the senses are geographical; each contributes to one's orientation in space, to an awareness of spatial relationships, and to the appreciation of the qualities of particular places, which include those being currently experienced (through residence or visiting) and those removed in time. It also follows that the senses are intricately tied up with the construction and reproduction of environments, each of which is, in effect, produced by the specific concatenation of the senses. Different societies place different emphasis on the senses, thereby effecting varying perceptions of a given environment. Rodaway suggests that the senses are connected to one another in five ways in relationship to the sensed environment: through cooperation among the senses, hierarchy, sequencing, thresholds of effect, and reciprocal relations with the environment.[5]

Not surprisingly, I deal here mainly with the visual sense, which seems to have played a major role in the development of travel and tourism in the West, especially recently in the growth of urban tourism. I also show that the denigration of the role of sight is echoed in the ways the "tourist" is denigrated as a contemporary subject. In French social theory in particular, the mere tourist is typically viewed as exceptionally superficial in his or her relationship with the urban form, because only the sense of sight is thought to be deployed. Buzard, however, has shown that the distinction between traveler and tourist has been characteristic throughout much of recent Western history; the denigration of the *sightseeing* tourist therefore says as much about those employing such a marker as it does about the poor benighted sightseers themselves.[6]

Vision and Tourism

Within Western philosophy, sight has been considered the noblest of the senses, as the basis of modern epistemology. Arendt neatly summarizes the dominant tradition: "From the very outset, in formal philosophy, thinking has been thought of in terms of *seeing*."[7] Rorty has famously demonstrated that post-Cartesian thought has generally privileged mental representations "in the mind's eye" as mirror reflections of the external world. He elaborates: "It is pictures rather than propositions, metaphors rather than statements, which determine most of our philosophical convictions . . . the story of the domination of the mind of the West by ocular metaphors."[8]

The dominant conception in philosophy has thus been of the mind as a great mirror that, to varying degrees and in terms of different epistemological foundations, permits us to "see" the external world. Vision has also played a crucial role in the imaginative history of Western culture. Jay points out the clusters of images that surround the sun, moon, stars, mirrors, night and day, and so on, and notes the ways that basic visual experience has helped construct efforts to make sense of both the sacred and the profane: "With the rise of modern science, the Gutenberg revolution in printing and the Albertian emphasis on perspective in painting, vision was given an especially powerful role in the modern era."[9]

There have, of course, been complex connections between this sense of sight and the very discovery and recording of place. Adler shows that before the eighteenth century, perception of other environments had been largely based on discourse and especially on the sense of hearing.[10] Particularly important was the way the ear provided scientific legitimacy. But this gradually shifted after the scientific revolutions of the sixteenth and seventeenth centuries, when eyewitness observation of the external world became more important. Observation came to be the basis of scientific legitimacy, and this position subsequently developed into the foundation of the scientific method of the West. Sense-data were typically perceived as produced and guaranteed by the sense of sight. And such sight came to be understood within "science" through what Jencks calls the "sanitized methodological form of 'observation.'"[11] As Foucault shows in *The Order of Things*, natural history involves the observable structure of the visible world and not the functions and relationships that are invisible to the senses.[12]

A number of sciences of visible nature developed, organized around essentially visual taxonomies, beginning with the Swedish botanist Carolus Linnaeus in 1735.[13] Such classifications were based upon the modern episteme of the individual subject, of the seeing eye and the distinctions that it makes. As Foucault claims: "Man is an invention of recent date" and such a man is one who sees, observes, and classifies as resemblance gives way to representation.[14] In the eighteenth century this increasing emphasis upon the scientific eye meant that mere travelers could not expect their observations to become part of scientific or scholarly understanding. No longer did a simple journey to another environment, normally beyond Europe, provide that authority. The first international scientific expedition took place in 1735. After that moment, the mere fact of traveling elsewhere did not provide *scientific* legitimacy for a traveler's observations.[15]

Travel with the specific purpose of scientific observation therefore became structurally differentiated from more traditional excursions. The latter came to require a different discursive justification, focused not on science but on connoisseurship, which meant being an expert *collector* of works of art and buildings, of flora and fauna, of landscapes and, later, of townscapes. Travel entailed a different kind of vision and hence a different visual ideology. Adler summarizes: "Travellers were less and less expected to record and communicate their emotions in an emotionally detached, impersonal manner. Experiences of beauty and sublimity, sought through the sense of sight, were valued for their spiritual significance to the individuals who cultivated them."[16] The amused eye increasingly turned to a variety of places that travelers were able to compare and through which they developed a discourse for the comparative connoisseurship of places in town and country.

This development had a number of important effects in the later eighteenth and early nineteenth centuries, initially in Britain and then in other parts of Europe and North America. First, there was increased travel to locales in England, Scotland, and Europe, places that were sufficiently amusing for the increasingly informed eye. Second, significant infrastructural developments occurred that produced specialized sites for travel; among these were ruins, literary landscapes, historic towns and, later, seaside resorts. Third, landscape painting developed; this naturalized the image of poor, agricultural laborers and other features that did not fit into touristic visions—particularly industrial blight and urban squalor. Finally, new social practices increasingly emerged through which places were to be sensed and experienced, especially the activities of walking, swimming, photography, shopping, and climbing.[17]

More generally, Green argues that people's interaction with nature increasingly involves "leisure and pleasure—tourism, spectacular entertainment, visual refreshment."[18] He documents the effects of leisure travel on the region surrounding Paris in the mid-nineteenth century. There was, he says, a prolonged "invasion of surrounding regions by and for the Parisian spectator."[19] Two innovations facilitated this invasion: the shortened trip out of the city and the increased ownership of country houses. These combined to generate around Paris what he terms a "metropolitan nature"—that is, spaces outside the city that could be easily accessed. Such spaces were turned into safe recreational and leisure sites for the city dweller to visit from time to time. Green notes that advertisements for houses in the countryside near Paris in this period emphasize the visual spectacle: "The language of views and panoramas prescribed a certain visual structure of the *nature* experience. The healthiness of the site was condensed with the actual process of looking at it, of absorbing it and moving round it with your eyes."[20] The establishment of various artists' communities represented a shift of an increasingly mobile middle class into the Parisian countryside and provided images of a metropolitanized nature that led to further colonization of rural space by many other visitors. Elsewhere I have described a similar process of the civilizing and metropolitanizing of nature that occurred in the English Lake District, although its location "in the north" meant that its cultural construction required complex discursive justifications.[21]

In the past century and a half, the sense of sight has been transformed by the widespread adoption of what Sontag calls the promiscuous practices of photography.[22] (It is interesting to speculate whether parallel transformations of the tactile senses will result from multisensual cybertravel.) Photography has democratized many forms of human experience by, as Barthes says, making notable whatever is photographed.[23] It gives shape to the very processes of travel, so that one's journey consists of moving from one good view to another, each to be captured on film. It has also helped to construct a twentieth-century sense of what is appropriately aesthetic and what is not worth "sightseeing"; it excludes as much as it includes. Wilson summarizes its impact: "The snapshot transforms the resistant aspect . . . into something familiar and intimate, something we can hold in our hands and memories. In this way, the camera allows us some control over the visual environments of our culture."[24] Until very recently, however, most cityscapes were not thought to be suitably photogenic.

Photographic practices reinforce and elaborate dominant visual gazes, including that of the male over the landscape-bodyscape of the female. Irigaray summarizes: "Investment in the look is not as privileged in women as in men. More than other senses, the eye objectifies and masters. It sets at a distance, and maintains a distance."[25] More generally photography produces the extraordinary array of circulating signs and images that constitute the visual culture of the late twentieth century. For Heidegger, the "fundamental event of the modern age is the conquest of the world as picture."[26] By this he does not mean a picture of the world but that the world is itself conceived of and grasped as picture. Visual "mastery" through "picturing" comes to be exerted over both rural and, increasingly, urban places.

Photography has come to enjoy exceptional legitimacy because of its power to present the physical and social world through what appear to be unambiguously accurate modes of representation. It is the most significant component of a new cultural economy of value and exchange in which visual images are given exceptional mobility and exchangeability. Photography is ineluctably bound up with the modern world, with the subjectivity of the observer, and with the extraordinary proliferation of signs and images that began during the first half of the nineteenth century, a process, incidentally, that substantially preceded the modernist Impressionism of the 1870s and 1880s.[27]

Sharratt describes the "present image economy"—according to which past objects and images are "now seen, looked at, predominantly if not exclusively, as potential mental souvenirs, as camera material, as memorable 'sights.'"[28] He distinguishes among three visual modes of producing these sights: the momentary glance, the gaze, and the enduring scan.[29] I have set out five forms taken by visual consumption of place which derive from these different modalities of the visual.

This transformation of vision into a modality of surveillance and discipline stems from the more general nineteenth-century process of "separation of the senses," especially the visual from the tactile. The autonomization of sight enabled the quantification and homogenization of visual experience, as radically new objects of the visual began to circulate (including commodities, mirrors, and photographs). These objects display not spiritual enchantment but a visual enchantment, an enchantment in which magic and spirituality have been displaced by appearances and surface features. The result is what Slater terms the "sanctification of vision"; modernity's disenchantment is based upon "seeing is believing" and "believing is seeing."[30] Cities themselves came to be remodeled so as to respond to and further enhance such a sanctification of vision. Architects and planners designed cities as places for the free play of the hegemonic visual sense.

The importance of the visual partly undermines the distinction between popular tourism and academic travel. Much academic work consists of producing and interpreting visual data. As tourists increasingly deploy photographic, cinematic, televisual, and other multimedia material, they parallel the ways academics produce and interpret the visual. The parallels are even closer in the case of disciplines that involve travel as a key research element. Thus, Gregory highlights the historical significance of the conception of the "world-as-exhibition" for the emergence of the discipline of geography in the eighteenth century.[31] This discipline appears to have developed on the basis of the visual representation of the world, through the world conceived of and grasped as though it were a picture. It is presented as an object on display, to be viewed, investigated, and experienced. Central to geography have been the culturally specific visual strategies of both landscapes or townscapes and maps. These have reinforced a particular Western view of the world. They reduce the complex multisensual experience to visually encoded features and then organize and synthesize these into a meaningful whole. They both capture aspects of environment and society through visual abstraction and representation; both express distance and objectivity from what is being sensed; and both organize and express control or mastery over what is being viewed, thereby ushering in new ways in which visuality is complicit in the operation of power.

Landscapes-townscapes and maps deploy the visual sense as a means of control and surveillance. Both therefore bring out what may be called the dark side of sight, the ways the visual is associated not only with metaphors of light or understanding or a clear view but with notions of surveillance, control, and mastery. Indeed much of Western philosophy in both the Anglo-American and Continental traditions has wrestled with this very contradiction between vision as lightness and vision as darkness (this is well demonstrated in Levin's analysis of "modernity and the hegemony of vision").[32]

Three of the twentieth century's most influential philosophers—Derrida, Heidegger, and Foucault—have all described the continued privileging of sight and, in different ways, of how such sight produces dark and destructive consequences. Foucault, for example, analyzes disciplinary power and the way it gradually replaces sovereign power. Such disciplinary power functions through normalization, surveillance, and observation, thereby gradually permitting the disposal of some of the more obviously authoritarian processes that had been employed up to the eighteenth century. Foucault's analysis of the power of the gaze shifts from the primacy of the individual knowing eye to its spatial positioning, especially via the panopticon, and of the relationship of that social vision to the operation of power.[33] Foucault disagrees with Debord and his concept of the "society of spectacle," according to which there is the "spectacularization of everyone," maintaining rather that "our society is one not of spectacle, but of surveillance. . . . We are neither in the amphitheater, nor on the stage, but in the panoptic machine."[34] Crawshaw and Urry discuss the diverse effects that the various senses have on the places that get visited.[35] Such places are subject to the inquisitive senses of visitors, especially that of the visual. Thus, living in a tourist honey pot is somewhat similar to being a prisoner in the Foucaultian panopticon.

This analysis clarifies how sight, which is often thought of as producing illumination and clarity (en*light*enment), also produces a dark side. A majority of the most powerful systems of modern incarceration in the twentieth century have involved the complicity of sight in their routine operations. Indeed it is often argued that we live in a surveillance society. Virilio, among others, has particularly emphasized the novel importance of video surveillance techniques to the changing morphology of the city.[36]

The fascination with *and* denigration of the visual that characterizes French social thought has its counterparts in the various discourses surrounding travel. We are aware that much travel involves, at least in part, the activity of sightseeing. Most such discourses emphasize the centrality of the seeing and collecting of sights—the operation of what was previously characterized as the spectatorial mode of visual consumption. Both townscapes and landscapes are subdivided and often appear as little more than the collection of a range of relatively unconnected sights, which may then be given an objectified form in photographs, postcards, models, and so on. In some cases, the process of collection dominates the process of travel.

Particularly ridiculed is the mere sightseer, who lets only the sense of sight have free rein. Such travelers are almost universally reviled as superficial in their appreciation of environments, peoples, and places. People are often embarrassed about being only sightseers. In the nineteenth century, for example, Wordsworth argued that the Lake District demands a *different* eye, one that is not threatened or frightened by relatively wild and untamed nature. It requires "a slow and gradual process of culture."[37] Much French social thought disparages the purely visual. Sight is judged not as the noblest of the senses but as the least penetrating, as getting in the way of real experiences that involve other senses and require the visitor to take much longer periods of time so as to be immersed in the site/sight.[38] Cultural criticism is leveled both at the tourists who are mere sightseers and at the companies and organizations that pander to them by constructing places for such superficial, contrived, and quick visual consumption.

In recent debates, some of the objects of the sightseer, paradigmatically Disneyland, are taken as illustrating hyperreality, forms of simulated experience that are more "real" than the original.[39] Such geographies rest upon hypersensuous experiences in which certain senses, especially that of vision, are reduced to a limited array of features, are then exaggerated, and finally come to dominate all other senses. This hyperreality is characterized by surface—where a particular sense is seduced by the most immediate and constructed aspect of the scene in question, whether it be the "eye" at a Disneyland or the "nose" and the sense of smell at a Fishing Heritage Center in Grimsby, England. This is a world of simulation rather than representation, a world where the medium is the message.

What such hyperreal places do not capture is another sense of the visual, what Jay characterizes as the baroque, the fascination with opacity, unreadability, and indecipherability, which has functioned as an alternative ocular regime within modernity. He talks of celebrating "the dazzling, disorientating, ecstatic surplus of images in baroque visual experience . . . [the] rejection of the monocular geometricalization of the Cartesian tradition. . . . The baroque self-consciously revels in the contradictions between surface and depth, disparaging as a result any attempt to reduce the multiplicity of visual spaces into any one coherent essence."[40] Jay talks of baroque planning being addressed not to reason but to the engagement and indulgence of all the senses, rather than to any one, dominant sense, or to the separation and exaggeration of each of them. Those few localities in the Western world still organized by a medieval street layout demonstrate something of this baroque sensibility.

Feminist theorists, who have also developed a critique of ocularcentric regimes, argue that concentrating upon the visual, or at least the nonbaroque versions of the visual, overemphasizes appearance, image, and surface. Irigaray contends that in Western cultures "the preponderance of the look over the smell, taste, touch and hearing has brought about an impoverishment of bodily relations. The moment the look dominates, the body loses its materiality."[41] Thus, the emphasis upon the visual reduces the body to surface and marginalizes the sensuality of the body. McClintock demonstrates the extraordinary intertwining of male power over colonized nature and the female body in the history of empire.[42] The male look over both can be seen as endlessly voyeuristic. She describes the tradition of male travel as an erotics of ravishment, in which the Western traveler conquers or fantasizes the conquering of both nature and women. She talks of the tradition of converting non-

European nature, the virgin territory, into a feminized landscape of the "porno-tropics."

By contrast, the claim is made that a feminist consciousness empha-sizes the dominant visual sense less and aims to integrate all the senses in a more rounded consciousness that does not seek mastery over the "other." Especially significant to female sexuality is the sense of touch. Irigaray argues that "woman takes pleasure more from touching than from looking, and her entry into a dominant scopic regime signifies, again, her consignment to passivity: she is to be the beautiful object of contemplation."[43]

City Life and Other Senses

I return briefly to nineteenth-century England and to the time around 1840 in which both photography and mass tourism were emerging. The House of Commons Select Committee of 1838 argued that because there were whole areas of London through which no thoroughfares passed, the lowest class of person was secluded from the *observation* and influ-ence of "better educated neighbors."[44] It was claimed that such people would be transformed and improved once they became *visible* to the middle and upper classes, both through surveillance of their behavior and through the inculcation of politeness. There were, of course, some crucial parallels in this argument with the rebuilding of Paris and the hugely enhanced visibility, the capacity to see and be seen, that emerged as medieval Paris was replaced by the grand boulevards of the Second Empire.[45]

These references in the mid-nineteenth-century British Parliament demonstrate how visibility was increasingly viewed as central to the reg-ulation of the lower classes. But at the same time that the "other" class was now to be seen in the massive cities of nineteenth-century Britain, it was definitely not to be touched. Indeed, Stallybrass and White argue that "contagion" and "contamination" became the tropes through which much nineteenth-century city life was apprehended.[46] As the "promiscu-ity" of the public space became increasingly unavoidable, so it was in-sisted that the upper and middle classes avoid touching the potentially contaminating other, the dangerous classes.

Two dichotomies operated here: gaze/touch and desire/contamination. The upper class sought mainly to gaze upon the other, for example while standing on their balconies. Stallybrass and White suggest that the bal-

cony took on special significance in nineteenth-century life and literature as the place from which one could gaze but not be touched, could
participate in the crowd yet be separate from it. The later development
of the skyscraper in Chicago in the 1880s led to further separation; its
panoramic windows enabled those inside to gaze down and across the
crowd, while being insulated from the odors and the potential touch of
those below. In Chicago the avoidance of the smells of the meat-
processing industry was an important spur to erecting buildings up into
the light. There are current parallels with the bird's-eye view provided by
the tourist bus: in but not of the crowd, one gazes down in safety, insulated from the heat, the cold, the rain, and the smells. It is as though the
scene is being viewed on a screen; sounds, noises, and the contaminating
touch are all precluded because the empire of the gaze, effected through
the screen of the bus, moves serenely over the disorderly other.[47]

The insulation of the upper classes, however, was never total.
Nineteenth-century novels and newspaper articles made the grotesque
visible while keeping it at a safe distance from the upper and middle
classes. Sons of the rich would often travel to areas of lowlife in the city
to gaze at sailors and prostitutes, rather like the late-twentieth-century
backpacker who visits the dark side of towns and cities of the global
marketplace. And, of course, some men did seek out the touch and feel
of the other by crossing to the dark side of the city and visiting (and
touching) prostitutes, opium dens, bars, and taverns. More generally we
have become familiar with the nineteenth-century phenomenon of the
urban flâneur, immortalized by Baudelaire and Benjamin, who sought to
immerse himself in the crowd but even then was not entirely at home.[48]
How travelers and visitors relate to the diverse sounds and sense impressions of a crowd of strangers remains one of the defining conditions
of the modern experience, involving an array of technologies, memories,
and selective use of the range of human senses.

One sense that became particularly significant in the cultural construction of the nineteenth-century Western city was that of smell.
Stallybrass and White argue that in the mid-nineteenth century "the city
. . . still continued to invade the privatized body and household of the
bourgeoisie as smell. It was, primarily, the sense of smell which enraged
social reformers, since smell, whilst, like touch, encoding revulsion, had
a pervasive and invisible presence difficult to regulate."[49] Smells, sewers,
and rats played key roles in the nineteenth-century construction of class
relations within large cities. Moreover, the popularity of the English sea-

side resort, which offered apparently clean, natural air, owed much to the desire to avoid the smells of the city. Such resorts were, in fact, some of the first urban places to adopt major public-health interventions.[50]

More generally, Lefebvre argues that if there is anywhere that "an intimacy occurs between 'subject' and 'object,' it must surely be the world of smells and the places where they reside."[51] Olfaction seems to provide a more direct and less premeditated encounter with the environment than do the other senses—and one that cannot be turned off. What needs investigation, therefore, are the diverse "smellscapes" that organize and mobilize our feelings about particular places (including what one might also call "tastescapes"). The concept of the smellscape effectively reveals how smells are spatially ordered and place-related. Indeed, the olfactory sense seems especially significant in evoking memories of specific places. Even if one cannot identify a certain smell, it can still be important in helping to create and sustain our sense of a particular place. In addition, a smell can generate both revulsion and attraction; as such it can play a major role in constructing and sustaining distinctions of taste. McClintock examines the nineteenth-century development of soap and the actual and metaphorical roles of cleanliness in the growth of the British Empire. She quotes a Unilever Company slogan from the period: "Soap Is Civilization."'[52]

The politics of smell not only enabled the production of new commodities for the mass market but also helped to construct the nature of the colonial encounter, to domesticate and purify it, and to invest it with intimate distinctions of bodily smell. The effect was that new notions of the natural hygienic body came to be imposed by the colonial power. Ruark effectively captures the paradoxical smellscape of the colonial city when he talks of "the smell of the white man, the white man's food and drink and clothing, the greasy stink of the white man's petrol fumes and belching diesel exhausts."[53] Bauman takes this argument even further, arguing that "modernity declared war on smells. Scents had no room in the shiny temple of perfect order modernity set out to erect."[54] For Bauman, modernity sought to neutralize smells by creating zones of control in which the senses would not be offended. Thus, zoning has become an element of public policy. Planners have accepted that repugnant smells are an inevitable by-product of urban-industrial existence. For example, refuse dumps, sewage plants, and industrial plants are all spaces in which bad smells are concentrated. But they are typically screened off from the tourist gaze by being situated on the periphery of cities. Tourist

sights are generally set at a distance from bad or offensive smells, although those for poorer visitors are less separated. The Indian Supreme
Court, for example, ruled in 1993 that two hundred factories should be
closed down in the town of Agra because pollution was posing a threat
to the Taj Mahal. But it was not only that the fine filigree work of the
white marble tiles was disintegrating; tourists were driven away by the
fumes of industrial and chemical processes.[55] Similarly, meeting places
in most hotels are regularly sprayed with scents. Flowers are arranged to
neutralize unwelcome smells and to endow the hotel experience with the
quality of fragrance.

Finally, Rodaway points out that although the visual world can be
turned on and off, rather like the photographs in a book or the images on
a television or computer screen, acoustic space cannot be turned off. Our
ears cannot be closed. Ihde argues that we are at the edge of the visual
sense, which in a way always remains partially distant from us, but that
we cannot avoid being at the center of acoustic sense.[56] Sound is simply
all around us. Moreover, as with smell, there appears to have been a
major historical shift from, in this case, aural to visual cultures. Aboriginal space has been said to be acoustic, for instance, whereas contemporary Western space is more visual. Still, aural culture within the West
seems to have been reinvigorated, as reflected in Muzak, loudspeakers,
boom boxes, telephone bells, traffic, motor boats, and so on. Few places
in contemporary cities are devoid of sound.

The Senses and the Tourist City

Even if tourism involves the superficial stimulation of a particular sense,
it does not follow that this is the only interaction taking place. Although
the production of a shared memory of an event, place, or person neces-
sitates cooperative work, often over considerable periods and within specific locales, this memory work may be prompted by a single sensual experience, such as a photograph, a smell, a taste, a sound, seeing some
artifact, and the like. But what gets recovered may involve a variety of
senses. Memories are often organized around artifacts and particular
spaces such as buildings, bits of landscape, rooms, machines, walls, fur-
niture, whatever. It is these spaces and objects that structure people's
capacities to reminisce, to daydream about what might have been, or
to recollect how their own lives have intersected with those of others.
The much-berated heritage industry may in fact play a significant role in

Street scene in Montmartre, with the white dome of Sacré-Coeur church in the background

This Parisian quarter is an archetypal bohemian milieu.

such reminiscence, especially where people encounter artifacts from their past that stimulate memories and dreams they once had. Places then are not just seen through the scopic regime of the sightseer but experienced through diverse senses. These may make us ache to be somewhere else or dread the prospect of having to stay put in a particular place for long periods.[57]

At the same time, some forms of institutional commemoration or official memories within societies silence alternative memories of the places and the past and involve particular senses, especially sight. Certain landscapes or distinctive buildings and monuments are often taken to represent a nation in ways that undermine alternative memories of other social groups, especially those of women and subordinate ethnic groups.[58] All sorts of social groups, institutions, and societies, in fact, develop multiple and often contradictory memory practices, although these may be excluded from view. Moreover, a complex rhetoric is often involved in the articulation of a discourse of memory that almost certainly engages a range of senses working across time and space.

The traditional concept of a tourist culture existing in sharp contrast with the rest of the society has become less plausible as symbolic representations bombard people in their daily routines. At the same time, as Venturi, Scott Brown, and Izenour's discussion of Las Vegas makes plain, tourist sites are increasingly using extravagantly inauthentic accessories to attract tourists.[59] Replicas of Egyptian temples, reconstructions of the Wild West or Victorian England, futuristic theme parks, Gaelic revival centers—all act as magnets to entice tourists. It is no longer enough for a tourist site to be merely a place of action or of dedicated relaxation. Now it must also distort time and bend space to produce the illusion of an extraordinariness or ecstasy of experience. The closer life in the tourist resort comes to resemble the pure play form, the more tourists will flock to visit. Because tourist cultures travel, the ante is never fixed. As we get more reconstructions of Mediterranean villages or Mexican saloons in shopping malls and more Thai and Chinese restaurants in city streets, so the tourist industry in the real Mediterranean, the real Mexico, Thailand, and China has to exert itself with ever more contrived representations of the apparent "reality" of these places.

The rate at which cultures travel varies; at the end of the twentieth century we are experiencing a speeding up of images and signs. The sheer density and velocity of signs and images have taken a quantum leap. One effect is that places and cultures are instantaneously communicated around the world, both intentionally through place marketing and more generally through the economy of signs. Recent events in the history of a place can become rapidly historicized and made part of its heritage for tourists, as in the demolition of the Berlin Wall. Sensational occurrence may invest ordinary places with the status of tourist attraction, mobilizing travelers to visit them while a larger audience of armchair travelers watch the sensation unfold on their television screens. Rojek's description of the effect of the O. J. Simpson trial exemplifies the phenomenon.[60] Sensational sights give the impression of history being made before one's eyes, producing what Rojek terms "collage tourism." Virilio also argues that the very representation of speed itself can distinguish one place from another.[61] He talks of the way a place may "dazzle," seducing the visitor with astonishing displays of image and information, simulacra and spectacle, people and products. He talks of the overexposed city without depth, beyond our senses, and of buildings as sites for the circulation of people, information, and images. These are places that appear full of "instantaneous" time.

All these processes affect historically established hierarchies among tourist locales. In the 1990s, a "consumption spaces hierarchy" encompasses an enormous array of places.[62] Within Britain, it certainly includes such resorts as Blackpool, Torquay, and Brighton but may also include inland leisure sites (Alton Towers), towns and cities (Bradford, Manchester), shopping centers (Merry Hill), museums and galleries (Tate Gallery of the North in Liverpool's Albert Dock), theme parks (Camelot), country areas (Catherine Cookson country), and heritage centers (Wigan Pier). Consumption spaces, which stretch across Europe and much of the rest of the world, compete to sell both themselves and often their reconstructed history and to provide the context for numerous other forms of consumption. The hierarchy is organized in terms of variegated distinctions of sense, taste, and fashion, distinctions mediated by the various senses.

Part II

Constructing Cities as Theme Parks

RICHARD FOGLESONG

Walt Disney World and Orlando Deregulation as a Strategy for Tourism

On November 22, 1963, Walt Disney and an entourage of top company officials flew in a borrowed jet from Tampa, Florida, to Orlando, fifty miles to the east. The night before they had stayed in a Tampa hotel under assumed names to avoid tipping off the press and stirring up land speculation. They were going to Orlando so that Disney could see the area one more time from the air before making a decision about buying a tract of land. The consultants' report on "Project X," as the stealth project was known among a handful of Disney executives, could take him only so far; ever the artist, he wanted to visualize the possibilities for himself.

Disney and his executives were close to selecting a site for their East Coast Disneyland. Marketing studies revealed that only 10 percent of visitors to Disneyland, in California, came from east of the Mississippi. An earlier plan for a theme park in St. Louis had fallen through, in part because the beer baron Augustus Busch had insulted Disney by arguing that beer should be sold in the park. In truth, Disney had never been keen on the St. Louis project, a multiparty venture tied to the rejuvenation of the city's waterfront. Company planners thereafter turned their attention to other locations—among them upstate New York, northern Virginia, and even New Jersey.

Interestingly, Niagara Falls was an early favorite, but it was rejected because its winter weather would have prevented the park from being operated year-round. Disney wanted to avoid having a seasonal workforce, fearing that he would end up with carnival-type workers like those in most amusement parks. So the search turned to Florida, which had the natural advantages of sunshine and water. Disney wanted to avoid the coasts, both to dissociate his theme park from an older genre of boardwalk amusement parks and to allow expansion in all directions. Ocala, located fifty miles northwest of Orlando amid white-fenced horse farms, was an early favorite because it was near the state's epicenter, in addition to having emotional appeal for Disney, who as a child had visited his aunt in nearby Geneva. But Ocala was soon rejected because, unlike Orlando, it lacked good road linkages.[1]

As their plane reached Orlando and circled south of the city, Disney looked down and saw a vast stretch of virgin land, much of it swampy and alligator-infested. What attracted him, however, were the roads: two major four-lane highways intersected southwest of the city. One was Interstate 4, then under construction, spanning Florida from Tampa on the Gulf Coast to Daytona Beach on the Atlantic; the other was Florida's Turnpike, running northward from Miami to Orlando and beyond. Disney's words were simple: "That's it."[2] Later, when asked what attracted him to Orlando, he would say: "The way the roads crossed."[3]

Roads were so important to Disney planners because tourists would have to be attracted from out of state to make the Florida theme park work. Even though the entire state of Florida had fewer people than the Los Angeles metropolitan area surrounding Disneyland, the Disney company wanted to build a park ten times the size of Disneyland. It would be not so much a Florida theme park as an East Coast tourist spa located in Florida. Disney planners called it a "total destination resort"; to make it work, they needed enough hotels, restaurants, and amenities to serve the many tourists who would travel down the East Coast to Florida.[4] Above all, that meant good road linkages, an advantage for Orlando since I-4 connected it with I-95, which runs along the Atlantic coast from Maine to Key West, and since Florida's Turnpike links via I-75 with I-10, which spans the country from Georgia to California. Whether tourists were driving south from New Jersey or eastward across the Gulf states, Orlando was well located—just what Disney consultants wanted.

From Orlando, the Disney entourage flew west, along the Gulf Coast to New Orleans, where they disembarked for the night. As they rode to their hotel, they noticed people crying on the streets, overwhelmed by the news that President Kennedy had been shot. It was a fateful day for central Florida, too, although Orlandoans did not know it until eighteen months later, when Disney revealed himself as the "mystery land buyer."

Disney's decision that day would transform Orlando from a sleepy agricultural community, more dependent on citrus than on tourism, into one of the most popular tourist destinations in the world. Orlando would also become one of the nation's fastest-growing urban regions, offering the amenities and developing the problems of other hypergrowth areas. Although Walt Disney World (WDW) alone did not transform Orlando, it was the most drastic agent of change; seldom has the location decision of a single corporation had such a colossal impact on a single community.

The Construction of Walt Disney World

The Disney World–Orlando story is not a case of industrial recruitment by an entrepreneurial government. Disney clearly chose Orlando, not the other way around. Yet he chose the site not only for its natural advantages—its climate, water, and inland location—but also for its transportation infrastructure, its compliant state government, and its local pro-growth regime. As explained below, Orlando's road system was formed by a leadership group that "baited the trap for the Mouse" without knowing which employer or industry, if any, they would snare.[5]

Luring Growth

Orlando in the 1950s and 1960s had a pro-growth regime headed by two men, Martin Andersen and Billy Dial. Andersen published the *Orlando Sentinel-Star* newspaper, and Dial was an attorney, deal maker and, after 1958, president of the city's largest bank. Going beyond the previous caretaker regime, these men organized what Clarence Stone terms a corporate regime, an informal leadership group dedicated to urban growth, especially in downtown Orlando, through a formula that emphasized roads, state and federal funding, and private-sector leadership backed by politically insulated institutions.[6] "We used to have a group that met once a week. There were about ten of us; some of them called us the movers and the shakers," said Dial. It was before Orlando had spread out, and the group concentrated on building the area's primary highway system. "We did everything we could to promote the city like that," added Dial.[7]

This group adroitly maneuvered to bring major roads to the area. Decisions on road construction were made by the five-member State Road

Board (SRB), appointed by the governor, and Andersen used his newspaper's political endorsements to gain advantageous appointments to the board. By the mid-1950s, Orlando had become the road hub of central Florida; then, in the 1960s, Dial and Andersen pursued bigger plans. They used Dial's appointment to the SRB to promote a plan to bring I-4 through Orlando, and they convinced state leaders to reroute Florida's Turnpike, so that it ran from Miami to Orlando instead of along the east coast. Although the road construction was not aimed at promoting tourism, the crisscross of highways was nevertheless what attracted Walt Disney.

Public investments, however, were only part of the bait for the Disney Mouse. The other part was deregulation and privatization, which correlated with Disney's desire for his own government, a desire generated by his experience of Southern California urbanization. Disney hated the ticky-tacky development of Anaheim, which surrounded Disneyland; he sought an alternative to the kind of urban growth wrought by fragmented land ownership and a weak public sector. His solution was, first, to buy a surfeit of land for his Florida theme park. Using dummy corporations based in Miami, his agents secretly purchased 27,500 acres southwest of Orlando for about two hundred dollars an acre. Second, he wanted private government, along with immunity from state and local regulations.

The idea of possessing his own government was part of Disney's larger plan for building a model city in Florida. From his first press conference in Orlando, Disney talked of building more than another Disneyland: a "city of tomorrow," he called it.[8] During early discussions of the Florida property, one company executive told Disney that he seemed to desire "an experimental absolute monarchy." "Can I have one?" was Disney's response. The answer was supposedly no, but the Disney company came close to getting what its chief executive wanted.[9]

With its tradition of ceding public powers to private firms, Florida offered fertile soil for kingdom building. Chapter 298 of the Florida Code permitted the creation of drainage districts that were controlled by the landowner rather than by residents and that could issue bonds and practice eminent domain. Acquiring such authority, the Disney company created the Reedy Creek Improvement District to carry out land reclamation work. It wanted more, however—immunity from building and zoning codes and a free hand in administering the theme park once it was constructed. These interests were apparent in a 1965 internal corporate memo from Paul Helliwell, a Disney attorney. Summarizing earlier conversations with Disney and other executives, Helliwell opined that to preserve their "freedom of action" in building the Florida park they needed a company-controlled government "superseding to the fullest extent possible under law state and county regulatory authorities."[10]

The company's desire to escape from popular as well as governmental control is even more apparent in their application for a "701" planning grant from the federal Department of Housing and Urban Development in 1966. There they proposed an experimental city that would "always be in a state of becoming," requiring that the city be "freed from the impediments to change, such as rigid building codes, traditional property rights, and elected political officials." The Disney company recommended a bifurcated government, in which planning and development would be under landowner control and only the remaining functions of government entrusted to elected officials.[11]

Before the legislative package could be formally presented, Walt Disney died unexpectedly, leaving control of the company to his brother, Roy, the corporation's financial manager. In February 1967, two months after Walt's death, Roy and his top executives presented their "demands," as Roy Disney called them in an apparent slip of the tongue, to a VIP audience of Florida's elected officials. They wanted municipal bonding authority, three highway interchanges, the widening of I-4 at the park entrance, increased trademark protection, and the creation of two municipalities together with an autonomous political district controlled by the company and empowered to issue tax-exempt bonds.[12] Roy Disney called the legislation "something that we would ask [for] in fairness for coming to Florida."[13] Said one of the government officials present: "It was as though they put a gun to our head. They were offering to invest $600 million, and there was the glamour of Disney. We were all just spellbound."[14]

The proposed two-tier government made it possible to comply with a court ruling that planning and zoning law be vested in a popularly elected government, while still permitting the Disney company to control the government and to enjoy regulatory immunities not available to other private developers or local governments. At the top tier of their government apparatus, embracing an area twice the size of Manhattan, was the Reedy Creek Improvement District (RCID). It would be controlled by the landowner, its board of supervisors elected on the principle of one acre equals one vote. Because the Disney company owned the land, it would elect the board. The bottom tier consisted of two municipalities, Bay Lake and Lake Buena Vista, each with a handful of residents who would be trusted Disney employees living in company housing. These residents would elect a government and then—ingeniously —transfer administrative responsibilities for planning and zoning to the Reedy Creek District, effectively circumventing the requirement that planning and zoning be controlled by residents.

The charter allowed the RCID to regulate land use, provide police and fire services, license the manufacture and sale of alcoholic beverages, build roads, lay sewer lines, construct waste-treatment plants, carry out flood projects—even build an airport and nuclear power plant, all without local or state approval. The company was creating a sort of Vatican with Mouse ears: a city-state within the larger state of Florida, privately owned yet enjoying regulatory powers reserved by law for popularly elected governments.

The Disney legislation sailed through the Florida legislature, passing without debate in both the House and Senate. Less than an hour after the vote, the SRB approved emergency funding of Disney's road request. Completing the approval process, the Florida Supreme Court ruled in 1968 that the RCID was legally entitled to issue tax-free municipal bonds. At issue was whether the bonding power permitted public funds to be used for private purposes. In a unanimous ruling, the court held that although the bonding power would "greatly aid Disney interests," it would likewise benefit the "numerous inhabitants of the district."[15] The district was thus free to issue $12 million in improvement bonds for reclamation, drainage, and road work on the Disney property.

These pivotal decisions in the 1960s set the framework for the Disney-Orlando relationship, imposing constraints on state and local government and giving a relatively free hand to Disney. Although the gifts of nature and state infrastructural investments first attracted Walt Disney to central Florida, it was a compliant state government—willing to satisfy his desire for kingdom building—that sealed the deal. The actions by the State of Florida have made WDW a model both of privatization (as an approach to city building) and of deregulation (as a strategy for stimulating tourist development). Both models are captured in Walt Disney's rhetorical ideal of creating a prototype city that would be a "showcase for free enterprise."[16] In reviewing the Disney World experience, we have an opportunity to examine the possibilities and contradictions of privatization and deregulation over a thirty-year period.

Consequences of Disney World

As a privatized model city, WDW works impressively well, at least on the inside. It was praised from the beginning as a model of urban planning; visitors were impressed by the scale and completeness of the coordination of themes, buildings, colors, landscaping, and transportation. David Brinkley, speaking on NBC at the park's opening, called it "the most imaginative and effective piece of urban planning in America." Brinkley was especially impressed with what had been done outside the amusement park in the planning of roads, transportation systems, stores, and hotels. "They all fit together in a setting of land, air, and water better than any other environment in America," he told television viewers.[17]

What made WDW so effective as a model city was not only the creativity of Disney designers but also the enormous power at their disposal: they had private power arising from centralized land ownership and public power deriving from Disney's government charter. The Disney company's ownership of forty-three square miles, an area about the size of San Francisco, gave them a kind of control not available to other land developers. And their legal authority exceeded that of local governments, including nearby Orlando, which, for example, had to comply with state land-use law, whereas Disney World before 1985 did not.

Through these combined private and public powers, the company fashioned an entire city, complete with fire stations, environmental protection, a phone company, landscape management, security, and dozens of other departments. On stage were exciting attractions, themed shops, restaurants, resort hotels, campgrounds, and recreation facilities. Backstage was a network of utilities, supply and maintenance facilities, and crisscrossing service tunnels that connected a vast underground hidden from public view.

As one Disney designer recalled, "We were very careful to avoid any contradictions in architecture and design. The challenge was not just in the theme park this time but outside the park because for this project we had total control. . . . We owned the immediate surrounding land."[18] Disney World's first two resort hotels, the Contemporary and South Seas, were built as architectural extensions of Tomorrowland and Adventureland, respectively. Whereas in California Disney planners had been shut out from designing the park's surroundings, in Florida the outside world of hotels, restaurants, shops, and the like still belonged to Disney; it could therefore be incorporated into the themed experience. In other words, the combination of privatization and vast land holdings gave Disney the political and economic capacity to internalize positive amenities.

Disney was thus able to overcome the barriers to effective planning created by fragmented land ownership and political democracy. One has only to look at the International Drive tourist strip, adjacent to WDW but not on Disney property, to appreciate the virtue of total control. I-Drive, which was "planned" under conditions of divided land ownership and political democracy, is a sprawling jungle of hotels, T-shirt shops, fast-food restaurants, and amusements—all mired in constant traffic congestion. Law enforcement officials complain of slow response time on I-Drive owing to traffic congestion, and county government temporarily imposed a moratorium on further I-Drive development in 1989 so that public planning could catch up with the steady march of private development.

For advocates of public planning, the disturbing message is that, outwardly, privatization seems to work better. However illiberal and undemocratic, centralized land ownership offers an effective antidote to the chaos of uncoordinated private interests. Likewise, the Disney company's central administration of WDW represents an antidote to the tendency of democracy to produce division and deadlock. It may indeed be easier to plan for the future, as the Disney company said in its 1966 grant application, without the "impediment to change of political officials."[19] In Disney's practices as landlord and urban administrator, both capitalist and government, we see the kind of enlightened planning that capitalists might practice if, as sometimes imagined, there were a cohesive capitalist class that could lay hold of urban government and impose its blueprint on the city.

Moreover, deregulation has clearly worked in the narrow sense of stimulating investment and job creation. Freed from local building codes, the whole twenty-five-hundred-acre complex was built in just eighteen months. Meeting the original deadline set by Walt Disney, the Magic Kingdom opened on October 1, 1971; by that time, the company had poured $500 million into the project, and nine thousand laborers had worked on it. Although the initial crowds were disappointing, by Thanksgiving the traffic backup on I-4 stretched for six miles to downtown Orlando, a harbinger of things to come.

Whereas only 3.5 million tourists had visited central Florida in 1969, only two years later, when the Magic Kingdom opened, ten million flocked to the Orlando area.[20] The Disney company immediately launched an

A fantasy castle, a themed escape within an escape, in the Magic Kingdom, Disney World

Disney enjoyed almost complete freedom from popular and governmental control.

ambitious expansion plan, Phase II, which added thirteen new attractions, as well as more guest accommodations, shops, and restaurants. By 1975, total investment stood at $700 million. Then, on October 1, 1982, the long-awaited Epcot Center was unveiled. It was not the residential city initially envisioned by Walt Disney but a sort of permanent World's Fair with industry-sponsored attractions displaying advanced technology in one section and pavilions underwritten by foreign governments that offered a glimpse of different cultures in another. By 1983, Disney had pumped $1.7 billion into the overall Disney World complex.

Six years later, Disney, in conjunction with MGM, opened a $500 million movie theme park. This 135-acre facility is both a functioning movie studio, with three sound stages, and a "gated attraction" where visitors can see movie stunts performed and watch re-created scenes from Disney and MGM films. The studio park was part of $1.3 billion in new Disney construction, including a water-thrill park, a nighttime entertainment and restaurant complex, and four new hotels with a total of forty-three hundred rooms. In 1990, the company announced a $1 billion plan for seven more hotels, an additional park, opened in 1998 as the Animal Kingdom, and twenty-nine new attractions at existing parks.

Even before Epcot, WDW had surpassed the Eiffel Tower, the Taj Mahal, the Tower of London, and the Egyptian pyramids in attendance. Welcoming 13 to 14 million visitors annually, the theme park in 1980 received 1.4 million foreign visitors, or 10 percent of all foreign travelers to the United States.[21] During Epcot's first year of operation, overall attendance at WDW shot up from 12.6 million to 22.7 million; because more than half of these visitors arrived by car, the area's traffic woes seriously worsened. In 1994, 33.2 million tourists visited the three-county Orlando metro area.

After the opening of the Magic Kingdom in 1971, Orlando became one of the nation's ten fastest-growing cities. The population of Orange County increased from 344,311 in 1970 to an estimated 670,000 in 1990, with new residents arriving at the rate of fifty per day. Within the three-county metro area, the population soared to 1 million by 1990 and was expected to reached 1.4 million by the year 2000. By the mid-1980s, Orlando had become the second fastest-growing city in the Sunbelt; in 1994, it was designated the nation's fastest-growing metro area.[22]

The Disney thunderbolt started a flash fire in real estate speculation. Between the announcement of plans for WDW and its opening in 1971, more than $200 million in real estate changed hands at the edge of the park, some of it selling for five hundred times 1965 values.[23] In turn, construction quickly became the area's leading industry after tourism. I-Drive, which was pushed through a pine forest in the month following Disney's arrival, along with a progression of new housing developments, from middle-class Goldenrod to upscale Tuscawilla to Arnold Palmer's exclusive Bay Hills, are the fruits of this building boom.

The explosion in hotel building is the best register of tourism's seismic impact. In 1965, the greater Orlando area had only eight thousand hotel rooms; yet by 1996, the three-county area had eighty-five thousand rooms—more than New York, Chicago, or Washington, D.C. Only Las Vegas has more. As local leaders like to say, "In Orlando our hotels are our factories." Besides attracting family vacationers, Orlando has become one of the nation's top ten convention centers, drawing more than $1 billion in convention business a year and providing work for approximately forty-five thousand central Floridians.[24] In 1993, almost 15 percent of foreign visitors to the United States made Orlando their first destination, placing mid-sized Orlando behind only Miami, Los Angeles, and New York among cities visited by foreign travelers.[25]

Impacts of the Development

In assessing Disney-style deregulation, it helps to consider the three sides to the growth issue: how to get it, how to manage it, and how to direct its costs and benefits. Privatization and deregulation, as WDW suggests, help generate growth, yet they thwart growth management and make it difficult to equitably apportion the costs and benefits of growth. As noted, WDW succeeds as a model city in part because its centralized powers permit it to incorporate positive amenities into the plan of development. But the reverse is also true: the powers enabling it to capture positive externalities allow it to impose development costs on the external public.

Consider traffic congestion. Disney World attracts an estimated 55,000 visitors per day, at least half of whom arrive by car. Many of its 35,000 employees compete with local motorists on I-4, which is both a commuter expressway in Orlando and the red carpet to Disney World. The downtown section of the roadway, which was intended for 80,000 vehicles, was receiving 140,000 cars a day by 1990.[26] Officials of the Florida Department of Transportation said in 1990 that I-4 needed $1 billion in improvements.[27]

Since then, Disney has contributed $12 million in funding and $21.45

million in land toward the construction of a beltway around Orlando, intended to relieve congestion on I-4.[28] At the same time, however, the company continues to seek infrastructure subsidies, in one case suing the state for not paying Disney enough for company land on which an interchange serving the property would be built,[29] in another case getting Orange County to pay half the cost—$53 million—for building its latest interchange.[30] Meanwhile, I-4 was handling upwards of 160,000 cars per day in 1995, with an expected growth of 12 percent per year.[31]

Consider the mismatch between tourist-industry wages and housing prices. Although housing prices in central Florida are only 82 percent of the national median, an Orlando city task force found in 1989 that two-thirds of the existing population could not afford the area's median-priced eighty-thousand-dollar home.[32] This problem has been aggravated by impact fees in Orange County and high land prices in the area around Disney. Because of a shortage of lower-priced homes and apartments, many Disney workers commute twenty-five miles north to Seminole County to find affordable housing. In the mid-1980s, Orlando Mayor Bill Frederick asked Disney to help rectify the shortage of homes priced between fifty thousand and seventy thousand dollars. But Disney's response was that it was a market situation and not its problem.[33] State government wanted Disney to assume responsibility for building affordable housing. The company resisted, however, for political as well as financial reasons: it did not want any more permanent residents—who could vote—on its property.

The continued growth of the complex heightened pressures on the housing market. The expansion plans announced in 1990 were projected to increase WDW's workforce from thirty-two thousand employees to more than sixty-seven thousand.[34] Plans for the new town of Celebration, revealed the following year, called for three golf courses, a massive shopping mall, a cultural center, and eight thousand private homes, though none of these would be affordable housing.[35] Under pressure from the state Department of Community Affairs, Disney first proposed to study the problem of affordable housing, then volunteered to produce a fourteen-minute educational film about affordable housing, and finally agreed to invest $13 million in two affordable housing complexes, neither on Disney property.[36] WDW thus gained a tax write-off for ten years, while Orange and Osceola counties gained affordable housing complexes, one containing 184 units, the other 280 units.[37]

Like other large corporations, the Disney company has sought to control its wage costs by reducing benefits and replacing full-time employees with part-time and contract employees who do not receive fringe benefits. In negotiations with the Service Trade Council in 1994, the company tried to get workers to contribute to their insurance premiums. The contract was overwhelmingly rejected, and after two weeks of negotiations the company agreed to pay 100 percent of the premiums of employees who chose a health maintenance organization.[38] During negotiations, a company document was leaked to the *Orlando Sentinel,* indicating that WDW hoped to save $79 million in employee benefits in 1988 by reducing benefits for full-time employees and increasing its part-time and contract labor staff, while expanding its workforce by nearly five thousand employees. The internal report called for a "shift toward a temporary labor base to help defeat the spiraling cost of EB [employee benefits]." At the time, nearly one out of every five employees already worked part-time.[39]

Consider the capacity of the local public sector to plan for growth. When the Disney company first came to Florida, it sought to prepare the private and public sectors for the impact of its theme park. Because Disney would initially build only two hotels, they encouraged the private sector to build additional hotels and restaurants and urged government to prepare for the effect on roads and public services, sharing information from its Disneyland experience. Yet, taxpayers were expected to pay for the needed facilities and services; the state even paid Disney for its land when it built the interchanges demanded by the company on I-4.

With subsequent expansion of the park, Disney's private powers impeded effective public planning. A key clause of the RCID charter specified that if a law was passed that conflicted with the charter, the charter "shall control" unless the law specifically repealed pertinent provisions of the charter.[40] Disney's cloak of immunity was thus extended into the future. In 1972, Florida adopted legislation requiring that "developments of regional impact" (DRIs) be submitted to advance plan review by regional planning agencies. This DRI requirement did not apply to Disney, however, because of the exemption in its 1967 charter. As a result, public planning was impeded, because local and state officials were denied the information needed to coordinate public infrastructure investments with Disney's private investments. County commissioners and public works directors learned about new Disney developments the same way everyone else did: from newspaper announcements.

Finally, consider the Disney company's thirty-year delay in building a prototypical residential community, as initially proposed in 1967. In a promotional film shown to the legislature when it was considering Disney's request for a governmental charter authorizing the RCID, the company described plans for an experimental community prototype—Epcot—with "an initial population of 20,000."[41] By 1997, however, there were more hotels than homes on Disney property. The population of the two cities within the RCID, Bay Lake and Lake Buena Vista, was forty-three; the residents, living in seventeen manufactured homes, were all nonunion Disney supervisors and their families, who safeguarded the company's control of the property.

As noted above, Disney began constructing the new town of Celebration in 1991. An example of the "new urbanism," this pedestrian-oriented, mixed-use development was located at the southern end of the Disney property in Osceola County. Although planned under the aegis of the RCID, it was de-annexed from the RCID so that its anticipated twenty thousand residents would not vote in Reedy Creek elections. Even before the first home was built in Celebration, demand exceeded supply. The company used a lottery to allocate the right to purchase the initial homes, which ranged from $140,000 town houses to $900,000 custom homes. Since mid-1996, when the first purchasers moved in, Celebration has been the hottest real estate development in the metropolitan Orlando marketplace. Buyers interested in a unique living experience could find it in Celebration. The town was designed to offer a blend of nostalgia and futurism, with front porches for rocking chairs and fiber-optic cabling for online communication between the community's eight thousand homes, all designed by top-name architects.[42] Its pricey housing was meant to offer neither affordability nor diversity; its location on the urban fringe was certain to contribute to urban sprawl and congestion; and its de-annexation from Reedy Creek ran counter to the Disney argument that governmental powers were needed precisely so it could build a model urban village.[43]

Political Reactions

The problems of transportation, affordable housing, and planning capacity provoked reaction from county as well as state governments. Political controversy was also fueled by the Disney company's more aggressive stance after Michael Eisner became chairman in 1984. Since then, Disney has exceeded its original mandate to create a "prototype community of tomorrow," building commercial facilities that compete directly with other area attractions. Disney World's new Pleasure Island competes with Orlando's Church Street Station, a downtown bar-and-dance complex, Typhoon Lagoon with an existing water-thrill park, and the Living Seas exhibition with Sea World. Disney has also moved headlong into the hotel business, becoming the area's leading hotelier. Because of the 1967 charter, all of this development was exempt from impact fees and regional plan reviews.

It was not until Disney began competing directly with public enterprise that Orange County became adversarial. In 1986, the company announced plans for a convention center that would compete with the county's convention complex. The county first threatened to sue, challenging the constitutionality of Disney's governmental powers, and then asked for payments in lieu of impact fees. After eighteen months of negotiations, an interlocal agreement between the RCID and Orange County was signed in 1989. The RCID agreed to pay $14.5 million over five years for the construction of roads to service WDW, the first time it has agreed to pay for roads serving Disney property. It also agreed to give the county forty-five days to comment "for informational purposes only" on proposed land-use changes and rezonings on its property. And the county agreed not to challenge Disney's governmental powers for seven years.

One of the two county commissioners who voted against the agreement labeled the RCID's $14.5 million payment "hush money."[44] The amount seemed small in comparison with WDW's transportation impact, the county's concessions, and the company's deep pockets (it made $703 million the previous year). But the agreement provided only a temporary lull in the Disney–Orange County conflict. Five months later, when CEO Eisner announced the company's expansion plans, county commissioners felt betrayed. Said one commissioner who had normally supported Disney, "I think in a way it may have been dishonest. We were bargaining in good faith . . . and this was an absolute surprise to Orange County. I didn't hear the plans from Disney, I heard it from reporters."[45]

Then, in January 1990, the RCID won $57 million in state bond money that the county had wanted to use for affordable housing. The Disney government used the money instead to enlarge its sewage-treatment plant, so that it could serve more tourists. The tax-exempt bond money was offered by the state on a first-come, first-served basis. By applying first, without coordinating its request with other governments in the area, Disney garnered all the bond financing for a six-county area. For this, the *Orlando Sentinel* called Disney "the grinch that stole affordable housing."

Even though Disney's actions were legal, they pushed to the fore a long-ignored question: whether Disney should be both sovereign government and private corporation. "It's terribly upsetting," said Commissioner Vera Carter, "that here we are trying to fight to get affordable housing, and we've got a private, profit-making enterprise using all of the resources."[46] Another commissioner was more direct: "It is un-American. They are a quasi-city not required to follow any growth-management. They can build whatever they please on that property and there isn't a thing we can do about it. . . . We can't even send out a building inspector."[47]

At the state level, the legislature adopted a Growth Management Act in 1985 that specifically applies to the Disney-controlled RCID. It marked the first time that a state land-use law was applied to Disney. The law, which took effect in 1990, required that local governments, including the RCID, project future development within their jurisdiction, formulate level-of-service standards, and demonstrate that service levels would not suffer with new development. As "the landowner," the Disney company was required to provide information regarding future construction, employment, affordable housing, and transportation needs. Made public through the RCID, this information was meant as an advance warning to area governments about Disney's expansion. Disney responded to these political challenges by creating the new position of vice president for government and community relations, filling the post with someone closely tied to Orlando and Orange County government leaders. In addition, it stepped up the level of fanfare surrounding its charitable donations.

Why were the Disney company's powers finally challenged in the 1980s? It was not because a new regime came to power; the local pro-growth regime in 1989–90 was essentially the same as before. What changed was that WDW's impact on public finance and public planning became more manifest, in part because of the arrogance of the Disney company. As Clarence Stone and other scholars have written, there may be consensus on growth in the abstract, but that consensus often breaks down over issues of finance, location, and other subsidiary issues.[48] That is what happened when Orange County sought to limit Disney's powers in 1989.

Yet the counterrevolution is far from complete. "The Mouse," as local residents call the Disney company, is hardly tamed. Protected by its private powers, it is still exempt from impact fees; it still has immunity from the requirement of having "development of regional impact" plans approved; and it still refuses to address affordable housing needs on-site. Owing to Disney's 1967 governmental charter, the county and state have little power to infringe upon Disney's freedom of action. As a result, the public sector is unable to impose linkage policies that would politically redirect the costs and benefits of growth.

Choices

The problem confronted by public planners is the unequal power relationship between the Disney company and the public sector. Although Disney is the largest taxpayer in Orange County, its exemption from impact fees and other growth-related assessments prevents the public sector from achieving linkage between the costs and benefits of growth. Disney's governmental charter institutionalized the power relationship that existed when Disney came to Florida in the mid-1960s. Then, Disney was in a controlling position; it could have gone elsewhere, and central Florida had not yet acquired significant locational advantages as a place to live and do business. Now, the de facto situation has changed. The Disney company has fixed capital investments in central Florida, and this section of the state has become an attractive site for business location and expansion. But the local public sector cannot use these locational advantages in bargaining with Disney over the scale and timing of the theme park's expansion. The Disney charter works like a prenuptial agreement, preventing the partners in this economic development marriage from bargaining as equals over the terms and conditions of their relationship.

This problem of unequal power is compounded by the transnational character of the Disney company. WDW is essentially a branch plant of an aggressive transnational corporation. When its founder, Walt Disney, was alive, it encouraged others to build hotels and tourist facilities in Orlando; under its present chairman, Michael Eisner, however, it has targeted local tourist facilities and hotels for competition. The same is true in Paris, where the company has built six hotels with fifty-two hundred rooms. A sense of economic partnership is lost when the regional economy's biggest actor is a transnational corporation without local, or even national, citizenship.

The WDW experience suggests that deregulation may help to stimulate urban growth, but it also constrains the capacity of governments to manage growth and to politically redirect the costs and benefits of growth. It might be termed the contradiction of deregulation: it fails when it succeeds. When it generates growth, it becomes a potential impediment to a community's ability to realize its collective interest. Even though some business and government leaders are demanding a more active role for government in development, market-oriented thinking continues to dominate the local political culture, influenced in part by a misreading of the WDW story. Loosening the hold of this viewpoint will necessitate more than an education in the requirements of urban development in the global era. It will call for a finer appreciation of the public investments that brought WDW to Orlando and of the constraints, and even harmful effects, of the prenuptial agreement signed with Disney in 1967. Symbolically and practically, revisiting that agreement is crucial to the area's economic future.

ROBERT E. PARKER

Las Vegas

Casino Gambling and Local Culture

The development of Las Vegas as a gambling-based destination for tourists can be divided into three periods. The first began with the legalization of casino gambling in 1931 and continued up until the late 1940s, when Benjamin (Bugsy) Siegel and other mobsters precipitated a larger, more sophisticated second phase. This era, characterized by the creation of lavish resort hotels (rather than just gambling halls) and the influence of organized crime, lasted until another notable Las Vegas resident, Howard Hughes, living in the Desert Inn penthouse, began negotiations for the casino in late 1966; he actually acquired a deed for it in 1967.[1] Finally, the past thirty years have witnessed intensified corporate control of the Las Vegas economy and diminished roles for organized crime and organized labor.

In the third period of development in particular, a loosely organized pro-growth coalition emerged to market the city as a tourist destination. Since the late 1980s, pivotal agents in the tourism industry have been wrestling with the city's image. There has been a movement to transform "Sin City" into "The All-American City," but most entrepreneurs in the gambling industry have determined that their earlier image was more profitable and are reemphasizing adult attractions and amenities. At any rate, their combined efforts have attracted a record number of visitors, many of whom travel to Las Vegas annually. At the same time, however, campaigns to entice and cater to tourists in a gambling-based economy divert attention from the needs and welfare of long-time residents and diminish the sense of local community.

From Legalized Gambling to Corporate Gaming

Legalized gambling has a relatively long history in the State of Nevada. From 1869 until Progressive Era reforms closed all casinos in 1911, gambling enjoyed great popularity in the state, particularly in silver- and gold-mining districts. Despite the prohibition, underground gambling continued and was well established in February 1931, when the state legislature legalized gambling for a second time. The chief motivation for legalization was the state's wish to tap into the underground gambling economy.[2] Still, during this early period, Las Vegas authorities were restrained in promoting the newly legalized gambling industry. They sharply restricted the number of licenses issued and confined the industry to a "red-lined" district. Moreover, gambling was largely limited to slot machines. Even in this limited form, however, gambling activity grew rapidly, thanks mainly to the infusion of massive expenditures by the federal government to construct Boulder (now known as Hoover) Dam and the Nellis Air Force Base. The dam, built between 1931 and 1935, required the efforts of five thousand workers who, together with their families, largely kept the Las Vegas gambling economy afloat during the Great Depression. Later in the decade, and particularly during World War II, the federal government again pumped vast resources into the local economy. Even more than gambling, this influx of funds transformed Las Vegas, originally a way station between Salt Lake City and Los Angeles, into a successful tourist destination.[3]

In December 1946 Bugsy Siegel opened the Flamingo at a cost of one million dollars. Although three other resort hotels were operating at the time, they were not major establishments. Siegel, who was reputed to be a cold-blooded murderer as well as a ladies' man, had become obsessed with building a lavish resort casino in Las Vegas that would transcend the Western-frontier-theme facilities. He wanted a venue attractive to Hollywood celebrities and competitive with international casinos. On opening night, the comedian Jimmy Durante performed before an audience filled with a host of Hollywood types. Cosmopolitan in design, Siegel's hotel essentially relegated competing facilities to the status of dude ranches. The Flamingo closed just one month later because of heavy losses but reopened in March 1947. After some shuffling of management personnel, it quickly became profitable. Although Siegel had just a few months to enjoy his success before being assassinated in Southern California, he was influential in setting the tone for the kinds of casino resorts that would shape Las Vegas's future. In the coming decades, gambling facilities were distinguished by their lavishness, their location on the outskirts of the Strip (as opposed to the downtown gambling district), and the influence of organized crime. Growth in the tourist trade during this period was greatly enhanced by postwar consumer culture. Pent-up demand for vacations and automobiles (particularly in nearby Southern California) created a whole new class of upscale consumers from which Las Vegas could effectively draw.

Despite stepped-up efforts to get rid of mob influence, fundamental change in the ownership structure of Las Vegas casinos awaited the arrival of Howard Hughes in 1966, when he began a reclusive existence that would last until late 1970. Hughes visited Las Vegas a number of times during the 1930s and 1940s and stayed for a time in the mid-1950s. He returned to Las Vegas on Thanksgiving eve, 1966, and left suddenly four years later, to the day. Within weeks of an unanticipated arrival at the Desert Inn, Hughes had started negotiations to buy his first Las Vegas property—the Desert Inn. The management of the inn had asked Hughes to leave to make room for some of the casino's high rollers. This prompted an angry Hughes to make an offer to buy the hotel, and he became the owner in spring 1967. Then, in a systematic, methodical way, he began to buy casino properties, including the Sands, the Frontier, and the Silver Slipper, all of which were near the Desert Inn. By 1968, Hughes was the largest casino operator in Las Vegas as well as in the state. As Moehring notes, "Like an invincible monarch, he pursued his quest to corner the casino market and transform Las Vegas into his personal fiefdom."[4] In expanding his corporate empire, Hughes also acquired vacant real estate, the local CBS television affiliate, two airlines, and two air terminals. He also intended to acquire Caesar's Palace, the Dunes, and the Riviera, as well as gambling properties in Reno and Lake Tahoe. U.S. Attorney General Ramsey Clark, however, blocked his buying binge (save the Landmark Casino in late 1968) on the grounds that he was in violation of antitrust laws. Stymied and disappointed by lack of support from his political allies in the state, Hughes left Las Vegas over the Thanksgiving weekend of 1970, never to return.

In spite of his inability to capture the entire market, Hughes and his numerous corporate subsidiaries had become the dominant city builders in Las Vegas. Their imprint remains today as a vital part of southern Nevada's residential and commercial development. Most important, Hughes, caught up in his own feverish obsession to monopolize Las

Vegas's gambling industry, did what gaming regulators had been unable, or unwilling, to do—largely rid the city of gambling properties that were overtly owned or controlled by organized crime. Hughes had, in essence, upped the ante in terms of entry costs for gaming-facility operators. Because of his enormous wealth and political influence, only entrepreneurs positioned to draw on corporate wealth could afford to match the increasingly lavish ambiance of Las Vegas casinos.

One such individual, Kirk Kerkorian (of MGM Studios and Western Airlines), was just emerging as a local competitor (with his completion of the International Hotel and Casino) when Hughes unexpectedly departed. At the time of its 1969 opening, Kerkorian's $65 million International was the world's largest resort hotel, with thirty thousand square feet of casino space and more than fifteen hundred rooms. Today, Kerkorian's corporate investments continue to alter the face of Las Vegas. When his five-thousand-room MGM Grand Hotel and Casino opened in 1993, Kerkorian could again lay claim to owning the world's largest resort hotel. A handful of corporate giants now controls some 60 percent of the gambling activity in Las Vegas.

Tourism in Las Vegas in the 1990s

In mid-1995, a survey conducted by the American Society of Travel Agents revealed that Las Vegas, for the second consecutive year, was the second most popular summer travel destination in the United States, behind Orlando, Florida. One year later Las Vegas was rated the most popular destination in the United States for domestic travelers, Orlando being a close second.[5] The society's president attributed the desirability of Las Vegas to the city's developers, who stay one step ahead of the competition "by building sights that attract more and more families for their vacations."[6] To be sure, more sights were being built and more people were visiting each year; however, the growth in the tourism trade had little to do with a rise in the number of family vacations. In fact, the proportion of tourists under the age of twenty-one had risen only slightly in the 1990s, from roughly 7 percent in 1990 to nearly 8 percent in 1995.

According to officials with the Las Vegas Convention and Visitors' Authority (LVCVA), 28.6 million tourists visited Las Vegas in 1995, an 8.7 percent increase over 1994's record 26.3 million. Following the World Trade Organization, Las Vegas defines a tourist as someone who stays away from home at least one night. This distinction is important when comparing Las Vegas with, say, Atlantic City, where most of the gambling is day-tripper activity. Las Vegas remains unique in being a true gambling destination for tourists. On average, 88.2 percent of the area's 89,594 hotel and motel rooms were occupied in 1995, representing a slight decline over the previous year's occupancy level, and most who visited were drawn because of the celebrated gaming casinos.[7]

Nevada's investment in gaming infrastructure is substantial. As of 1995, the state had nearly 400 casinos offering the gambler 5,877 table games and 164,625 slot machines.[8] For the fiscal year 1994, gambling in Nevada increased by nearly 11 percent over the previous year. Gaming profits amounted to $6.6 billion in 1994, of which less than $390 million was turned over to the state in taxes.[9] Nationally, gambling patrons spent more than $44.4 billion in 1995, an advance of more than 11 percent over 1994. Casinos took in the highest revenues among all types of commercial gaming: winnings in 1995 amounted to $18.0 billion. The "handle"—the amount of money that flowed through all forms of gaming—increased even more rapidly, at a 14 percent clip, reaching more than $550.3 billion.[10]

The Corporate Casino Culture

In the 1940s and 1950s, the major casinos and hotels in Las Vegas were owned and operated by individual entrepreneurs, such as Benny Binion and Sam Boyd, with underworld operators playing a major role. Today, however, large corporations dominate the gaming-based tourist trade in Las Vegas. Although vestiges of organized crime may remain, the listing of the ten largest hotels and casinos (and their owners) clearly highlights the transformation from individual proprietorship to corporate dominance under shareholder ownership and control. Indeed, in 1993, when ITT purchased the Desert Inn Hotel and Casino, the transnational firm (among other ventures, ITT operated a casino in Greece and a hotel and resort in Mexico) joined seven other corporations that together generate more than 60 percent of Nevada's earnings from gaming. Thus, the 1967 purchase of the Desert Inn by Howard Hughes's Summa Corporation in 1967 began a trend toward corporate domination of the Strip.[11]

New projects and major expansions added nearly ten thousand new hotel rooms to the city between 1996 and 1998. Three major casino resorts, the Luxor, Treasure Island, and the MGM Grand Hotel and Casino, opened in 1996; in addition, several existing facilities expanded, one of

A section of the Strip in Las Vegas, Nevada, one of the most popular destinations in the United States

The five-thousand-room MGM Grand Hotel and Casino, a centerpiece of this gambling mecca, opened in 1993.

which, the nine-hundred-foot-high, $400 million Stratosphere, featured thrill rides at its apex. Since then, other corporate projects have included New York, New York, a $500 million casino based on the theme of Manhattan, featuring twenty-one hundred hotel rooms and suites. A joint project of Primadonna Resorts and MGM Grand, Inc., the facility consists of ten New York–style towers and a nine-story parking garage. Yet another significant Las Vegas casino project is the Orleans Hotel and Casino, a $165 million investment of Coast Resorts, Inc., and Tiberti Construction. The facility, modeled after New Orleans's French Quarter, showcases a Bourbon Street shopping mall and one hundred thousand square feet of casino space and adds more than eight hundred hotel rooms to the city's growing inventory of tourist accommodations. Additionally, there was a major $250 million expansion at the Luxor, and a more modest $60 million Reserve casino.[12] The Monte Carlo, a thirty-two-story tower, was another joint venture involving two major actors in the gaming industry—Circus Circus Enterprises and Mirage Resorts. This development added 3,024 additional rooms to the area's hotel stock and provided ninety thousand additional square feet of casino space. Finally, the $150 million Sunset Station Hotel and Casino, a joint development of Station Casinos, Inc., and Tiberti Construction, offered eighty-five thousand square feet of casino space, more than five hundred hotel rooms, and retail and nongaming entertainment amenities.[13] Although some of the new casinos devote less space than older ones to gaming, the greater area devoted to slot machines, as compared with table games, permits the casinos to use the space more efficiently.[14]

Conventions and Conventioneers

Las Vegas is, above all, a destination for those seeking adult entertainment and a gaming milieu. But it is also one of the most highly ranked convention cities in the country. In 1995, Las Vegas was host to 2.9 million convention delegates, up from 2.6 million in 1994. According to convention officials, business in Las Vegas doubled between 1985 and 1995 and grew by 30 percent more in 1996 alone.[15] At least a dozen of the conventions held in 1996 attracted a minimum of 40,000 conventioneers each.[16] The largest single convention each year, the computer exhibition known as Comdex, drew over 225,000 industry officials and business consumers in 1996. Of this number, 35,000 were estimated by the convention bureau to be international visitors. Despite the hefty influx of tourists that Comdex generates, casino operators generally benefit little from it.[17] Traditionally, a disproportionate number of attendees have been nongamblers and penurious tippers, so much so that hotel executives raise room rates during the Comdex convention to compensate for the lack of gaming revenue. For instance, in 1996 single and double rooms at the Las Vegas Hilton and MGM Grand went for $225 a night during the convention, more than twice the usual charge. Other hotels that normally rented rooms for $40 per night were asking (and getting) $125. Although conventioneers were expected to leave some $320 million behind, proportionately the biggest economic beneficiaries were small businesses, such as area restaurants and dry cleaners.[18]

A Fleeting Family Flirtation

Early in the 1990s, many Las Vegas gaming facilities began experimenting with a high-profile marketing transformation. Owners and operators of large resorts, believing that they faced competition from Native American casinos, riverboat gambling, state lotteries, and other forms of legalized gambling, concluded they needed to broaden their market if they were to maintain their preeminent position in the tourist industry. Their objective was to discard the traditional portrayal of Las Vegas as an adult-centered playground and to embrace a new, wholesome image conducive to family entertainment.

A spokesperson for the LVCVA proclaimed that "Las Vegas is really a good value for the family. It'll get even better when we complete some new family-oriented projects."[19] Cam Usher, general manager of sales with the city's convention and visitors' association, stated: "The emphasis is and will continue to be on the family market." Elaborating, Usher commented that "family theme parks are especially important to Las Vegas in the wake of the opening of casinos in Phoenix, Biloxi, Missouri, and New Orleans. As more cities compete for the gambling dollar, Las Vegas will have to become more diverse in order to stay ahead of the competition."[20]

Although Circus Circus began to offer family entertainment in the 1970s, the real move in this direction came in 1989, when both the Mirage and the Excalibur casino resorts began operations. At the Mirage, patrons can view an exploding volcano, white tigers, and dolphins between gambling binges, and at the Excalibur, visitors have a wide range of nongambling activities to choose from, including the re-creation of a medieval jousting duel. Both enterprises attracted a lot of attention and did indeed produce the intended effect of attracting more families and couples to the city. The trend continued in the early 1990s, with casinos reserving sections of their facilities for youth- and family-oriented attractions. At both the MGM Grand and Circus Circus casinos, developers constructed entirely separate structures and built theme parks within them (the Land of Oz theme park at the former, and Grand Slam Canyon at the latter). At the Luxor, a winding Nile River excursion and state-of-the-art virtual-reality novelties are interspersed throughout the casino. As will be noted later, this blurring of casino space with nongambling recreational space contributed to a growing problem associated with a gambling-based economic infrastructure—underage wagering. Nonetheless, gaming as well as nongaming entertainment entrepreneurs in Las Vegas continued to nurture the image of Las Vegas as a place to bring the entire family.

By 1993, this new family orientation appeared to have become a rousing success. According to a 1994 report by Christiansen Cummings Associates Inc. of New York, Las Vegas was the nation's pacesetter in making entertainment attractions at casino properties an essential element in prolonging a customer's visit to gaming facilities. Although expressing caution about the expense involved in constructing and maintaining indoor roller coasters, among other attractions, the president of the consulting firm highlighted the Luxor and the MGM as two casinos that successfully integrated gaming and nongaming entertainment.[21] In mid-1993, Circus Circus completed its $90 million, 350,000-square-foot, climate-controlled, pink-hued Grand Slam Canyon. Some five thousand youngsters attended the opening of the entertainment facility, in spite of its being held on a school day. The Canyon theme park featured motorized dinosaurs, a roller coaster, and a flume ride.[22] During this period, other entrepreneurs were developing self-standing sports complexes, bowling alleys, pool halls, and multiplex cinemas.

The marketing campaign emphasizing family entertainment in Las Vegas was picked up and amplified by the mass media. In early 1994, *Time* magazine carried images of the Luxor on the cover with the headline: "Las Vegas: The New All-American City."[23] In the same month, *U.S. News and World Report* carried a prominent piece titled "Las Vegas Gamboling: The Neon City Has Reinvented Itself as a Vacation Mecca for Families."[24] The national media attention given to transformation helped seal the belief in many operators' minds that substantial profitability lay in entertaining the entire family. At the same time, however, others in the industry were questioning the new sanitized approach to marketing Las Vegas. The realization that, despite heightened numbers of tourists, Las Vegas was losing its unique reputation as an adult tourist destination began to dawn on key actors in the industry. Marc Grossman, vice president of communications for Hilton Hotels Corporation, says the trend toward theme parks and water rides may be just an industry fad. Grossman makes plain the intentions of Hilton Hotels regarding future expansion of their gambling properties: "Changes in store for the Las Vegas Hilton do not include amusement rides or other family attractions. Hilton is not going to be a kid's place."[25]

In sum, in the 1990s powerful agents within the gaming industry debated the path Las Vegas should pursue. One development in particular appeared to turn the tide against the family entertainment image—a widely circulated report by the LVCVA detailing the differences in gambling behavior exhibited by patrons with children and those without. The data clearly indicated that Las Vegas casinos are more profitable when they invest in adult attractions rather than in those aimed at youth. First, gamblers with children make up only about 7–8 percent of the gambling population. And, significantly, this figure changed little in the first half of the 1990s, during which time the number of Las Vegas tourists rose from 21 million to more than 28 million. This finding means that hotels, casinos, and resorts are investing substantial amounts of capital (to maintain high-tech theme parks and similar youth-oriented attractions) for a relatively small part of the tourist market. Formal and informal surveys of professional gamblers in Las Vegas also revealed little patience for the city's new family-values orientation to tourism. But perhaps the most compelling findings focused on the differences in the amount of money individuals brought to Las Vegas to wager, broken down by type of patron. Gamblers with children allocated themselves an average of $296 for wagering, compared with $504 for individuals who visited Las Vegas without children. Childless gamblers, the report showed, also spent more time gambling, gambled a higher amount of money per wager, and were three times more likely to place keno or bingo bets than were those with children. The study revealed only two categories in which people with children spent more money than childless individuals—sightseeing and retail trade, neither of which are directly connected to casino investments.[26]

Faced with the fundamental economic reality that the family-orientation strategy was not very profitable, many of the larger hotels and casinos hastened to distance themselves from those advertising themselves as family friendly. For example, executives of Mirage Resorts, which presently operates the Mirage, has made it clear they would actively discourage families when they opened Bellagio (a $1 billion resort) later in the decade. Other companies highlighted adult themes in their advertising, and several casinos remarketed themselves as facilities that catered to adult gambling patrons—period. The Riviera, for instance, changed its advertising and slogans to unmistakably differentiate itself from the "wholesome family" image: in 1994, the casino began using the slogan "We're the entertainment center of Las Vegas and the alternative for grown-ups."[27] Even the MGM Grand Hotel and Casino modified its thirty-three-acre theme park by jettisoning some youth-oriented rides in favor of such adult nongambling amenities as musical and comedy shows. The consensus among the corporate decision makers was that families just got in the way. Reflecting the turn away from families, the LVCVA's 1995 tourism campaign was strategically aimed at adults: "Las Vegas —Open 24 Hours." A spokesperson for Circus Circus Enterprises, which had initiated the movement to lure the family trade, commented: "Our primary goal always has been, and still is, to bring in good gaming customers."[28]

Clearly, Las Vegas's retreat to its adult-centered roots was driven by financial considerations; opposition to broadening the city's appeal, however, came from other sources as well. A number of religious and other antigambling crusaders (such as the National Coalition against Legalized Gambling) had been attacking Las Vegas ever since the visible shift toward the family orientation. Six years after they began their struggle, they could claim some measure of success despite the political weakness of their constituency. Certainly the family-marketing approach, even while exposing new elements of the population to the city's temptations, had not cleaned it up. For all of the emphasis on families, the city remained notorious for underemployment, prostitution, and the myriad social problems associated with compulsive gambling. Whether the present reemphasis on adult attractions will succeed in increasing profits remains to be seen.

The city remains vulnerable to competition from the many forms of legalized gambling that have spread across the United States. According to an annual report prepared for *International Gaming and Wagering Business*, numerous casinos opened or expanded in 1995 in both the

Las Vegas—Sin City or All-American City?

Tourists in Las Vegas can experience this simulated New York City.

United States and Canada, and revenues were up sharply in states with existing facilities. The number of riverboat casinos also increased. But perhaps the greatest threat to Las Vegas's tourist economy came from the aggressive establishment of casinos by Native Americans. As of April 1996, 130 Native American tribes had successfully negotiated gaming compacts in twenty-four states.[29]

The Underside of the Tourist-Driven Economy in Las Vegas

To many outsiders, Las Vegas might appear to be an unambiguous success story. In fact, the Vegas Valley endures many social costs resulting from the prevailing casino culture. The imprint of the tourist-based gaming economy is manifest in widely touted job-creation figures.[30] At the same time, however, it has fostered the spread of compulsive and un-

Table 1 Leading Occupations, Las Vegas, Metropolitan Statistical Area

Occupation	No. of Individuals Employed
Waiter	18,110
Retail salesperson	17,140
General office clerk	12,760
Janitor, cleaner	11,980
Maid	11,510
Blackjack dealer	10,860
Carpenter	9,910
General manager, executive	9,490
Security guard	9,180
Bookkeeper, accountant, accounting clerk	7,900
Bus person, bar helper	7,420
Secretary	6,610

Source: State of Nevada 1996.

derage gambling;[31] in the struggles of everyday citizens to afford housing while earning service-sector wages;[32] in the diminution of public space in favor of private;[33] the bankruptcy of mom n' pop stores;[34] the ever-present fiscal crisis of the local government as it attempts to simultaneously subsidize large, profitable gambling establishments and provide the material and immaterial infrastructure needed to service the local citizenry;[35] and the degradation of the natural environment.

Despite the seductive impression created by Hollywood films, television, and popular periodicals, working in the Las Vegas tourist economy usually means earning low wages, receiving few benefits, and tolerating unpredictable work schedules and stressful working conditions. Understanding the impact of gaming-based tourism on Las Vegas workers requires a close look at the kinds of positions that provide the greatest number of jobs (see table 1).

These data reveal that the occupational structure of Las Vegas is heavily dependent on service-sector employment. In 1994, 45 percent of employment in the state of Nevada was in the service industries, compared with 27.5 percent nationally.[36] The importance of the service sector is even more profound in the Las Vegas metropolitan region, which essentially relies on a single industry—tourism—to support its economy. Just over half of the five-hundred-thousand person labor force in southern Nevada is employed in the hotel, gaming, and resort sector of the Las Vegas economy.

Looking at the twelve major areas of employment in Las Vegas, one can generalize about the conditions of most casino jobs. As a rule, these jobs require neither a formal education nor specific occupational training. Indeed, the occupations that account for a disproportionate amount of casino employment do not even warrant a high school diploma. Even fewer occupations demand postsecondary education. Similarly, the occupations projected to grow the most rapidly in the 1990s tend to be low-skill, low-wage, dead-end service jobs—among them, janitors, preschool and kindergarten teachers, and home health aides.[37] Further, according to Census Bureau data released in 1994, of all major cities Las Vegas had the lowest percentage of workers in skilled occupations, such as executive, managerial, or technical positions.[38] A study two years earlier, prepared by the market research firm of Boyd Company, Inc., cited "vast underemployment" in southern Nevada, defined as employees "working below skill and education levels." Reacting to the report, Keith Schwer, director of the Center for Business and Economic Research at the University of Nevada, Las Vegas, commented: "In the final analysis, with the service industry being the dominant employment sector . . . and until more entry-level, high-wage jobs are created, college-educated and skilled workers in Southern Nevada may have to settle for positions which may be below their skill level, and a lower wage than they are accustomed to."[39] In 1992, service workers employed in the hotel, gaming, and entertainment industries earned an average of $19,960 annually.[40]

Because of the low wages in casino employment, the opportunity to own a median-priced house is beyond the resources of many southern Nevadans. Housing affordability is a key element in the message that Las Vegas boosters use to sell the city, and the popular media has echoed and reinforced the notion of inexpensive housing in Las Vegas. In fact, however, according to a 1995 canvas conducted by the National Association of Home Builders, Las Vegas ranked 139th out of 175 metropolitan areas surveyed for housing affordability.[41] The rapid growth of the Vegas Valley, strongly stimulated by the demand for new tourism workers, has caused prices to rise for all types of housing in the region. Between 1992 and 1994, the average wage increased one-quarter of 1 percent, while in roughly the same period new home prices increased by 8 percent (to just under $122,000). Conditions have not been any better for renters. Southern Nevadans, who were already paying an average of more than $600 a month for rent, endured an increase of 16 percent in rental costs between the first quarter of 1994 and that of 1995.[42] The mismatch between the kinds of jobs generated by the gambling economy and the available housing stock in the metropolitan region has created a difficult hurdle for migrants seeking to find a permanent home. A major portion of housing construction in Clark County has been aimed at the upscale market, whereas most of the jobs being created have provided relatively low incomes.

To a large extent, the financial welfare of these low-wage workers has been heavily dependent on the generosity of tourists who augment service-worker incomes with tips and "tokes" (a local synonym for tips, derived from the days when it was conventional for gambling patrons to give casino dealers a gambling token following a winning hand).[43] In the past two decades, visitors have grown less liberal in offering these traditional forms of supplementary income. Moreover, the Internal Revenue Service makes tips a problematic income source for workers; federal agents, who investigate each establishment and determine the average tip amount for a given period, work on the dubious assumption that workers consistently earn that income level, then tax them regardless of the actual amount earned, and audit taxpayers in Nevada at a rate 2.5 times the national average.[44]

Despite the tremendous wealth that pours through the Las Vegas economy, very little of it, compared with other states and cities, is reinvested in the community. Instead, from land development to pedestrian crosswalks, the public sector seeks to accommodate the wishes of the gaming industry and often does so at taxpayers' expense. At 7 percent, taxes on gaming revenues are the lowest in the nation. In many tourism-based cities, hotel-room taxes are used to help develop the community's infrastructure. In Nevada, however, room-tax dollars must be used to promote tourism.[45] Las Vegas-based casino corporations, in bidding to develop facilities in Chicago and New Orleans, offered to pay a tax rate approximately twice that mandated by Nevada. With sales taxes constituting the only other significant source of state income, it is not surprising that Nevada's social welfare programs rank among the nation's lowest. Even in boom times, the state has trouble paying for education, as revenues are sparse and the population has grown so rapidly.

In the southern Nevada area, the local growth coalition long ago popularized and legitimized a gospel of unregulated economic activity. No downside is recognized. To illustrate, consider this excerpt from an article in the city's leading newspaper: "Las Vegas' sizzling economy, bolstered by a strong gaming industry, sustained population growth, and business development, was the envy of the nation in 1995. The metro area's job growth, low taxes, booming tourism market, and growing retirement base made headlines in a slew of national media reports. When all the numbers are gathered for 1995, Las Vegas will show strong growth in employment, gaming revenue, business sales, home sales, and population."[46] In addition to the local media, the Nevada Resort Association (a powerful group of thirty-two of Nevada's largest hotel-casino operators), local chambers of commerce, the Nevada Development Authority, the Las Vegas Convention and Visitors' Authority, the airline industry, and allied public officials are all important elements of the growth coalition in southern Nevada.

To transform Las Vegas into a money machine, a loosely organized growth coalition has assiduously promoted Las Vegas (and Nevada) as a place with a "good business climate"; by this they have meant it is a profitable locale for businesses and a tax haven for residents. Nevada has no corporate or income taxes, no inheritance, estate, or gift taxes, and no franchise or inventory taxes. Another important feature of the good business climate is the ready availability of an abundant pool of low-wage labor. Nevada is a right-to-work state, a fact economic development officials stress in contrasting their business climate with that of neighboring California and Idaho, as well as nearby New Mexico and Colorado. Consequently, few workers are members of labor unions (only 7 percent of the local labor force compared with 15 percent nationally). Various subsidies and incentives are routinely offered to real estate developers by jurisdictions in southern Nevada. For example, Bob Snow, the developer of Church Street Station in Orlando, received nearly $18 million in cash and real estate from pro-gaming politicians in Las Vegas to subsidize his development of a casino known as Main Street Station. The Victorian-styled facility opened in September 1991, closed in June 1992, and registered just one profitable month. Snow was an unknown entity in Las Vegas when he applied for the subsidies, yet city authorities risked and lost nearly $20 million on one project as a demonstration of their commitment to attracting outside capital.

The social costs of tourism are easy to identify. Traffic congestion was just a harbinger of larger problems. At peak times, it takes up to thirty minutes to travel the two blocks from Tropicana Avenue to Flamingo Road on the Strip. As a result of the traffic glut—made worse by the vast numbers of cars rented by tourists—air quality has deteriorated. More vehicles emitting more carbon monoxide, together with construction activity and high winds stirring up dirt and dust, is an ever-increasing problem in the metropolitan area. According to a 1996 report by the Environmental Protection Agency, Las Vegas and New York City tied for fifth place in their levels of carbon monoxide pollution. In 1996, Las Vegas was out of compliance with federal standards for both dust and carbon monoxide.[47]

Perhaps the most damaging aspect of the tourist trade will turn out to be the degradation of the natural environment. This desert city appears surrealistically punctuated with man-made lakes, streams, fountains, and golf courses. In spite of its desert location, the Las Vegas metropolitan area consumes far more water than nondesert regions of a similar size: in 1995 it used 360 gallons daily per capita, compared with 110 in Oakland, 211 in Los Angeles, and 160 gallons in Tucson.[48] That this was a largely tourist-induced problem can be seen in the considerable amount of water used to maintain the twenty-nine (and counting) golf courses owned by the city and its hotels. The tremendous amount of space devoted to this tourist-related activity contributed to a dearth of public space; in the mid-1900s Las Vegas had fewer than 1.5 acres of park per thousand residents. That figure was roughly one-tenth of the area recommended by national recreation officials.

The lesson is that progress has its price, even—or perhaps especially—in a city that makes its living by producing and selling fantasy.

DANIEL HIERNAUX-NICOLAS

Cancún Bliss

The development of Cancún began in the mid-1970s. Thirty years later it was the biggest resort in Mexico, having surpassed even Acapulco, the country's other tourist mecca.[1] Cancún's idyllic image, which differs dramatically from that of the rest of Mexico, derives from the enchantment of the Caribbean environment combined with the concept of a totally new city devoted to leisure. Always intended as a resort, Cancún was conceived in the mid-1960s as a large-scale project promoted by the Mexican government. At that time, new initiatives were designed at the federal level for economic and regional development: a steel plant on the South Pacific Coast and petroleum refineries and petrochemical plants on the Gulf Coast. As part of this broad effort at development, a group of bankers decided to promote a risky strategy: to improve Mexican tourism through an entirely new, planned project on the Caribbean side—Cancún.

This ambitious enterprise began in 1976. It was a substantial element of Mexico's pre-1984 development strategy, which depended heavily on public investment. Cancún, now a long-term exemplar of tourism policy in Mexico, has passed through various stages of national development and through intermittent crises, sustaining and even improving its niche in national tourism. Recently it has been shifting from a resort enclave to an open urban center, integrated more than ever into the Mayan region around it, although it has not produced a substantial improvement in regional conditions.

After twenty years of ongoing development, even during Mexico's worst economic crisis, Cancún has changed; its present status reflects modifications of the tourism model in Mexico. This reorientation is a sort of accommodation in the face of new tendencies in international tourism. Moreover, further transformation is likely. Among the new policies being proposed in the country is the legalization of gambling, still not allowed in Mexico. Cancún would be a potential site for a casino, and tourism activities could change markedly if this decision was to be made.[2]

Mass Tourism in Mexico

The social reforms that spread throughout the Western world during the late 1930s were crucial in introducing free time and leisure activities for the working class, in addition to the notion of spending money on holidays. Since then, tourism has grown worldwide.[3] These changes have been reflected in the volume of Mexican tourism. In 1929, only 19,000 tourists entered Mexico. Following World War II, this number reached 164,000 and continued to increase steadily. In 1963, tourism passed the one million mark and by 1969 the number of visitors had doubled to two million. By 1970, arrivals by air were exceeding land travel into Mexico. In general, the number of tourists to Mexico has been rising, although some flattening occurred after 1974 as a result of Mexico's economic and political situation (see table 1).[4]

Mexico entered a new stage of growth after World War II. Its manufacturing sector had been stimulated by the war-generated demand, as a complement to the United States economy, and this expansion initiated a long phase of development. Miguel Alemán, the first civilian president (1946–52), was deeply committed to Mexican modernization.[5] During this period, economic expansion was the main objective of the strongly nationalist administration, which promoted protectionism to ensure the development of a national industrial base within the country. Between 1945 and 1970 the economy grew at an annual rate of about 9 percent.

The economic development model adopted by Mexico was intensively oriented toward modernizing industry and developing the infrastructure needed for that purpose. Agriculture, traditionally a subsistence sector, was only partially transformed through the green revolution. Salaries increased for white-collar workers, and within three decades, the size of the middle class had grown substantially. The consumption patterns of the middle class were increasingly affected by in-

Table 1   International Tourists Visiting Mexico, 1929–76

Year	No. of Tourists (in thousands)
1929	19.2
1945	164.8
1963	1,057.8
1969	2,064.8
1976	3,107.2

Source: Jiménez 1992, 278–79.

ternational standards. Mexicans, perhaps more than Europeans, were anxious to participate in the American way of life.

At the same time, tourism was being organized on the basis of geographic clusters.[6] The largest source of tourists to Mexico was, of course, the United States (see table 2). The first major contact with American tourism occurred in the Tijuana–San Diego area during the Prohibition Era. In response to a demand for leisure activities by the U.S. population, Mexicans began to offer everything from prostitution to gambling at the secluded Casino de Agua Caliente. From the Marines based in San Diego to the Hollywood stars, everybody had reasons to cross the border.

Acapulco started in the 1930s as a small-scale resort.[7] During World War II, it was seen as a safe place for tourism. After the war, Mexican elites became patrons of the resort. As the country's bourgeoisie expanded, it selected Acapulco as its holiday destination. New hotels, luxury residences, and a yacht club were developed with government subsidies and private investment. A glamorous image of Acapulco was quickly spawned, thanks also to the development of the Mexican film industry and, later, of television, which introduced a "new geography of desire and pleasure."[8]

In the meantime, Veracruz, a traditional resort on the Gulf Coast and the principal port of Mexico, started to lose its appeal for the Mexican masses as their principal holiday destination.[9] Acapulco offered them a definitive image of modernization: a collection of high-rise buildings constructed in the 1950s and 1960s, set along a breathtaking coast and boasting impressive hotels and first-rate restaurants. Present, too, were all those small symbols of American modernity, such as fast food, miniature golf, and discos. Finally, in the 1960s, Mexican tourists were able to afford their own dream city, which was a reflection (pale but real) of American modernity.

Table 2   Percentage of Tourists to Mexico from the United States, 1960–95

Year	American Tourists (%)
1960	87.1
1965	87.9
1970	93.4
1975	86.6
1980	83.4
1985	84.2
1990	87.5
1995	86.9

Source: Jiménez 1992, 308; SECTUR 1996.

In the mid-1960s, Acapulco was the only modern tourist resort in Mexico. Of course, some adventurous tourists headed for different, wilder places, for example, a gorgeous, unpopulated coastal location or an inaccessible archaeological site in the rain forest of Yucatán. Mexico City was also a favorite destination for tourism, for three reasons: its comfortable accommodations, its cultural and historical importance, and, finally, the existence of the only international airport in Mexico, which had been modernized in the 1950s to meet increasing international demand.

In the 1960s, however, the country began to run into economic difficulties. Because exports of agricultural and raw materials were not supplying a sufficient surplus volume of domestic capital, the Mexican government started to engage in state-sponsored development, in an effort to stimulate industrial production, but the increase in goods manufacturing was not enough to improve the economy in the short run. A different solution was needed at the same time that industrial projects were being developed. Tourism therefore became central to Mexican public policy, and Cancún was pivotal to these plans.

Cancún as an International Project

The federal government has closely followed the development of tourism. Beginning in the 1920s the federal government became involved through the granting of visas and the establishment of consultative commissions to propose ways of developing the industry. Toward the end of the 1950s, it opened its first tourism office abroad.[10] Miguel Alemán continued his support for tourism with the establishment of the National Council for Tourism, created in 1961. In 1962 the first National Tourism Development Plan was proposed.

During the 1960s, younger officials concluded that traditional approaches to tourism were inadequate, arguing that more federal involvement was needed if the country was to fulfill its three main objectives: the continued growth of international tourism to Mexico, improvement in the quality of infrastructure, and the development of new resorts. Meanwhile, the Mexican government had established two official institutions to finance the development of tourism. The first was charged with the improvement of infrastructure, the second with the financing of new hotels. Both entities were part of the Mexican central bank, the Bank of Mexico.

As mentioned earlier, in the 1960s Acapulco was the only Mexican resort that more or less met international standards of acceptability. But Acapulco was growing chaotically: urban growth was taking place with no control and planning, poverty was rising, and the city and tourist zones lacked necessary infrastructure.[11] It was likely that foreign tourists would be increasingly repelled by such conditions. Although no other major resort was under development at the time, it was clear that new sites had to be considered. Young technocrats like Antonio Enriquez Savignac began an overview of Mexico's coastal areas. (The term *overview* is not an exaggeration: they actually flew by helicopter to select the sites.) The Caribbean coast offered one of the most gorgeous prospects, and of the thirty-five sites considered, Cancún was one of the best. The glimpse from above gave an excellent idea of the charming conditions of the environment but, as we shall see, not of the crucial problematics of the zone.

Cancún was thus selected as a possible new resort project. Bankers convinced the director of the Mexican central bank, as well as the secretary of finance and the president, of the advantages of the project. At that time, international banking organizations were encouraging large-scale projects for economic development, and Mexico's plans for Cancún fit perfectly. Mexico proposed Cancún as a project, and its plan was accepted by the Inter-American Development Bank (IDB) in 1964.[12] The Mexican government justified the project by arguing that it would provide a substantial increase in the flow of convertible currencies into Mexico, generate many new jobs outside of existing, overtaxed urban centers, especially Mexico City, and counter patterns of regional inequality.

In part, the selection of Cancún also reflected geostrategic conside-rations. The government feared a threat from the Left in the Yucatán, which had barely developed, except around Mérida; it also faced prob-lems in its main export, sisal, for which demand was dropping (see map 1). Worst off was the state of Quintana Roo, which had no important urban center and no prospect for economic development. The area bor-dered the politically troubled neighborhood of Central America. Fear of indigenous uprisings therefore contributed to the desire to find develop-ment alternatives for the southeast. The same reasoning later led to the impulse to jump-start projects in Mexican California and also to develop Ixtapa, where guerrillas had operated since the 1960s.

Financing from both the IDB and the Mexican government sup-ported infrastructure development for Cancún, which is a barrier island, a long, straight stretch of land dividing the Caribbean Sea from the Nichupté Lagoon. Only two narrow inlets connect the sea and the brack-ish lagoon. According to initial projections, 85 percent of visitors to the area would be international tourists. Facilities were designed only for high-income guests.[13]

The initial plan defined two main zones: a tourist zone, reserved ba-sically for hotel structures, and an urban service center. A large avenue was to mark the edge of the tourist zone, with hotels facing the sea. No development was considered for the side facing the lagoon. The cost of such a layout was, of course, terribly high, since all the infrastructure would serve only one side of the avenue. The layout was a clear reflection of the dominant tourism design of the 1960s: the sea was the main tour-ist attraction; the tourist area was to be isolated from the urban zone containing the central business district (CBD) and residences of service and administrative workers; and middle-class housing was slated for four-story buildings, with standard layouts and construction materials.

Tourists were expected to arrive in Cancún through the international airport and be transported directly to the hotel resort. Then they would spend all their holiday at the same place and return home. This classi-cal tourism model also separated the work space from the leisure space: like Le Corbusierian urbanists, the designers of Cancún were very strict about segregation. Low- and medium-skilled workers would travel to the hotel zone by bus, and those with higher skill levels by car. The ideal or-ganization of space would provide special locations for work and allow a minimum interface between workers and the public. Room cleaning, for example, would be done when tourists were out (on the beach); ser-

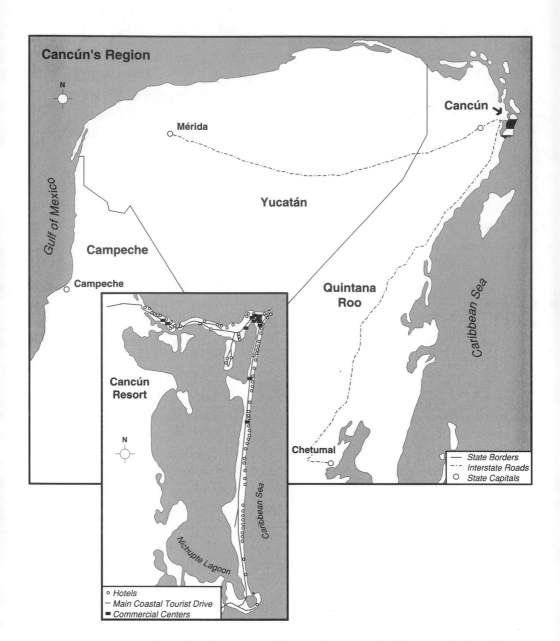

Map of the Cancún region (inset: map of the Cancún resort showing areas developed for tourism)

Cancún's original development was oriented in one direction—to the sea—and faced away from the Yucatán region.

vices for the hotel were in the basements or not visible. In these ways, Cancún was the most authentic expression of Taylorist principles of efficiency applied to hotel space: it reflected an idealistic, quasi-utopian spatial organization, with a total division between labor and leisure, workers and tourists. At least until the mid-1980s, Cancún could be considered as a paradigm of a totally Fordist tourist resort, if Fordism is defined as large-scale production of a uniform product according to inflexible organizational principles. This model of space was present not only in the organization of the hotel but also in the relation between the tourist and the broader environment. The lagoon, for example, was not considered a tourist attraction. Although the sea was obviously a crucial visual and esthetic attraction, it provided only a venue for cautious swimming in front of the hotel: interaction with the surroundings was clearly restricted to the fringe of sand and the immediate sea. The visual landscape was a backdrop for sitting or lying on the beach.[14]

The luxury of the hotels was a clear reflection of the resort's catering to a foreign, upper-income clientele. The design also reflected the expectation that people vacationing in Cancún were seeking privacy and tranquility. All the land was offered at the same time: the infrastructure development of the tourist zone was therefore conceived and built at one moment. An analysis conducted in 1984 indicated that sufficient land had been supplied with services to accommodate an increase in visitors for the next twenty-five years.[15] Until 1984, no restrictions forced developers to cluster; because the whole length of the island was built to the highest standard, projects could be located anywhere, and the Land Department was ready to permit any project. In fact, the density of occupancy of the tourist zone and the efficiency in the use of the infrastructure was not relevant. The main goal was to attract new hotels, which would develop like bubbles along the fringe.

Cancún's image came from the quality of its structures and its environment. As some authors have recognized, no distinction can be made between one resort of this sort and another: Gay-Para, for example, wrote about this kind of development as "high rise public housing structures with feet in the water," while de Ventós described his confusion in not knowing if he was in Honolulu or elsewhere.[16] Augé proposed the concept of the "no-place," meaning a space without history, identity, or any possibility of being appropriated by social groups.[17]

The resort began operations in 1976, when the first hotel the public. The year 1984 is considered a turning point in th

The hotel-zone tourist "bubble" in Cancún, Yucatán, Mexico

Cancún pioneered the sun-and-sand vacation, with the sea as a scenic backdrop.

ment of Cancún because the utopian project began to be overwhelmed by new factors: mass tourism and an overall change in tourist preferences. These factors would transform the original project into a much more open, but also more complex, resort.

The National Impact

From a national perspective, Cancún was a success from the beginning. The main objective was to eliminate Acapulco's monopoly in international deluxe tourism, not only because of its deterioration but also because, as Urry has observed, variety is one of the basic purposes of tourism.[18] Indeed, the extraordinary was no longer available in Acapulco. New sites had to be designed to insure a new look for Mexican tourism.

The entrepreneurial response to the project was outstanding: in 1984, around six thousand rooms were available, the vast majority in the highest luxury categories. By 1995, Cancún was the largest hotel resort in Mexico, at least for high-end accommodations.[19] By 1994 Cancún accounted for 20 percent of international tourists in Mexico, while Acapulco dropped from 21 percent in 1975 to 4 percent. Even more important, official calculations show that Cancún has become the main source of foreign exchange flowing to Mexico through tourism. Estimated as a mere 18 percent in 1988, the figure for 1993 was around 32 percent. Unlike other resorts developed later by FONATUR, the government's development arm, such as Ixtapa-Zihuatanejo, Loreto, or Los Cabos, Cancún was immediately accepted by national and international development capital as an investment opportunity.

The role of FONATUR was decisive in promoting a certain image of the development and insuring the start of tourist activities. By 1983, FONATUR owned six hotels in Cancún, with a total of 1,063 rooms (18.6 percent of the rooms in Mexico), as well as two restaurants, two malls, the only golf course in the resort, and the convention center. FONATUR's main purpose, however, was not to make profits for itself but rather to invest public funds to promote private investment. Among those profiting from this initiative was the nation's political class, which invested heavily in the project. As Fernando Martí points out, President Echeverría (1970–76) at first opposed the project, but he soon fell in love with it—and invested.[20] As the scandals surrounding the Salinas family have shown, the popular suspicion that politicians were the real owners of Cancún was not so far from the truth.

The growth of Cancún as the most important resort in Mexico required expensive government-financed advertising. Additional government support included infrastructure development, extremely large offers of land to private investors, and guarantees of continuous official backing for investment in the area. According to FONATUR's figures, in 1994, 4,629 acres were accessed by more than 99 miles of roads. The costs of this project ran high, and expenditures to support tourism contributed substantially to the country's debt burden. Even after the mid-1980s, when the national government abandoned or privatized a large number of its industrialization projects, tourism remained a priority because of its foreign exchange earnings.

City or Resort?

After 1982 Mexico's rate of economic growth became erratic, with significant effects on tourism. The peso, which had been devalued only once since the 1950s, had been maintained in an overvalued position throughout the 1970s, making Mexico a relatively expensive destination. During the oil boom, the Mexican tourism balance reversed (Mexicans were spending more money outside the country than were foreigners visiting Mexico). Greater affluence, however, also resulted in an increased flow of Mexicans to their national resorts. The ratio of Mexican to foreign visitors in Cancún ceased to be the 3:17 originally forecast; instead, in 1975 three Mexicans visited the resort for every foreigner, and indigenous expenditures contributed substantially to the development of Cancún until 1982. After that year, however, repeated devaluations made the Mexican peso such a bargain that Cancún was no longer restricted to high-income external groups. Flying to Cancún for a week's vacation was suddenly possible for a large sector of U.S. society. In addition, direct flights to Cancún allowed lower air fares and led to the development of a more intensive package system. By 1994, almost half of the arrivals by air were through charter planes. Consequently, control over Cancún's future fell into the hands of tour operators, mainly Americans.

At the same time, the construction industry became involved in a boom never even imagined in 1984. With incredible speed, the open spaces in Cancún's tourist zone began to fill up with new structures. Until 1984, the idea had been to preserve a certain image: high buildings were not allowed to block the view to the sea, a clearly exclusive model. The strong market, however, stimulated a new vision of the resort by the Mexican authorities. It was time to increase the densities, to impose new standards on building height, and to reinforce the market with a diversification of facilities. Mass tourism overtook Cancún after 1984, causing enormous growth. Even though occupancy had fallen in all Mexican resorts, Cancún still maintained the highest rate nationally (around 72 percent in 1994) and therefore remained as the most profitable resort in the country for tourism entrepreneurs.

Mass tourism, though a welcome development for the Mexican economy, forced a change in the Cancún model. Motivations for traveling had changed at the international level. The hotel-beach-waterfront program of past decades was no longer acceptable, because the public had come to fear the health consequences of intense exposure to sun, and other vacation activities such as sports, nature, shopping, and culture disrupted the traditional model of the "three esses"—sand, sun, and sex. Attracting people to the beach without complementary activities became difficult. Shopping had become more integral to the vacation experience and, moreover, offered new opportunities for profit. The commercial centers initially conceived by FONATUR required expansion as they became tourist attractions in their own right and not simply service facilities.

The lagoon gained a new importance as a tourist attraction; not only were new restaurants and services installed on this side, but boat trips, waterskiing, and windsurfing gained in market share. The development thus shifted from a completely sea-oriented design to a sea-lagoon orientation. Finally, both sides of the main avenue were marketed and considered appropriate for commercial development. To promote the lure of the "wild sea," scuba diving, deep-sea fishing, submarine excursions to view coral reefs, and other commercial ventures were developed. Finally, the urban center itself started to become a tourist attraction. Tired of remaining in the hotel bubble and of using cabs or buses to get downtown, visitors who had discovered the new restaurants, boutiques, and services that gave the city center a more exciting atmosphere than the beachfront began to stay in the former service area. Thus, new, lower-level hotels and restaurants in the city drew a new group of visitors, both domestic and foreign.

Can one therefore conclude that a segregated resort has become a complex urban seaside center? In part the answer is yes, since the urban district has become part of the resort, supplementing the hotel development of the island fringe. But Cancún remains completely different from Acapulco, where the resident population lives just a few blocks from the tourist zone and where residents and tourists have traditionally inter-mixed. In Cancún the tourist population is still segregated from local res-idents, even though the city has become the main urban center of the state of Quintana Roo and continues to draw population from the sur-rounding region.[21]

Back to the Region

One of the surprises of the Cancún project is the new relation the resort has developed with its region. At the beginning, Cancún was an isolated development that required a migrant labor force. The largest number of jobs were low paying and were filled mainly by Mayan workers who were born in villages and small towns on the peninsula. Often this migration occurred in two steps. The first, and intermediate, stop was Mérida, where the Indians worked in low-paying tourism-related jobs. Through their exposure to restaurants, hotels, and tourist services, many learned to speak Spanish and to dress like Westerners, preferring modern syn-thetic fabrics to their beautiful traditional garments. Sometimes, En-glish words—the key to jobs in Cancún—were added to their sparse Spanish vocabulary. With this informal training, Mayan workers then traveled to Cancún, the final destination and the mythic site of a new life. There they ended up as help in the hotel kitchens (which were not air-conditioned, of course), as workers servicing the underground systems, or as gardeners. Frequently, migrants returned home for some holidays, bringing with them new costumes, electronic devices, and home appli-ances, symbols of their integration into modern life.[22]

The skilled workforce that operated the hotels was more urban in ori-gin. And sometimes its "migration" was imposed, as when an enterprise transferred workers from other facilities to a hotel or business in Can-cún. Voluntary migration to these jobs was also common, however. The hope of a better income or a more glamorous life was sufficient incentive to insure a constant source of labor. Middle-class singles or people open to risk and entrepreneurial endeavors went freely to Cancún, finding jobs as medium-level employees in hotels and in businesses. Some became part of a growing "Californian class," a group consisting of nativos and foreigners that was beginning to assume leadership roles in the city.[23] (The use of drugs and the adoption of a "cool life" clearly mixed well with leisure lifestyles and combined to define this complex and interna-tional set of people.)

Table 3   Tourism vs. Other Economic Activities in Cancún, as a Percentage of Economic Activity in the State of Quintana Roo, 1989 and 1994*

Indicators of Tourism Activity	1989 (%)	1994 (%)
Share of business establishments	15.3	6.1
Share of employment	38.9	30.1
Share of wages	44.2	49.9
Share of assets of business establishments	57.2	71.2
Share of gross added value	37.2	45.7
Share of gross capital formation	66.1	42.5

Source: National Economic Census 1989, 1994.
*Manuel Rodríguez Woog is responsible for developing the methodology that defines the activities that are included in tourism. I wish to thank him for providing the information in this table.

A 1984 study showed that the demand for goods in Cancún could not be satisfied locally.[24] In fact, not only food but also construction materials had to be imported from outside the region. In the 1990s, however, an important change began to take place as more goods were supplied from within the region. The growing resort had spawned development of new industries, not only in Cancún but in and around nearby municipalities; in fact, the Yucatán peninsula was one of the fastest-growing industrial regions from 1988 to 1994. Entrepreneurs from Mérida began taking an interest in the resort as hotels, restaurants, and various services offered new opportunities for smaller enterprises. New accommodations, in the form of apartments and condominiums, were also being developed, again involving regional enterprises. Thus, Cancún, though originally a "bubble resort," affected the whole region. The consequences of this spillover was to make tourism less dominant in the state's economy (see table 3). This reflected the effectiveness of tourism in generating new activities in the rest of the state. At the same time, workers in Cancún saw their wages rise, and they began to spend it in the region. Tourism is still the most profitable business in the state of Quintana Roo, but it is not limited to Cancún.[25]

In the late 1980s, tourism began to sprawl throughout the region. Accommodations in various categories started to appear in the coastal zone of Quintana Roo, toward Chetumal and Belize. This new development caused a complex diversification of Cancún's original focus as an upscale resort; now the more luxurious and exclusive small resorts were being built away from Cancún, for example, at Puerto Aventuras. These

resorts attracted the richest segments of the market, those people looking for a quiet place with first-class accommodations. At the same time,
inexpensive accommodations could still be found all along the coast. A
growing demand for this type of accommodation is visible even at international levels: many Canadians, Americans, and Europeans are pleased
to find themselves in an environment that is more exotic and less geared
toward mass tourism, where they are isolated not only from technology
but from comfort. Cheaper air fares facilitate the arrival of new social
groups who are more interested in the landscape and extraordinary
qualities of the Caribbean Sea than in the five-star comforts of the luxury
hotels in Cancún or elsewhere along the coast.

The tourism model is therefore changing in and around Cancún. Even
within the original resort, most of the tourism packages offer visits to the
archaeological zones or other side trips inside the region. Journeys to
the ancient Mayan sites of Chichen Itza, Tulum, and Uxmal now compete with the traditional sea-hotel-city trip. These developments have
partly been the result of the Mexican government's steady withdrawal
from Cancún. Initially a state-sponsored resort offering a uniform product, Cancún has been left to market forces. This economic process of
"touristification" has in turn created a variety of new market niches.[26]

Perspectives

The deluxe Fordist utopia of the 1960s and 1970s has been transformed
into a model of mass tourism based on a broader view than the traditional sand-sea concept.[27] The transition was achieved by making the
enclave into a regional city resort with heterogeneous attractions, a
trend opposite to that described by Judd in Chapter 3. This transformation took place not just through a physical restructuring but also
through a reconsideration of tourism functions inside the city of Cancún
and through regional colonization; the region is now a supplemental resource to the resort.

The result, however, is not a clear success in terms of regional development, even though the impact is substantial. The distance continues
to grow between the local winners and the remaining population, which
has been impoverished by national and regional economic crises. The
vast majority of Mexicans living within the region have not benefited
from Cancún's development. More than ever, Cancún is inaccessible to
the peasant population, as most jobs now available there are no longer

open to unskilled migrant workers. Low wages, unstable labor markets, racism, a high cost of living, and poor housing are some of the conditions that would-be migrants have found in Cancún.

The changes that have occurred in Cancún reflect a clear departure from the carefully planned, government-sponsored development of the past. Planning efforts have been supplanted by the desire to use Cancún as a platform for profits. With the current flow of drug money into Cancún, disorganized capitalism offers new activities for entrepreneurs. In fact, all tourist activities in Mexico seem to have been penetrated by drug investment and money laundering.[28] There is increasing pressure to open casinos, even though this is a risky strategy for a country trying to wipe out flagrant corruption and bolster democratic processes. The threat to the natural environment is also growing. Water activities, for example, are increasing in Cancún, despite their detrimental effect on the lagoon, and more and more food, drink, and other services are being offered by buildings erected directly in the lagoon. Tourist development along the coastal region may also be environmentally devastating, even in the near future.

Clearly the new tourism model for Cancún is creating a postmodern city and tourist experience. Whereas in the past tourists went mainly to relax on the beach, now a kaleidoscope of activities awaits them, not only in Cancún but also in the coastal region. A hyperaccelerated way of life during vacations is now available as an alternative to just relaxing. Originally conceived as a deluxe enclave serving wealthy foreigners in splendid seclusion, Cancún and its environs now encompass a complex mix of residents and visitors. Additionally, the integration of its economy with that of the region has tightened ties with other towns and cities. These advances, however, have not yet mitigated the inequalities separating those able to take advantage of the new economic opportunities from those who cannot.

Part III

Converting Cities into Tourist Sites

SASKIA SASSEN AND FRANK ROOST

The City

Strategic Site for the Global Entertainment Industry

Major cities, in addition to being centers for finance and business services (i.e., industries that serve other businesses, such as corporate law firms, management consultants, and the like), are strategic sites for the coordination of global entertainment conglomerates. The entertainment industry, like the finance industry, requires access to multiple highly specialized inputs that are available only in large diverse places. The same cities that produce entertainment also consume it, giving rise to a new form of urban tourism, one that is media related and uses the city itself, especially the global city, as an object for consumption—the city as theme park. Now that most people in the highly developed countries reside in suburbs and small towns, the large city has assumed the status of exotica. Modern tourism is no longer centered on the historic monument, concert hall, or museum but on the urban scene or, more precisely, on some version of the urban scene fit for tourism.

Since the 1980s, there has been a rapid growth in the use of urbanity as an advertising tool and the ascendance of urban music and lifestyles as an object for consumption. Now, in the 1990s, large entertainment firms are among the leading investors and developers in major urban projects that emerge as destinations for tourists and suburbanites. This process has brought with it a growing participation by the media industry in urban planning and development. It is particularly evident in the redevelopment of New York City's Times Square, where the key investor is the Walt Disney Company, and of Potsdamer Platz in Berlin, with the massive Sony entertainment complex as its anchor.

The production and marketing needs of the global entertainment industry thus reconfigure the urban setting, particularly its emblematic sites, as well as strengthening the global city dynamic. Even though the specific entertainment complexes of major cities involve only a fraction of the industry's total employment and sales, they are strategic in a double sense: as sites for the management and coordination of a global industry and as magnets for urban tourism. In the latter role, entertainment production, in contrast to the reproduction of material produced elsewhere, is becoming defined and marketed as an exotic item of consumption.

The Globalization of the Media Industry

Technological innovations and government deregulation have led to the extraordinary growth of international media markets and the globalization of the entertainment industry. As in other parts of the economy, this process is characterized by concentration and internationalization. Major firms seek to diversify through investment in and acquisition of various entertainment-related industries—as evidenced in the large mergers and acquisitions of the past few years. The German company Bertelsmann, the world's largest publisher, acquired RCA records and thereby fostered its growing music and entertainment business. Viacom, a major television producer, merged with Blockbuster, the home-video giant, and then took over Paramount, the movie studio and theme-park owner. The most important theme-park operator, the Walt Disney Company, already a major television and movie producer, merged with the Capital Cities/ABC network. And Time Warner Inc., already highly diversified, merged with Turner Broadcasting Corporation, the leading international news corporation.

This strategy has enabled the entertainment corporations to optimize their marketing: characters and themes from their productions foster customer loyalty and help promote the consumption of other products in all kinds of media. Besides the familiar synergy among music, movies, television, and print media, the most recent new form of telecommunication, the Internet, is also becoming a part of this circle of consumption.[1] For example, Walt Disney is introducing its famous characters in a number of Internet sites.[2] More generally, a whole new version of tourism is being developed for consumption on the Internet and in virtual-reality environments.

As a second strategy, entertainment corporations have intensified their transnational activities, which enables them to sell their standardized products in more and larger markets. Major investments reflect this trend. Time Warner internationalized its pay-TV activities by founding HBO Asia and HBO Olé in Latin America and, expanding into the theme-park industry, recently opened Warner Bros. Movie World in Germany. Having built EuroDisney in France, now called Disneyland Paris, the Walt Disney Corporation then introduced the Disney Channel in Europe. Viacom took its MTV and Nickelodeon channels to Europe, while Bertelsmann's and Sony's most important strategic investments since the late 1980s were their acquisitions of U.S.-based entertainment corporations.

The globalization of the entertainment industry leads to "a process of homogenization of the kind that Hollywood has already made familiar" and a concentration of economic activities because "new media giants are gobbling up the smaller giants everywhere from Buenos Aires and Hollywood to Paris and to Tokyo."[3] In combination with deregulation, diversification and mergers are bringing about a dual structure to the media industry, whereby a limited number of major conglomerates dominate the industry, while numerous small specialized firms operate in niche markets.

The telecommunications industry is also undergoing rapid change—the key forces being globalization, deregulation, digitalization and, for most of the world, privatization. Deregulation and privatization are facilitating the formation of megafirms and global alliances. Technological developments are facilitating the convergence of telecommunications, computers, and television, leading to the formation of a mega-multimedia sector.[4] Globalization is a key feature of this sector, and all signs indicate that it will continue to grow. By 1997 three major global alliances of telecommunications firms had occurred, gaining control of the industry through strategic partnerships. Such alliances are geared to deliver not only computer and telephone services but also data transmission, video conferencing, home shopping, television, news, and entertainment. Mergers and acquisitions also rose sharply in the specialized information technology sector, as small companies sought to achieve the size and technology necessary to compete in global markets. In 1995 transactions reached a record number of 2,913 deals, a 57 percent increase over the

1,861 recorded in 1994. The combined value of these deals was $134 billion, a 47 percent increase over the $90.5 billion of 1994. Deregulation is a vital element in the expansion of service and the formation of global alliances. Experts are forecasting that after a period of sharp global competition, a few major global players will monopolize the business.[5]

The global entertainment industry is characterized by a drive to enter consumer markets worldwide and the intensive use of technology. In spite of the dispersive effects of new technologies and internationalization, production and marketing factors have caused the entertainment industry to keep its production facilities in traditional locations. American soap operas and sitcoms are an example: the simple technical level of these shows—which seldom require special effects, vast studios, or a large number of actors—would suggest that this kind of entertainment can be produced almost anywhere. Nevertheless, the majority of these programs are produced either in and around Los Angeles or in New York City. Television production declined in New York City during the 1980s relative to that in Los Angeles, which could offer more flexible production space. It is, however, once again a growing sector there, as new studios continue to be built, especially on the West Side of Manhattan.[6] These two cities have remained dominant because they are among the few places in which the entertainment industry can find enough creative professionals (actors, directors, and writers as well as marketing specialists) to ensure the product's international success.[7]

Access to a wide range of talent, top-level specialists, and advanced technology is evident in the concentration of multimedia enterprises in Manhattan.[8] As with international finance, it is ironic that such concentration should occur in an industry based on digitalized processes, which know no bounds geographically. Yet the production process itself requires a particular kind of place and, as in finance, an extreme spatial concentration—in the case of New York City, the so-called Silicon Alley in Lower Manhattan.[9] Silicon Alley firms can simultaneously access the financing capacities and creativity of Wall Street, the multiple resources of the city's publishing, television, and radio sector, and the anarchic creative talent one finds concentrated in the city.[10] In this regard, the multimedia complex of New York City has strategic advantages over the same sector in San Francisco and the newly emerging one in Los Angeles. The increasingly specialized knowledge necessary for innovation and coordination within the industry heightens the importance of traditional centers. The locational choices of the Bertelsmann group show the effect of this magnetism.[11] Although the holding company is still headquartered in the small German town of Guetersloh, where it was founded a century ago, after intensifying its efforts to diversify, the company restructured its organization and founded the Bertelsmann Music Group, with headquarters in New York City.[12] The United States is now its largest foreign investment site, and the company has transferred its publishing ventures to New York City as well, having recently moved into a building located at Times Square.

As with international finance and some advanced corporate services, the globalization of entertainment raises the level of complexity of certain aspects of the market insofar as the legal, accounting, advertising, management, and marketing systems of various countries are different and need to be rationalized. In turn this process raises the need for access to multiple and often simultaneous high-level professional inputs.[13] Thus, the preexistence of the vast business-services sector in global cities increases their locational advantages to the entertainment industry.

Cities as Sites of Consumption

For the entertainment industry, cities are not only strategic sites for production and coordination but increasingly important sites of consumption. For years the industry focused expansion activities on nonmetropolitan areas in the form of theme parks aimed not just at direct sales of products but also at fostering the customer's loyalty. Theme parks are an integral part of the circle of entertainment consumption.[14] The Walt Disney Company has a long tradition in this business; as well as offering amusements, its parks are vast shopping malls for goods with tie-ins to Disney movies. Paramount (now part of the Viacom group) is also a major player, having taken over five theme parks in 1992. Time Warner Inc. now owns a chain of nine theme parks (Six Flags Entertainment), where it is introducing its famous Warner Brothers cartoon and movie characters.

Since the 1980s the industry has begun using urban sites for the same purpose. Identifying new possibilities for developers, the Urban Land Institute has labeled these places "urban entertainment destinations" and categorized the most important ones as follows:

- Entertainment-oriented retailers, like the Disney Store and the Warner Bros. Studio Store chains, which sell anything related to the media industry's products, such as videotapes, books, CDs, and simple consumer goods that bear the images of their famous characters.

The marquee of NBC Studios at Rockefeller Center, New York City.

An NBC studios tour allows visitors to view an entertainment production site.

- High-tech entertainment centers, like Sega Arcades, which offer state-of-the-art virtual-reality technology—known as "immersion experiences."
- Themed restaurants, like the Hard Rock Cafe and Planet Hollywood, whose environments feature memorabilia of media stars.
- Cinema complexes and specialty-film venues, which are renowned either because of their size or because of their special technologies.

These urban entertainment destinations cannot be characterized in familiar terms, like the well-known department stores that act as anchor tenants within shopping complexes. Rather, for the entertainment corporations, these investments, as well as being profit-making entities in themselves, are means to other ends, becoming integral parts of marketing strategies intended to "fully exploit the value of their intellectual properties and brand identities."[15] However artificial those attractions might be, this market segment is likely to materialize increasingly within urban settings.[16] At times the strategy has led to conflict, as when com-

The Beatles (in wax) at Madame Tussaud's, London

Liverpool's fab four are on perpetual display.

munity organizations and other urban actors have resisted the takeover of city streets by film and video production companies.[17] Public officials, however, have welcomed this trend toward urban entertainment, in the belief that entertainment is a growth industry and creates good public relations for their cities.

Certain traditional locations have extraordinarily high concentrations of entertainment destinations. For example, MCA's 222,000-square-foot "Universal CityWalk" in Universal City, California, is a mixture of entertainment destination, tourist attraction, shopping center, and artificial Main Street, attracting visitors and residents alike; it is located within an even larger complex that includes the MCA world headquarters and Universal Studios.[18] Perhaps most striking is the concentration of such businesses in midtown Manhattan. Although it has always been a major tourist destination, during the last few years the importance of entertainment-related attractions has grown dramatically: the area around Fifty-seventh Street has numerous themed restaurants, and some visitors go to New York solely for the experiences offered in them.[19] In addition to these artificial sights, midtown Manhattan offers the special appeal of "real" media locales like the NBC News Studio at Rockefeller Center or David Letterman's "Late Night Show" on Broadway.

The success of this unique mixture of media production and traditional tourist destination seems to be why the entertainment industry is increasingly exploiting and shaping this market. After buying the former AT&T building on East Fifty-Sixth Street, Sony transformed the open public area at street level into Sony Plaza. The complex includes shops selling Sony electronics and accessories related to performers under contract with its music or film division as well as an interactive science museum. Sony is following the same strategy in other cities: in Berlin the company has built a huge complex that covers a fourth of the Potsdamer Platz, once a center of business and entertainment that remained empty while the city was divided.[20] The complex contains Sony's European headquarters, a library of Sony media, and a glass-roofed plaza for events, dominated by a mega-screen featuring Sony's entertainment products.

In midtown Manhattan other entertainment corporations are following similar entertainment strategies. In 1994, the Walt Disney Company produced its first Broadway musical, *Beauty and the Beast,* the movie version of which had been released some years earlier, based on the well-known fairy tale. The stage production has attracted people from all over the country who, it seems, have seen the movie or video several times, who know the story and the songs, and who are enjoying a show that tries hard to bring onto stage the visual effects that earlier had been possible only in animated movies.[21]

Times Square Redevelopment: Urban Theming

The redevelopment of Times Square reflects the recent shift in strategies of urban economic development planners, who, until a short time ago, focused single-mindedly on finance and business services as the key to future growth. The Times Square area has had a long tradition as New York City's, and probably the nation's, most famous entertainment district: at the turn of the century, the area began to attract theaters, restaurants, bars, hotels, and movie palaces—whose advertisements illuminated the area at night. The growth of radio during the 1920s added to the mix: "As network radio became big business, virtually every operation of primary importance in the radio industry was in Midtown Manhattan. . . . Radio executives, like movie producers, were eager to evaluate theatrical talent."[22] The area's outstanding concentration of entertainment businesses made it important as a location for production, innovation, and coordination as well as for consumption.

The postwar era brought dramatic changes to Times Square, however. With the exodus of the urban middle class to the suburbs and the introduction of television, cinemas and legitimate theaters lost many of their customers, and a large number of businesses had to close. Cheap carnival amusements and prostitution (which had always existed there) became more prevalent; sex shops and theaters showing adult movies soon appeared following the legalization of pornography. As part of this economic and social transformation, the area generally decayed, eventually attracting homeless people and drug dealers.

In an effort to change the specific character of the area and to bring more investment to the western edge of midtown Manhattan, New York State's Urban Development Corporation (UDC) and New York City's Public Development Corporation were eager to find investors for a redevelopment of the area around Times Square and Forty-Second Street.[23] In 1982, the city and the UDC selected several developers for parts of the project. The most important component was to be the building of four large office towers at the intersection of Forty-Second Street, Seventh Avenue, and Broadway. The design of the towers was intended to change the character of the area by reflecting the sobriety of the new tenants, who would make Times Square a less frivolous and less menacing place. In exchange for permission to build the towers, the developer was required to pay for a public-amenity package. Park Tower Realty won the competition for this overall project, which was to be designed by the architects Philip Johnson and John Burgee. To finance its part of the project, Park Tower Realty began to cooperate with the Prudential Insurance Company, and the two companies formed the Times Square Center Associates (TSCA) consortium. A number of problems occurred after the city had approved the project. Dozens of lawsuits and objections were filed by the inhabitants of the nearby low-income neighborhood, who feared that gentrification would drive up property values. The project ended up being delayed for years.[24]

Faced with a much later completion date than originally promised, the prospective tenants of the office towers withdrew. Nevertheless, in 1989 Prudential posted a $241 million letter of credit for the condemnation of a large part of the redevelopment area. In 1990, condemnation, relocation of businesses, and some demolition began. By 1992, over two hundred businesses (mainly small retail shops and sex-related enterprises) had been closed or relocated. By this time the market conditions had dramatically changed: New York City's office boom of the 1980s, which had been spurred by the extreme growth in producer and financial services, was over. But a number of office towers had already been built around the project area. Because any other solution had become impossible, TSCA was released from some of its obligations, and the UDC agreed that the developers could wait until market conditions improved before starting construction of the planned office buildings.[25]

In the early 1990s, construction of the office towers seemed unlikely in the near future. Because most businesses had been relocated, the buildings on West Forty-Second Street—once the heart of the entertainment district—stood empty. In 1993 the UDC and the city released a new plan, designed mainly by the architect Robert Stern. The plan, named "42nd Street Now!" consisted of three major parts: the construction of a hotel on Eighth Avenue (where a hotel had been planned originally), with retail shops on the adjacent lots; a renovation of theaters in the middle blocks; and, the most innovative part of the concept, a renovation of the empty ground-floor buildings on the office sites for intermediate use as retail shops and restaurants, to be financed by the developers. The plan also suggested more fanciful designs for existing and future buildings, achieved through altering building heights and placing large neon signs on all structures in the area. The aim was to generate excitement and to reflect the area's specific character as an entertainment district.[26]

In 1994, after much negotiation, the new plan began to approach realization: the Walt Disney Corporation, close on the heels of its first Broadway musical, agreed to renovate the landmark New Amsterdam Theater on Forty-Second Street for its own stage productions on the condition that the city attract two other entertainment-oriented tenants to the area. This proviso eventually was met, but Disney then proceeded to bargain for a $26 million low-interest loan from the city government, so that the company would only have to invest $8 million of its own capital for the renovation.[27] The office developers also gained concessions from the city: $9.2 million of the funds TSCA had agreed to grant as part of its public-amenity package was used for the renovation of one of the theaters. Under the aegis of "The New 42nd Street," a nonprofit organization overseeing the renovation of the historic theaters along that street, the century-old Victory Theater was rebuilt and opened in December 1995 as a "young person's theater."[28]

The Disney commitment produced a snowball effect. In July 1995, it was announced that Forest City Ratner, a development firm specializing in central-city projects, would develop an entertainment complex on Forty-second Street for American Multiplex Cinemas Entertainment and Tussaud's Group Ltd. It was to include the restoration of the facades of the Empire, the Harris, and the Liberty Theaters and the opening of a large retail complex inside, complete with an entertainment center comprising a twenty-five-screen movie theater, a high-tech show, and possibly a restaurant where Mme. Tussaud's famous wax figures would function as waiter-robots.[29] Livent, a Canadian company and the producer of such successful musicals as *Show Boat* and *Kiss of the Spider Woman*, was another major investor. The company combined the Lyric and Apollo Theaters and restored them into a state of the art, 1,850-seat theater for live musical productions.[30]

Further, a new competition was held in which various investors presented their suggestions for the site on Eighth Avenue where a hotel had been planned. The group that won had been formed by the Disney Development Company as the "anchor entertainment retail tenant," working with the Tishman Urban Development Corporation as the developer. The Tishman proposal was designed by Arquitectonica, the Miami-based firm famous for its glitzy-looking buildings. The success of the winning combination derived from the fact these firms seemed prepared to create a high-profile entertainment center capable of attracting tourists and suburbanites, thereby contributing to the city's economy and tax base.[31] If built as planned, the $303 million project will include a 680-room tourist and convention hotel, a 100-suite vacation club and time-share, a 12,000-square-foot two-story restaurant, an entertainment and retail complex, and possibly a 28,000-square-foot Sega entertainment center.[32]

Cities as Entertainment Products

The economic and spatial structures of the entertainment industry increasingly call for the specific functions provided by cities. Global cities, in particular, are emerging as strategic sites for both consumption and production. The production and marketing needs of the entertainment industry result in a remaking of the global city as a tourist mecca on a previously undreamed-of scale. Whereas the production sites of other industries are rarely magnets for visitors (except when retrofitted as historic or tourist sites), the actual fabrication of the entertainment product —and the themed stores and restaurants that give the visitor a vicarious feeling of participation in the creative process—become major attractions in themselves. Further, urban culture becomes an exotic object of tourism increasingly mediated through the entertainment industry. This outcome undercuts old distinctions between sites of production and sites of consumption, a point that may apply to urban tourism everywhere.

BRUCE EHRLICH AND PETER DREIER

The New Boston Discovers the Old Tourism and the Struggle for a Livable City

Boston is among America's premier tourist cities, placed by surveys among the top five U.S. cities to visit.[1] Each year, the city attracts millions of people. They come for business, academic conferences, and special events like the Boston Marathon. They come to see colonial-era sites such as the Paul Revere house and to wander through its well-preserved historic neighborhoods. They come for graduation ceremonies at one of the area's many colleges and universities and to tour the New England countryside. They come to shop in one of the city's notable retail areas, such as Faneuil Hall Marketplace, to enjoy one of several nationally ranked museums, or to attend the theater or symphony.

What is remarkable about Boston's success as a tourist destination is that it occurred almost by accident. That is, it was not the result of a carefully planned strategy by government officials, business executives, or civic leaders to develop tourism as a key component of the city's economy.[2] Rather, various political, cultural, social, and economic forces, moving along somewhat different trajectories, converged to make Boston a highly desirable destination.

Tourist-industry leaders and organizations have played only a minor role in the city's recent emergence as a tourist location. During the first two decades of urban renewal, the industry was small. It lacked its own distinct political organization, operating as a committee within the Boston

Chamber of Commerce until 1974, when the Greater Boston Convention and Visitors Bureau was created. Obviously, some key business and political decisions—such as building and then expanding the convention center, increasing the number of hotels, and setting up a visitors' and convention bureau—were linked directly to promoting a tourist economy. For the most part, however, Boston has thrived as a tourist city because it has naturally drawn visitors eager to participate in its economic life, learn about its historic and cultural features, and take advantage of its innate urban qualities.

Hotel owners in Boston, in comparison with those in other U.S. cities, have been less concerned with improving the city's attractiveness to visitors. Their relative passivity resulted from their enviable economic position. The high demand for a limited number of rooms has made the hotel business there highly profitable; occupancy levels and room rates have been among the highest in the United States. Between 1975 and 1994, the number of hotel rooms in Boston doubled to 12,400, while average daily room rates (in constant dollars) more than doubled. Thus, until it mobilized to construct a new convention center in the late 1990s, the visitor industry had not organized to promote the development of major new attractions, gaming, or other tourist venues and had given only limited support to recent efforts to upgrade the Freedom Trail. In fact, industry opposition, along with powerful neighborhood opposition and fiscally conservative legislators, stopped the development of a proposed megaplex in 1995 that would have combined a football stadium with the convention center. The stadium, which few considered essential to the city's economy or image, was seen by hotel owners as a financial and political liability, standing in the way of the smaller and more economically important convention center.

The evolution of Boston's modern tourist and visitor industry is tightly interwoven with broad economic and cultural developments that have taken place within the city since the 1950s. The preservation of historic sites and older downtown neighborhoods—two of Boston's most highly regarded features—had been, until recently, only reluctantly accepted as a necessary, though secondary, public policy. The primary strategy focused instead on the creation of the "New Boston." Only in the mid-1970s did many begin to realize that one of the most valuable aspects of the New Boston is the Old Boston.

Yet if tourism planning is underdeveloped in Boston, urban planning and design, historic preservation, and struggles over urban space are not. Not surprisingly, then, tourism in Boston does not stand far apart from the city's other commercial, cultural, and recreational activities; to a great extent it is absorbed into the daily life of the city. In this respect, Boston is much like European cities. Mixed-use districts and development define the city's visitor spaces. Indeed, the appeal of the Boston experience—both for tourists and local nontourists—is largely related to its not having been planned mainly for tourists, even though better planning may be necessary to preserve its success.

The Growth Coalition and Redevelopment

During the eighteenth and nineteenth centuries, Boston was a leading maritime trade, finance, and industrial center of the emerging nation. By the turn of the twentieth century, however, the city's economy was already in eclipse, as trade and finance activities agglomerated in New York and the nation's industrial center shifted to the Midwest. Boston's economic decline proceeded through the Great Depression and continued for another quarter century. By the end of World War II, the city was at a crossroads. Between 1950 and 1960, population fell by 13 percent (from 801,000 to 697,000), and employment was flat (at 551,000). Meanwhile, suburban population and employment grew, by 9 percent and 22 percent, respectively.

The emergence of Boston's growth coalition during the 1950s and its implementation of a massive urban-renewal program have been richly chronicled elsewhere.[3] For more than twenty years, it entailed an extremely close cooperation among the city's business leaders, mayors, and the powerful Boston Redevelopment Authority (BRA). Private elites and government leaders have played a significant role in connecting larger economic forces to the revitalization of downtown Boston. Some actions such as the razing of the West End neighborhood were highly controversial, but the general success of the coalition in reversing decline is not in doubt.

Boston's urban-renewal program, combined with broader political and economic shifts, triggered an economic recovery by the mid-1960s.[4] By the mid-1970s, the private economy had replaced federal programs as the catalyst for Boston's downtown development. It was no longer necessary to lure office developers with local property-tax breaks. By the early 1980s, Boston had forged what might be termed a "growth management" coalition built on somewhat fragile, but nonetheless resilient, foundations and composed of segments that had different reasons for resisting unbridled growth.

The growth of Greater Boston's tourism business, though largely unforeseen by the planners, has been driven by the city's economic revitalization over the past four decades. This was largely the result of three dominant forces: the restructuring of the global economy, with its impact on urban economies;[5] increased federal spending on health, higher education, and defense; and implementation of an aggressive, federally financed urban-renewal program. The city—historically a center of finance, business services, higher education, and medicine—has become an important regional node in the new international division of labor: it is the primary location for government and business services in New England; a leading site for health care and medical research; an important international academic center; the hub of a large regional defense and computer industry; and a finance center based on its large mutual-fund and insurance industries. Boston stands fourth, behind New York, London, and Tokyo, in the value of stock funds under management there.

Who Visits Boston?

An estimated 11 million people visit Greater Boston each year. Domestic visitors, most of whom come from the northeastern United States, account for 90 percent of that figure.[6] The average visitor to Boston, whether there for business or pleasure, has traveled no more than five or six hours and will stay for only three or four days. Even long-distance travelers typically stay just a few days, passing through Boston on their way to other major American destinations. Tourists coming for business or meetings and conventions make up approximately 45 percent of Boston's overnight visitors. Their economic impact is relatively greater, however, accounting for an estimated 70 percent of hotel stays. Most of the conventions and large group meetings that utilize the city are closely connected to dominant local industries. Educational, legal, governmental, scientific, technical, health, and medical meetings made up 65 percent of room sales in this sector.[7] As the city's leading industries have grown, so too has the visitor industry. Between 1972 and 1994 employment in services and in finance, insurance, and real estate (the sector known as FIRE) grew by 55 percent, but hotel employment increased by 70 percent.

Overnight leisure tourists, domestic and foreign, account for slightly more than half of all visitors to Greater Boston. Yet because an estimated 40 percent of these tourists are visiting friends or relatives, they account for only about 30 percent of visitor revenues and 20 percent of hotel stays. Hotel-room bookings during spring graduations and fall home-comings are among the highest of the year. Many leisure tourists, especially family vacationers, often find room rates in Boston prohibitive and stay in lower-priced accommodations outside the city.

Boston's tourist facilities reflect the dominant corporate and professional character of travel to the city. Many of the large hotels are incorporated into mixed-use projects that also include office, retail, and residential space: the Sheraton at Prudential Center; the Westin and Marriott at Copley Plaza; the Boston Harbor Hotel at Rowes Wharf; the Marriott at Cambridge Center; and the Charles Hotel at Charles Square represent almost 30 percent of the hotel rooms in Boston and Cambridge. Ninety-four percent of the hotels built between 1978 and 1995 were in the luxury or first-class categories, and many lower-priced hotels have been upgraded. As a result, the overall share of budget and mid-priced hotels has dropped from 43 percent to less than 30 percent of rooms. In 1997 average room rates in Boston exceeded $145 per night.[8]

Despite the relative strength of the Boston visitor market, the supply of hotel rooms and meeting space lags far behind that of most large metropolitan areas in the United States. With 3.2 million people, Greater Boston is the eighth largest metropolitan area in the country. But among twenty-four major market centers for convention and trade shows, Boston ranks sixteenth in the number of hotel rooms and twenty-second in meeting space. The city's principal meeting venue, the Hynes Convention Center, built in 1963 as part of the Prudential Center project, ranks twenty-second in size among the nation's major convention halls.[9]

Although Boston's visitor industry is integral to its economy, tourism is not among its top four economic sectors (FIRE, health, professional services, and government); regionally, education and high technology also surpass tourism in importance. Visitors to Boston spend between $2.8 and $4.6 billion annually, representing between 8 and 13 percent of the city's economy. Employment in travel and tourism businesses accounts for just 6–7 percent of jobs, which is average among U.S. cities.[10]

The various public and private agencies organized to promote tourism in Boston and Massachusetts have only recently begun to coordinate their activities, which consist mostly of marketing efforts. The agencies include the Massachusetts Office of Travel and Tourism (MOTT), Massachusetts Port Authority, Greater Boston Convention and Visitors Bureau (GBCVB), Massachusetts Convention Center Authority, and Massachusetts Lodging Association. MOTT works in close concert with, and provides major funding to, GBCVB and other private tourist bureaus across the state. Until recently, Boston's city government played only a limited role in promoting tourism. Unlike the state government, which put approximately 20 percent ($14.5 million in 1996) of the revenues generated through the hotel-motel tax back into tourist promotion and marketing and which subsidizes the Hynes Convention Center, the municipal government spends very little, although it took in approximately $17 million in hotel-motel taxes in 1995.

The municipal government has only recently begun to play a significant role in tourism development. A collaboration in 1997 between the city and state governments to construct a proposed $700 million convention center included a pledge of $158 million in city funding, its first significant investment in tourism infrastructure. State legislation authorizing the financing of the convention center also required the development of an additional forty-eight hundred hotel rooms in Boston and Cambridge, the tax receipts from which will be used to repay state construction bonds. This requirement is expected to result in a 33 percent increase in hotel rooms in just five years and will ensure that the city and the BRA aggressively promote the rapid planning and permitting of new hotels.

This decision stood in sharp contrast to the BRA's actions during the 1980s real estate boom, when it assisted existing hotels by using its zoning and design review authority to restrict the supply of new hotels. At one point, in 1981, the BRA had twenty-five proposals for new hotels under review. It approved only a few of these, allowing for continued growth but without producing higher vacancy rates and, thus, lower profits for hotel owners.[11] By 1997, however, the pent-up demand for hotel space, along with the requirements of the convention-center bill, had prompted a deluge of new hotel development proposals.

What Do Visitors Do in Boston?

Beyond the immediate practical purposes of visiting Boston—to do business, to see friends or relatives, to attend college graduations, and the like—visitors are drawn to Boston for the completeness of its urban ambience: the vitality of its newer developments blend with the richness of its historical and cultural attractions, architectural delights, interesting shopping venues, restaurants, theaters, and nightclubs. Most of these experiences are concentrated in a small number of well-preserved downtown neighborhoods and revitalized business districts and are easily traversed on foot. Dense and intact, Boston is surely the most European of the nation's cities.[12]

At a time when many American cities are seen as places to avoid rather than visit, Boston stands as an exception. If Boston's promotion of itself as "America's Walking City" seems mundane, it is as much a reflection of its desirable urban qualities as it is a judgment of other American cities—where walking is perceived as unsafe, unpleasant, or pointless. Boston's competitive advantage in tourism lies in the fact that it is still a *city*, where the past, present, and future coexist in reality and the imagination. To attract tourists, many cities have contrived nostalgic entertainment and shopping sites, such as South Street Seaport in New York, Laclede's Landing in St. Louis, and the Cannery Row shopping mall in Monterrey, California. Although Boston is not totally immune to these trends, it draws primarily on its innate and more substantive qualities. It may be, as some have observed, "the ultimate theme park—the Tomorrowland tourist attraction—reality itself."[13]

Until the mid-1970s, the historic sites in and around the city were Boston's main tourist attractions, not its residential neighborhoods and commercial areas. In fact, a 1967 survey found that only 8 percent of visitors thought the best thing about the city was its overall appearance, and those who found it attractive were praising its new construction. The city's "squalor—its filthy streets, its slums, the air of decay that hangs over many of its sections"—was cited as a major detraction.[14] In the past twenty years, however, motivations for going to Boston have changed. People now go to Boston to see the city as well as to do things in it; by 1994, the "city visit" and shopping had surpassed historical sightseeing as the most popular visitor activities.[15]

Increasingly, Boston's appeal rests on its well-preserved historic neighborhoods and buildings, its cultural assets, and its retail and entertainment districts. Boston's South End, Back Bay, Beacon Hill, North End, and Charlestown neighborhoods offer tourists a unique collection of preserved nineteenth-century neighborhoods. Other staples are the

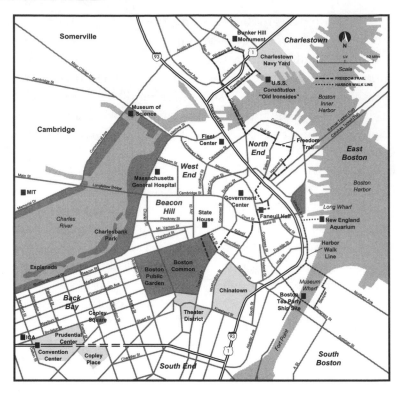

Map of Boston

With so many tourist attractions crowded on a point between the Charles River and Boston Harbor, Boston is an ideal walking city.

Boston National Historical Park, Museum of Science, New England Aquarium, Museum of Fine Arts, and Freedom Trail (a walking trail that connects sixteen colonial- and revolutionary-era sites). The most heavily patronized establishment of any type is Faneuil Hall Marketplace, which occupies three restored nineteenth-century market buildings and is located adjacent to historic Faneuil Hall on the Freedom Trail. Other important shopping venues are Copley Place and the Prudential Center, two modern indoor malls in the heart of the city's main hotel district, and Newbury Street in Back Bay, seven blocks of boutiques, specialty stores, exclusive clothing shops, and restaurants and bars, most of them housed in restored Victorian-era buildings. The recent introduction into Boston of numerous luxury retail shops has become yet another major selling point to tourists, especially European travelers. Significantly, all the above attractions serve the local market as much as, if not more than, the tourist and visitor market.

The fifty-nine colleges and universities in the Boston area have also had an effect on the economy that extends well beyond graduations, college tours for high school seniors, and sporting events. Harvard University, for example, is one of the essential attractions for European travelers, as is, to a lesser extent, the Massachusetts Institute of Technology for the Japanese. Harvard Square has become a major student and visitor shopping district. The large number of wealthy foreign students, especially those at Boston University, has had a pronounced effect on the city's nightlife and luxury retail trade.[16] And, most significantly, graduates from area schools, especially Harvard and MIT, have been a driving force in the growth of the region's high-technology and information industries, both major magnets for business travel.

Boston does have one area exemplifying many features of the so-called tourist bubble described by Judd in his essay: the combined Copley Place and Prudential Center complex. The Copley-Prudential complex includes three hotels and a convention center along with office, retail, and residential space. With the inclusion of four adjacent hotels, one-third of the city's hotel rooms are located here. Yet, the complex, although physically set off from its environment on superblocks, does not segregate tourist activity from the city. It is surrounded by attractive neighborhoods and spectacular public spaces that bring visitors out into the streets, and it is also heavily used by locals for shopping, dining, and entertainment. Still the enclosed private spaces here do represent a departure from the dominant Boston tourist experience, and a recent proposal to construct a third such hotel-entertainment-retail complex over nearby rail and highway air rights could further challenge the traditional city of streets.

The Historic City and the United States Bicentennial

Long before Boston established itself as a popular tourist destination, it was widely recognized as a principal site of the American Revolution and a key city in the nation's early history. The effort to preserve and memorialize this history began in 1818, when land was first acquired to build a monument on Bunker Hill, site of the first major battle of the Revolution, and continued through the early twentieth century with the

The historic Copley Plaza Hotel (right) flanked by the modern John Hancock Tower

Copley Square is situated at the eastern edge of a luxury hotel district and shopping complex in Boston's Back Bay.

disparate efforts of historical and preservation societies to save significant buildings and ships from demolition and convert them to public museums. In 1951, the Freedom Trail, a concept linking many of these sites, was proposed by a local newspaper columnist and a member of the Old North Church.[17] That same year, the federal government initiated preservationist efforts when it restored and designated Dorchester Heights as a national historic site.[18]

Congress created the Boston National Historic Sites Commission in 1955, whose members included Representative Thomas (Tip) O'Neill of Cambridge, future Speaker of the House, and the noted historian Walter Muir Whitehill, whose writings, advocacy, and planning efforts would have great influence in Boston through the next decade.[19] By 1959, the commission's work had already led to the creation of the Minute Man

National Historical Park in the nearby towns of Lexington and Concord. Its final report, in 1960, clearly established the need for greater preservation in the midst of the urban-renewal efforts already under way. It proposed creation of a Boston National Historic Sites Advisory Board to manage eight key sites and oversee development of a visitors' center.[20] Soon afterward, under Whitehill's leadership, the city created the Boston Historic Conservation Committee, representing the first systematic local effort to survey and evaluate Boston's historic sites and buildings and to integrate this knowledge within broader redevelopment plans. According to a 1966 visitors' survey, historical sightseeing was the most popular tourist activity in the city and a key factor in drawing nonbusiness tourists to Boston.[21]

The impending national celebration of the United States' Bicentennial, in 1976, became the vehicle through which Boston's political and corporate leaders first organized around tourism development. The evolution of this effort over the course of thirteen years paralleled broader changes occurring in Boston's development approach. The first plan, initiated by Mayor John Collins and the Chamber of Commerce in 1963, was conceived as a World Exposition. Far from celebrating the city or its history, however, this plan envisioned the creation of an experimental new community in Boston Harbor; Boston's historical and cultural resources were considered "collateral events."[22]

Following Boston's failure to obtain the designation for an "Expo," the city government, under Mayor Kevin White, took an entirely different approach. The "Boston 200 Master Plan," written in 1973, spoke richly about the city's historical resources and its livable urban environment as the center of its tourism strategy.[23] The plan called for the development of few tourist-specific facilities; rather, it insisted on the inseparability of the urban environment for tourists, residents, and workers. The city's Bicentennial plan and associated efforts led to the improvement of public spaces and increased historic preservation and the formation of both the Boston Landmarks Commission and the Greater Boston Convention and Visitors Bureau. It also led, finally, to new federal investment, when in 1974, John McCormack, congressman from South Boston and Speaker of the House of Representatives, obtained passage of the Boston National Historical Park Act, which called for the preservation of several key sites and the establishment of a National Park Service visitors' center.[24]

Between 1985 and 1995, the U.S. Department of the Interior invested an additional $45 million toward the restoration of Freedom Trail sites. But, despite the importance of Boston's historical legacy as a catalyst for the growth of its modern tourist economy, the historical Boston has not kept pace with the New Boston. Attendance at Freedom Trail sites was low between 1980 and 1993, at the same time that the number of visitors to the city increased by more than 50 percent.[25]

Neighborhood Resistance and Preservation

That Boston is now known for promoting and preserving its history may seem ironic to anyone familiar with the contentious politics of Boston's early redevelopment experience. Indeed, among historians of urban planning, Boston may be best known for the bulldozer-style urban renewal chronicled by Gans in his classic study *The Urban Villagers*.[26] A number of Boston's older residential neighborhoods, including Roxbury, Charlestown, the Fenway, Chinatown, and the South End, experienced both demolition and rehabilitation efforts. The net effect was to reduce the overall number of housing units in the city.

The early successes of the coalition supporting renewal galvanized the opposition, which prompted the city government to change the direction of its revitalization strategies and focus on preservation and the management of growth. Despite strong pressures from property developers that could have led to both overbuilding and the destruction of much of the city's historic fabric, the BRA eventually responded to countervailing voices from civic-minded business leaders, neighborhood organizations, and preservationists. They mobilized enough power to redirect the Authority's efforts, causing it to restrict "Manhattanization" of those neighborhoods that visitors and tourists now find so appealing. To understand these forces, it is necessary briefly to describe the political struggle over redevelopment in postwar Boston.

Many residents of Boston's older neighborhoods resisted renewal efforts. Two kinds of opposition emerged: a working-class movement to stop the socially disruptive effects of urban renewal, and an effort by middle-class professionals to occupy and upgrade attractive, centrally located areas. Many poor and working-class residents saw urban renewal as a threat to the social fabric of communities. They also doubted that they would be recipients of its benefits. More affluent residents believed that urban renewal would destroy the historic city and its architectural heritage. Despite divergent motives, the common goal was to challenge efforts by the municipal government and developers to raze buildings or erect projects within residential areas.

In the mid-1960s, Charlestown and the South End, two working-class neighborhoods with exceptional architectural and historic significance, were confronted with BRA urban-renewal plans. Community mobilization in both neighborhoods led to major public conflicts over displacement, the loss of low-income housing, and the disruption of community life.[27] In the South End, with a growing population of downtown professional workers, historic preservation also emerged as a theme. In 1964 the BRA first included staff devoted to preservation planning in its redevelopment efforts. The Charlestown Preservation Society and the South End Historical Society were founded in 1965 and 1966, respectively. Although approximately 25 percent of the South End and 10 percent of Charlestown were bulldozed, neighborhood resistance helped prevent further destruction. The BRA shifted its approach to emphasize rehabilitation more than demolition and helped finance the renovation of thousands of dwelling units.[28]

A precedent had been set in 1955, when affluent Beacon Hill became the first neighborhood to obtain protection by the Commonwealth of Massachusetts through historic district status. In 1966 Back Bay achieved similar status. Back Bay residents, many of them early back-to-the-city pioneers, initially organized in 1964 to defeat a residential tower proposed for Commonwealth Avenue, a mile-long stretch of stately, but deteriorating, Victorian-era mansions and town houses, and then to turn back a zoning amendment that increased building height limits along the avenue. Following these victories, residents convinced the state legislature (with no opposition) to create the Back Bay Architectural District. In 1972, community efforts resulted in the designation of the South End and parts of Roxbury as National Register districts, which meant that a public review process would now be required before federal funds could be used for building demolition in those areas.

In 1975, preservationists also succeeded in obtaining state legislation to create the Boston Landmarks Commission (BLC). This effort avoided a direct confrontation with real estate development interests by excluding most of downtown from its initial jurisdiction (which grew over time).[29] The mission of the BLC is to "protect the beauty of the city of Boston and . . . [the] areas, sites, structures, and fixtures which constitute or reflect distinctive features of the political, economic, social, cultural or architectural history of the city . . . [and to] resist and restrain

A stop along Boston's Freedom Trail

The old State House (1713), seat of the Colonial government, is now surrounded by highrises. The nineteenth-century Custom House Tower (in the background) was built atop the original Custom House in the early twentieth century. It has recently been developed as a Marriott Vacation Club Resort.

environmental influences adverse to such purposes."[30] The Boston
Preservation Alliance, the first citywide preservation organization, was
founded in 1980.

Only a few of Boston's historic neighborhoods are designated historic
districts, however; Charlestown and the North End, as well as other
nineteenth- and early twentieth-century neighborhoods and enclaves
throughout Boston have been largely preserved without the imposition
of mandatory codes. In these places, social commitment, neighborhood
attachment, and community development have been key forces. And although gentrification has also been an important factor, so has the work
of neighborhood groups, such as nonprofit community development corporations and grassroots tenants' organizations in protecting and preserving affordable housing from both market forces and the urban-
renewal bulldozer. What is significant here is that most city neighborhoods have remained physically intact, retaining large portions of their
late nineteenth-century and early twentieth-century building stock, and
that only a few areas suffer from the concentration of blight and aban-
donment that plague most older American cities.

Critical struggles during the 1970s laid the groundwork for later
management of growth. They include the mobilization of neighborhoods across Boston and Cambridge to stop a major inner-city highway
plan, which eventually led to the creation of new park land and major
mass-transit improvements.[31] Another massive renewal effort, the Park
Plaza project, facing the Public Garden and Boston Common, was defeated in 1974 by a broad opposition of local businesses, residents, and
environmentalists. Although this area was redeveloped in the 1980s
with superluxury housing, a hotel, and retail establishments, it was at
a vastly reduced scale. By the mid-1980s, with the support of Mayor
Raymond Flynn, neighborhood councils and other citizen advisory groups
gained unprecedented influence over real estate development and zoning policy. The commitment and active participation of residents across
the city to protect their communities ensured that governmental action
and private development would not destroy the residential base of the
city as real estate entrepreneurs sought to increase its value for commercial development.[32]

Public spaces, whether in the downtown core or in outlying neighborhoods, are today a key part of Boston's reputation for livability. As
Sorkin has noted, "In the 'public space' of the theme park or shopping
mall, speech itself is restricted. There are no demonstrations in Disney-

land. The effort to reclaim the city is the struggle of democracy itself."[33]
Maintenance of public space is important primarily for its effect on the
quality of life for the city's residents, but it also serves to make Boston a
more attractive city for visitors and tourists.

Faneuil Hall: Commerce Rediscovers Historic Boston

Faneuil Hall was the key meeting hall for Boston organizers of the American Revolution. Two hundred years later, the redevelopment of the Faneuil Hall and Quincy Market area into the Faneuil Hall Marketplace,
designed by Benjamin Thompson and Associates for the Rouse Corporation, was the single most influential project in Boston, and perhaps in
all urban America. Early urban-renewal plans had originally targeted the
market area for clearance, but when the Marketplace opened in 1976, it
proved to be a transformative event in historic preservation and urban
revitalization. This evolution, however, "was more the result of close
calls and lucky breaks than of a calculated choice in city hall."[34]

Quincy Market and two adjacent warehouse buildings, situated between Faneuil Hall and the waterfront, were constructed by the city in
1825. The buildings were initially marked for clearance in 1956 by the
Boston City Planning Board, but by 1963 planners, preservationists, and
historians, including Whitehill, convinced the BRA they should be saved.
The 1964 urban renewal plan drawn up by the Boston Chamber of Commerce recognized the importance of this area in terms of history, architecture, and urban design, although an economically feasible reuse was
not yet apparent.[35] Several years later, the city obtained a $2 million
preservation grant from the federal government, which it used to stabi-
lize and restore the buildings and to relocate four hundred wholesale
produce dealers to a new market outside of downtown.[36]

In 1973, the city selected the Rouse-Thompson team to develop the
market area; this decision was heavily influenced by local business leaders, as well as by Rouse's financial commitment to pay the City at least
six hundred thousand dollars a year in lease payments and to donate an
additional five hundred thousand dollars for the Bicentennial. The city
gave the developer an initial three-year property tax abatement and a
ninety-nine-year lease for the buildings.[37] Over the years, this deal has
produced a modest profit for the city.[38]

Rouse and Thompson's initial concept was geared to the local retail
market. The project was principally intended to serve city residents,

downtown office workers, and suburban shoppers, who might be lured back to the city with an exciting shopping experience. It was intended to be "real," selling useful goods in an authentic environment (not a "pseudo-period commercial design") and to relate with "genuine meaning" to its urban context.[39] Tourists, who were also expected to utilize the Marketplace, were early identified as a likely threat to its success, as they would tend to push the merchandising toward frivolousness and sameness.

Faneuil Hall Marketplace became a major attraction the day it opened in 1976. Along with the Bicentennial celebration, which included the arrival of Queen Elizabeth of England and a flotilla of Tall Ships, and the recent completion of several new office towers, among them the massive yet elegant John Hancock Tower, it signaled both the rising potential of the New Boston and its link with the historic Boston. Hotel demand grew 42 percent between 1975 and 1978.[40] (At the same time, because of declining employment in manufacturing, transportation, and trade, Boston's total employment reached a postwar low of 526,563 in 1976.) Nationally, the Marketplace's success overturned widespread skepticism about urban shopping malls and inspired imitations across the country, including other Rouse malls in New York City, Philadelphia, and Baltimore.

Twenty years later, the Marketplace remains a success. Standing at the crossroads of the financial district, Government Center, the Freedom Trail, the North End, and the waterfront, it is the most visited place in the city, attracting more than 12 million customers annually. Yet the concern over tourism has been borne out: tourists account for more than a third of its customers and half of its revenues, while local residents and workers do relatively little retail shopping, using the Marketplace primarily for food and drink. Rising rents and large national retailers, including the Disney Store, have pushed out many of the original local merchants.[41]

Nevertheless, criticism of Faneuil Hall Marketplace as too theatrical or Disney-like misses a critical point:[42] good cities have always included elements of public theater, and good city planning can stimulate this theatrical realm, both its aesthetic and social pleasures, through the development of active and entertaining public spaces. Despite its touristic trappings, the Marketplace still succeeds on these terms for the most part. The Marketplace also managed to establish a new benchmark in the design of urban public spaces, replacing the barren, windswept plaza

The South Market building of Faneuil Hall and Quincy Market, redeveloped into a festival mall by James Rouse

When the Quincy Market mall opened on August 26, 1976, it drew a crowd of one hundred thousand and became the model for Rouse malls in other cities.

that had dominated the previous two decades of urban development in America.

The restored Faneuil Hall is still used as a public meeting space. It has been the scene of political rallies and debates among candidates for president, governor, and mayor and of forums sponsored by community groups on a wide range of public issues, including housing and homelessness. The public spaces around Faneuil Hall and the Marketplace are principally designed to stimulate shopping and consumption and are somewhat regulated (with carefully selected street performers). Consequently, they are criticized for artificiality and pandering to a purely consumptionist ethic. Nevertheless, the success of this project encouraged the development and improvement of other, arguably more authentic, public spaces based on the principles of adaptive reuse pioneered in the original Marketplace development.

Waterfront and Harbor Development

Some of Boston's key tourist destinations—including Faneuil Hall Marketplace, the Children's Museum, the New England Aquarium, the World Trade Center, the U.S.S. *Constitution*, and several hotels—are located on or near its waterfront. In fact, the success of redevelopment in the Faneuil Hall area helped ignite a renewed interest in Boston's waterfront, much of which had decayed as the port lost business to New York and other cities. In the 1970s, investment along the waterfront picked up, but because plans were not well coordinated, some big architectural mistakes were made. During the mid-1980s, the BRA developed a comprehensive waterfront plan and imposed stricter design guidelines on major projects. The long-dormant Charlestown Navy Yard was redeveloped into a large complex of mixed-income residential buildings, offices, a marina, and parks. Water transportation across the harbor was revived, along with sailing and harbor cruises. A Harborwalk allowed pedestrian access along the three-mile waterfront. Although some of this activity contributed to tourism, the predominance of private commercial and residential developments, as well as the presence of inappropriately sited public facilities such as a county jail and a federal courthouse, has largely inhibited access to and use of the waterfront by city residents and tourists.

Some federally supported efforts currently under way, however, should have major positive impacts on the long-term development and use of the waterfront and harbor. These include the court-mandated $3.5 billion cleanup of Boston Harbor, which has already led to the opening of beaches and other recreational sites; the replacement of an elevated highway, which, when constructed in the 1950s, cut off the waterfront from downtown, with an underground artery; and passage of legislation in 1996 creating the Boston Harbor Islands National Recreation Area.

Finally, by the late 1990s the South Boston "Seaport District," situated across a narrow channel from the financial district, emerged as the principal locus for the planning and development of new office, residential, and tourist facilities. City planners and property developers hope to transform this area's abandoned piers, industrial spaces, and vacant tracts into a major extension of the New Boston, while retaining what industrial and port activities remain. The area already contains hundreds of artists' lofts, several small museums, the World Trade Center exhibition facility, and a new hotel and is the intended site of the new convention center. If and when these plans materialize, the Seaport District will surely become a significant new feature of the Boston tourist experience.

Convergence of Growth and Preservation Politics in the 1980s

The main ingredients for preserving Boston's traditional urban fabric included historic preservation, gentrification, maintenance, neighborhood mobilization, and new urban-design concepts, along with city planning and corporate civic leadership that sought to reconcile these factors with the imperatives of economic growth and redevelopment. Three factors emerged in the mid-1970s to produce an economically significant tourist location. One, the economic restructuring and physical revitalization of the metropolitan region, entailed dramatic growth in business services, FIRE, health care, education, and high technology, along with a vast expansion of office space, hospitals, shopping centers, hotels, museums, and modern cultural facilities. The second was increased attention to the preexisting richness of the city's historic landmarks in connection with the United States Bicentennial celebration in 1976. Third was the movement by working- and middle-class residents to maintain Boston's livability by resisting urban renewal and preserving the city's traditional urban qualities and community life.

One by-product of Boston's expanding service-sector-based economy, including its tourism and visitor sector, has been increased labor militancy, particularly in the hotel industry. Beginning in 1981, Boston's moribund Hotel and Restaurant Workers Union was revitalized under the militant leadership of Dominick Bozzotto, who turned the local union around by mobilizing the predominantly female and minority membership through community organizing, confrontational tactics, and tough bargaining.[43] The union also became highly involved in city-wide affordable housing efforts. Thus, tourism did not, as in some cities, contribute to a downgraded labor force.

This characterization is not meant to downplay Boston's many serious social and economic problems, from the polarization of incomes to racial segregation and redlining to such correlates of poverty as crime, homelessness, and infant mortality. Although Boston was one of the few major American cities whose poverty rate declined during the 1980s, almost one-fifth of its population remained below the poverty line.[44] The restructuring of the Boston region's economy, and the sharp escalation of its housing costs, exacerbated the city's problems. Some of these problems, especially the homeless population in the city's downtown areas, were quite visible to visitors and residents alike. But tourists were less likely to set foot in some of Boston's more troubled high-poverty areas such as Roxbury, Dorchester, or South Boston. At the same time, Boston's vibrant and contentious civic life, including its neighborhood activism, helped to pressure both public- and private-sector leaders to address these problems more forcefully than in most other cities.[45]

By the late 1970s, growing numbers of middle-class professional workers, tourists, and downtown businesspeople were drawn to the city's livable environment and rich urban milieu. Private investment in preservation was given an important boost in 1976, with the enactment of the federal Historic Preservation Tax Credit program, and again in 1981 with passage of the Economic Recovery Tax Act of 1981, which further increased tax incentives specific to rehabilitation of historic properties as well as for real estate investment in general.[46] Thus, by 1981, neighborhood residents, developers, architects, government planners, and politicians were finding an increasing appreciation of the economic, social, and cultural values of preservation and good urban design.

The timing was propitious. The economic restructuring of the national economy required greater geographic consolidation of its corporate-finance and business-service functions, elevating the locational importance of key regional cities such as Boston and increasing the pressure for new commercial development. During the 1980s, the downtown residential neighborhoods were also the locus of intensive gentrification and restoration of older buildings, which served as a base for expanding the political constituency for preservation. The city was about to embark on its largest construction boom in more than a century. Whatever had been learned over the past three decades of urban revitalization would be put to a major test in the 1980s.

Pressure from preservationist and neighborhood interests ensured that buildings were preserved and that towers were shorter and set back from the street to minimize shadow and wind effects. Some of Boston's prominent business leaders, while strongly supportive of economic growth, understood the dangers of unchecked development and the threat of overbuilding the city's small core, helping give the city government more political room to manage development than in any major American city except, perhaps, San Francisco.

Contextual design, reduced scale, and active streetscapes became the hallmarks of Boston architecture and urban design during this era. According to the American Institute of Architects (AIA) Guide to Boston, "Boston's most significant achievement in this century may have been in urban design and planning, in integrating new architecture with that of the past and at the same time maintaining an emphasis on human scale. More than any other American City, Boston has retained or adapted its physical past while allowing new landmarks to take root. . . . The Faneuil Hall Marketplace reuse project has become a symbol of the new Boston development philosophy."[47] From 1984 through 1992, the BRA, under the direction of Stephen Coyle, also implemented new zoning regulations that restricted allowable building heights in most of downtown and encouraged further preservation of the existing building stock. There was remarkably little opposition to these initiatives by real estate and business interests.[48] Edwin Sidman, chairman of Beacon Properties, which owns many downtown properties, including two hotels, commented that "the zoning made eminently good sense. Cities don't operate well on a boom and bust mentality. Boston doesn't need to sell itself out." Because much of downtown still consisted of buildings constructed during the late nineteenth and early twentieth centuries, even many real estate owners supported efforts to maintain their increasingly profitable older buildings and reduce the impact of new developments.

What's Next?

Boston, through a combination of civic leadership, strong planning, economic growth, neighborhood activism, and luck has succeeded in positioning itself as a leading city in North America for living, business, and travel. Yet, as the foregoing analysis has demonstrated, the forces of change are neither stable nor predictable over time. The economic and cultural values that underlie Boston's recent transformation are currently strong, but they are far from certain. For the future, the book is still open.[49]

In the past, as we have emphasized, little effort has gone into planning or developing alternative growth strategies for tourism. As a result, tourism has stayed largely within the boundaries and spaces of everyday

life, sharing amenities and attractions with the city's residents and workers, supporting business growth, and contributing to the retention of a
large middle-class population. Future tourist development that follows
this integrated and balanced path is surely the preferred course. Yet at
present it is uncertain what the effects will be of the projected new growth
in tourism.

Boston's tourist economy tends to be constrained by regional growth
patterns. Since 1980, growth in visitation to Boston has lagged behind
national trends.[50] This lag is largely tied to the relatively slow pace of
economic and population growth in the northeastern United States. In
1995, for example, while national tourism grew by 8 percent, in Massachusetts it grew by just 1 percent and in Boston by just 3 percent.[51] A regional recession between 1989 and 1992, marked by an 11 percent drop
in city employment, was accompanied by an even sharper falloff in hotel
employment. Although the new convention center now in development
may help increase the number of convention visitors to Boston, the future size of the city's convention market is unpredictable.

Boston's tourism and economic development leaders seek to expand
the city's share of national and international tourism. To capitalize on
the long-term growth of this market, however, they must give greater attention to those qualities that will have the broadest and most enduring
appeal, namely, the city's historic and cultural heritage. Without treating
the old city as a museum piece, planners taking a more vigilant stance in
favor of preservation and history will likely broaden and sustain the
city's appeal to the world's growing tourist market. Otherwise, economic
forces, which until now have energized the visitor industry, can, in time,
also generate more demolition and overdevelopment and thereby erode
the aesthetic and historic qualities that visitors find so attractive.

Arthur Frommer, a leading authority on tourism, points to the European experience as a guide for American cities: "Because of historic
preservation and only because of historic preservation, the travel industry is now the single largest industry in Europe."[52] Only the cities that initiated "draconian measures in support of preservation" became leading
tourist destinations, says Frommer, while cities such as Brussels and
Milan, which did not adequately protect their historic environments,
turned into tourist backwaters.

Boston's policy makers did not seem to agree with Frommer's hard
line on preservation and, up to a point, they made correct decisions. The
nature of postwar urban development in the United States made it un-

likely that Boston could have regained its economic vitality were it constrained by draconian historic preservation laws. And Boston's success has been tied principally to the unique integration of its new developments with the old. Boston was also lucky that many of its historic buildings were saved from the wrecking ball by a period of prolonged economic stagnation during the 1930s, 1940s, and 1950s and that urban redevelopment did not start too soon or progress too far before public sentiment and support for preservation took root.

In the long run, however, Frommer may be right. Although the future growth of the city and regional economy cannot be predicted, the continued historical and cultural value of the city's built environment seems more certain: along with the largely untapped potential of Boston Harbor, it is what truly distinguishes the city and provides its competitive advantage in tourism. It can be presumed that these qualities will take on even greater significance in the years ahead.

LILY M. HOFFMAN AND

JIŘÍ MUSIL

Culture Meets Commerce
Tourism in Postcommunist Prague

Prague made a dramatic leap into the international tourist circuit after the "velvet revolution" of 1989 displaced state socialism. By 1993, Prague was one of the most frequently visited cities in Europe, first among the former socialist cities and a rising international star.

Prague's experience represents a different phenomenon from that of cities restructuring to capture tourism or built as tourist centers. For Prague, tourism has been an integral part of post-1989 democratization, marketization, and privatization. The emerging structure of tourism cannot be understood apart from this larger context nor without understanding the significance of continuity amid change. Observers have noted that East Central Europe is dealing with a complex reshaping or transformation rather than a simple transition.[1] In this sense, Prague represents a naturally occurring experiment that allows us to examine the interplay of history, culture, and political economy and to see, more clearly, how tourism articulates with global market forces.

Continuity and Change

The key to Prague's seemingly rapid transformation is the cultural capital embodied in a relatively intact central core.[2] As one guidebook puts it, "There are few other cities in Europe that look so good—and no other

capital where six hundred years of architecture are presented so completely untouched by natural disaster or war."[3] Fodor's 1992 travel guide
to Czechoslovakia describes the benefits of underdevelopment: "The sense
of rediscovering a neglected world . . . the sense of history, stretching
back through centuries of wars, empires, and monuments to everyday
life, remains uncluttered by the trappings of modernity. . . . Crumbling
facades, dilapidated palaces, and treacherous cobbled streets both shock
and enchant the visitor used to a world where what remains of history
has been spruced up for tourist eyes."[4]

The preservation of Prague's historic core is the result of several factors. Prague had the good fortune to emerge unscathed from World War
II. In addition, strong planning cultures, both presocialist and socialist,
helped protect the core. A preservationist tradition, institutionalized in-
formally as the Club for Old Prague, dates back to the late nineteenth
century and the controversial renewal of the old Jewish ghetto. Despite
extensive urban development during the First Republic (1918–38), there
was no radical intervention into the structure of the inner city, which
kept its fourteenth-century layout.[5] The Club for Old Prague survived in-
formally under the socialist regime, often mitigating harsh bureaucratic
rulings. Under state socialism, urban development was centrally managed and integrated into overall economic planning.[6] In 1971, the core
was designated a legally protected area, in part to illustrate the superiority of the socialist system. These historic-preservation codes still protect over one-third of the seventeen hundred buildings in the core and
make redevelopment difficult.

State socialist regimes also had a distinctive urban ecology that dis-
couraged urban growth and further conserved the core.[7] In the absence
of a market in land, new development was shunted to the outskirts to facilitate mass-production methods of construction. The inner city was neglected and for the most part preserved, retaining some artists and intellectuals but increasingly becoming home to the elderly, the poor, and
the Romany minority. The net result was that Prague's population in
1980 was approximately the same as in 1940. Describing the lack of
change in the core over the past forty years, one city planning official
listed only two new department stores, a new railroad station and metro,
some demolition and modernization.[8]

As closed societies concerned with political security, the socialist
states constructed formal barriers to travel and tourism not only with
the West but among the cities and countries of the East. Despite this

generic attitude and the former Czechoslovakia's extremely repressive regime, Prague became a tourist destination. Socialist tourism to Prague included organized tours from other socialist countries, congress tourism (conventions, professional meetings, and trade fairs), and a form of political tourism. Because Germans from the former German Democratic Republic could travel to Czechoslovakia without a permit, Prague became a popular meeting place for relatives and friends separated by the wall. Statistics show that the number of foreign visitors increased prior to 1989. Before 1970, the annual number of foreign visitors ranged from 2 to 4 million. Those numbers increased throughout the 1970s, peaking at 19.4 million in 1978, and decreased slightly thereafter. In 1985 there were 16.5 million visitors, 95 percent of them from the former socialist states and the rest predominately from neighboring Austria and Germany.[9]

The economic benefits of tourism ultimately outweighed political resistance and led to a common decision among the socialist countries to use tourism as an economic tool. Urban-based congress tourism was encouraged along with regionally based spa and recreational tourism. For Prague, this translated into infrastructure development—hotel building, improved transportation, and the renovation of facades in the historic core. During the last phase of the Communist regime, hotel building was prioritized within the construction sector, and in 1988 laws enabling tourism development were enacted. Almost half of Prague's top forty-nine hotels, as listed in 1992 guide books, were built after 1945.[10]

Tourism: Work and Play

With the opening to the West, Prague became a destination for the international flow of travelers. Statistics show that the number of foreign visitors grew dramatically in the first three years after 1989, an increase that stabilized at about 100 million visitors per year in the mid-1990s (table 1). Using the official Czech government definition of a tourist—a person who stays overnight in a registered bed—some 15.5 million of these visitors were classified as tourists in 1994. Ninety-two percent, or 14.3 million of these tourists, went to Prague, the political and cultural capital of the country and by far the largest city. In a city of only 1.2 million residents, more than 14 million tourists per year make a large impact.

People may travel exclusively for pleasure or in connection with work;

Table 1   Foreign Visitors to the Czech Republic, 1985–96

Year	Foreign Visitors (in millions)	Annual Change (%)
1985	16.5	—
1989	23.24	+41
1990	36.57	+57
1991	50.86	+39
1992	69.41	+36
1993	71.73	+3
1994*	101.14	+41
1995	98.06	−3
1996	109.40	+12

Source: Ministry of Economy of the Czech Republic 1995, 27; 1996, 29. Figures for 1985 from Musil and Pohoryles 1993, 186.

*The border with the Slovak Republic was statistically monitored beginning in 1994.

between these two poles are travelers who combine work and play. This last group of tourists has been particularly important in shaping Prague because of their dynamic interaction with the city. These visitors bring more than consumer dollars to the local economy, and as a result their impact is more complex than that of tourists who simply consume the city.

In the relatively short period since 1989, one can identify several shifting patterns. Immediately after 1989, business and professional visitors and the politically interested went to Prague. Traditional sightseeing and mass tourism began in 1991, and by 1993 mass tourism, mixed with specialized types of congress and study tourism, dominated. More recently, Prague seems to have drawn more of those who combine work and sightseeing, perhaps because of its basic attraction as an economic, political, and cultural frontier. To understand Prague's emerging tourist sector, we must examine how it is being shaped by the motivations, interests, and activities of such visitors.

One important group is the international corporate and business class—consultants, lawyers, accountants, developers, and entrepreneurs—for whom Prague is a venue for expanded business and professional activity. As early as 1993, a survey of future location decisions for branch offices of fifteen thousand large European firms revealed that Prague was the first choice within Europe.[11] Attracted to Prague for its gateway location, its relative economic and political stability, and its historical legacy, this group has fueled a demand for upgraded accommodations and services, thereby linking Prague's rapidly growing financial, business, and real estate sectors with tourism.

Business and commercial tourism has also been stimulated by Prague's return to its prewar tradition of hosting fairs and exhibitions.[12] After 1989, the number of such events increased dramatically. In 1995, one of the two major exhibition halls held fifty fairs—approximately one a week—and the other forty. Another specific feature of Prague's post-communist tourism is its professional and cultural character. This is conditioned in part by the city and in part by the particular history of Czech universities, research centers, and professions, all trying to make up for forty years of relative isolation. Foreign educational and cultural institutions have linked up with local universities and cultural organizations to create programs for tourists, including students, in topics such as Czech architecture, photography, music, and literature. During the summer, Prague hosts many summer schools and special courses. In the summer of 1995, for example, these included three programs in architecture sponsored by American universities; a writing program cosponsored by the Central European University in Prague, an American university, and prominent Czech writers; a joint American-Czech photography program; Slavonic studies organized by Charles University; and many language and literature programs. Western students and faculty profiting from contact with their Czech counterparts and immersing themselves in the city are now a given part of everyday life.

Prague quickly joined the ranks of the top twenty conference sites worldwide to become an intellectual meeting place and center, hosting hundreds of lectures, congresses, and professional meetings each year. This is due, in part, to Prague's preexisting convention infrastructure. The six-thousand-seat Convention Palace, the former Palace of Culture, is, ironically, a legacy of the former regime and was originally intended for use by the Communist Party. In 1993, sixty-three thousand conference participants each spent an average of $623, or a total of almost $40 million, in this one building. Another major site—an exhibition park—is a legacy of the earlier Austro-Hungarian period. Congresses and professional meetings have hastened the incorporation of Czech professionals and businesspeople into the mainstream while simultaneously opening the Czech Republic to Western models and training. A notable example was the 1997 announcement that Prague will host the annual meeting of the World Bank and International Monetary Fund in 2000.

A related aspect of postcommunist tourism is Prague's expatriate community. After 1989, a community of foreigners quickly established itself in Prague—touted as the Paris of the 1990s—replete with avant-garde publications and coffeehouses. This represents an authentic and evolving cultural scene, existing alongside the Kafka T-shirts and Mozart posters of "tourist" Prague and drawing an international population of students, artists, and young professionals in search of alternative work and lifestyles at a time when the United States and Western European countries were laying off such people. During 1995–96, there were an estimated twenty thousand to thirty thousand Americans in Prague. Young U.S. journalists helped found and staff two English-speaking newspapers. As of 1996 there were five English-language newspapers and two English literary journals, as well as French and German newspapers. Various English publications described business and real estate opportunities. Two American bookstores function as meeting places for foreigners abroad as well as for the local expatriate community. This community has multiplier effects, generating more tourism as each expat is visited by several persons and as the community itself becomes a tourism attraction.

The Emerging Tourist Industry

How has Prague met the demands for a tourist infrastructure? After the borders opened in 1989, demand for hotel space in Prague quickly overwhelmed capacity. The response has been two-tiered: on one level, there has been a hotel boom dominated by foreign investment, and on the other, a decentralized pattern of private accommodations.

Immediate demand was met by private flats—both registered and unregistered—accessed through housing services. This lodging pattern, common to other former socialist countries, existed during the previous regime and is stimulated by residents' desire for hard currency.[13] The net effect has been to decentralize and redistribute tourists throughout the city, encouraging the growth of restaurants and services not only in the historic core but in outlying neighborhoods. It has also helped distribute tourism's economic benefits to a broader, more diverse population and has brought residents and tourists into direct contact, affecting the expectations and worldview of both.

Obviously Prague needed and pursued foreign capital. Tourism in general and accommodations in particular have attracted more foreign investment than other branches of the economy and triggered a dramatic cycle of hotel building and reconstruction.[14] By 1995, accommodations in Prague were comparable to those in European cities like Munich and Vienna, with 170 hotels and between 35,000 and 50,000 beds (including private lodgings), a substantial increase over the 10,000 hotel beds available in 1989.[15] By January 1996, most of the older hotels had been renovated, and at least thirty were newly built or converted from apartment buildings or dormitories. Major international chains that have competed to build or acquire hotels in Prague include the Four Seasons, Moewenpick, Ritz-Carleton, Hilton, Holiday Inn, Best Western, and Renaissance.

Because of high demand, privatizing Prague's large hotels, in the words of an official in the Ministry of Privatization, was "one of the easiest parts of the privatization process." The largest hotels, such as the Atrium, were offered to the public by means of coupon privatization to insure a continuing Czech share. Most large hotels, however, are now joint ventures involving foreign capital. The Atrium, for example, is a Hilton. In the words of one hotel owner, "Czech hoteliers have lost ground; we are no longer dominant in our own land."[16] A significant factor contributing to foreign ownership has been the difficulty Czech entrepreneurs have had in borrowing money at reasonable rates.

But while credit has been a major problem, it is not the only motivation for joint ventures. Foreign know-how is also an issue. Critics are concerned with quality and the lack of a service ethos. Under the former regime, services were defined as a nonproductive part of the economy and generally disparaged. This attitude, internalized by individual workers, is still widespread. The leaders of the local tourism industry cite the need for a Czech-based training institute to train managers in modern Western methods and to instill a service ethos. They also point to a need for accommodations that offer standardized services at a range of prices and for an information system for reservations. The situation of the Hotel International, built in the monumental Stalinist style of the 1950s and set in a suburban district of Prague, illustrates these dilemmas. Although the hotel was fully privatized in 1994 during the second wave of privatization, the manager has stated that "in this market, we can't stay alone." A franchise with Holiday Inn will bring with it a reservations system, a well-known name and standard of accommodations, and training for staff. Citing the Frankfurt Holiday Inn, nineteen miles from the center of Frankfurt, as an example of what a name can do, he felt more reassured about his 240 rooms located in suburban Prague.

In a rather short time, a tourism industry has evolved that begins to exhibit familiar Western trends and tensions regarding competition, cor-

Table 2   Citizens of the Czech Republic Traveling Abroad, 1989–96

Year	Czech Tourists Abroad (in millions)
1989	7.80
1990	13.38
1991	30.66
1992	32.67
1993	30.98
1994*	45.84
1995	44.87
1996	48.61

Source: Ministry of Economy of the Czech Republic 1995, 33, table 4.1; 1996, 31.
*The border with the Slovak Republic was statistically monitored beginning in 1994.
Note: The population of the Czech Republic in 1994 was 10.3 million; that of Prague, 1,214,584. Ministry of Economy of the Czech Republic 1996, 7.

porate domination, and the loss of local control. After several decades of economic and political subordination to the former Soviet Union, as well as to a centralized state, Czechs are extremely sensitive to issues of dominance and subordination. As the Czech economy gets more robust and capital markets become more accessible to local entrepreneurs, it is likely that the Czech market share of accommodations and travel agencies will grow. Indeed, the country's privatization policy has sought to balance foreign and local interests and to replace foreign with local capital. Local capital is beginning to invest in tourism accommodations (and services in general) in the form of smaller hotels and bed-and-breakfasts, both in Prague and regionally.

The growth of the tourism industry, and particularly of tourist agencies, has been fueled by outbound as well as inbound tourism, and travel agencies servicing outbound Czechs have been one of the most common entrepreneurial start-ups. After forty years of travel restrictions, every man, woman, and child wanted to visit the West. This has revived the Central European tradition of *Wanderen,* which typically occurs in the summer months when foreign visits peak, making summertime Prague look like other large European cities. The number of trips abroad by Czechs in 1990 amounted to 1.3 times the total population in 1990, almost three times in 1991 and 1992, and more than four times in 1994 (table 2).

Initially, tourism bookings were divided between local and international agencies. Only Cedok—the former official state travel agency, with offices in eleven countries—had the preexisting network and resources to bring tourists to Prague. Small Czech agencies were limited to organized outbound travel by motor bus, often to a single destination. But as Czech travelers have become more sophisticated consumers and as incomes have risen, they have turned to larger, sometimes foreign, agencies in search of higher quality and more standardized services. The large Western-based internationals such as Thomas Cook and Co., American Express, and Fischer Reisen have increased their share of Czech business.[17] At the same time, Czech agencies have grown rapidly in size and services. In 1995, more than half of the twenty largest travel agencies in Prague were Czech.[18] But the resurgence of the Czech tourism industry is dependent upon the Czech economy, and in the summer of 1997 when the Czech crown was devalued, many small agencies went bankrupt, stranding their clients abroad. As the 1998 travel season began, big agencies, both local and foreign, increased their market share.

Tensions in the tourist industry do not run simply along local and foreign lines. Although Czechs like to support Czech business, there is a strong political bias against the former socialist institutions and organizations. This works to the disadvantage of Čedok. Viewed as a symbol of the past, the agency has had trouble getting competitive rates from hotels and recruiting new personnel. Indeed most of Čedok's business has been with foreign tourists traveling to Prague. These political tensions are reflected in the existence of two parallel associations of travel agencies: one is composed of small, newer, postcommunist operators and uses the word *private* to distinguish itself from the second organization, whose members include larger operators "from the past." To counter negative public opinion, Čedok advertised its seventy-fifth birthday on posters in the metro, thereby notifying the Czech public that its origins were pre-World War II.

Government Policy and International Politics

The Czech government has been equivocal about tourism. The first postcommunist government established a Ministry of Internal Trade and Tourism, which gave tourism ministerial status. This administration commissioned prognostic studies from foreign firms, Japanese as well as European. After the elections of 1992, a neoconservative government led by the economist Václav Klaus dissolved the ministry and placed tourism within the Ministry of Economy. In 1996, the Ministry of Economy and the Ministry of Economic Competition were abolished and their

Table 3   Foreign Currency Income from Tourism, 1989–96

Year	Income (in millions of US$)	Annual Change (%)
1989	492.2	—
1990	418.5	−15
1991	713.7	+71
1992	1,126.1	+58
1993	1,557.8	+38
1994	1,965.6	+26
1995	2,875.0	+46
1996	4,075.2	+42

Source: Ministry of Economy of the Czech Republic 1995, 39, table 5.1; 1996, 33.

functions combined within a newly created Ministry of Local Development, responsible for housing—its predominant concern—as well as for regional policies and tourism.

As during the socialist regime, tourism is being recognized primarily because of its economic performance. A Department of Tourism and the Czech Tourist Agency were created in 1993 to promote regional tourist development at home and abroad and to deal with related legislation. Financial support for promoting tourism increased to approximately $2.7 million in 1996. The Minister of Economy prefaced the 1995 government publication on tourism by declaring tourism "an important branch of the Czech Republic's economy." In 1994, foreign currency revenue from incoming tourism was approximately $2 billion, 14 percent of exports from the Czech Republic and 6 percent of the gross domestic product (GDP). The 1995 figure of approximately $2.9 billion represented a 46 percent increase over 1994, and the 1996 figure of $4 billion a 42 percent increase over the preceding year (table 3). Over and beyond the official figures, there is an underground tourist economy estimated at over $1.5 billion. More than two-thirds of the total tourist income (official and black market) is generated in Prague.[19]

Although there is increased recognition of tourism's growing economic importance, a consistent national policy does not exist. In this context, there is a tendency for grants to drive tourism policy. International organizations that promote tourism as a tool for economic development and global integration press for political and economic standardization and for the integration of Czech tourism into European and worldwide systems.[20] These organizations have funded projects to regionalize tourism and to develop an information infrastructure to link up with European systems. Both projects have generated debate.

Ninety-two percent of tourists to the Czech Republic go to Prague and stay for a relatively short time. The tourism business community in Prague has emphasized the need for more visitors, longer stays, and fuller hotels and has been wary of promoting cultural activities outside the city.[21] At the same time, smaller historic cities such as Český Krumlov, Telč, and Kutná Hora have been designated UNESCO World Monuments and are pushing for regionalization to attract more visitors. A typical regionalizing project creates a package that includes two days in Prague and then eco- or agro-tourism such as farm visits into the surrounding regions. Its proponents claim that this will lengthen the average stay in the Czech Republic and increase the Czech share of the international tourist economy; draw new groups into the tourist circuit by diversifying the offerings; and distribute the economic benefits of tourism to the many small towns and villages whose future is no longer secured by state-supported agriculture or industry.

International organizations have also supported projects to create an information system that would both service the Czech Republic internally and connect it with European systems. Despite the acknowledged need, this too has been controversial within the local tourist industry and at the governmental level. Municipalities and hotels favor the introduction of a reservations system to help decentralize and regionalize the flow of tourists. But local travel agencies, particularly small firms, fear that such a system will cost them their local advantage. The Ministry of Economy did not support an earlier attempt to create such a system. Mindful of these tensions, the Czech Tourist Authority has gone another route. Together with a local company, they have begun a pilot project to create a regional information system that will make standardized data from the seventy-six regions of the Czech Republic available internationally via the Internet.

The tourist industry has given rise to interest groups and political action. A tourism lobby composed of associations of hotels and restaurants, travel agencies, and other provider groups is coalescing around an agenda that favors tourist-friendly policies and increased financial support.[22] Tourist providers want a decreased value added tax (VAT), more funding for advertising abroad, the regulation of guides and terms like *information services*, and state support for a three-year training institute for tourism-industry professionals (so as not to have to train them abroad). Many in the industry feel that Czech tourism is at a crossroads. Having captured initial interest worldwide, the sector must standardize, expand,

and diversify to maintain and strengthen its position in a global market. The Department of Tourism and the tourism industry argue that direct state support is essential for this effort and that current funding levels are inadequate. They propose following the example of states in the European Union, which use 1–2 percent of tourism profits for infrastructure development, and contend that tourism profits, rather than supporting the industry, have been used to support less profitable parts of foreign trade, just as under state socialism.

Postcommunist Tourism and Prague's Social and Spatial Structure

The rapid introduction of a market economy marked by privatization and property restitution has had its greatest impact on Prague's historic and commercial center. Development pressures are strongest at the core, where visitors have been attracted precisely because of underdevelopment—by urban landscapes that maintain the charm of an old city. This area, which we refer to as "tourist Prague," falls within Prague 1 and 2 on either side of the Charles Bridge and includes Old Town and Josefov (Jewish Town); Lesser Town and Hradčany (the Castle); and Wenceslas Square and the surrounding streets. Although there are several other islands of tourism, most tourists concentrate there, as do the restaurants and tourist shops. How do these new forces interact with the inherited structures and institutions, and what are the social and ecological consequences?

Historically, the area that makes up contemporary tourist Prague has been the site of many urban functions. From the medieval period to the nineteenth century, it was a center for trade. Charles University, founded by Charles IV in the fourteenth century, is located here. One also finds national libraries, theaters, concert halls, museums, major schools for the applied arts, and numerous government buildings. Because of the abundance of educational institutions, this area has traditionally been known for its book stores and has served as the center of the printing industry. In the midst of this mélange are historic buildings and monuments such as the Jewish Town and Tyne Church. From the socialist period, this area also retained a relatively large residential population of the elderly and the poor, as well as some artists and intellectuals who remained in Lesser Town. Few hotels existed within the old urban core. This part of Prague, with its mixture of functions and people, most closely

Old Town Square, Prague, Czech Republic

The old section of Prague, which occupies the center of the city, is an architectural treasure.

resembles the Latin Quarter in Paris. Mass tourism has been added to this rich functional mix, multiplying the daily population and the number of tourist-oriented stores and restaurants.

Prague's social and spatial structure has been deeply affected by property restitution and small privatization—the first round of which involved shops and businesses. This takes the form of commercialization (the substitution of offices and businesses for residential use) and the beginning processes of gentrification (the displacement of low-income by higher-income residents). The result has been an acceleration of the continuing decline in number of residents in Prague 1 and Prague 2, the two administrative units that form the historic and tourist area of Prague. In the period from 1989 to 1994, the population of Prague 1 declined by 10.9 percent and that of Prague 2 by 15.7 percent.

In Prague 1 and 2, between 70 to 75 percent of the housing stock was reprivatized.[23] Restitution along with small-scale privatization has provided the base for a developing entrepreneurial sector of shops, restaurants, and other small businesses. Rising rents jump-started the processes of renovation and redevelopment. As privatization and property restitution began, rents rose to the levels of other major European cities, fueled by speculation in the property market by scores of new real estate offices in Prague, many of them branch offices of foreign firms or Czech firms backed by foreign capital.[24] The net result has been a dramatic and rapid transformation of Prague 1, the core of tourist Prague. In October 1994, *The Economist* wrote: "Visit Prague . . . and you see a city center that is booming and indubitably bourgeois. The hauntingly beautiful period buildings now house the engines of a modern market economy. Stockbrokers' computers hum beneath hand-painted 17th century ceilings. The Ministry of Economy inhabits a palace overlooking the Old Town Square. Bustling shops flank the branches of local and foreign banks. Smartly dressed women take coffee in elegant cafes."[25] Then-Prime Minister Václav Klaus proudly described Prague as "the capital of an ordinary European country."

Although it is difficult to separate the effects of privatization from those of tourism per se, they clearly reinforce each other. Because of demand, rising rents lead to replacement of the cheap shops and restaurants serving local residents and workers by boutiques, galleries, and upscale restaurants that cater predominately to tourists.[26] These processes create a tension between old patterns based on a different population and social structure and new patterns emerging not only from tourism but from the market economy to which it is related; this economy brings with it a more westernized division of labor and social structure.

Let us examine the employment structure of this area where one-fifth of Prague's workforce are employed. First, there are the many public-sector workers whose places of employment are in tourist Prague (the university, offices of the municipal and national government, libraries, and hospitals). These individuals now have difficulty affording a beer or a noon meal. At the same time, a new and rapidly growing private-sector labor force in business, financial services, and real estate, with salaries two to three times higher than public-sector professionals, is beginning to use the same restaurants as the tourists. The growing number of luxury shops in the area is frequented by newly wealthy Czechs as well as by the guests of nearby hotels.[27]

The costs of rapid urban restructuring are being borne most directly by central-city residents and workers but also by the population of all metropolitan Prague. Reflecting the urban ecology of the former regime, central-city residents were mainly the old and poor. The sudden, dramatic change in the character of the district forces them to commute out for food and basic services. Although rents are still regulated, these long-time residents are nonetheless being forced out as buildings are bought, sold, and renovated for expanding commercial and tourist related activity. Overall, residential use is declining, and retail and commercial space increasing.[28] Another cost is the public amenities foregone. In the prewar period, the public sector was a competitive bidder for choice building sites; now, remaining building sites have been awarded to a hotel, a bank, and a mixed office-retail project. Other public costs more directly related to tourism include the rise in crime, crowding, noise, loss of privacy, gambling casinos, and an increase in various types of informal economic activity, often illegal, such as prostitution or street vending.

Preservation, Development, and Local Politics

Faced with rapid change, many argue that Prague needs a comprehensive approach to both development and tourism. There are, however, barriers to making use of the planning and preservation tools that helped safeguard historic Prague in the past. After 1989, planning was so deeply identified with the former regime that the public planning apparatus was for the most part dismantled. The 1990 Act on Municipalities decentralized local government and gave responsibility for planning to municipalities, who view planning as antidemocratic and anti–free market and fear it will restrict their right to develop their newly privatized property.[29]

The meaning of historic preservation is also in flux and illustrates the complex interplay of continuity and change. Although there is a tradition of historic preservation for Prague dating back to the late nineteenth century, preservation took on different connotations and received widespread public support under state socialism. Ordinary people began to support the preservation of historic buildings and even existing buildings of no special value, because preservation represented continuity with the Czech past. The public often fought, through pressure groups, the demolition of buildings in symbolically sensitive parts of the city— as in the case of a building near the National Theater. Although this building had no architectural or historical value, the public protested its demolition because it stood next to the National Theater, a structure that symbolizes Czech nationhood. At the same time, the urban policy of the Czech Communist Party was to support the preservation of old cities and historic monuments to show the cultural superiority of socialism over pragmatic and brutal capitalism. Thus, the public as well as the Party supported preservation, though for entirely different reasons.

In the new market economy, historic preservation comes right up against market pressures and free-market ideology, which have altered the former consensus. This makes for the more typical Western scenario of residential concerns conflicting with business and political interests. In 1990, Old Town residents turned out en masse to protest plans to build hotels in their area, as did residents of Lesser Town in 1993. What the public accepts, in the historic core, is a reconstruction that returns a building to its historical usage without changing the basic facade. One example of this is the reconstruction of the Ungelt. In the Middle Ages this structure served as an inn for traveling traders; later, it housed office buildings and a medical center. At present, the whole complex is being returned to its former function and reconstructed as a luxury hotel.

Although professionals, local politicians, and a majority of the public generally support a policy of respect for the past, laws and fines are sometimes disregarded and some architectural designs have been carried forward in the face of significant dissent. Myslbek, one of the last unbuilt sites in the core, is a case in point. In 1996, the design for Myslbek was roundly criticized by the Club for Old Prague and President Havel, among others, as an architectural disaster equal to some of the communist-era buildings.[30] Speculation as to why Myslbek was built as designed points to municipal profit. Despite Prague's generally hands-off policy, Myslbek was developed innovatively as a joint-stock company with 20 percent participation by the city of Prague. Another explanation is the lesser symbolic importance of the Myslbek site. These conflicts underline the types of battles being fought in Prague.

Some professionals in the Chief Architect's Office believe that too much preservation hinders the transformation of the historic core into a functional part of the city. In this view, tourism combined with privatization and development is the main factor reviving the historic core, because these economic activities bring renewed vitality; old buildings become viable economic units as they begin earning money in the form of shops and cafes. This, they suggest, has led to a more effective revival of Prague's "historic slums" than have any of the formal mechanisms of planning or legal protection used by previous regimes, which, ironically, were a factor in their neglect and subsequent decline. Thus, the contradictions and dilemmas make it difficult to strike a balance between functional needs and cultural values.

The city of Prague seems ambivalent about tourism. The authorities have conducted no studies of tourism, and tourist-related issues do not figure in the master plan or in prognostic studies. Municipal ambivalence is rooted in the political economy of tourism. At present it is the central state and the overall economy that benefit most directly from tourism; the city bears added costs but gets little direct financial benefit. Czech municipalities still have limited fiscal independence. They collect little direct revenue and cannot set tax rates, and most of their operating funds still come from the central state.[31] Even the small tourist fee for hotel accommodations goes first to the central state, where it is then redistributed on the basis of population, not tourism activity. Although several small Czech cities operate tourist services for profit, the mayor and Council of Prague are free-market proponents who do not believe the municipality should itself engage in profitable enterprise. There is a general consensus within municipal government that if Prague is not able to capture a greater share of the tourism income in the near future, the central state should take over the burden of supporting the tourism infrastructure. As it stands, Prague is vulnerable to losing services and quality of life.

Different Paths to Tourism Development?

Mass tourism exists in Prague as elsewhere, but it is the more complex forms combining work and play that give postcommunist tourism its particular dynamic character. One factor differentiating tourism in Prague from that in Paris and London is Prague's status as a newly opened economic, political, and cultural frontier. Professional and cultural interactions, in particular, have helped to integrate Prague quickly into international circuits. The case study of Prague allows us to view tourism as the cultural mechanism that accompanies and enables political and economic globalization. Indeed, the high degree of interaction raises questions about the adequacy and usefulness of the concept of tourism as it is commonly used.

One theme of the globalization literature is that tourism provides an entry point that allows transnational corporations and homogenized mass culture to overwhelm local differences. The evidence from the tourist sector in Prague is mixed. It is true that transnational organizations and capital (nonprofit as well as for-profit) are attracted to the tourism industry and are important actors in the emerging tourism sector. Yet, not all international players are equal. The major foreign actors in Prague, for example, are regional—Austrian and German companies with shared cultural roots—and anecdotes abound regarding the difficulties of dealing with large U.S. or Canadian developers who do not understand the mentality of small countries. Furthermore, Czechs have actively sought to retain control and regain market share in the tourism sector. More important, the tourist sector has served as a major channel for entrepreneurial start-ups, and both black and gray markets have had notable redistributive effects, spreading the benefits of tourism broadly. Whether, and to what extent, this is a transitional or one-time phenomenon remains to be seen.

Cultural homogenization is a more difficult issue. On the most general level, Prague has quickly become a typical Western city. Yet tourism has also motivated Prague to display its rich heritage of art, architecture, and music. Rather than yielding to cultural homogeneity, Prague is repositioning itself within the international community on the basis of its unique cultural contributions. In addition to reclaiming an older heritage, a new and evolving intellectual and countercultural scene has emerged and draws its share of tourists alongside the more touristic constructions centered on Kafka or Mozart. It remains to be seen how more recent global implants such as Planet Hollywood will fit within this already nuanced cultural arena. The view from within suggests that after the experience of the past forty years, many Czechs are happy to be part of the world that includes McDonald's, Marks and Spencer, and tourists.

The issue of social-spatial impact is similarly complex. We have emphasized the difficulty of analytically isolating tourism from privatization and economic development in general. The modern sectors, which include financial and producer services as well as tourism, tend to support one another and are part of an emerging whole that exhibits some signs of the social polarization that we find in Western cities.[32] Tourism has its costs: it has exacerbated existing inequalities, particularly for public-sector employees and the elderly, and it has increased the pressure on the historic core. Yet, it has also had positive redistributive effects and has contributed to reweaving the fractured tissue of urban life in Prague. Many of the overwhelming number of historic buildings in need of maintenance and renovation have been restored to use, including more than one hundred palaces in the central core. This in turn attracts business and becomes a locational factor. Privatization and tourism have become genuine economic generators that combine to bring back the diverse functions and uses of a living city.

This study of postcommunist Prague illustrates the complex interplay of continuity and change. Although the former prime minister delighted in describing Prague as "the capital of an ordinary European country," Prague is far from ordinary. Its legacy of historical structures makes it particularly vulnerable to developmental pressures, leading one to wonder why the outcome has not been worse. Just as many of the structures and mentalities of the prewar period continued during state socialism, statism—as an administrative style of centralized control—persists amid the official erosion of planning and preservation. Of the different paths to tourism development, perhaps the Czech Republic and Prague—supported by public sentiment—are taking a state managerial route, despite appearance (and ideology) to the contrary.

ARIE SHACHAR AND NOAM SHOVAL

Tourism in Jerusalem
A Place to Pray

Walk around Zion, circle it; count its towers, take note of
its ramparts, survey its places.
—PSALM 48:13–14

Jerusalem: the city which miraculously transforms man
into pilgrim; no one can enter it and remain unchanged.
—ELIE WIESEL

Tourism in Jerusalem has had a distinct character
throughout the long history of the city. It is a phenomenon in which the
components of the city itself—its sights, views, architecture, people,
food, and smells—have almost no bearing on why people visit the city.
The last time Jerusalem was built on a monumental scale, before the
present period, was during the reign of Herod the Great, when it was
known for the magnificent Second Temple as well as its multitude of impressive palaces, roads, bridges, and highly sophisticated urban infrastructure. It took two thousand years before the city, through the efforts
of Mayor Teddy Kollek, regained some character in its built environment. With the exception of the Dome of the Rock, a well-known architectural masterpiece, Jerusalem had no building, palace, temple, shrine,
church, mosque, garden, fountain, or any other man-made structure or
natural phenomenon that was unique. Simply stated, from its destruction by the Romans in A.D. 70 up until recently, Jerusalem was a small,
poor, neglected place, barely surviving at the periphery of various empires. One might say that Jerusalem as a global center for pilgrims and

visitors was not an earthly city but Heaven on High, a spiritual city venerated in visitors' minds and hearts.[1]

In 1996, Jerusalem marked the three thousandth anniversary of King David's conquest of the city and its transformation into his capital. The transfer of the Ark of the Covenant to Jerusalem by David, and especially the building of the First Temple by his son, Solomon, changed Jerusalem into a religious center and a focus of Jewish pilgrimage. This status continued and was strengthened during the period of the Second Temple, reaching a peak in the first century of the Common Era. Within the same period, Jesus and his disciples came as pilgrims to Jerusalem during one of the Passover festivals. This event transformed Jerusalem into one of the holiest of Christian sites, making it a focal point for Christian pilgrims. About six hundred years later, Islam, too, adopted Jerusalem as one of its most sacred places, identifying it as the site of significant events in the life of Muhammad, including his Night Journey and his ascension to heaven. The increasingly sacred character of the city for the three monotheistic religions brought with it the notable activity of pilgrimage. As a consequence, Jerusalem presents a singular case among all sacred places, in that it attracts pilgrims from diverse religions, nations, and cultural traditions. The significance of Jerusalem to followers of these three religions, and their many denominations, has created spatial and organizational competition and fierce ongoing conflicts over rituals, sites, and itineraries. Whereas Rome, Mecca, and Varanasi (India) are associated with only one religion, Jerusalem is a multireligious center of unique character, spiritual meaning, and universal appeal.

Modern secular tourism, which took shape in Europe in the form of the Grand Tour, began trickling into Jerusalem in the sixteenth century and grew at an ever-increasing rate during the nineteenth century.[2] The change from individual tourism to organized tourism in Jerusalem and the Holy Land occurred in spring 1869, when Thomas Cook and Son began operations in the region with an organized tour for thirty tourists to Egypt and the Holy Land—a tour guided by Cook himself. By 1882, the company had led more than five thousand tourists to see the two locations.[3] Still, until the mid-twentieth century, obstacles restricted the flow of tourists, including the long distance to the Holy Land from European countries, problems of security (until mid-century, Bedouins regularly attacked urban and rural settlements and terrorized tourists), and the lack of a suitable infrastructure.[4] By 1995, more than 2 million tour-

ists and pilgrims visited Jerusalem in a single year, making it by far the
most popular destination in Israel.

From Holy Places to Tourist Space

Tours to Jerusalem were, at least up to the second half of the nineteenth
century, intended to serve a moral and spiritual purpose and to satisfy a
religious obligation. A visit to Jerusalem was aimed at allowing the pilgrim to identify with its history, its moral leadership, its agonies and suf-
ferings, and its promise of salvation, personal purification, and peace on
earth. Not simply a place for intellectual contemplation or aesthetic observation, it incorporated fantasy, prayers, and dreams.[5] To quote Urry,
"The city is the repository of people's memories and of the past; and it
also functions as a receptacle of cultural symbols."[6] Jerusalem's importance lay in the symbolic meanings attached to it. The issue of the authenticity of sites was of only minor significance, as long as the visitors
accepted the beliefs of their creed about the historical and religious geography of Jerusalem. Consequently, the personal and spiritual experience of the pilgrim-visitor has been molded by the social constructions
of holy places according to the narrative of a particular religious belief.
Once in Jerusalem, the pilgrim can realize and give concrete meaning to
the spiritual world in which he or she was bred. In this way Jerusalem
became an omphalos of the world, an *axis mundi*—the point of intersection between the mundane and transcendental.

Because pilgrims visit different sites at different times and practice
different rituals, several holy cities make up the entity called Jerusalem,
with each configuration defined by the religions and denominations that
sacralize the city.[7] The various sites that are visited and worshiped are a
prime example of what might be termed conferred authenticity; the au-
thentication process takes place by virtue of the continuous stream of
pilgrims and tourists over long periods.[8] Pilgrims and tourists do not
aim at a universal tourist space in Jerusalem but focus and limit their
gaze, their worship, and their personal spiritual experience to the particular sacred space as shaped and defined by their religious denomination.[9] In modern times, nationalism has been superimposed on the old
religious divides; thus, the national monuments and symbols of Jews
and Arabs are completely different and markedly separated. Consequently
the contest for political dominance over the city further divides the
tourist space.

Urban Tourism and Urban Structure

The Dutch researcher Miriam Jansen-Verbeke proposed the division of urban tourism into primary and secondary elements.[10] The primary elements are the attractions that draw visitors to cities, the secondary ones the various services that cater to their needs (hotels, restaurants, travel agencies, tour operators, and the like). When the primary and secondary elements converge spatially, a tourism district is created.[11] Jerusalem, rather than containing a single tourism district, encompasses a constellation of spaces, each of which is composed of sites specific to a particular group of pilgrims and tourists. In addition, a small number of sites are visited because of their universal appeal, which transcends their specific religious, cultural, or national significance. Among the examples of this type of site are the Wailing Wall, the Temple Mount, the Mount of Olives, and Mount Zion.

The Politics of Tourist-Space Segmentation

The segmentation of Jerusalem into distinct sacred spaces, which were initially pilgrim spaces and in modern times have become tourist spaces, has been a highly political process, molding the entire urban fabric of Jerusalem. During its two thousand years, when it was not the capital city of an empire, kingdom, or nation—between A.D. 70 (the Roman conquest and the destruction of the Second Temple) and 1949 (when the State of Israel unilaterally declared the city to be its capital)—the various religions and sects shaped the physical growth and structure of the urban-built environment.[12] This process occurred in two steps: first, the identification of the "sacred space and its validation by an ongoing stream of pilgrims"; second, the transformation of the "sacred space into a tourist space."[13] Sacred space included not only sites of historical-religious significance but areas adjacent to them, such as the headquarters of religious organizations and institutions that managed the holy places. In turn places of worship and prayer gave rise to the establishment of schools—the public institutions charged with instilling principles of belief and of moral behavior. Combining a holy place and an institution of learning created a forceful nucleus that stimulated development around it; development around the nucleus of a sacred space thus established the base of the ecological structure of the Old City of Jerusalem, where one finds the Muslim quarter around the Dome of the

Rock and the Al-Aqsa Mosque; the Christian quarter around the Church of the Holy Sepulchre; the Jewish quarter adjacent to the Wailing Wall (or Western Wall)—the only remains of the Temple Mount complex; and the Armenian quarter around St. James Cathedral.

This process of segmented development has been strongly reinforced by visitors who, in addition to fulfilling their own quest for moral uplift, have served a major political function: pilgrims, and more recently many tourists, carried a message of support, material and symbolic, to members of their group residing in the city. Pilgrims and tourists visit Jerusalem to identify in body and soul with their religion, denomination, or nationality. The tour of Jerusalem is a sort of temporary mobilization of the believers and followers who join the ongoing and everlasting struggle for the strong presence and domination of their own version of Jerusalem on Earth.

The political nature of the pilgrimage to Jerusalem has been evident throughout the past two thousand years, culminating in the nineteenth century, when the various European powers rushed to appropriate pieces of the city from the weakening Ottoman empire. They achieved this goal not through military power but by establishing physical bridgeheads in Jerusalem in the form of services to pilgrims and tourists, such as churches, hospices, and hospitals built in splendid complexes of quasi-monumental scale. Their construction of these required the acquisition of large tracts of land, which created foreign strongholds in Jerusalem. An example of such development is the Russian Compound, which comprises the magnificent dome-shaped Holy Trinity Church, extensive tourist accommodations, and a hospital. Another instance is the French Compound. Located between the Russian Compound and the northern wall of the Old City, Notre Dame de France à Jerusalem is composed of a huge hospice, a large modern hospital, and an impressive church.

These European outposts produced new tourist spaces of a grand scale and appearance. They had a decisive influence in establishing and shaping the growth of New Jerusalem outside the walls of the Old City, and up to the present day they constitute the most remarkable landmarks in the city's landscape. Because of their visual and aesthetic qualities and their historical significance for Jerusalem, these sites have gradually changed from simply providing services and accommodations to pilgrims and tourists to becoming primary tourist attractions in themselves.

Tourism to Jerusalem took on new meaning in the second half of the

| 1 Via Dolorosa | 2 Dome of the Rock | 3 Mount of Olives | 4 Holy Sepulchre |
| 5 Wailing Wall | 6 Old City Walls | 7 Jaffa Gate | 8 Mamilla |

Jerusalem landmarks, from the air

The Old City walls, Mamilla, and the Jaffa Gate closely bound a tourist space. A complex of shops, housing, and parks, the Mamilla Project provides a transitional space between the old and new cities.

twentieth century: the creation of the State of Israel gave rise to persistent efforts at reinforcing the Jewish presence and dominance over Jerusalem. The urban landscape of the city changed dramatically once it became the capital. After 1948, when west Jerusalem became the part of the city that remained under Israeli rule following partition of the city during the Arab-Israeli war, the government built several national monuments that created new tourist spaces of the highest symbolic nature. The most important of these were the Knesset (Parliament) building and, adjacent to it, the Israel Museum, whose archaeological artifacts highlight the links between modern-day Israel and its long history of Jewish settlement; the museum does not chronicle the history of the Arabs in this region. The compound comprising the Knesset, the Israel Museum, and the new campus of the Hebrew University forms the new national center of Israel and stands in antithesis to the Old City. Secular in nature and representing political power, historical roots, and modern science and learning, the new center counterbalances the Old City, once the epitome of religious beliefs and moral values.

Another preeminent national symbol is Mount Herzl, the highest mountain in the city and the site of memorials and national cemeteries; at its summit is the tomb of Theodore Herzl, the founder of modern Zionism. In a supreme example of "staged authenticity,"[14] not only were Herzl's remains moved from Vienna to Jerusalem, but his study and library were restored in order to re-create the physical milieu for his creative dreams and programs. Near Herzl's tomb is the resting place of Israel's presidents and prime ministers. Former Prime Minister Yitzhak Rabin's tomb has already become a national memorial that attracts large numbers of visitors. The cemetery and Yad Vashem—the memorial and museum to the millions who died in the Holocaust—are located on the lower slopes of Mount Herzl. The Military Cemetery and the Holocaust memorial are sacred spaces of the highest order in a civic religion, symbolizing the painful road to Jewish national revival. The entire Herzl compound, within the new Jerusalem, mirrors the Mount of Olives Cemetery just opposite the eastern walls of the Old City. In the same way that the Mount of Olives was the major destination of Jewish pilgrims for two thousand years, the Mount Herzl memorial, especially Yad Vashem, is currently one of the foremost attractions, second only to the Wailing Wall. The visit to Yad Vashem, always a shocking and deeply moving experience, can be regarded as a secular pilgrimage that has strong national and political motivations.

Table 1 International Tourism to Israel, 1970–95 (in thousands)

Year	Tourist Arrivals by Land and Air	Cruise Passengers*	Total	Tourists Visiting Jerusalem
1970	419	22	441	352
1975	559	61	620	496
1980	1,066	110	1,176	940
1985	1,264	172	1,436	1,148
1990	1,132	210	1,342	1,073
1995	2,215	315	2,530	2,024

Source: For the years 1970–90, Central Bureau of Statistics, Israel 1995, 7; Central Bureau of Statistics and Ministry of Tourism, Israel 1996, 9; Municipality of Jerusalem et al. 1996, 9.
*A cruise passenger is defined as a visitor on a cruise who enters Israel for a day or two and returns to the ship at night; includes personnel from cruise ships and military ships as well.

Urban Tourism in Jerusalem

Surveys indicate that about 80 percent of tourists to Israel visit Jerusalem;[15] one can therefore estimate the volume of tourism to Jerusalem using national statistics (table 1).[16]

There is no way to determine the number of visitors to such important tourist sites as the Wailing Wall, the Church of the Holy Sepulchre, the Temple Mount, Yad Vashem, the markets of the Old City, Mount Zion, the Mount of Olives, and the like, since no tickets are issued at these places. Based on rough estimates, however, of the more than two million tourists to Jerusalem in 1995, 89 percent (1.8 million) visited the Wailing Wall, and 60 percent (1.3 million) the Via Dolorosa, among the most popular Christian sites. A similar pattern was noted among cruise travelers.[17] In 1994, about 1.5 million visitors viewed Yad Vashem, about half a million of whom were tourists and the rest Israelis.[18] In the same year, about 700,000 people entered the Israel Museum, and about 200,000 the Tower of David Museum;[19] these figures include both tourists and Israelis.

Of travelers to Israel in 1995, 56 percent were part of organized tours; only 29 percent were traveling on their own; and the rest were visiting relatives and friends. The dominance of group travel further strengthens segmentation among the religious groups traveling to the city, since in the case of organized groups the itinerary reflects the outlook of the tour organizers rather than personal choice, which is likely to be more eclectic.

To describe the different tourist spaces in Jerusalem, it is essential to identify the major groups of visitors and tourists. Religion is the main demarcation; in turn each of the three monotheistic religions is subdi-

Table 2   Tourists to Israel, by Religious Affiliation

Year	Christians (%)	Jews (%)	Moslems (%)	No Affiliation (%)	Other (%)
1986–87	49	41	NA	NA	10
1995	59	27	1.3	12	1

Source: Ministry of Tourism and Israel Airport Authority 1988, 13; Midgam 1996, 66.

vided into denominations or by the level of orthodoxy of religious belief (see table 2):

- Jews
    Secular followers and moderates
    Ultra-Orthodox sects
- Christians
    Roman Catholic
    Orthodox
    Protestant
    Monophysite
- Muslims

A second defining characteristic is length of stay, which is partially related to age. Young tourists, the backpackers, remain for long periods, usually several weeks; their tourism is highly individual and reflects interests and patterns of behavior typical of youthful tourists all over the world. A significant group, the cruise tourists, visits Jerusalem and its vicinity without spending even a single night in the city. They are shepherded about in bus convoys and, because of the limited time allowed, visit only the most famous attractions, without conforming to any religious or national group preferences. In between are those traveling in groups or by themselves, who usually spend several days or a week. Clearly, these groups have less impact on Jerusalem than those who visit for religious reasons.

It is possible to analyze the tourist spaces visited by each group.[20]

Jewish Visitors

Secular and Religious Jews

Secular and moderate Jews (Conservative and Reform Jews from the Diaspora, "national religious" Jews living in Israel) tend to identify themselves with modern Israel and, while in Jerusalem, to visit sites of Jewish national

Table 3   Sacred Tourist Sites for Christian Visitors

Site	Protestant	Roman Catholic	Orthodox
Basilica of the Ecce Homo		X	
Chapel of the Condemnation		X	
Chapel of the Flagellation		X	
Church of All Nations		X	
Church of the Holy Sepulchre	X	X	X
Church of St. Mary Magdalene			X
Church of Visitation		X	
Crusader Church of St. Anne		X	
Dead Sea Scrolls	X	X	
Dome of the Ascension		X	X
Dominus Flavit Chapel		X	
Dormition Abbey		X	
Ein Karem, The Spring	X	X	X
Franciscan Church of St. John the Baptist		X	
Garden of Gethsemane	X	X	X
Garden Tomb	X		
Greek Orthodox Patriarchate and Museum			X
Greek Praetorium			X
Holy Land Model of the Second Temple Period	X	X	
Latin Patriarchate		X	
Monastery of the Cross			X
Mount Zion, Room of the Last Supper	X	X	X
Orthodox Church of St. John the Baptist			X
Panorama from Mount of Olives	X	X	X
Pater Noster Church		X	
Pool of Bethesda	X	X	
Pool of Shiloah	X		
Russian Church and Convent			X
Russian Church of the Ascension			X
St. Alexander			X
St. Salvadore		X	
St. Stephens Church		X	X
St. Peter in Gallicantu		X	
Shrine of the Book	X	X	
Temple Mount	X	X	X
Tomb of Mary			X
Via Dolorosa	X	X	X
Viri Galilei			X

character. Within the Old City these include the Wailing Wall, the Jewish quarter, and, south of the present walls of the Old City, the archaeological excavations related to the Temple area and to the City of David. Western Jerusalem, the location of all the national monuments, offers the main tourist attractions for secular and national religious Jewish tourists.

Ultra-Orthodox Jews

Most of the locations visited by ultra-Orthodox Jews are religious sites, especially tombs. The two main exceptions are recreational areas: the zoo, one of the few forms of entertainment allowed ultra-Orthodox families, and the ultra-Orthodox quarter (the Geula and Mea She'arim area, a place of recreation and shopping). The typical main motivations of ultra-Orthodox tourists—that of staying in the vicinity of a particular rabbi and of visiting family—only strengthen the tendency of this group to congregate in a specific space, which to a large extent is in north Jerusalem, where the ultra-Orthodox population is concentrated.

Christian Pilgrims and Visitors

The most important Christian sites are generally shared by all Christian denominations. The emphasis and rituals of the various denominations differ, however. Regardless of the shared sites, each denomination has a particular focus, a location where pilgrims can pray en masse with members of their own denomination. There is little interest in national and Israeli sites, since Christian pilgrims are indifferent to the political contest for Jerusalem. For them, the holy places are of exclusive importance.[21] Christian pilgrims frequent institutions connected to their specific religious denomination or their country of origin (such as churches, orphanages, schools, and research institutes). For example, Romanian pilgrims visit the Romanian Orthodox Church; Greek Catholics, the Greek Catholic Patriarchate; French Catholics, the Ecole Biblique; Swedes, the Swedish Theological Institute; and Mormons, the Mormon University.

Since Protestants do not have a defined hierarchy, each tour leader is free to guide a group according to his or her priorities. There are, therefore, many Protestant groups whose itinerary resembles that of the typical urban tourist, without the designated routes and sites mandated for pilgrims.

Christian tourist spaces are organized according to the three major religious divisions: Protestant, Catholic, and Orthodox. The usual Christian tourist space comprises a large number of sites that are traditionally included in organized tours and guidebooks and recommended by tour guides. Mapping the list of sites visited by Christian pilgrims and tourists produces the Christian tourist space. The area is curvilinear, stretching from the Mount of Olives, in the east, extending along the Via

Model of King Solomon's Jerusalem at the Holyland Hotel site

The son and successor of King David, Solomon was king of the ancient Hebrews from ca. 970 to ca. 930 B.C.

Dolorosa (Way of the Cross) to the Holy Sepulchre, and then turning south to Mount Zion (the site of the room of the Last Supper). Almost all sites visited by the various Christian denominations fall within this tourist space.

Muslim Pilgrims and Visitors

Until it began to unravel, the peace process brought a new segment of tourism to Jerusalem—the Muslim pilgrimage. The size of this group was never large—only about 1 percent of incoming tourists at its peak— and the breakdown of the peace talks has undoubtedly slowed it considerably. In 1995, eighty-five thousand visitors crossed the Jordan River to the West Bank and Gaza, usually as part of a family visit.[22] The most popular sites visited were the Mount of Olives; the Haram-es-Sharif, including the Dome of the Rock and the Al-Aqsa Mosque; Mount Zion, including the mosque in the room of the Last Supper and King David's tomb;[23] the Suq; the Jerusalem shopping mall at Malcha; and Orient House, the unofficial office of the Palestinian Authority.

Muslim tourist space includes religious as well as Arab sites that signify nationalist aspirations. The large Jerusalem shopping mall at Malcha, of little interest to tourists from Europe, North America, and Japan, attracts many Muslims from countries less developed than Israel.

The Delicate Balance

The cultural and religious character of Jerusalem, in addition to its unique position as the contested capital of two nations, has resulted in the establishment of segmented tourist spaces. These well-demarcated zones have been created by distinct groups with distinct programs and activities. Though segmented, each of these areas, because of its attractiveness to large numbers of tourists, acquires great economic value. Each is controlled by the institutions of a particular religion, and each has a strong local political character that identifies it as a sort of enclave or mini-city within the general municipal jurisdiction. The common historical roots of the three main religions mean that the tourist spaces are physically close and sometimes overlap. The small size of the Old City and its surroundings gives the combined map of the tourist spaces its tightly knit and condensed character.

The political and economic worth of each tourist space makes it a highly valued and well-guarded asset. Because competition among the various spaces cannot include territorial expansion, it is expressed through specific improvements in an area's tourist services, the guidance system, and the auxiliary services. Any attempt to expand into another's realm or to create a bridgehead from one space to another could cause a serious shock to the delicate and finely tuned spatial system. In September 1996, for example, an attempt by the government to uncover the northern exit to the Western Wall tunnels caused a severe political upheaval; although the tunnels began within the Jewish tourist space, they ended within the Muslim tourist space. This episode is tragic proof of the resistance that any changes in territorial control of the mosaic would engender. It can therefore be concluded that the well-structured pattern of tourist spaces in Jerusalem is kept intact through the balance of mutual interest and common survival, which forces each group to play strictly according to the rules of the game. This delicate balance of power and spatial organization enables Jerusalem to maintain a precarious status as a major destination—a status that could be instantly compromised by an escalation in conflict and violence.

Part IV

Tourism Strategies

CHARLES C. EUCHNER

Tourism and Sports
The Serious Competition
for Play

A famous cover of the *New Yorker* displays New York through the jaundiced perspective of someone who has never crossed the Hudson River. Midtown Manhattan is the colossal center of the world. Across the Hudson, New Jersey appears as a diminished presence on the horizon. The rest of the world recedes into a vanishing distance, with China, Japan, and Russia mere specks on the far horizon.

In the eyes of its boosters in cities across the United States the sports industry occupies a similar status. Sports boosters tend to view their industry as the defining feature of any city's economic and social life. The booster's map places stadiums front-and-center, with service and entertainment businesses—restaurants, hotels, nightclubs, souvenir stores, parking garages, theaters, museums, aquariums, and waterfront malls—clustered in the immediate environs. In the near distance a few office buildings loom over the horizon. Farther out on the periphery, highways, warehouses, manufacturing plants, residential areas, schools, hospitals, churches, and parks appear as bumps on the earth's curvature. Receding in the distance are the suburbs, the countryside, and the rest of the insignificant world.

Proponents of major stadium projects claim that sports bring a dramatic infusion of outside dollars into a community. Gregg Lukenbill, the protagonist in efforts to bring football or baseball to Sacramento, gushed that "the Raiders coming to Sacramento would be an event the magnitude of the Gold Rush."[1] Mayor Rudolph Giuliani of New York commented that revenues from a new stadium for the New York Yankees "would be off the charts"—even though the team would simply be shifted from one part of the city to another.[2] David Garrick, the former vice president of Toronto's SkyDome, recalls speaking to an African couple on a tour of the edifice: when asked what had made them visit the SkyDome, "of all places," they replied that they had seen "all the Jays games from a [satellite television] dish, and it made them interested in seeing Toronto." "Think of it," Garrick said; "we had 100 million viewers for the All Star Game. NBC was in town for days doing shots of the city, and the Goodyear blimp took aerial views of the city."[3]

In virtually every major American city, expectations of enormous inflows of investment have led to construction of expensive new stadiums. In a three-year period in the 1990s, some $7 billion was committed or spent to build or refurbish stadiums and arenas.[4] Politicians and policy makers justify this level of governmental support with the dubious argument that sports franchises contribute to the economic vitality of the city and the less dubious argument that sports provide a symbolic boost to the city. The ability of team owners to command this level of governmental support results in part from their success in persuading the public of the economic and symbolic importance of their activity. But it also derives from their extraordinary power. Major league sports operate as a cartel, with individual teams cooperating to help unify policies on labor relations and to create basic rules for league competition and size, broadcasting, marketing, and the requirements for team ownership.[5] When individual franchises seek better lease terms with their host cities, the collective power of the league supports those demands. League commissioners and presidents set minimum standards for facilities and leases, and cities have little choice but to meet the stadium demands or risk losing the team. What drives the modern stadium-building boom is not the search for tourism and urban development but a reactive relationship with a monopolistic industry. Stadium construction is a defensive, not an offensive, strategy.

Sports as an Industry

The baseball and football leagues strongly influence both the supply and demand for their product—and increase the cost of doing business. First consider supply. Both baseball and football have expanded the size of their leagues, but not nearly enough to keep pace with cities' demands for teams. Since 1969, major league baseball (MLB) has increased from

The Toronto Skydome, home of the Toronto Blue Jays baseball team

Completed in 1989, the stadium cost $400 million to construct.

twenty-four to thirty teams; in that same period, the National Football League (NFL) has increased from twenty-two to twenty-eight. Given the growth in U.S. population (from 203 million in 1970 to 255 million in 1992), the emergence of new cities and metropolitan areas (especially in the South and West), and the expansion of sports internationally (increasing the supply of players), each sport could field a dozen or more teams. The economist Andrew Zimbalist has remarked: "Expansion to thirty-five or forty teams by the end of the century would mean that more cities have their demand for a team satisfied, *a more equitable relationship would develop between existing teams and host cities,* and there would be a greater number of . . . players. This outcome sounds like something economists call a welfare maximizing solution."[6] Despite the grousing of old-timers who claim that expansion has diluted the talent of the major leagues, the athletic abilities and talent of modern players are probably greater than ever.[7] Nevertheless, the leagues add new teams only when they confront a direct threat from either Congress or the courts.[8]

Now consider demand. The leagues have succeeded in boosting demand with a strategy of delocalization. Before 1960, no major league or NFL team played in a stadium outside a central city. But with the movement to the suburbs and the growing importance of broadcasting revenues, centrality ceased to matter. League officials have encouraged teams to look to suburban localities and even relatively small towns for possible playing sites. By 1996, seven teams—the NFL's Giants, Jets, Lions, Dolphins, and Patriots, and baseball's Angels, Rangers, and Marlins—played outside the central city. Towns like St. Petersburg, Florida, never would have been considered for a major league team a generation ago, but the city built a stadium and intensely pursued the Chicago White Sox in 1988 and the San Francisco Giants in 1992. In 1998, St. Petersburg finally fielded a team. Even exurban areas have entered the bidding: Irwindale, a town in eastern Los Angeles County with a population of one thousand, became a major player in 1987 when it announced an agreement to build a new stadium for the Raiders football team. That deal eventually collapsed, but this episode demonstrated that any of hundreds of localities could serve as sites for professional sports teams. The only prerequisites are access to a major media market and a freeway system.

Sports franchises exert great leverage over public officials because they can control the timing and the tempo of negotiations, because supply is restricted, and because expansion or movable teams can always attract multiple bidders. When political conditions are unfavorable— when, for example, budgetary constraints or public opposition make public officials reluctant to spend hundreds of millions of dollars for sports—the owner can retreat from demands for better facilities and lease terms. Then, when conditions are ripe, the owner can make more demands and put pressure on key figures. In fact, it often takes franchises years to gain the benefits they seek. But they usually succeed, partly because civic elites convince themselves that big-time sports are an essential tool for promoting tourism and development.[9] At all times, the unique nature of the commodity gives sports a special caché for local media, fans, and members of the growth coalition. As Janet Lever remarks in a study of Latin American soccer, "Where else do we meet with 50,000 others?"[10]

In a superficial way, major league franchises belie the cartel argu-

ment. The franchises compete with one another for league championships, and team owners clash on a wide range of issues such as revenue sharing, broadcasting strategies, labor relations, and strategies for
international development. But this internal competition actually increases the league's cartel power vis-à-vis cities. When one team gets a
new stadium that brings in millions more in revenues, rivals seek to
catch up with a stadium of their own. Soon after the Colorado Rockies
signed a lucrative deal to play at the new Coors Field, Bill White, president of the National League, flew into town to proclaim the facility as the
new standard for the rest of the league. One of the most lucrative stadium deals—the Rams' lease at the TransWorld Dome in St. Louis—
allows the Rams to break the thirty-year lease after ten years if the stadium is not among the "first tier" of all facilities in the NFL. How such
a standard would be interpreted is open to question, but it destabilizes
the city's long-term investment in pro football. The Rams, in essence,
have a threat to move built into their lease.[11]

League rules that govern the revenues that teams may keep to themselves and the revenues they must share reinforce the desire of team
owners for new facilities. The NFL's near-equal sharing of all ticket,
broadcasting, and merchandising income drives teams to look for revenues sources that need not be shared. Luxury seating is one of the loop-
holes. Teams can keep all of the income from annual leases of "personal
seat licenses" (ranging from $250 to $2,000 per seat) and skyboxes (from
$15,000 for a group of seats in Green Bay to $250,000 in Dallas). Because
these luxury seats usually require specific structural configurations, new
stadiums are often necessary to get this money.[12] In major league baseball, a different dynamic drives the stadium-building mania. Teams are
granted exclusive control over territories, which vary dramatically in
local television revenues. The New York Yankees, for example, received
$45 million annually in local television deals in the early 1990s, while the
Seattle Mariners received only about $8 million. "Small market" teams
like the Milwaukee Brewers and San Diego Padres felt extra pressure to
get the new income that new stadiums could generate.

Even organized labor—which challenges the leagues' hegemony over
sports through the collective bargaining process—serves to strengthen
the sports industry's power. Despite rancorous labor disputes that have
caused strikes and lockouts in baseball, football, basketball, and hockey,
management-labor conflicts make each side richer. The leagues' refusal
to allow players to move freely at the end of each contract limits the

number of players. This restriction of supply drives up the salaries of those players who do become eligible for arbitration or free agency. Exploding salaries, in turn, put pressure on franchises—especially those operating in small markets—to seek more revenues. This pressure, which has also forced sports to professionalize office operations, marketing, talent evaluation, and so on, is the main factor behind the drive for new stadiums with luxury seating and better lease terms.[13]

League bylaws also intimidate host cities—and up the ante in negotiations over facilities. If they wanted, both football and baseball leagues could change their internal rules to reduce the pressure for new stadiums. The NFL, for example, could close the loophole that has fostered the skybox frenzy, and baseball could end its unfair territorial exclusivity or develop a revenue-sharing plan. Major league baseball could also allow teams to sell the contracts of expensive players to the highest bidders, so that small-market teams could properly profit from their investment in player development. The leagues could hold down player salaries—the major financial pressure on teams that spurs stadium demands—by allowing freer movement of players. Limits on the number of free agents restrict the supply of quality players and drive up costs.[14] Cities, in effect, subsidize the inflationary costs built into the structure of the industry.

Frenzy of Movement

Whatever the costs and benefits of a sports-based tourism strategy, virtually every major metropolitan area in the United States has become involved in stadium projects and bidding wars for NFL and MLB franchises. It is precisely this frenzy of activity that makes sports such an expensive and risky strategy for promoting tourism and development.

Since the early 1980s, an unprecedented wave of stadium construction has followed team owners' threats to move. Virtually every team in baseball and football has engaged in the stadium game. Although several football teams had moved within their metropolitan areas, it was the Raiders' move from Oakland to Los Angeles in 1982 that changed the whole dynamic of city-sports relations. The team's owner, Al Davis, defied the NFL's attempts to stop him. His successful legal battles not only won him $42 million in damages from the NFL for antitrust violations but also sent a signal to other NFL owners that they could abandon their home cities at will. In the following thirteen years, five more teams moved, creating a crisis of confidence in the NFL's commitment to its host cities. In the same period, nineteen teams demanded and got new stadiums by threatening to move, and five cities got expansion teams by making commitments to build new stadiums. Two cities won franchises by promising to spend hundreds of millions to renovate stadiums.

It was not the actual franchise shifts that prompted the stadium-building boom as much as the *threat* to move. (No baseball team, in fact, has moved out of its area since the Washington Senators moved to Arlington, Texas, after the 1971 season.) In city after city, state and local authorities responded by devising elaborate schemes to finance and build new stadiums. Creative financing schemes include establishing special enterprise and taxing zones, sports lotteries, sales of rights to luxury seating, sin taxes (levies on liquor and cigarettes), travel and tourism taxes, increases in sales taxes, sales of a variety of bond offerings, and the reshuffling of capital budgets. With the Rams' move to St. Louis in 1995, personal seat licenses (PSLs) became the latest gimmick, giving fans the right to buy a season ticket sometime in the future.

Stadium politics has extended to smaller cities and towns, which have invested millions of dollars in new facilities for minor league teams, exhibition seasons, and training facilities. When designed well and located strategically, stadiums could conceivably foster economic activity during hours when smaller cities and towns normally roll up their sidewalks for the night. But in the only major study of the economics of the minor leagues, Arthur Johnson found that ad hoc and reactive policy making characterized decisions to build minor league stadiums.[15] Also hurting the potential for tourism and development were the restrictions on the use of stadiums when baseball games were not being played. Johnson concluded: "The economic impact of a minor league team is not sufficient to justify the relatively large public expenditure necessary for a minor league stadium. This conclusion is implicitly supported by the absence of any significant local corporate funding of stadium construction costs."[16]

One sign of the stadium frenzy is the refusal of baseball and football teams to share facilities. To reduce construction and maintenance costs and achieve greater usage, stadiums built between the 1950s and the 1980s were designed for both sports. Starting in the 1980s, however, franchises demanded and got public financing for single-purpose facilities. Ironically, the refusal to share stadiums came at a time when architectural technology had made dual-purpose facilities better than ever.

Movable stands, for example, enable parks to be configured to fit the dimensions of both baseball and football fields.[17] Nevertheless, in 1996, when Mayor Giuliani suggested building a multipurpose stadium in New York, critics attacked the idea as passé.[18]

The new facilities almost never result from any master plan to enhance a city's tourism. Stadiums are not a means toward the end of tourism but a means toward the end of responding to team owners. Once state and local governments embark on stadium-building projects, they often depict them as necessary means to boost tourism and other service industries. But that ex post facto reasoning is a fig leaf to cover the reality of capitulation to the sports industry. Thus, one major study concludes that cities building stadiums for minor league teams, "with the exception of Indianapolis, . . . had neither a planning process nor a development strategy formally based on the business of sports."[19] Furthermore—and most important—once city officials begin bargaining with leagues and teams, the demands of the teams overshadow the tourist- and economic-development interests of the city, despite rhetoric to the contrary.

Sports in Local Economies

Sports boosters claim that major league and NFL franchises attract tourist business. The Baltimore Orioles have estimated that almost half of their fans (46 percent) come from outside the Baltimore area. Similar claims have been made by the Minnesota Twins (47 percent) and Toronto Blue Jays.[20] Estimates of the out-of-towners attracted to games and their impact on local businesses are, however, usually overstated. Team estimates always include visitors from nearby towns and cities that are properly understood as part of the same metropolitan area.

Tourism officials themselves are skeptical of the claims made for professional sports. Some say they cannot conduct scientific surveys of the role of sports in tourism because public officials and businesspeople do not want the limited impact of sports to be documented. Richard Webster of the U.S. Travel Data Center has stated that professional sport "has nothing to do with tourism or development." Joseph R. McGrath, president of the Greater Pittsburgh Convention and Visitors Bureau, dismissed claims that sports boost tourism: "It's the emperor's new clothes. We do packages and promote the Pirates [baseball team], and the reality is that it's nice to have a team. But it does not draw huge numbers of people. We don't have a comprehensive survey. We'd even be chastised if we did such a survey because of what we'd find out. . . . We'd *like* it to be a big deal, because it's already there. . . . But groups rarely ever do group ticket purchases. We rarely have ticket requests [from tourists] unless people ask whether *their* team is in town." Pittsburgh draws 3.8 million tourists annually. The Convention and Visitors Bureau sells about one thousand baseball packages, involving about ten thousand tickets, a year. Far fewer tourists go to Steelers' football games, because the team's eight games are always sold out through season tickets.

Alan Rickard, vice president of communications for the International Association of Convention and Visitor Bureaus (IACVB), has observed that public investment in sports stadiums has become "a major concern of members" because of the taxes that many tourism-related businesses pay for such projects, compared to their minimal impact on tourism. A 1993 report of convention-goers commissioned by IACVB found that far less than 1 percent of all convention spending was devoted to sporting events. Rickard noted that "when a convention comes to town, they typically have their own events. Of course some organize outings to a stadium, but they're usually more interested in other things."

The tourism industry's concern over public investment in sports facilities peaked in June 1996. A coalition of car-rental agencies and other tourism-related businesses embarked on a ten-city barnstorming tour to mobilize opposition to sports-related projects. Roger Ballou, chief executive officer of Alamo Rent-A-Car and the chairman of the Tourism Industry Association of America (TIA), conducted radio interviews to rally public opinion against what one TIA official called the unfairness of taxation without representation. "Very few travelers are attending these games, but they're going to be called on to pay for these facilities," observed Richard Webster. "Even when the city has a team that people want to see, most of the seats are [for] season-ticket holders." The tourism industry's attack is part of a larger backlash against subsidies to large firms at the expense of small firms. The backlash is fueled by studies that find that three-quarters of all subsidies go to projects that do not create any new permanent jobs.[21]

The hard fact is that when tourists want to see a team, they often cannot. Most NFL teams sell out their stadiums long before games. The baseball stadiums that would be good drawing cards for tourists—like Baltimore's Camden Yards, Cleveland's Jacobs Field, and Denver's Coors Field—have few if any tickets left on the day of the game. Teams seek advance sales so that ticket payments gather interest in banks. The small contemporary bandbox stadiums are designed, in part, to encourage advance ticket purchases; in contrast, fans never felt an urgency to buy advance tickets for the huge old facilities, like Cleveland's Municipal Stadium. A team's gain from advance sales is tourism's loss, except for the relatively few visitors who buy tickets before their trip.

Deciding where to go on vacation involves a dynamic that is different from the decision-making process for selecting a place to live. Nonetheless, surveys of the factors involved in home selection can be instructive. In 1995, *Money* magazine asked a sample of Americans how they would rank forty-one factors (on a scale of one to ten) when choosing a place to live. Some of the factors concerned amenities that also matter to tourists. Major and minor league sports finished thirty-ninth and fortieth, respectively, in the survey. Weather conditions, proximity to forests or parks, access to a big city, availability of museums, zoos, and aquariums, and access to music all finished ahead of sports.[22]

Despite media reports of sports as big business, the industry is in fact a minor part of any local economy. In 1994–95, all the teams in the four major professional sports leagues—baseball, football, basketball, and hockey—had combined revenues of less than $5.5 billion. In a national economy of $5.5 trillion, such figures seem almost insignificant—representing less than 1 percent of the total economy. By way of comparison, in 1993, the sanitary tissues industry earned $9.4 billion, the surface active-agent cleaning industry $6.5 billion, and the pickles and sauce industry $6.22 billion.[23] Sport is also, almost by definition, a notoriously seasonal industry. Team sports "do business" a small fraction of the year; the number of games played may range from a low of eight for football to a high of eighty-one for baseball during the regular season. Moreover, players' salaries account for the greatest expenditures by far—almost 70 percent of the NFL's budget and more than 60 percent of major league baseball's. And because most players live outside the city, and even the region, where the team plays, most of their salaries are exported.[24] The Boston Red Sox, for example, have had only one player who actually lived in the city in the 1990s. Although other full-time and even part-time personnel—management, stadium employees, concessionaires—do live in the area, they usually reside in the suburbs.[25]

The critical test of an industry's importance to an economy is whether it feeds into the web of other local economic activities. As it turns out, the sports industry exerts a negligible effect on local economic activity less because of seasonality than because of physical isolation.[26] Even when new sports facilities are adjacent to other tourist attractions, as in the case of Baltimore's Camden Yards and Toronto's SkyDome, the complexes to which they belong are as separate from their surroundings as a suburban mall. Economic linkages therefore occur within a relatively small and sealed-off portion of the local economy.

Much local economic theory emphasizes the importance of exports and interconnected business activities. Exports help the local economy by bringing in outside money which then creates an economic multiplier if it gets respent locally. The question is how much sports—and tourism in general—can contribute to export industries that depend on local linkages and clustering. One good example of linkage-rich sports tourism is hiking and camping. These recreational activities do not require huge public expenditures by private firms and allow public access at a reasonable price. New Hampshire's White Mountains attract seven million visitors a year—more than Yosemite and Yellowstone Parks combined. The various facilities of the Appalachian Mountain Club (AMC) account for about 14 percent of visits to the White Mountains, and AMC visitors directly spend about $24 million annually. More important, about 84 percent of that spending occurs outside AMC facilities, meaning that visitors spend millions on camping and hiking equipment, other lodging (rooms purchased before and after the trip), gas, food, and other goods and services during stays in the area that last from several days to several weeks. Consequently, their presence ripples through local economies.[27]

A recent analysis of the 1994 baseball strike on areas surrounding stadiums sheds some light on the impact of professional sports on tourism. John Zipp found that the cancellation of games because of that strike did not appear to hurt local retail economies; indeed, some cities experienced a slight increase in economic activity during the strike. In thirteen of the seventeen cities for which data were available, sales of nondurable goods actually increased during the seven-week strike period, compared with the same period the previous year. In seventeen of twenty-four cities surveyed to assay the strike's impact on overall retail sales, activity increased during the two-month strike period, as compared to the previous two-month period. The cities thought to be most vulnerable to a baseball strike—the ten cities with the highest ratio of fans to overall population—"did better than expected in both strike months." Comparisons with the economic activity of control cases—cities without teams—showed no significant differences.

Zipp also considered the impact of the strike on nearby hotels. Sports boosters claim that games draw overnight visitors. Operating on an estimate by the Orioles management that 12 percent of the team's fans stayed overnight when they went to see a game, Zipp estimated that the strike would have cost the Baltimore metropolitan area 14,850 hotel-room stays in August and 13,789 stays in September. But such an estimate clearly would be absurd. "It is difficult to attribute these losses to the strike . . . since these figures represent 47.9 percent of all lost August hotel rooms in the metro area and 137.9 percent of all lost September sales." It is irrational to hold the baseball strike responsible for more losses in room sales than even occurred in September. A more likely explanation for the two-month drop-off was the unrelated decline in convention business and the team's having overestimated the number of overnight stays for which it was responsible.[28] Another study conducted for Wisconsin Independent Businesses found that 80 percent of the businesses in the Milwaukee metropolitan area said they did not benefit from activity associated with the Brewers baseball team, whereas about 2 percent said they benefited "greatly" from the team.[29]

These results suggest a blowout effect—namely, sporting events that attract large crowds, paradoxically, might drive out other business. The surprising increase in overall retail activity implies that when downtown areas are not overwhelmed with game traffic, people may have a greater opportunity to engage in other activities and spending. The crush of traffic and crowds drives people away not only from the neighborhood of the stadium but also from all the nearby streets that serve as arteries to the stadium. On game days, the areas near stadiums are unusable during the hour before and after the game. Local radio stations warn drivers to stay away from the roads leading to the stadium because of game traffic. During games, activity at nearby restaurants and other businesses comes to a near standstill.

Baade recently studied forty-eight cities in the United States to measure their economic activities between 1958 and 1987 with and without teams. His findings are instructive. In thirty of thirty-two cities where a change in the number of sports franchises occurred, there was "no significant relationship" between those teams and the overall income growth in the city. In the thirty cities with stadiums less than ten years old, there was also no significant change in overall income levels. Baade calculated percentages of variation in "regional, trend-adjusted, real per capita personal income" in the thirty-six cities where economic activity could be attributed at some time to new sports stadiums and franchises. Those figures range from a positive 26 percent impact in St. Louis down to a minus 6 percent impact in Miami. The sum total effect for all cities in the survey averaged out to zero.[30]

Much of the economic activity associated with sports franchises and stadiums involves the provision of goods and services to fans—food, drinks, and souvenirs. Most of these are produced outside the city, meaning that the revenue generated is immediately exported. Overall, Rocky Mountain and southern states are net exporters of such services, while western and New England states are net importers. "Nevertheless, after accounting for national trends, neither teams nor stadiums explain much of the variation in a region's relative, real, per-capita personal income," Baade concludes.[31]

Sports Impact in Two Cities

An examination of the impact of sports strategies in two cities points to the potential benefits and pitfalls of using sports as a development tool. Indianapolis and Toronto have both sought to promote sports-oriented tourism. Indianapolis has earned a unique niche in urban America because of its efforts to attract both amateur and professional events. Some evidence suggests that this niche strategy may have contributed to tourism and economic growth. Toronto's SkyDome, however, presents a problematic case for sports-based tourism strategies. After an early period of excitement over the novelty of the facility, attendance figures declined significantly.[32] Torontoans must now reckon with the facility's $572 million price tag and the city's neglect of other possibilities for stimulating recreation and tourism.

Indianapolis has been a real success story because of its creativity in defining itself as the amateur sports capital of the world, as well as its early commitment to the sports strategy. In the 1970s and 1980s, the city attracted a number of amateur sporting events, in addition to having several major sports organizations make their headquarters there. A wide range of sporting activities, resulting in year-round events, took place in the heart of the city. In all, the city invested $172.6 million in sports projects—less than 10 percent of total capital investment in the downtown area. For every dollar that Indianapolis invested, the State of Indiana and corporate and philanthropic donors contributed $5.33. The city also invested in other attractions, the most important being higher education, to create a synergy in an urban space previously considered dead. James Owen concludes in a study: "The multipurpose dimension of the Hoosier Dome dramatizes the point that the community's investment in sports infrastructure is just one symbiotic element of a complex matrix of cultural, entertainment, business, and government projects operating in concert to attract people to the downtown area."[33] Indianapolis also attracted millions in corporate and philanthropic money, including $25 million from the Lily Endowment Foundation. And the city built its facilities early enough in the cycle of modern urban revitalization that the costs were kept comparatively low.

Indianapolis's greatest achievement seems to have been a change of perception. Before adopting its aggressive and coordinated sports strategy, the city was derisively referred to as "Naptown" and "Indiana-No-Place"; now it is widely viewed as a sports hub. Until the 1970s the Indianapolis 500 was the only sporting event there that attracted national attention; subsequently the city has hosted professional football (the Colts) and basketball (the Pacers), Olympic tryouts, the Pan American Games, and a variety of other events. Between 1981 and 1989, annual attendance at events increased from 2.7 million to 7.5 million.[34] Nevertheless, the independent economic impact of sports has been slight. A study commissioned by the city's Chamber of Commerce concluded that the sports strategy attracted $1.05 billion in *outside* spending between 1977 and 1991; that amount, the boosters say, should be multiplied to account for the additional spending that "spun out" to the local economy.[35] But those estimates assume that the money spent at a sports facility stays within the city limits. This is manifestly not the case in an age of national and even international capital and spending flows. An independent academic study, in fact, found that the impact of sports on the local economy was almost nonexistent. Sports jobs represented .32 percent of all jobs in the city in 1989, an increase of only .03 percent since 1977. The number of downtown jobs increased from 95,562 to 105,500 between 1970 and 1990, but job growth in the suburbs was much greater.[36] Overall, one study concluded that Indianapolis's strategy did not produce more growth than other midwestern communities experienced and did not lead to a concentration of high-paying jobs in the region.[37]

Toronto more closely typifies the consequences of sports-based development strategies. The opening of the SkyDome in 1989 caused a sensation in urban and sports circles. With its retractable roof, direct linkages with hotels and restaurants, and convenient downtown location, the SkyDome seemed to exemplify the best and most romantic in sports facilities. The facility's major tenants, baseball's Blue Jays, set attendance records for the major leagues, attracting 3.8 million fans in 1990—an all-time record—and more than 4 million for each of the next three years. In the SkyDome's first five years, the Jays won four division, two league, and two World Series championships.

SkyDome supporters scoffed at the argument that the record attendance figures could be attributed to a novelty effect and that attendance would diminish once people got a look at the new facility. But that is exactly what happened. Once the Blue Jays fell from championship to second-division status, SkyDome attendance dwindled to just over 2 million in 1995. Before the 1994 baseball strike, the Blue Jays averaged 50,000 fans per game; in the first month of 1996, the team averaged 29,300.[38] In discussing the attendance decline, Blue Jays officials undermine the sports-tourism argument. George Holm, the team's director of stadium and ticket operations, noted: "The fact that the team was winning, the fact the stadium was new, the roof was unique, played a role. Everything came together." Studies support the idea that success on the field directly translates to higher attendance levels.[39] Paul Beeston, the team's president, argued that the existence of other attractions detracts from baseball attendance. "Now you've got the Raptors [of the National Basketball Association] in town, you've got *Beauty and the Beast* in town. You've got new competition." The implication is clear: tourist attractions do not always reinforce and sometimes undermine each other. The bigger the event, the more it might detract from other activities.

Rethinking the Politics of Sports

Somehow, if sports is to play a more constructive role in tourism and economic development, it is necessary to reduce the leverage of professional leagues and teams. Sports and cities do have benefits to offer one another, if bargaining occurs on a level playing field. The demands of the sports industry have to offer a reasonable match with the needs and capacities of host cities. Ultimately, achieving such a balance requires challenging the monopolistic nature of the sports industry.

There are a number of possible approaches to the problem. The first is to feed the monster: accept that the sports industry has power over a unique commodity. A second is to somehow restrain the power of the sports industry. A voluntary-treaty approach would require states and cities to reach agreements on acceptable behavior in bidding for teams; signatories would promise not to raid other cities' teams. During the conflict over the NFL Browns in 1995 and 1996, Mayor Michael White of Cleveland championed such a "good neighbor" policy. This approach is doomed, however, because of the logic of competition. Even if some cities agreed to a set of basic standards, there would always be a renegade willing to violate those standards if the chance to get a team arose.

A third approach is to challenge the industry with competition. Rival leagues have often forced the NFL and MLB to create new teams. Baseball's first round of expansion, in 1961 and 1962, occurred after the creation of the Continental League. Rival leagues could arise in other sports. The Major Soccer League (MSL), which began play in eight cities in 1996, has a cooperative structure that restrains expenses.[40] A city might be better off working with a nascent league with low costs, like the MSL, than with major league baseball or the NFL, with their hyperinflated costs.

A fourth approach is to confront the industry in Congress and in the courts. Baseball has always responded to serious threats to its cherished antitrust exemption. Congressional hearings about baseball's antitrust exemption, franchise relocations, and slow movement on expansion prompted the sport to add two new teams for the 1993 season. But a divided Congress cannot be expected to pass bills that block team movement or require teams to honor commitments to host cities.[41] Legal strategies include eminent-domain condemnation and challenges to the league's monopolist practices. Oakland and Baltimore both attempted to condemn the wayward Raiders and Colts in the early 1980s to prevent their relocation, but failed on legal technicalities. The strategy remains viable but risky.[42]

Given the nature of the problem—a monopolistic league that exerts extraordinary control over both supply and demand—one final alternative might be the only viable strategy. Using the model of the judicial breakup of the telephone monopoly in 1982, victims of sports monopolies could employ antitrust law to dissolve them. If leagues were forced to compete with one another, they might try to offer the best terms to host cities rather than pressure the cities to respond to their demands. American civic leaders or sports fans find it difficult to imagine a different configuration for pro sports, just as it was hard for people to conceive of a different way of providing telephone service. A transformed structure might resemble that of the National Collegiate Athletic Association (NCAA), with dozens of leagues offering competitive frameworks for teams across the country. It might also look like European and Latin American soccer leagues, which provide one team, and often more, to every city. Both the NCAA and soccer models are intriguing because they offer stability and openness at the same time.

The minor leagues present yet another model. Their teams have successfully operated as public corporations, with individual citizens often holding shares in the team; the NFL's Green Bay Packers also operate this way. But the major leagues of baseball and football have banned such arrangements for other teams and would need to be coerced to allow them in the future.[43] These approaches would not improve sports as a tourist strategy, but they might make resources available for other tourism strategies. Without some kind of coordinated attack on the sports industry, the value of sports as a tourist and development tool is likely to be minimal and even negative. If sports is to play a small but effective role in a city's overall mix of tourist and other activities, the price must be right.

Looking back on the changes wrought by visible development projects like the Hoosier Dome, one Indianapolis insider wrote: "One could see signs of deterioration everywhere, even within the shadows of the Hoosier Dome and the tall downtown buildings that symbolized the emergence of Indianapolis as a growing entrepreneurial city. Rates of drug abuse, gang violence, infant mortality, child and spousal abuse, homelessness and acquired immune deficiency syndrome were rising. Some neighborhoods looked almost bombed out. Many people believed that the public schools were performing below expectations. Growth was uneven, and the central-city population was declining."[44] That insider, former Mayor William Hudnut, deserved credit for a frankness that matched his optimism. Of all the cities using sports as a tourism strategy, Indianapolis probably enjoyed the greatest success. But, as Hudnut himself acknowledged, sports and stadiums cannot contribute much if anything to a real urban renaissance.

Tourism has a place in local economic development. A constructive tourism strategy requires that cities escape the monopolistic logic of competing for professional sports teams by building expensive infrastructure. A nest of accessible sporting events and activities, which feed into other tourist attractions and economic activities, may make more sense for some cities than attracting big-time sports.

SABINA DEITRICK,

ROBERT A. BEAUREGARD, AND

CHERYL ZARLENGA KERCHIS

Riverboat Gambling, Tourism, and Economic Development

Riverboat casinos are the most recent addition to the list of tourist attractions in the United States. For state and local governments with anemic economies and stagnant or sagging tax revenues, riverboat casinos promise a quick fix.[1] In the industrial heartland, where manufacturing job losses continue to mount, economically depressed cities such as Joliet, Illinois, and Davenport, Iowa, are using excursion-boat gaming to develop a new industry and promote themselves as tourist destinations. The Gulf Coast city of Biloxi, Mississippi, hopes that riverboat casinos will revive a moribund tourist sector and turn a low-rent vacation resort into a gambling mecca, much as casinos did in Atlantic City more than two decades ago.[2] In places like New Orleans, with an already vibrant tourist trade, riverboat casinos provide an additional attraction, and in other states and localities, officials view them as a defensive move to keep tourists from elsewhere.[3]

But to what extent will riverboat casinos encourage tourism in a community and create the social and economic benefits promised by industry proponents? Despite great fanfare and contrary to industry promises and the hopes of many state and local officials, riverboat casinos are unlikely to anchor an economically integrated and diversified local tourist sector or to provide sustained and widespread economic prosperity. The political economy of these casinos, understood in a spatial context, provides the framework for our assessment.[4] Legal gambling is highly regulated by state governments, and riverboat casinos are extremely dependent, at least in their start-up phase, on local politics. In addition, riverboat casinos have relatively small market areas compared to large, land-based casinos, and their economic performance is sensitive to the presence of nearby competitors and the size and density of the surrounding population. Our analysis of these themes draws on recent research, public discussions, and a burgeoning literature on casino gaming.

Casino Development

Although land-based casinos have been legal in Nevada since 1931 and in Atlantic City since 1976, Iowa, in 1989, became the first state to pass legislation permitting riverboat gambling. By the end of 1997, six states permitted some form of riverboat gambling: Illinois, Iowa, Louisiana, Mississippi, Missouri, and Indiana. Mississippi led the states with thirty casinos; the six states together operated more than eighty riverboat gaming establishments.[5] Given that Iowa, Mississippi, and Missouri do not limit the number of licensed riverboat casinos and that Pennsylvania, West Virginia, and Ohio, among other states, are debating their legalization, the number of boats is likely to increase.

Riverboat casinos have benefited from the recent history of legalized gambling. Over the past few decades, thirty-seven state governments and the District of Columbia have turned to state-run lotteries as sources of new revenue. In 1985 Montana legalized slot machines, and in 1988 Congress passed the Indian Gaming Regulatory Act, recognizing the rights of Native Americans to operate casino gambling on their lands. By 1993, eighty-one class 3 gaming facilities (those that allow casino gambling and slot machines) were open for business in seventeen states. In 1997, casino gambling was legal in twenty-seven states, most of it occurring in rural areas.

The expansion of legalized gambling in general was fueled by, and contributed to, increased consumer spending on casino gambling.[6] From 1991 to 1993, money spent on legal gambling in the United States grew twice as fast as overall consumer spending. By 1993, gambling revenues accounted for 8 percent, or $28 billion, of all recreational and entertainment expenditures. Casino revenues, in particular, grew even more rapidly, increasing by 36 percent between 1990 and 1993.

Pros and Cons

Because few cities can compete with Las Vegas as a casino-resort destination, riverboat casinos become an attractive alternative, either drawing visitors on their own or augmenting existing tourist attractions. Among their advantages, they are less expensive to construct than land-based casinos and more quickly put in place, they often utilize empty or derelict riverfront land, and they act as a magnet for tourists from other regions. Theoretically, those attracted to the gambling tables will wander outside the casinos to enjoy the city's other tourist activities or will return later to do so. As tourists, they will spend dollars not already in the local economy. Not to be overlooked, given the need for enabling legislation, riverboat casinos seem more acceptable to the average voter than land-based casinos.[7]

Like gambling and tourism more generally, riverboats enable state and local governments to increase revenues without raising existing taxes or imposing new taxes on residents. Casino taxes are hidden and, in theory, borne by casino operators. Because riverboat casinos are often located along political boundaries, many patrons come from outside the municipality and even outside the state.[8] Consequently, they are a low-cost political path to new taxes. Casinos also fit neatly into the prevailing emphasis on services, as communities have increasingly shifted away from manufacturing and made recreation, entertainment, conventions, tourism, dining, and travel the major focus of their economic initiatives.[9] Tourism is the new export sector, one that brings not heavy industry but clean, pleasant places to play. Floating casinos, however, do not fit comfortably within the current economic-development interest in local linkages—the various buyer and supplier networks that knit together industrial clusters.[10]

Opponents have challenged the optimistic scenario of gaming, calling it a curse rather than a blessing. One commentator described riverboat casinos as "the urban developers' equivalent to crack cocaine, a way to get an intense high at low initial cost."[11] In this version of events, riverboat casinos take money from the local economy, transferring it to corporate coffers outside the community. They attract mainly day-trippers, people who live within a few hours' drive and who do not stay overnight; most gamblers are local residents who shift their spending from local goods and services to slot machines and betting tables. Some become compulsive gamblers who proceed to ruin their lives and break up their

The Lady Luck, a riverboat casino, moored at Natchez, Mississippi

This photo seems to illustrate the fact that riverboats often fail to stimulate surrounding economic activity.

families. Critics also claim that the jobs generated by casinos are not only low paying, seasonal, and unstable but vulnerable to competition from nearby cities and states. Crimes such as prostitution increase, and traffic congestion worsens.

Legalized gambling has, in fact, experienced problems. By early 1995, four riverboat casinos had closed in Mississippi, and two others in New Orleans were bankrupt.[12] Following much hoopla, the only land-based casino in New Orleans failed less than six months after it had opened, when the Harrah's Jazz Company filed for Chapter 11 bankruptcy. Harrah's temporary casino closed, and construction was halted on its $823 million permanent facility. A proposed casino in Bridgeport, Connecticut, to be operated by an Indian tribe, was rejected by the State Senate. Proponents of riverboat casinos in Ohio, Pennsylvania, and West Vir-

ginia were unable to pass enabling legislation, and casino legislation in
Florida, Massachusetts, and New York failed to obtain the necessary political support. Between 1988 and 1992, more than half of Atlantic City's
casinos filed for bankruptcy; one closed permanently.[13] Moreover, at the
end of the century, after decades of casino activity, residents of Atlantic
City were still awaiting the promised spin-off from gambling, a promise
revived in the mid-1990s by a new round of casino investment.[14]

Politics and Geography

Casinos are one of the most regulated industries in the United States.
States grant licenses (often limiting them in number and by location) for
the operation of casinos, set limits on bets, regulate odds, investigate the
backgrounds of employees, and monitor all casino operations. Limits on
the number of licenses and locations affect competition, a point of great
importance to casino operators.

The complexity of the regulatory process generates a spatial politics
that affects individual casinos and the industry as a whole. The politics of
riverboat casinos begins when state legislators propose enabling legislation, generally in response to similar legislation being debated in neighboring states and lobbying by local officials and industry representatives.[15] The legislative process involves balancing the negative image and
the costs of gambling with the potential tax and economic benefits. Legislators generally face intense pressure from both industry lobbyists and
casino opponents. The latter include groups protesting perceived negative moral, social, and environmental influences; those with investments
in other gambling arenas (for example, thoroughbred racing associations); and retailers and restaurateurs fearing the displacement of limited consumer dollars.

Central to the debate is the possibility that neighboring states might
legalize casino gaming and thus lure residents and their gambling dollars across state borders, resulting in a loss of in-state expenditures and
tax revenues. From the industry's perspective, certain states are considered linchpins. If they legalize gambling, a domino effect will cause
other states in the region to do the same simply for defensive purposes.[16]

Two key elements of casino legislation are the number of licenses and
the places of operation. Some states (for example, Illinois and Louisiana)
have allocated a specific number of licenses and assigned them to particular localities. Other states (Iowa and Mississippi) do not limit the

number of licenses, but since the casinos must be on navigable water-ways, the number of eligible localities is relatively small.[17] Numerical limits set up competition among locales vying for a casino and among casino operators vying for licenses. Even unlimited licenses do not pre-clude casino operators from competing for the best sites. Because river-boat casinos attract mainly day-trippers, the most desirable locations are in or near heavily populated areas with good highways.[18]

Municipalities and casino operators have an interest in avoiding harmful casino competition and in maximizing market share. Individu-ally, however, each municipality wants more rather than fewer licenses, and each operator wants to secure the best location. Opposition groups attempt first to prevent the legalization of casino gambling and then, as a fallback position, attempt to limit the number of licenses. Competition is not simply among places for investors but also among investors for places.

When legislation was proposed in Pennsylvania in the mid-1990s, casino operators and developers began to investigate sites in Philadel-phia and Pittsburgh, the two largest cities (and markets) in the state and therefore the most likely to receive licenses. By early 1994, five sites were being considered in Pittsburgh. Resistance appeared soon thereafter: a group called No Dice organized to oppose a casino complex proposed for a former steel-mill site adjacent to its South Side neighborhood. The group held public hearings, lobbied local officials, and joined a statewide coalition of fifteen antigambling groups called PAGE, Pennsylvanians Against Gambling Expansion. No Dice wanted the site developed with housing and objected to any further intrusion on a neighborhood that had become noted for its barrooms, nightclubs, restaurants, and coffee-houses.

The mayor of Pittsburgh, however, was not about to turn aside an op-portunity to create jobs and meet part of the city's fiscal needs, particu-larly given the anemic condition of the local economy and the weak tourism sector. The city began writing guidelines for riverboat casino development. Hospitality Franchise Systems, Inc. (HFS), a major hotel operator with an option to buy the site, also worked with South Side rep-resentatives to develop a workable plan.[19] By mid-year, major casino op-erators such as HFS, Harrah's, Trump, Bally's, ITT Sheraton, Ladbroke, and Players International were all negotiating to secure sites.

The activity abruptly slowed by year's end. The newly elected governor, Tom Ridge, pledged that he would sign a riverboat gambling law only if a statewide referendum was passed on the issue. In the years since, the state legislature has yet to pass a bill calling for a referendum. The shift in interest in riverboat gambling extended beyond Pennsylvania. Nearby Ohio defeated a ballot proposal allowing riverboat casinos in 1996 by an overwhelming margin, 62 percent to 38 percent. The supporters of gambling in the Pennsylvania state legislature tried to strike a compromise by sponsoring legislation to add slot machines at the state's four race tracks, but groups such as PAGE and antigambling forces in the legislature managed to keep that off the ballot as well.

Indiana attempted to depoliticize the site selection process by requiring municipalities to give the license to the casino that was predicted to have the largest economic impact as determined by an independent, university-based analysis. But it also allowed municipalities and casino operators to make side deals, in the form of subsidies from the developer (or exactions, depending on your perspective) as payments for road improvements. In some eligible communities, the preferred developers were those who offered the best side deals; the overall economic impact and financial stability of casino operators were ignored.[20] This, of course, returned politics to the equation, generating political friction between the localities and the Indiana Gaming Commission.

In smaller market areas with the potential for market saturation, the location of riverboat casinos is critical. Because one riverboat casino is generally indistinguishable from another, competition is shifted from the casino's product to the casino's location. Although geographic concentration of riverboat casinos might increase the draw of an area and establish a strong image that could be marketed more widely, too many riverboat casinos in one area might overload the market. Given that the number and location of licenses are regulated by the state, interindustry competition is more political than economic.

Location is also important to state and local governments, particularly if the sites of riverboat casinos are in adjacent states and near one another, a distinct possibility when states are separated by a lake or river. A study done for Pittsburgh estimated that two casinos in the city would produce $14.9 million in local tax revenues annually, but only $8.9 million, or 40 percent less, if West Virginia and Ohio legalized riverboat casinos.[21]

Economic Development Impacts

At first glance, the economics of the casino industry is straightforward. Firms invest in gaming facilities, pay wages to their employees, buy goods and services, generate revenues from people wagering their money, and pay taxes on their earnings. The public sector increases its revenues through taxes and fees from the casino operators and sometimes from entrance fees paid by patrons. Gamblers wager money and win or lose, depending on the odds of the games they play and the limits they set on their losses. With billions of dollars bet, what does this circulation of capital and money mean for local economic development?

The investment appeal of all types of casinos is a function of both their high cash flow (which provides investors with financial flexibility) and their high profitability. In Illinois, for example, in the first five years of operations, riverboat casinos averaged annual adjusted gross gambling receipts of $70.3 million and annual gross receipts per square foot of $4.15 billion. Compared to the sales volume per square foot for retail space in Midwest shopping malls—$116 for a department store and $604 for a jewelry store in 1993—the cash flow of casinos is significantly greater.[22] As one observer put it: "Casinos mean cash. . . . There is probably no type of business in the world where as much paper money is handled on a daily basis by more people under more security than in a casino."[23]

For corporations investing in gaming, the returns are huge. Between 1992 and 1994, legal casino gambling revenues increased by 51 percent, to $15 billion. In 1992, gambling revenues from riverboats totaled $415 million, and by 1994, with the addition of dozens of new boats, they reached $3.26 billion, a 687 percent increase in current dollars. This raised the boating share of all legalized casino gaming revenues from 4 percent to 21 percent, nearly twice the share accounted for by casinos on Indian reservations but less than one-third of the share accounted for by the land-based casinos in Nevada and Atlantic City.[24] The gross revenues of riverboats for 1994 increased 135.2 percent over those for 1993, a percentage unmatched by any other form of legalized gambling, and made up 8.2 percent of the gross gaming revenues for casinos, pari-mutuel betting, lotteries, legal bookmaking, and other forms of gaming such as charitable bingo.[25]

Casinos offer new revenue sources to state and local governments, although industry projections often exaggerate their size.[26] Localities may levy property, admissions, and sales, wage, and business taxes. States levy licensing fees and receive sales-tax payments. The biggest increase to state and local coffers comes from taxes on gaming operations. Tax rates vary from a low of 12 percent in Mississippi to around 20 percent in most other places. A five-year projection of local riverboat tax revenues for Gary, Indiana, fell between $25.8 million and $53.8 million per casino, depending on its size.[27] An industry-based study for Pittsburgh projected that five dockside facilities would generate an average of $124 million annually in state tax revenues over the first five years of operation, with an additional average of $57 million per year for city and county governments.[28]

New revenues from gaming can be used to reduce tax rates or to fund public services. In Joliet, Illinois, for example, the city eliminated a $5.50 monthly water fee for sewer improvements and a $25 annual motor vehicle tax. New gambling revenues were to provide $27 million for neighborhood improvements, $10 million for sewer construction, and $8 million for improvements to schools and police headquarters. The city has also paid down $8.9 million in debt.[29]

Counteracting these fiscal benefits are various costs associated with riverboat casinos.[30] First, all taxes impose burdens, and gambling taxes may be exceptionally costly. Although governments may not calculate the social costs of taxes, economists have. The marginal welfare cost of an ordinary tax dollar is estimated to be between $1.17 and $1.57, whereas gambling taxes cost between $2.25 and $4.75 for each dollar collected, assuming that 40 percent of all gambling revenues are taxed.[31] Second, a riverboat casino, like any firm, uses public services. The major costs are road improvement and greater police presence to handle traffic, general public safety, and casino-related crimes such as drunkenness and prostitution.

In addition to promises of a tax bounty, casino operators offer jobs. Riverboat casinos are relatively large employers and have the potential to reduce the local unemployment rate. An Indiana study estimated an annual local employment impact of between 922 and 1,879 jobs per casino for Gary, which was slated for two riverboats.[32] In Joliet, Illinois, three riverboat casinos employed approximately 4,000 workers in 1995, 90 percent of them full-time, and paid wages of about $100 million per year. The city's unemployment rate in early 1996 had fallen to 5 percent, nearly two percentage points below the national average.[33]

In addition, casinos generate jobs among local and nonlocal firms that sell goods and services to the casinos or benefit from any induced growth in the local economy. The more local the linkages between casinos and other businesses, the greater the economic-development benefit will be. Unlike land-based casinos, riverboats are usually built not only outside the locality but outside the state, at a cost of between $12 million and $70 million per boat. As a result, the local economy does not gain construction jobs and spending.[34] Concern over the absence of local linkages has been the impetus behind encouraging or requiring casino operators to build landside facilities. Likewise the capital machinery of the gambling industry—the slot machines, video game terminals, and game tables—are also purchased from outside firms, thereby creating few connections to local suppliers and reducing the potential multiplier effect.

The casino industry usually does invigorate the local economy through local purchases of noncapital goods and services, for example, utilities, food and beverages, uniforms, musical talent, office products, and construction services for docks and parking lots. Other important business services, such as advertising and finance, are likely to be purchased elsewhere, even in a well-developed gambling location such as Atlantic City.[35] The extent to which casino expenditures leak out of the community depends on the size and diversity of the local economy. A city like New Orleans will have more suppliers than a small community like Natchez, Mississippi.[36] As a result, the small communities, having lower multipliers, will reap a lower proportion of casino outflows than New Orleans.

A study of Atlantic City found that of the $2.2 billion in casino purchases in 1994, 62.5 percent were made in New Jersey and 25.5 percent in other states; the remainder were made outside the United States.[37] Atlantic County, the location of Atlantic City, captured 41.6 percent of total purchases, but many of the casinos' suppliers were warehouses and distributors that added little value to goods originally produced elsewhere.

In sum, riverboat casinos provide a number of significant economic benefits for states and localities. They also come with fiscal costs and questions as to the extent of their linkages with the local economy. Before attempting an overall assessment, we should look at the potential of riverboat casinos to contribute to local tourism and, then, at the social costs imposed on the community.

Assessing the Impacts

The desirability of a riverboat casino as a tourist attraction depends on the number of visitors it brings into the community and on the degree to which it complements the community's other tourist sites. Specifically, it should expand and diversify the local tourism sector.

Riverboat casinos appear to perform well on the first criterion. In Joliet, less than one hour's drive from Chicago, close to eighteen thousand people on average visit the three riverboat casinos every day, a significant number when compared with the city's population of eighty-three thousand. The average annual attendance for all of Illinois's riverboat casinos is 1.4 million patrons per boat.[38]

On the other hand, riverboat casinos do not attract visitors who engage in other tourist activities. Casino patrons are notoriously focused on gambling. Dubbed the "Atlantic City effect," the impact of casinos on tourist or leisure-time activities is negligible.[39] Riverboat casino gamblers are not on a family outing, nor are they sightseers, adventurers, or sun worshipers. Gambling is an adult activity seldom combined with family activities involving children, although for a brief time casino operators in Las Vegas tried to make the tourist sector there more family-friendly.[40]

The confinement of gambling tourists to the riverboat environment is reinforced by the operation and design of the boats themselves. By law in most states, but not all, the boats must leave the dock periodically. (In Illinois, they make six to seven cruises per day.) When traveling on the river, gamblers are not physically able to visit other tourist attractions. Moreover, operators design casinos to capture as much related spending on food and beverages, entertainment, and trinkets as possible. Their goal is to keep the casino patron within the casino environment in order to maximize betting.

Opponents of riverboat casinos pay particular attention to the social costs of gambling.[41] For them, increases in gambling addiction, crime related to gambling (for example, thefts committed to bankroll a gambling habit), public disorderliness, child and spousal abuse, driving under the influence of alcohol, and prostitution are the major concerns. Studies have clearly indicated that these crimes escalate with the presence of casinos. Estimates show that between .75 and 2.25 percent of an area's population become problem gamblers. Problem gamblers generate social costs estimated to be $13,200 per person per year in 1993 dollars.[42]

In Iowa, which has experienced a gambling boom, the percentage of problem gamblers is reported to have risen from 1.7 in 1989 to 5.4 in 1995.[43]

Even for gamblers who keep their impulses under control, betting (and losing) surely substitutes for other purchases. When gamblers are mainly from the local area, as with riverboat casinos, local gambling is generally not a net addition to the economy but a loss.[44] Spending is shifted from other consumption activities and from savings, and no new goods are produced. The export benefit, that is, the import of dollars from outside the community and region, is thus diminished. Furthermore, when the gamblers are local residents, the tremendous profits that firms make represent a direct transfer of money out of the local economy.

In an ideal scenario, a desirable industry is linked to other businesses within a community. What emerges is an integrated cluster of activities that is difficult to replicate and hard to relocate. This is not the case with riverboat casinos. Controlled from outside the community and needing relatively little to make its product, gambling is essentially a service designed to capture as much of a patron's discretionary money as possible. Success in doing so may actually undermine not only a community's economic vitality but its tourist sector as well.

The major contributions of riverboat casinos to local tourism are their visual presence and advertising. A riverboat provides an image of entertainment and fun and suggests a vibrant community. However, riverboat casinos attract mainly day-trippers and have a much smaller market area than do land-based casinos. Adding a floating casino to an already large and diversified tourism sector, such as one might find in New York, San Francisco, Los Angeles, or New Orleans, is likely to have little impact. To expect that riverboat casinos are the core around which to build a tourism strategy or through which to energize a moribund tourist sector is to place hope far beyond reality.

PATRICK MULLINS

International Tourism and the Cities of Southeast Asia

Although there is a growing body of literature on the rapid economic development of Southeast Asia, on the role played by international tourism in this development, and on the region's rapid urbanization and the growth of its largest cities, little is known about the link between international tourism and urban development there.[1] Of particular interest is the question of whether international tourism is having the same impact on Southeast Asian cities as on the cities of the developed world.[2]

In Australia, Europe, and North America, private and public investments have built unique infrastructures of consumption, both within restructured older cities and as the basis of new resort communities. The result is a distinctive sociospatial clustering of convention centers, festival shopping malls, casinos, sports stadiums, and heritage areas that provides the physical basis for tourist competition. I use the term *urban tourism* to refer to the process of restructuring existing cities.[3] In contrast, *tourism urbanization* refers to the process of building entire cities and towns to function exclusively as centers of tourism.[4] Such development is clearly seen along the Mediterranean littoral from southern Spain to the former Yugoslavia, around the Florida coastline in the United States, in Japan, and down the eastern seaboard of Australia. The concept of tourism urbanization parallels that of industrial urbanization. Whereas the latter refers to the labor-intensive focus of cities and towns in nineteenth-century Europe and North America following the Industrial Revolution, tourism urbanization is primarily a late-twentieth-century phenomenon whereby cities and towns have been specially built for the satisfaction of wants and desires—for fun—rather than for production.[5]

Contemporary tourism, and international tourism in particular, is primarily the product of three major social forces. The first is the globalizing demand to consume as many goods and services as possible. Travel offers a way to expand consumption opportunities. Southeast Asia —and specifically its tourist-oriented cities and towns—has become a new and rapidly growing destination for satisfying consumption urges.[6] In addition to tourists, who provide the demand for tourism products, two other groups contribute to urban tourism and tourism urbanization in Southeast Asia: economic suppliers and political actors. The first group includes those who manufacture, market, and sell goods and services to tourists. Transnational corporations provide the leadership for the tourism industry, although local producers and merchants are more likely to sell goods and services directly to tourists and thereby become important economic players in this game as well. Political actors use political means to control the rate and trajectory of development, although local people sometimes contest this development. It is the actions of these three groups—the tourists, the tourism industry, and the political sector—that have brought about an urban-based Southeast Asian tourism. Parts of the largest cities, Bangkok, Kuala Lumpur, and Singapore, have been socially and physically transformed by urban tourism. At the same time a rudimentary tourism urbanization, in the form of coastal resorts, is emerging around the Gulf of Thailand and extending down the Malay peninsula to the Singapore-Indonesian border.

Tourist Flows

International tourism is an important component of Southeast Asia's development. It is arguably the most important component of Singapore's economy,[7] and even in the economically weak nations of the region, specifically those of Indochina, it is becoming increasingly critical. International tourism is central to the development of the region's largest and fastest-growing cities, such as Bangkok, Jakarta, and Manila, and most particularly in purposefully built coastal resorts like Pattaya and Phuket in Thailand, Cebu in the Philippines, and the Denpasar area of Bali in Indonesia.[8]

The major flow of international tourists to Southeast Asia began around 1970, following ten or so years of mass tourism in Europe and

North America. New technology, along with cultural and social changes, was the catalyst for this growth. Earlier, most tourists had arrived by passenger ship en route from the Pacific to the Indian Ocean, the primary stopover being the city-state of Singapore. The introduction of the Boeing 747 in 1969 made relatively cheap, long-haul flights possible. Since then tourism has increased rapidly, even though, by world standards, Southeast Asia remains a minor destination. Its position parallels that of the wider East Asia and Pacific region: the fastest-growing tourist destination in the world, it nonetheless commands only a small share of world tourism. In 1970, East Asia and the Pacific accounted for 3 percent of world passenger arrivals; by 1980 the region received 7 percent and in 1990 15 percent.[9] In 1993, the region received 16 percent of all international tourists, an estimated 41 percent of whom were traveling to Southeast Asia.[10]

In 1993 Malaysia, Singapore, and Thailand were the principal Southeast Asian destinations, each accounting for about a quarter of arrivals. They were followed by Indonesia and the Philippines (table 1). The latter has a surprisingly small share considering its demographic and geographic size. One of the more important destinations in the early 1970s, the Philippines lost ground dramatically around 1980 as a consequence of persistent political instability and social chaos and has not regained its position.[11] Even Vietnam, a very small and new destination, is challenging the Philippines as a place to visit.[12] The remaining countries— Cambodia, Myanmar (formerly Burma), and Laos—attract almost no international tourists, although their recent shifts to market economies may eventually make them more attractive, particularly after necessary infrastructure is put in place.[13]

The majority of tourists to Southeast Asia come from other parts of Asia, most often from neighboring countries and nearby regions (table 2).[14] Japan, however, is the single most important market, even though it is not the largest single source of tourists for any of the main destinations. Mass international tourism by the Japanese began in the 1970s but increased dramatically during the 1980s, partly in response to growth in disposable income and partly because the government had encouraged citizens to travel internationally so as to reduce the country's huge trade imbalance.[15] In 1990, half of Japanese tourists traveled to four principal destinations: the United States, Hong Kong, Korea, and Taiwan; with the exception of Singapore, Southeast Asia remained relatively low on the list of preferred destinations.[16] Although not as important a source as

Table 1 Tourist Arrivals in Southeast Asia, 1989–93 (in thousands)

Destination	1989 No. of tourists	1989 %	1990 No. of tourists	1990 %	1991 No. of tourists	1991 %	1992 No. of tourists	1992 %	1993 No. of tourists	1989–93 Percentage of change[a]	Population of country (in millions)
Brunei	393	2.3	377	1.8	344	1.7	500	2.3	NA	27.2	0.3
Cambodia	20	0.1	17	0.1	25	0.1	88	0.4	118	490.0	8.0
Indonesia	1,626	9.3	2,178	10.2	2,570	12.9	3,064	14.1	3,403	109.3	191.0
Malaysia	4,846	27.9	7,446	34.9	5,847	29.3	6,016	27.7	6,504	34.2	18.0
Myanmar	14	0.1	21	0.1	22	0.1	27	0.1	55	292.9	42.0
Philippines	1,076	6.2	893	4.2	849	4.3	1,043	4.8	1,246	15.8	60.0
Singapore	4,397	25.3	4,842	22.7	4,913	24.6	5,443	25.0	5,804	32.0	3.0
Thailand	4,810	27.6	5,299	24.8	5,087	25.5	5,136	23.6	5,761	19.8	56.0
Vietnam	215	1.2	250	1.2	300	1.5	440	2.0	670	211.6	66.0
Total	17,397	100	21,323	100	19,957	100	21,757	100	—[b]	25.1	444.3

Source: World Tourism Organization 1995.

Note: Data for Laos are not available.

[a] Percentages for Brunei and the total reflect only 1989–92.

[b] Incomplete because of lack of 1993 data for Brunei.

Table 2 Principal Sources of International Tourists to Leading Southeast Asian Destinations, by Country of Origin

To Indonesia (1990)	Percentage of Tourism	To Malaysia (1992)	Percentage of Tourism	To Philippines (1993)	Percentage of Tourism	To Singapore (1992)[a]	Percentage of Tourism	To Thailand (1993–94)	Percentage of Tourism
Singapore	26.7	Singapore	62.3	United States	19.7	ASEAN	30.2	Malaysia	14.6
Japan	11.9	Thailand	7.2	Japan	17.7	Japan	16.7	Japan	11.2
Australia	8.1	Japan	4.3	Taiwan	12.3	Taiwan	6.5	Taiwan	7.3
Malaysia	6.5	Taiwan	3.4	Hong Kong	5.6	Australia	6.4	Singapore	6.3
United States	4.4	Indonesia	2.6	South Korea	5.1	United Kingdom	5.1	Germany	5.7
Netherlands	4.1	Brunei	2.4	Australia	4.4	United States	4.8	Hong Kong	5.0
United Kingdom	4.1	United Kingdom	2.4	United Kingdom	3.7	Hong Kong	3.9	United States	4.7
Total for Asia[b]	49.4	Total for Asia	83.8	Total for Asia	44.7	Total for Asia	68.9	Total for Asia	63.3

Source: EIU 1991; 1994a,b,c, 1995.
[a] Singapore does not distinguish among members of the Association of Southeast Asian Nations (ASEAN).
[b] Totals are likely to be greater than indicated here because only major Asian countries have been identified.

Asia, Western countries have also contributed significant numbers of tourists.

Southeast Asian tourism is a mass, urban-based phenomenon that offers the pleasures of sun, sea, sand, sex, shopping, drugs, food, and entertainment.[17] Attractions for the more discriminating traveler are, of course, available—from heritage buildings and historic monuments to cultural rituals and ecotourism—but these are minor relative to the goods and services offered on the mass market. Male-oriented packaged tours draw large numbers, mostly from Japan, to the sex markets of Bangkok and Manila and to the various resort centers like Cebu and Phuket. Given the extent of illegal drug production in this region, drugs are probably a significant draw. The harsh penalties for taking drugs out of the country may limit purchases, but although not well documented, drug use among tourists is probably common.

The urban systems of countries in Southeast Asia are dominated by their largest cities, especially in Cambodia, Laos, and Thailand, as well as by the city-state of Singapore.[18] Urban primacy inevitably means that the character of these leading cities either predisposes or blocks the success of a country in attracting tourists. The more dynamic and capitalist the economy, the more urbanized the country and the greater the likelihood of having the infrastructure and facilities to cater to international tourists. Of particular importance are international airports and other types of transport infrastructure (such as freeways), international-class hotels, modern electrical, sewerage, and drainage systems, and good water supplies. The early and extensive development of this infrastructure in Singapore helps explain why this city has long been the most important international tourist destination in the region, relative to its size.[19] Moreover, Singapore has been the only Southeast Asian city initiating urban tourism programs of the types common in Australia, Europe, and North America. Meetings, incentive travel, conventions, and exhibitions are now being encouraged, and the city is beginning to exploit its unique historical importance by promoting its heritage, rebuilding its markets (which were destroyed in the urban renewal schemes of the 1970s), and reconstructing its ethnic enclaves. State-directed conservation and heritage organizations are guiding this process and marketing their product not just to tourists but to local consumers as well.[20] The sophistication of Singapore's effort is a direct result of its being a developed country.[21] And, as in other developed

The exotic Grand Palace (ca. 1782), Bangkok, Thailand

Despite its well-publicized sex tourism, Thailand offers much to the tourist interested in its cultural history.

societies, a large, resident middle class also enjoys the goods and services offered by urban tourism projects.

Apart from Singapore, Thailand is the best known of the Southeast Asian tourist destinations, perhaps because of Bangkok's (in)famous and varied nightlife, particularly its sex tourism and the entertainment and shopping opportunities that go hand-in-hand with this product. These services are largely segregated in certain quarters of the city. After Bangkok, the most important tourist centers in Thailand are the rapidly developing resort cities and towns spread around the coasts, notably Pattaya, to the east of Bangkok; Hua Hin, in the southwest; and Phuket, in the south.[22] All offer seaside holiday pleasures, including sex tourism. Moreover, Chiang Mai, in the far north of the country, in addition to providing sex and drugs, offers local culture, in the form of handicrafts and the rituals and ceremonies of nearby hill tribes.[23]

It is important to mention the role of the military—particularly the U.S. military—in the development of Southeast Asian tourism.[24] The presence of military bases during the Vietnam War, and the extended recreational leaves available to military personnel, initially encouraged the growth and diversification of urban commerce in sex in Thailand and the Philippines.[25] When the war ended in 1975, the presence of a well-established industry, in conjunction with male demand, as well as the ability of international male tourists to access the goods and services available, further expanded the industry, whose major customers soon became the Japanese. By the early 1990s, an estimated eight hundred thousand prostitutes (10 percent male) were working in the Thai sex industry, around seventy thousand of whom were children under the age of fifteen.[26]

The remaining countries have relatively few tourist destinations. Most visitors to Malaysia gravitate to Kuala Lumpur, the country's largest city, to two or three resorts on the Malay peninsula, and to some of the offshore islands.[27] Bali is the best known of the Indonesian destinations and one of the most famous international tourist centers in Southeast Asia. Tourism there centers around the beach resort areas adjacent to the city of Denpasar.[28] The largest international airport is in Djakarta, the country's business and political center, making the city a major international tourist destination in its own right.[29] In the Philippines, Manila plays a role similar to that of Bangkok, and Cebu resembles Thailand's resort areas, although it is small by comparison.[30] Of other Southeast Asian countries, only Vietnam has shown a significant growth in tourism, the majority of tourists being expatriate Vietnamese returning to see family and friends.[31]

The Urban Impact of International Tourism

Sklair explores the globalizing effects of tourism upon the cities and towns of Southeast Asia, placing consumerism within a broader theoretical framework defined by transnational social relations.[32] The totality of these social relations lead to what he calls "transnational practices." These mechanisms for change are of three types: cultural-ideological, economic, and political. Each type tends to be tied to a major institution. Transnational cultural and ideological practices emerge from consumerism; transnational economic practices are institutionalized within transnational corporations (TNCs); and transnational political practices emanate from a transnational capitalist class (TCC) composed of political actors who seek to control the trajectory of development.

The culture-ideology of consumerism, says Sklair, constitutes the core of contemporary culture for peoples of the developed world, and increasingly for those in less developed countries as well.[33] It refers to a demand—a cultural imperative—to consume as many goods and services as possible, not just to fulfill needs but to satisfy wants and desires as well—through fun, enjoyment, and pleasure.[34] Our lives, he notes, are now defined by the things that we consume, and this is an obsession from which few of us wish to escape, whether rich or poor, whether living in developed or less developed countries.[35]

Tourism presents itself as a major avenue for people to satisfy the cultural imperative to consume. Some of the commodities thus attained may be new merely because they are packaged differently. Of course, not everyone has the financial means to become a tourist, but for those who can afford it, an international network of cities is emerging to satisfy their demands. The globalized middle class has played a central role in establishing the relationship between consumerism and tourism. The high disposable incomes of middle-class men and women and their predisposition to consume a variety of goods and services set them apart as major players in domestic and international travel. Significant differences exist within this class: some individuals, such as business executives, tend to consume as an overt expression of their social standing and privileged position, while others, such as professionals, are more ascetic in their orientation.[36] These differences influence the types of tourist offerings available to them and the destinations to which different members of the middle class gravitate.

On the supply side, the actions of TNCs, the link between TNCs and indigenous economic actors, and policies of governments and international institutions further shape the character of Southeast Asian tourism. In the international tourism literature, it has been assumed that TNCs limit the revenues flowing to local peoples.[37] This conclusion has come primarily from observations of the tourist-dependent island states of the Caribbean and the Pacific, regions with weak market economies.[38] Dependence, in conjunction with the need to import goods and services for the industry, has inevitably meant a marked leakage of tourist earnings overseas. Nevertheless, leakage is not simply an outcome of a TNC presence, and the extent of the problem varies. In Singapore, for instance, the loss of revenue has not been sufficient to seriously harm the industry or, more broadly, the economy. The extent of TNC influence is greatest in three areas of tourism: international transport, specifically the airline industry; marketing and ticketing, particularly of packaged tours; and food and accommodations, notably the international hotel chains.[39] In other tourism sectors there may be a much greater local presence and consequently compensatory benefits for the local company.

In the case of the airline industry, TNCs began to play a more marked role in Southeast Asia during the 1980s, as governments around the world deregulated their aviation industries and privatized their airlines.[40] Although a number of Southeast Asian carriers are still state-owned, privatization is under way. With operators fighting for market share, stronger airlines are absorbing weaker ones, and an increase in interlocking ownership in the industry has emerged. For example, of four airlines operating in Southeast Asia, British Airways purchased a quarter of the Australian carrier Qantas, and Qantas, in turn, owns part of Air New Zealand, which owns part of the Australian domestic carrier Ansett, an airline that has recently begun to fly into Asia. With the exception of Ansett, all of these airlines had been government-owned. Airlines owned by TNCs do not yet monopolize air routes into and out of the region, but as privatization continues and as the Southeast Asian tourism market expands, TNCs will undoubtedly play an increasingly important role. Already there are clear indications of highly lucrative intercity routes. Indeed, three of the top twenty intercity international routes are in Southeast Asia, the most important being Singapore–Kuala Lumpur.[41]

The marketing and ticketing of international tourist trips more clearly suggests the dominance of TNCs in the Southeast Asian industry, although detailed data are not readily available. This dominance can be surmised, however, from the fact that most international tourists travel to the region on packaged tours, and because most of these tours are sold by TNCs, the role of these organizations must be significant.

Much of the discussion of the TNCs' involvement in international tourism has focused on the hotel industry. In the case of Southeast Asia, although TNC hotel chains have a growing presence, they do not overwhelm the local industry, particularly in the largest countries, such as Thailand and Indonesia. In Bali, for example, small, inexpensive, and locally owned accommodations (known as *losmen*) have played, and continue to play, an important role in the island's international tourism.[42] In Indonesia as a whole, the classified hotels (which include those owned and operated by TNCs) account for only 7.5 percent of hotels and 30 percent of rooms, although in the Philippines, 44 percent of hotel rooms are estimated to be owned by TNCs.[43] Current trends suggest that future TNC involvement in the hotel industry will be more indirect, coming in the form of franchising and leasing, as well as management and technical-assistance contracts. These arrangements reduce financial risks to TNCs but still enable them to profit from the local tourist industries.[44] At the same time they may ensure that a larger share of revenues goes to local entrepreneurs. The tourism sector with the least TNC participation is the merchandising of goods and services to international tourists. TNCs do provide some food, entertainment, tours, and shopping through the wage labor they hire. The limited data we have, however, suggest that locals disproportionately produce these goods and services through both the formal and informal economies.[45]

The major role played by local businesses and the local petit bourgeoisie is not surprising considering the labor-intensive, "high touch" nature of the tourism industry. Moreover, its volatile nature makes it conducive to petit bourgeois enterprises, which tend to be more flexible than large-scale TNC operations. Because tourism fluctuates wildly through seasonal demand and changing consumer preferences, it becomes difficult to establish traditional capitalist-class relations between owners and wage labor. This situation predisposes the industry toward smaller enterprises, particularly family-based operations.[46]

Governments and international organizations often promote the interests of globalized capital. The linkages are complex. TNC executives and their local affiliates interact with government bureaucrats, politicians, and professionals and with entrepreneurs who market, advertise, and sell goods and services to tourists. The ties linking these groups form a global network, though it would not be accurate to label the participants a *class* in the usual sociological sense.[47]

Within Southeast Asia, this transnational network has played a distinctive role. Beginning in the early 1970s, national governments began introducing policies to promote international tourism. More recently, government-related tourism organizations, such as the Tourism Authority of Thailand, have strengthened their role. National governments have also been active in developing large-scale tourism infrastructure, especially airports and related systems of transport. In 1997 Bangkok began building a new airport, the Singapore airport had been recently modernized, and Vietnam was starting a program of airport construction. Moreover, freeway networks have been constructed to enable the rapid movement of tourists and businesspeople from airports into the congested central business districts of the major cities.[48]

International organizations also take part in the formulation of tourism policies. For example, the United Nations Development Projects (UNDP) assisted the Philippine government in devising a tourism marketing plan for the period 1991–2010, and the World Tourism Organization (WTO) formulated a tourism master plan for Vietnam.[49] These individualized policies have been directed at attracting more tourists to the region's cities, getting them to stay longer, and encouraging them to spend more money. Such achievements, it is hoped, will increase foreign exchange earnings, expand business and employment opportunities, and generate greater tax revenue. More attention is also being given to using international tourism to promote regional growth in the less developed parts of Southeast Asia, although as of 1997 it was too early to notice any effects.[50]

Coalitions of business, industry, government, and the military have been formed to promote tourism. In Thailand, for example, the traditional aristocracy, the military, government bureaucrats, the commercial elite, local urban developers, and TNCs came together in the late 1970s to promote the country's tourism, particularly in Bangkok and the resort centers, and they have achieved considerable success.[51] Equally important, beginning in the 1980s, the Association of Southeast Asian Nations (ASEAN) introduced systems of cooperation to promote tourism in the region as a whole. The aim is to ensure that all countries benefit from international travel, based on the concept that if tourists go to one country, they can be encouraged to go on to other, nearby nations as well. This co-operation is now being extended to Myanmar and Laos, as new ASEAN members, as well as to the non-ASEAN nation of Cambodia, with Thailand playing the pivotal role in this promotion.[52]

International tourism is having a distinct, though still relatively minor, effect on Southeast Asia's sociospatial structures. Urban tourism, on the one hand, and tourism urbanization, on the other, are becoming increasingly evident in a network of cities and towns linking Thailand, Malaysia, Singapore, and Indonesia. Urban tourism is clearly seen within Bangkok, a mega-metropolitan region, and within Kuala Lumpur and Singapore, two other major metropolitan centers. The largest cities boast refurbished palaces and temples, casinos, shopping precincts, nightlife districts, and the like, whereas the resort areas offer high-rise apartments, marinas, and hotel-based integrated resorts. This tourism infrastructure is integrated into a wider coastal tourism urbanization that is spreading in a discontinuous arc around the Gulf of Thailand. Large distances separate most of the centers; still, linkages are developing among the four countries. Moreover, the three main entry points into this system for international tourists—Bangkok, Kuala Lumpur, and Singapore—have a redeveloped railway line (now being marketed as an Orient Express) linking Singapore in the south with Bangkok in the north. Planned road improvements will contribute significantly to this expansion of tourism urbanization.

A relatively extensive literature chronicles the impact of tourism on the peoples living in and near tourism-dependent centers.[53] Much of the early research on Southeast Asian tourism (with a strong focus on Bali) cast it in a negative light, as destructive of indigenous culture. More recent analyses and discussions, however, justify some caution in assuming uniformly negative impacts, since it is now acknowledged that local peoples can adapt selectively to outside influences. On some occasions, interactions have produced positive benefits: the local peoples have adapted parts of their culture in response to outside influences and have rejected other intrusions.[54]

Judgments about economic impacts have also been mixed. The unstable nature of tourism as an industry and its limited contribution to economic growth have provoked the strongest criticisms. Those places shown to be most negatively affected are tourism-dependent island-states where TNCs have marked control over the industry. In such cases, tourism appears to have few linkages with other sectors of the local economy, and therefore few multiplier effects, and tends to displace rather than employ local workers, bring high inflation, and complete the commodification process of these islands' subsistence economies. It is the ownership and control by TNCs that is said to lead to such effects. Yet, these conclusions are based upon a limited number of studies; detailed longitudinal analyses are needed to capture shifts in costs and benefits to both these tourism-dependent island-states and to tourism-dependent urban areas.

Some Southeast Asian research suggests that when direct, indirect, and induced effects of tourism are considered, the industry has major positive outcomes nationally and within cities.[55] At a national level, tourism is said to be valuable for the foreign exchange earned, the employment provided, and the wages made available, relative to the other new labor-intensive industry, export-oriented manufacturing. Furthermore, the level of leakage in tourism-dependent areas may be much lower than many have claimed. Walton, for example, has said that leakage is greater from Malaysian and Singaporean manufacturing than from those countries' tourism industries.[56]

The main criticism involving tourism's social effects has been directed at the sex industry, which undermines family and kinship ties and weakens the social fabric in general. A combination of demand and poverty has made prostitution one avenue open to poor people in that it allows them access to money in countries where it is difficult to obtain a decent, stable cash income.[57] It is worth noting that sex tourism does not take the sole form of prostitution. When sexual relations—so-called "romance tourism"—develop under certain circumstances between tourists and locals, such contacts appear to be planned and intended by both the tourists and by the locals. In a limited number of cases, a local person may return home with the tourist and become either a temporary or permanent resident, or even a spouse.[58]

As a related effect of the sex trade, traditional family structures are said to change, with women being grossly exploited.[59] It is important to note that such negative impacts are not confined to tourism. Family structures and gender relations have also been fundamentally transformed by other new industries, notably export-oriented manufacturing, but it is difficult to map the nature and magnitude of the change for the tourism industry. In an intriguing study of small-town industrialization in West Java, Wolf recorded the positive benefits women received from factory employment.[60] The economic independence brought by access to wages led to some changes in patriarchal relations, which probably benefited the women concerned. Similarly income earned through employment in the tourist sector, even through prostitution, can potentially enhance women's autonomy.

Corruption also appears to be a social consequence of the tourism industry, particularly because tourists often seek goods and services that may be illegal or morally questionable.[61] The real estate speculation typical of tourist centers also tends to breed corruption as property owners seek to influence government selection of development sites for subsidies. Unstable and speculative industries, like urban real estate, are attractive to the money-laundering activities of global organized crime.[62] Moreover, the nature of the tourism industry inevitably means that tourists' security will always be threatened, in the form of terrorism, scams, and other types of theft, because tourists are high-spending, temporary residents in these poor countries.[63]

All countries in Southeast Asia have political volatility emanating largely from conflicting definitions of democracy.[64] This problem is aggravated by governments' inconsistent approaches to certain tourism products, notably drugs and prostitution. Although frequently illegal, or at least criticized on moral grounds, they are tolerated to a degree because of their importance to the countries' economies.

Finally, Southeast Asian tourism has brought negative environmental impacts.[65] In mega-metropolitan areas like Bangkok, Djakarta, and Manila, tourism is but one source of environmental damage. More direct environmental effects occur in coastal resort cities and towns, such as Pattaya and Phuket, where the absence of adequate land-use planning, infrastructure, and environmental regulations has threatened the local ecology. Fortunately, these centers are small in number, so that environmental impacts have been limited. However, the continuous, rapid growth of these centers, specifically the expansion of the coastal tourism urbanization of Thailand-Malaysia-Singapore-Indonesia, is potentially devastating. Without adequate environmental protection, widespread disaster is possible, which, in turn, could destroy the tourism industry. Such threats have led to calls for smaller, alternative projects, ones that are environmentally friendly and more beneficial to local populations.[66] Such developments, however, can cater only to small numbers of tourists, not to the mass market that defines Southeast Asian tourism today.

The region's urban-based tourism is currently under attack for its extreme hedonism; its disproportionate emphasis on sex, particularly the sexual use of children, has elicited moral outrage both within and outside these countries.[67] Not only has this reaction forced authorities within host countries to toughen laws, but tourists are now being prosecuted by their own governments for their involvement in this type of tourism, especially when child abuse is involved. Moreover, host nations are following various strategies to diversify their tourism product.[68] First, there has been the construction of mega-malls in all the major Southeast Asian cities, the largest in Asia (Seacon Square) having recently been opened in Bangkok. Indeed, this Thai city has undergone a shopping revolution over recent years, with retail space doubling between 1990 and 1994, and by 1994 it had two of the world's five largest shopping malls.[69] Tourists were a major target, even though the malls had been built primarily to capture the disposable income of the rapidly expanding native middle classes. Second, casinos have been constructed in a number of the cities as part of a worldwide trend to capture the gambling dollar, both from residents and from international tourists.[70] Third, there is now a greater emphasis on marketing the material culture of the region—for example, Bangkok's temples and palaces and Thailand's handicrafts. Finally, large numbers of golf courses are being built in resort areas and in rural sections of mega-metropolitan centers. This expansion is being driven from Japan, with a swath of courses having been completed within and outside that country. All along the western rim of the Pacific, from Japan as far south as Australia, one finds a growing concentration of golf courses aimed at international tourists.[71] No longer aimed solely at a male-oriented market, Southeast Asia tourism is now enlarging its focus, targeting three potentially lucrative markets: families, Japanese honeymooners, and the growing number of business and professional women with high incomes.[72] In doing so, tourism in the region will increasingly resemble the phenomenon in the rest of the world, and the area's unique niche as a destination for males in search of forbidden pleasures will gradually disappear.

SUSAN S. FAINSTEIN AND

DENNIS R. JUDD

Cities as Places to Play

Tourism has been a central component of the economic, social, and cultural shift that has left its imprint on the world system of cities in the past two decades. Theorists have variously termed it the move from Fordism to post-Fordism, from the industrial to the informational mode of development, from modernism to radical modernism, from modernity to postmodernity, and from internationalism to globalism. In spite of considerable debate over the newness of the tendencies revealed and the extensiveness of the changes, there does seem to be a degree of consensus that the present epoch involves a different, more flexible organization of production, higher mobility of both capital and people, heightened competition among places, and greater social and cultural fragmentation. Within the city the unity previously imposed by a manufacturing-driven economy has disappeared, and urban culture itself has become a commodity.

The authors in this book have described the growing importance of tourism in the late twentieth century, with a particular focus on the effects of tourism on cities. Some of the authors have examined physical redevelopment, tourism marketing, and sports, entertainment, and gaming as components of the industry. Others have traced the development and outcomes of tourism growth by looking at individual cities. In this conclusion we seek to generalize from these various contributions.

Tourism and Urban Spatial Structure

Economic activities have always shaped cities, and this is particularly the case for tourism. We define tourism as an activity demarcated by the interaction of visitors with the tourism industry; we expect that the motives of tourists in choosing to visit a city may be highly varied. Along with the corporate-office complex, tourism has been a primary force in determining contemporary urban form, as facilities for tourists have increasingly become interwoven with other structures. The appearance and extensiveness of spaces for tourists, as well as the degree to which these spaces blend into the fabric of the city, depend upon the historical and social circumstances within which they are embedded. Cities that are not built initially for tourists must be retrofitted, often at considerable cost in new infrastructure.

It would take many more cases than we have included in this book to adequately cover the full range of possibilities, but three basic types of tourist cities can be identified:

- Resort cities are places created expressly for consumption by visitors. Mullins, in his chapter, employs the term *tourism urbanization* to describe the development of such places.[1]
- Tourist-historic cities lay claim to a historic and cultural identity that tourists can experience.[2] Sometimes these cities have been sites of tourism for a long time (e.g., Venice and Athens), but in many cases a program of conscious promotion and reconstruction of heritage has transformed them into tourist sites.
- Converted cities have built an infrastructure for the purpose of attracting visitors, but the tourist space brought into being by this infrastructure is insulated from the larger urban milieu within a process of uneven development.[3] Typically, sites of production, such as manufacturing and port facilities, are either adapted to new uses or replaced, and a standard menu of new facilities is constructed specifically for tourists.

A brief discussion of these three types of tourist cities will place the case studies in this book into context.

Resort Cities

The metropolitan areas of Cancún and Las Vegas and the environs of Disney World, which all began as resorts, share a number of characteristics. At their core is an intentional, exclusive space devoted wholly to lodging, dining, entertainment, and shopping. The success of these tourist venues has stimulated further activity, making them become more than mere tourist locations. Cancún has spawned an adjacent city in which tourism intermingles with indigenous activities. A tourist economy has rippled outward from Cancún in such a way that the official tourist space has increasingly become a base from which tourists emanate rather than a self-contained and isolated resort. Las Vegas's extraordinary growth is reflected in the development of one of the United States' fastest-growing universities, and the gaming industry has spawned economic sectors that will inevitably constitute a diversified local economy. Disney World is giving birth to a new town, Celebration, which incorporates the tenets of neotraditional urban design. As Foglesong points out, over time the Disney Corporation will likely become subject to regulation by local and state governments. As at Cancún, additional economic development not controlled by the founder is taking place in the surrounding area.

Although Cancún, Las Vegas, and Disney World were all designed for tourism, the auspices under which they were developed were quite different. Cancún started out wholly as a public enterprise, in which private developers responded to the Mexican government's request for proposals. Infrastructure was entirely a governmental responsibility. Major Mexican and multinational corporations were the developers of hotels along the beach, although small business has found numerous opportunities in the urban center across the lagoon from the beachfront. Las Vegas's growth was the product of multiple private actors, with little planning involved. Its tourism sector, however, continues to be dominated by large multinational gaming corporations. Disney World, like Cancún, is the result of a detailed plan, but the source of the scheme was a private corporation, and the public sector has been mainly the passive facilitator of Disney's projects. This pattern of domination by one corporation has continued in the design of Celebration, although Disney will necessarily relinquish some of its dominance as the town grows.

Tourist-Historic Cities

Of the places featured in this book, Prague represents the purest case of the tourist-historic city.[4] Its magnetic attraction for tourists has been enhanced by its rediscovery after the demise of the Soviet bloc, which both increased its accessibility and suddenly opened up opportunities for entrepreneurs to exploit its tourism potential. Interestingly, one of its greatest assets is that it had not gone through U.S.-style urban renewal that might have destroyed much of its historic architecture or been heavily damaged during World War II, like so many Western European cities.

Jerusalem likewise attracts visitors because of its historic monuments, but as Shachar and Shoval note, with a few exceptions it is less the inherent qualities of the structures than their symbolic meanings that constitute the appeal. Jerusalem represents a particular type of tourist-historic city, a place of religious pilgrimage. The cities of South Asia draw travelers because they are associated with antiquities and exoticism but also because they have become venues for sex and drug tourism. In this latter use, their historical and cultural identity is completely irrelevant. For tourists seeking sex and drugs, these locales are just like the resort cities, the only difference being that they offer a unique entertainment strategy.

Tourist-historic cities differ from those cities expressly built for tourism as well as from those in which some well-demarcated spaces have been converted from previous activities to tourism uses. Instead, tourist sites and uses are built into the architectural and cultural fabric of the city, and tourists mix with residents and workers rather than restricting themselves to purpose-built spaces. We can observe this spatial integration in Jerusalem, Prague, and Boston. Nevertheless, even though tourism has been absorbed into cities such as these, it has changed their character. The meaning of religious structures, government buildings, or castles changes when they cease being encountered in the course of worship, business transactions, or political interaction and have instead become objects of the tourist gaze. Such transformations need not be interpreted negatively, and indeed many churches and synagogues, even when invested with religious significance, have always been sightseeing attractions as well.[5] Still, even when spaces retain the same configuration as in times past, changes in their use imply a rupture in historic continuity. Thus, in Prague, as Hoffman and Musil note, in a sharp break from the days of the Communist rule, business travelers now mingle with residents and vacationers within the confines of the old city. Holcomb's chapter on city marketing and Urry's on the sense perception of urban culture show that the appeal of tourist-historic cities is not a straightforward consequence of their mere existence as resurrected historic sites; rather, promoters manipulate and improve on what these places originally had to offer. Urry's observation is perceptive: as the number of reconstructed Mediterranean villages and Mexican restaurants in shopping malls proliferates, and as Thai and Chinese restaurants become common features of urban culture, tourist entrepreneurs in the real Mediterranean countries and in Mexico, Thailand, and China

The marble Leaning Tower of Pisa, in Italy

Completed in 1350, the tower became a tourist icon because of an engineering error.

are forced to provide ever more stylized interpretations of "authentic" culture.

Converted Cities

Judd describes a type of tourist city in which specialized tourist bubbles are carved out of areas that otherwise would be hostile to or inconvenient for tourists. To remake places with few obvious or easily advertised attractions into tourist cities, standardized tourist spaces are constructed. The aim is to create an illusory world within an otherwise ordinary setting. Sassen's portrayal of the redevelopment of Times Square is a case in point, where giant billboards, movie multiplexes, superstores, and themed restaurants combine to create a kinetic environment that overwhelms the visitor. Its spectacular quality virtually insists that to be there is to participate in excitement, to stand at the crossroads of an exotic urban culture. Times Square, however, though an artificial environment, does not fully exemplify the concept of the tourist bubble, both because of its long history as an entertainment mecca and because of New York City's overall character.[6]

Within a converted city, tourist spaces are isolated from the ordinary fabric of daily life if the city outside the tourist enclaves seems hostile or uninviting to a visitor. Ehrlich and Dreier claim that with the exception of the Prudential-Copley complex, Boston was converted from a decaying port into a dynamic service and tourist city without such segmentation. If they are correct in this assertion, then Boston has achieved the kind of tourist development that is characteristic of European cities but is rare in the United States (San Francisco, Portland, Oregon, and Seattle may also fit into this category, but certainly not Cleveland, St. Louis, San Antonio, or Atlanta). Boston possesses several advantages that have allowed it to sustain an extensive redevelopment program without succumbing to artificiality—namely, it has a number of historic sites connected by the Freedom Trail and an important business-travel component as part of its tourist economy.

Often, tourism is thoroughly mixed with other economic activities; this is particularly the case in relation to the downtown corporate-office complex. Along with service industries, tourism has contributed to a transformed urban core that no longer contains the port and manufacturing facilities of former times. Together, tourists and businesspeople support urban amenities, ranging from restaurants to symphony orchestras to professional sports. The tourism-services complex provides economies of scale that cluster together high-level consumption services used by the resident middle class, business travelers, and vacationing tourists alike.

In this respect, as Sassen demonstrates, global cities have particular advantages in the competition for tourists. For not only are they the premier sites for financial and business services, but they are also host environments for the entertainment industry, which plays a crucial role in attracting visitors. The agglomeration economies offered by the sectoral mix of New York (as well as Tokyo and London) include huge capital resources, a labor force of great flexibility, an extensive market for entertainment, and a high level of entrepreneurship, particularly within the property development and entertainment industries. Moreover, the amount of wealth that exists in global cities, along with the assets of the visitors it attracts, is sufficient to support a Madison Avenue or a Regent Street, which offers everything a festival market does and more, but on a fantastically bigger scale and in a less artificial environment.

Tourism and Culture

Reflexivity, according to Giddens, is the quality of modern culture that results from the ability of people to know what is happening elsewhere in the world and to change their behavior because of expectations of particular consequences.[7] In his discussion of modernity, Giddens refers also to the removal of phenomena from their original context ("disembeddedness")—for example, money allows the purchase of a product removed in time and distance from its production. Tourism quintessentially involves reflexivity and disembeddedness and is therefore fundamental to the making of modern culture.[8]

Tourism partakes of the complexity of late modernity.[9] It is simultaneously a provider of shared and distinctive experience. Whereas each kind of music now has its own following, and most films are directed at niche markets, certain tourist attractions cut across the usual boundaries of race, class, gender, and ethnicity. The iconic images discussed by Judd and by Holcomb, ranging from the various towers (Eiffel, Tower of London, Empire State Building) to sacred places like the Dome of the Rock and Notre Dame, are widely known and evoke shared sentiments of awe or stimulate similar fantasies of the past. These fabled sites, as well as the newly created tourist haunts like the Disney parks and the Rouse festival markets, are visited by a broad spectrum of people. Obviously tourism is not a recreation of the poor, but among those who travel at all there appears to be a remarkable agreement about the top attractions. Both the masses and the classes, if they have sufficient means to travel, will pay their respects to the most famous monuments, will take their children to the theme parks, and will shop for souvenirs. Contemporary tourism still has within it the routines of the pilgrimage: certain places constitute the sacred sites that must be visited, whether still holy like the Wailing Wall or secularized like Disney World. The standardization of the tourism experience therefore provides common symbols and shared memories within otherwise fragmented cultures.

At the same time, however, much of tourism is segmented by class and culture. Only the wealthy and business travelers on expense accounts can regularly afford to stay in luxury hotels and eat in three-star restaurants. The people who make a special trip to The Hague to see the Vermeer exhibit differ from those who take the Jack the Ripper tour of London's South Bank or who journey to Cleveland's Rock 'n Roll Hall of Fame, and doubtless they, in turn, are different from the visitors to Saint Louis's Bowling Hall of Fame. Broadway musicals, Bangkok brothels, and defunct coal mines—to cite several of the attractions mentioned in this volume—appeal to dissimilar clienteles.

Tourism, in certain respects, creates a supranational culture by forging connections among people from different milieus, and it thus contributes to the formation of a global culture. Hiernaux comments that one of the impulses initially inspiring the Mexican tourist industry was a desire to promote international friendship. Although friendship may overstate the usual case, travel does require a tolerance of diversity and a participation in the life of others not to be achieved by staying at home. As much as the Ugly American and his or her counterparts elsewhere have been caricatured, the boorish visitor is probably more the exception than the rule.

Travel, as well as affecting the collective culture of tourists, marks the culture of the place that is visited in several ways. As discussed by Urry in this volume and in *The Tourist Gaze*, it provides people with a reflected image of themselves, which then leads them to conform to that image. It also does so by providing a globalized space within the local community; when local residents use this space, they become, in effect, tourists.

The spaces frequented by tourists, whether they be by the beach or in the heart of downtown, have acquired many of the connotations that go with the image of a theme park.[10] This term has been applied broadly to refer to actual theme parks (such as the Disney ventures, which constitute the archetype), to festive marketplaces, to entertainment centers like Times Square. The phrase tends to be used pejoratively and has incorporated within it a view that tourist spaces, by disguising or excluding the harsher sides of reality, reinforce the dualism of a world divided between work and play, production and consumption, wealth and poverty. The undeniable purpose of leisure is to escape from life's unpleasantness. Accordingly, the designers of tourist spaces understandably avoid the troubling aspects of life.[11] Regardless of how we evaluate the social consequences, however, we can assume that the main spatial effect of urban tourism is to produce spaces that are prettified, that do not feature people involved in manual labor (except when engaged in historical reenactment or entertainment), that exclude visible evidence of poverty, and that give people opportunities for entertainment and officially sanctioned fun.

This aspect of tourism makes it an easy target for criticism. In evaluating tourism and its impacts, therefore, it is particularly important to avoid a facile regress into a critique based on prejudice rather than on knowledge. We offer, then, some final comments on the socioeconomic effects of tourism.

Images of Tourism

In the 1980s studies of global restructuring concentrated on the movement of capital and industry away from older industrial cities and regions of the Western countries to developing nations offering low labor rates and relaxed regulatory environments. Although the service sector has taken up much of the slack in employment, considerable anxiety has been expressed about whether service jobs were as good as jobs in manufacturing. At some level, service-sector jobs did not seem as real as the jobs being lost. It was easy to understand that people need automobiles, washing machines, farm equipment, and toilet paper. These are tangible products that make the comforts and security of modern life possible. In the new economy, however, most of the labor force is involved in the creation of intangibles. At the high end, people trade securities and provide investment advice, advertise products, design new computer software, and offer consulting, accounting, and legal services. At the other pole of the services spectrum, low-wage and seasonal labor in fast-food joints and tourist shops has replaced the kinds of employment that produced a durable physical product.

Many commentators have said that this transformation involves a switch from production to consumption as the main economic force shaping cities.[12] We do not think this characterization is accurate. Sassen, in *The Global City*, contends that the financial industry, still centered in cities, does not simply offer a service but *produces* financial products, and her chapter in this volume discusses the entertainment industry as a site of production as well as consumption.[13] It would be useful if the production-consumption dichotomy gave way to a recognition that cities increasingly specialize in types of production in which products are either intangible or immediately consumed. According to this interpretation, cities have in many respects reverted to their preindustrial economic roles as marketplaces, sources of finance capital, and producers of intangibles.[14]

There is no reason to assume, a priori, that a services- or tourism-based economy has worse effects than the economic structure and employer-employee relations that characterized the industrial age. As it recedes further from view, recollections of the industrial economy become constantly more nostalgic. The received images are of a highly paid army of unionized workers marching off to the factory in the morning and returning in the evening to a home with all the creature comforts, which are made possible not only by personal affluence but also by the constantly changing technological advances of the products pouring forth from the factories.

The tendency to romanticize the industrial age was energized by the dislocations associated with the abrupt deindustrialization that swept through and devastated communities in the industrial belts of all the Western countries in the 1970s and 1980s. In their book *The Deindustrialization of America*, Barry Bluestone and Bennett Harrison paint a dramatic portrait of the "fundamental struggle between capital and community" initiated when industrial firms closed down factories: "No one appears to be immune to job loss, no matter how well placed. Popular conceptions notwithstanding, displacement respects neither educational attainment nor occupational status. . . . When a plant shuts down, or operations are permanently curtailed so that some workers receive layoffs without recall, engineers lose their jobs along with janitors."[15] According to Bluestone and Harrison, part of what had gone awry was that corporations were engaging in a frenzy of mergers and downsizing, a process driven as much by investors who were milking companies of profits and assets as by an economic imperative to make economic processes more productive. In the 1980s, part-time employment replaced full-time jobs with benefits, and average wages fell, as low-wage service jobs replaced factory employment. It is therefore not surprising that the age of industry soon became regarded as a golden bygone era.

One ought to be careful, however, when thinking of the industrial age. For most of its history it was characterized by bitter and often violent conflicts between capital and labor; at most, the rapprochement that brought about some measure of harmony in some industries (but by no means all) lasted from the mid-1930s to the early 1970s. Aside from the deplorable work conditions in many industries, even after unionization (e.g., in mining and timber) periods of relative prosperity were offset by serious recessions and depressions, with their high rates of joblessness. In the twentieth century, two world wars helped fuel prosperity, and in the United States the high growth rates of the post–World War II *Pax Americana* were sustained by America's global economic hegemony, which began to erode in a quite predictable way by the late 1960s. Competition from abroad was bound to reduce industrial employment in the United States, as were the revolutions in transportation and manufacturing processes. Even in regions where manufacturing output did not decline—and there are many of these throughout the Western countries   the number of jobs plummeted because manufacturing became much more efficient. It takes fewer and fewer workers to keep the world awash in a surplus of goods. In this respect, the industrial sector has become similar to agriculture and like agriculture, it has become the subject of a romanticized mythology of the good life.

The refurbished image of the industrial economy is matched by a tendency to paint the service sector in a negative light, and this is applied with particular force to tourism. As we pointed out in the introduction, the tourist has often been the object of contempt—and the study of tourism is not exempt. The analysis of factories and industrial workers is manifestly important; everyone so involved walks in the footsteps of Marx, Engels, and Lenin, and also of Carnegie and Ford. There is more than a little suspicion that to study tourism is to study something frivolous. A job is work, but to be a tourist is to have fun. Is it legitimate to study fun? The only way to answer such a question is to point out that tourism has become a large-scale capitalist industry central to the world economy and to national and urban economies. It is a prototypic late twentieth-century industry—both a service-sector industry and an archetypal post-Fordist-style industry, able to vary price, quality, content, and market by niche. We may know little about its overall social and economic impacts, but it is time that we did.

The chapters in this volume permit only an impressionistic account of the economic impact of tourism on cities. We know that tourism has become a fundamental economic sector in cities and, in areas like Cancún, it has been a significant engine of regional growth. We see that it is symbiotic with other industries, especially entertainment and office-based services, and that there is a strong interactive effect between business development and tourism. We can say that on economic terms stadiums and gaming are not a wise investment for most cities. Important questions concerning the labor market remain: What kinds of jobs are created? How well do they pay, and can they be constituted into careers? It is important that studies of just these sorts of questions be undertaken.

We asked our authors to focus primarily upon the way cities compete for tourists and how tourism has reshaped the spatial ecology of cities. We find that the modes of competition—the construction of facilities, the marketing of a city—are quite similar from place to place. Striking differences emerge, however, in the objectives that visitors pursue—sin in South Asia, family entertainment in Disney World, personal fortunes on the riverboats and in Las Vegas, spiritual redemption in Jerusalem, business and history in Prague and Boston, urban exotica in New York, sun, sand, or ancient ruins in Cancún. Tourism is not a zero-sum game, with every city competing against every other, but rather an industry that affords a variety of niches. The variations in the tourism product from place to place mean that much more detailed empirical investigation is required for an understanding of the tourism economy. Our analysis has revealed a wide spectrum of possible outcomes from tourism; the task remains to spell out the conditions under which its economic effects can be most beneficial and its homogenizing and marginalizing tendencies can be kept in check. This is an important undertaking, unless one believes that tourism is a passing fad. It is not. Tourists are everywhere, and they are here to stay.

Contributors

Robert A. Beauregard is a professor in the Milano Graduate School of Management and Urban Policy at the New School for Social Research in New York City. His current work concerns the dynamics and meanings of urban decline, the economic development of cities, the nature of urban life, and the role of urban intellectuals. He has also written extensively on planning theory. His most recent book is *Voices of Decline: The Postwar Fate of U.S. Cities* (Blackwell, 1993).

Sabina Deitrick is an assistant professor in the Graduate School of Public and International Affairs at the University of Pittsburgh. Her work focuses on regional planning, economic development, and urban revitalization. She is coeditor with Peter Meyer of a special-focus issue on brownfields revitalization in *Public Works Management and Policy* 2 (January 1998).

Peter Dreier is the E. P. Clapp Distinguished Professor of Politics and director of the Public Policy Program at Occidental College in Los Angeles. From 1984 through 1992 he served as senior policy adviser to Mayor Ray Flynn of Boston and as director of housing at the Boston Redevelopment Authority. He has written extensively on urban policy, community development, community organizing, and American politics. He received a Ph.D. from the University of Chicago.

Bruce Ehrlich lives and works in Boston, where he is senior project manager with the Department of Neighborhood Development. Since

1992 he has been responsible for the coordination of homeless policy and programs for the City of Boston. He has also been involved with other affordable housing and community development initiatives in the city. He has previously written on the politics of housing and economic development and holds a master's degree in city planning from the Massachusetts Institute of Technology.

Charles C. Euchner is the coordinator of Boston 400, the comprehensive planning initiative of the City of Boston. Euchner has taught political science at the University of Pennsylvania, the College of Holy Cross, and St. Mary's College of Maryland. He is author of *Extraordinary Politics: How Protest and Dissent Are Changing American Politics* (Westview Press, 1996) and *Playing the Field: Why Sports Teams Move and Cities Fight to Keep Them* (Johns Hopkins University Press, 1993). A former journalist, he received a B.A. from Vanderbilt University and an M.A. and Ph.D. from Johns Hopkins University.

Susan S. Fainstein is professor of urban planning and policy development at Rutgers University. She is coauthor of *Restructuring the City: The Political Economy of Urban Redevelopment* (Longman, 1983), author of *The City Builders: Property, Planning, and Politics in London and New York* (Blackwell, 1994), and coeditor of *Divided Cities: New York and London in the Contemporary World* (Blackwell, 1992). She has written extensively on issues of redevelopment, comparative public policy, and urban social movements.

Richard Foglesong is professor of politics and director of Project Governance, a community outreach program supporting democracy and effective government, at Rollins College in Florida. He is writing a book on Walt Disney World and Orlando, supported by a grant from the National Endowment for the Humanities. He is frequently quoted in the national and international media regarding Disney World. In addition to numerous magazine and op-ed articles, he is author of *Planning the Capitalist City* (Princeton University Press, 1986), a history of American urban planning, and coeditor of *The Politics of Economic Adjustment* (Greenwood, 1990). He is extensively involved in community activities in the Orlando area.

David Gladstone is a Ph.D. candidate in the Department of Urban Planning and Policy Development at Rutgers University. He has published on tourism urbanization in the United States and on theories of the state and civil society. His dissertation concerns the nature and impact of tourism in developing countries.

Daniel Hiernaux-Nicolas is Professor Investigador Titular at the Autonomous University of Metropolitan Xochimilco. For several years he directed a tourism bureau for the Mexican government. He has written extensively on tourism and economic development in Mexico and elsewhere.

Lily M. Hoffman is associate professor of sociology at City College and the Graduate Center of the City University of New York and former director of the Rosenberg-Humphrey Program in Public Policy. Her research interests include urban redevelopment, with a comparative focus on the Czech Republic, where she has been monitoring changes in urban planning and urban social and physical structure since 1989. Hoffman's current interest in tourism grows out of her work on urban redevelopment and comparative policy. Author of *The Politics of Knowledge: Activist Movements in Medicine and Planning* (SUNY Press, 1989), she is currently completing a historical study of ghetto tourism in Harlem and is involved in an ongoing study of tourism and revitalization in northern Manhattan.

Briavel Holcomb is professor and chair of the Department of Urban Studies and Community Health at Rutgers University. She has written extensively on urban regeneration and gender issues and is coauthor of *Revitalizing Cities* (Association of American Geographers, 1981) and coeditor of *Women's Lives and Public Policy: The International Experience* (Greenwood, 1993). After two decades of concentrating on urban redevelopment, poverty policy, and women's issues, her interests turned toward tourism, stimulated by the experience of circumnavigating the world with five hundred young Americans in the University of Pittsburgh's Semester at Sea program. Since then her research has included the marketing of the Caribbean to U.S. tourists, gay tourism in the United States, and gender and the heritage industry.

Dennis R. Judd is a professor in the Department of Political Science, University of Missouri-St. Louis. He is editor of the *Urban Affairs Review* (formerly the *Urban Affairs Quarterly*) and of the Globalization and Community book series for the University of Minnesota Press. He has published extensively on urban politics, urban redevelopment, and related subjects and is coauthor, most recently, of *City Politics* (2d ed., Addison-Wesley, 1998) and *The Politics of Urban America* (2d ed., Allyn and Bacon, 1998).

Cheryl Zarlenga Kerchis is a Ph.D. student in public policy at the Graduate School of Public and International Affairs, University of Pittsburgh. Her research interests include U.S. welfare and employment policy and urban poverty.

Patrick Mullins is a reader in sociology at the University of Queensland in Australia and has published extensively on tourism urbanization in southeast Queensland. He is extending this work as a member of an international collaborative research team that is examining consumerism and sustainable development in Australia and Korea.

Jiří Musil is professor of social geography at Charles University, Prague, and at the Budapest and Warsaw branches of the Central European University. He is also president of the Czech Sociological Association. His main professional fields are urban and regional sociology and the sociology of culture. In 1992–93 he served as academic director of the Central European University, Prague, and in 1990–92 as the first director of the renewed Institute of Sociology, Czech Academy of Sciences. He is a member of "Academia Europea," a founding member of the Czech Learned Society, and member of the Bauhaus Scientific Board, Dessau, Germany. Musil has served as a consultant with the United Nations, UNESCO, and several other international and professional associations. He has published thirteen books in a number of languages and lectured at various Western universities.

Robert E. Parker is associate professor of sociology at the University of Nevada, Las Vegas. He is the coauthor (with Joe R. Feagin) of *Building American Cities* (2d ed., Prentice-Hall, 1990) and the author of *Flesh Peddlers and Warm Bodies: The Temporary Help Industry and Its Workers* (Rutgers University Press, 1994). In addition, he is the author of numerous articles and chapters on urban-, work-, and race-related topics. His current research focuses on the political economy of cities and developments in the U.S. workforce.

Frank Roost has studied urban and regional planning at Technische Universitaet Berlin and Columbia University. He has published several articles about the Walt Disney Corporation's urban planning projects and, as a Nafoeg scholar, is currently researching the global media industry's activities in Germany, Japan, and the United States.

Saskia Sassen is professor of sociology at the University of Chicago. She is the author of *The Mobility of Labor and Capital: A Study in International Investment and Labor Flow* (Cambridge University Press, 1988), *The Global City: New York, London, Tokyo* (Princeton University Press, 1991), *Cities in a World Economy* (Pine Forge/Sage, 1994), and *Immigrants and Refugees: A European Dilemma* (Fischer Verlag, 1995). Her current projects concern immigration in the United States, Western Europe, and Japan and governance and accountability in the world economy.

Arie Shachar is professor of urban geography and urban planning at the Hebrew University of Jerusalem. His main research interests involve economic globalization processes and urban development and the urban impact of the culture industry. Among his publications are *Society, Culture and Urbanization* (Sage, 1986), written with S. N. Eisenstadt, and the edited volume *European Cities in Competition* (Avebury, 1996). Since 1995, Professor Shachar has been director of the Strategic Plan for the Metropolitan Tel-Aviv project. In 1998 he became director of the planning team for the New National Master Plan for Israel.

Noam Shoval is presently a Ph.D. candidate in the Department of Geography of the Hebrew University of Jerusalem, specializing in the field of tourism, with special emphasis on urban tourism and urban development. His Ph.D. dissertation deals with differentiated urban spaces for tourism in Jerusalem.

John Urry received his B.A., M.A., and Ph.D. from Cambridge University. He has taught at the Lancaster University since 1970, where he is professor of sociology. Recent books include *The Tourist Gaze* (Sage, 1990); *Economies of Signs and Space* (Sage, 1994), written with S. Lash; *Consuming Places* (Routledge, 1995); *Touring Cultures* (Routledge, 1997), coedited with C. Rojek; and *Contested Natures* (Sage, 1998), written with P. Macnaghten. He is editor of the International Library of Sociology (Routledge) and Schools of Thought in Sociology (Edward Elgar) book series.

Notes

Susan S. Fainstein and Dennis R. Judd,
"Global Forces, Local Strategies, and Urban Tourism"

1. Urry 1990, 24. Although Thomas Cook was not alone in inventing the group excursion, he was the first to offer it as a form of mass merchandising. He began by leading groups of working-class families to British resort areas in the interest of promoting temperance through wholesome recreation. Later he expanded his choice of destinations to the European Continent and eventually shifted his market by offering grand tours to the wealthy. See Feifer 1985.

2. Britton 1991, 454.

3. World Tourism Organization 1995a, 1.

4. Ibid., 4.

5. Ibid., 1. Receipts from international tourism in 1994 totaled $335 billion (World Tourism Organization 1995b, 2). Expenditures by domestic tourists are notoriously difficult to estimate. Undoubtedly they are much less on a per capita basis than those of foreign travelers. Nevertheless, even the most conservative estimate would indicate that combined domestic and international tourism expenditures amount to well over a trillion dollars.

6. World Tourism Organization 1995b, 2.

7. Britton 1991, 457.

8. Readers of Jane Austen will remember that Sir Thomas Bertram was absent from Mansfield Park so that he could supervise estates in the West Indies.

9. Consultant's report to TWA, read by one of the authors over the shoulder of a TWA manager while en route, September 25, 1996.

10. Britton 1991, 463.

11. In this vol., see Sassen; Deitrick, Beauregard, and Kerchis; and Euchner.

12. MacCannell 1976, 10.

13. Theroux 1995, 1, 5.

14. In this vol., see Fainstein and Gladstone; and Urry.

15. We wish to thank Lily Hoffman for her reminder, when reading the initial draft of this introduction, that tourism should be appreciated as a complex phe-

nomenon incorporating a variety of motives, many very positive, and that its transforming effects can be simultaneously positive and negative.

16. See the discussion by Foglesong, this vol.
17. MacCannell 1976.
18. Urry 1995, 10.
19. Urry 1990.
20. Zukin 1991, 221.
21. Graburn 1994, 46.
22. Britton 1991, 463; also see Urry 1990, 12.
23. Urry 1990, 12.
24. Ibid., 109. According to Ashworth and Tunbridge (1990, 245), the heritage industry is the principal new industry in Great Britain.
25. Raban 1987, 210. The author of this description reports that he inquired of the British National Coal Board as to whether he should take this proposal seriously: "The press officer was huffy. There was, he said, nothing at all original in that idea; the NCB had been doing it for years."
26. Urry 1995, 123.
27. Britton 1991, 463.
28. Ioannides 1995, 56.
29. Holcomb 1993, 124.
30. See Beauregard 1993, 257.
31. Edsall and Edsall 1991; Judd 1994.
32. Beauregard 1993.
33. Boyer 1992, 192.
34. Urry 1990, 58.
35. Ibid., 138–39.

Susan S. Fainstein and David Gladstone, "Evaluating Urban Tourism"

1. Judd, this vol.
2. Shaw and Williams 1994.
3. Ashworth and Tunbridge 1990, 264–65.
4. The Rouse Corporation developed Boston's Faneuil Hall, Baltimore's Harborplace, New York's South Street Seaport, and numerous other festival marketplaces in American cities. See Frieden and Sagalyn 1990.
5. Guskind and Peirce 1988; Fenich 1992a.
6. Fenich 1992b; Law 1992.
7. Thus, in his study of Baltimore's Inner Harbor redevelopment, Levine (1987) found that despite the arrival of over 400 million tourists, incomes of Baltimore's lowest income groups actually declined during the 1980s.
8. Bianchini 1993, 9.
9. Bianchini 1993 discusses the co-optation of the avant-garde and alternative artistic movements of the 1960s–70s by the commercial cultural entrepreneurs of the 1980s.
10. Zukin 1989; Fainstein, Fainstein, and Armistead 1986.
11. On gentrification, see Smith et al. 1994. Gans (1993, 36) criticizes Jane Jacobs for equating urban vitality with the exotic quality of immigrant neighborhoods: "If such districts are near the downtown area, they may attract intellectuals, artists, and Bohemian types. . . . The street life, the small stores that traditionally

serve ethnic groups and other cultural minorities, and the area's exotic flavor then draw visitors and tourists, whose presence helps to make the district even livelier. . . . But visibility is not the only measure of vitality, and areas that are uninteresting to the visitor may be quite vital to the people who live in them." Ethnic neighborhoods like Manhattan's Little Italy and Detroit's Greektown often lost their residents and became simply restaurant zones.

12. Mullins 1994. The Gold Coast is the name given to the northeast coast of Australia, an area extensively developed for tourism, leisure homes, and recreation.

13. Davis 1994; Parker, this vol.

14. Foglesong, this vol.

15. Mullins 1991.

16. Garcia 1994; Ashworth and Tunbridge 1990.

17. Gladstone 1998.

18. Harvey 1987.

19. See Eco 1986; Sorkin 1992b.

20. Venturi, Scott Brown, and Izenour 1977, 8.

21. Debord 1994, 45.

22. Watson and Kopachevsky 1994, 646–47, emphasis in original.

23. Mike Davis's 1990 *City of Quartz* has been perhaps the most provocative book on this theme. See also Sennett 1990; Sorkin 1992.

24. Zukin 1991.

25. MacCannell 1976; Pretes 1995.

26. Sedaris 1994.

27. Debord 1994, 120.

28. Two novels that capture particularly well the effect of tourism on what were once isolated fishing villages are John Casey's *Spartina* (1989), which describes a town in Rhode Island, and Mary Lee Settle's *Blood Tie* (1977), which relates the story of residents of a village on the Turkish coast.

29. Boorstin 1992.

30. Baudrillard 1984; Eco 1986; Sorkin 1992.

31. Watson and Kopachevsky 1994, 655

32. See Fainstein 1994, chap. 10.

33. Lash and Urry 1994, chap. 10.

34. Ibid., 260.

35. Ibid., 276.

36. MacCannell 1976.

37. Giddens (1991, 5), in his discussion of reflexive modernity, seemingly contrasts "lifestyle choices among a diversity of options" with "standardising influences . . . most notably, in the form of commodification." His argument contradicts the ideologists of the market, who assert that its principal function is to offer choices. The two differing conceptions are best synthesized in examinations of flexible specialization, which accept post-Fordist systems of commodity production as simultaneously offering both standardization and choice.

38. McCarthy 1963, 7–8, emphasis in original.

39. Ibid., 34.

40. Ibid., 35.

41. Bohlen 1996.

Dennis R. Judd, "Constructing the Tourist Bubble"

This chapter is a revised version of a paper delivered at the International Conference on Urban Tourism and City Trips, sponsored by the European Center for Comparative Urban Research, Erasmus University, Rotterdam, April 28–29, 1994. An earlier version of this paper was published in *Tourism Management* 16, no. 3 (May 1995) 175–87.

1. U.S. Department of Housing and Urban Development 1982, 14.
2. Hill 1983, 105.
3. Convention centers spark civic wars, 1986, 16.
4. Fainstein, Fainstein, Hill, Judd, Smith 1986.
5. Strauss 1961, 76.
6. Hula 1990, 191–215.
7. Ashworth and Tunbridge 1990, 153.
8. Urry 1990, 8.
9. Bottoms and Wiles 1995, 42.
10. Ashworth and Tunbridge 1990, 176.
11. Strauss 1961, 8.
12. Ibid., 72–73.
13. Ashworth and Tunbridge 1990, 245.
14. Boyer 1992, 189–90.
15. Boyer 1992.
16. Barthes 1979, 3.
17. Ibid., 8.
18. D. Smith 1980, 46; cited in Shaw and Williams 1994, 169.
19. Urry 1995, 135. Here, I have inverted Urry's concept of "coerced consumption," in which the tourist is always looking for something that seems new and unique.
20. Frieden and Sagalyn 1990, 43–47.
21. Successful Meetings 1993, 32–33.
22. Ibid., 11.
23. Sanders 1992, 139–59.
24. Tabak 1993, 30.
25. Fenich 1992a, 34.
26. Law 1994, 47.
27. Ibid., 61–64.
28. Successful Meetings 1993, 60–61.
29. Teibel 1994, 33–37.
30. Ibid., 37.
31. Successful Meetings 1993, 7, 32, 44.
32. Guskind 1987.
33. Tabak 1993, 30.
34. Ibid., 62.
35. Judd and Swanstrom 1998, 374.
36. Baade and Dye 1988.
37. Euchner 1993, 12–13.
38. Ibid., 67.
39. Phares 1996.
40. Baade and Dye 1988; Euchner 1993, 71; Zipp 1996; Euchner, this vol.

41. Davis 1992, 155.
42. Frieden and Sagalyn 1989; Teaford 1990.
43. Urry 1995, 123.
44. Zukin 1991, 232.
45. Eadington 1995, 159–60.
46. Quoted in Goodman 1994, 29.
47. Ibid., 26–27.
48. Quoted in Harrah's Entertainment 1996, 13.
49. Goodman 1994, 91–94.
50. Beauregard, this vol.; Goodman 1994, 51–57; Hornblower 1996, 31.
51. Perlman 1996, 52.
52. Perlman 1996.
53. Pagano and Bowman 1995, 74.
54. A Dog Eat Dog Films Production, written, produced, and directed by Michael Moore (Warner Bros. Pictures).
55. McRee 1994, 189.
56. Urry 1990, 7.
57. McRee 1994, 189.

Briavel Holcomb, "Marketing Cities for Tourism"

1. Bramham et al. 1989, 4.
2. Gilbert 1989, citing the British Institute of Marketing.
3. Jefferson 1990, 85.
4. Greene 1990, 44.
5. Hall 1992a, 1.
6. Appledome 1996b, 4.
7. Appledome 1993, A18.
8. Appledome 1996a.
9. Longman 1995, B12.
10. Myerson 1996a.
11. Quoted in ibid., 155.
12. Law 1994, 101.
13. Hall 1992a, 145.
14. Hall 1992a.
15. Recent books on tourism marketing recommend such strategies as analyzing and targeting markets, environmental and resource analysis, goal formulation and mission statement development, market segmentation, positioning, product development, pricing, identifying target audiences, determining promotional mix, and the evaluation of marketing effectiveness.
16. One study estimated a 90 percent "wastage rate" on U.K. commercial tour brochures, based on the approximately 200 million brochures that resulted in 15 million bookings (Hodgson 1993). Another reviewed "conversion" research, which attempts to measure the correlation between advertising and visitation, and found that although such studies are appealing to the trade for their value in justifying public expenditure on advertising, their accuracy is often questionable (Messmer and Johnson 1993).
17. See Judd, this vol.
18. Cosco 1986.

19. Schmalz 1987.

20. Holcomb and Luongo 1996.

21. Drummond 1995.

22. Port Authority of New York and New Jersey 1994, 43.

23. Grimes 1995.

24. Ibid., B1, B4.

25. Tighe 1985, 242.

26. Davies 1987.

27. John 1995, 42. See Judd, this vol.

28. Jones 1946, 132.

29. For a more complete account, see Holcomb 1990.

30. Burd 1977, 130.

31. Glaab 1967.

32. Organization for Economic Cooperation and Development 1993, 13.

33. Davies 1987.

34. Bramwell and Rawding 1994.

35. Page 1995.

36. Hall 1994, 152.

37. Ibid., 160.

38. Mommass and Van der Poel 1989, 255.

39. Roche 1994.

40. Neill 1993.

41. Jean Holder, secretary general of the Caribbean Tourism Association, quoted in Owen 1992, 358.

42. March 1994.

John Urry, "Sensing the City"

1. Rorty 1980; Jay 1993; Levin 1993.

2. Bermingham 1994; Urry 1990.

3. In the romantic form of the tourist gaze, the emphasis is upon solitude and spirituality; in the collective form a place becomes the object of the gaze precisely because of the presence of other people, who provide an aura of excitement.

4. Rodaway 1994.

5. Ibid., 36–37.

6. Buzard 1993.

7. Arendt 1978, 110–11 (emphasis in original). More generally, on the senses, see Macnaghten and Urry 1997, chap. 4.

8. Rorty 1980, 12–13.

9. Jay 1986, 179; Jay 1993.

10. Adler 1989; Urry 1995, 194–96.

11. Jenks 1995, 3.

12. Foucault 1970.

13. Gregory 1994, 23; Pratt 1992.

14. Foucault 1970, 221, 312, 386.

15. Pratt 1992, chap. 2.

16. Adler 1989, 22; and see Urry 1995, chap 13.

17. Ousby 1990; Urry 1995; Macnaghten and Urry 1997, chap. 6.

18. Green 1990, 88.

19. Ibid., 76.
20. Ibid., 88.
21. Urry 1995, chap. 13.
22. Sontag 1979; Crawshaw and Urry 1997.
23. Barthes 1981, 34.
24. Wilson 1992, 122; and see J. Taylor 1994; Parr 1995.
25. Irigaray 1978, 50.
26. Heidegger 1977, 134.
27. Crary 1990, 149.
28. Sharratt 1989, 38.
29. Sharratt 1989; and see Bryson 1983.
30. Slater 1995, 220, 226.
31. Gregory 1994; Mitchell 1989.
32. Levin 1993b; and Jay 1993.
33. Foucault 1977; Jay 1993; Urry 1992.
34. Foucault 1977, 217; Jenks 1995, 155.
35. Crawshaw and Urry 1997.
36. Virilio 1988; Barry 1995, 44.
37. Quoted in Ousby 1990, 194.
38. Baudrillard 1981; Eco 1986; Rodaway 1994.
39. Boorstin 1964.
40. Jay 1992, 187.
41. Irigaray 1978, 123; Mulvey 1989.
42. McClintock 1995.
43. Quoted in Jay 1993, 531.
44. Stallybrass and White 1986, 134.
45. Berman 1983.
46. Stallybrass and White 1986.
47. Ibid. See Edensor 1996 on the impacts of this in the case of tourism in India.
48. Tester 1995.
49. Stallybrass and White 1986, 139.
50. See Shields 1991, on nineteenth-century Brighton.
51. Lefebvre 1991, 197; Rodaway 1994; Porteous 1985, 1990.
52. McClintock 1995, 207; Porteous 1985.
53. Quoted in Rodaway 1994, 72.
54. Bauman 1993, 24.
55. Edensor 1996.
56. Ihde 1976.
57. Urry 1996; Jay 1992; Urry 1992.
58. Wright 1985; Carter, Donald, and Squires 1993; Bhabha 1990.
59. Venturi, Scott Brown, and Izenour 1972.
60. Rojek 1997.
61. Virilio 1977, 1991; Urry 1994.
62. Urry 1995.

Richard Foglesong, "Walt Disney World and Orlando"

1. Fowler 1968, 1984.
2. Fowler 1984.

3. Walt Disney Productions 1981.
4. Ibid.
5. Foglesong 1991.
6. Stone 1987b, 272.
7. B. Dial, interviewed by R. Foglesong, 1990.
8. Disney maps $100 million plan, 1965.
9. Thomas 1976, 364.
10. Paul Helliwell 1965.
11. Economic Research Associates 1966.
12. Walt Disney Productions 1967.
13. Walt Disney Productions 1981.
14. Howden 1990.
15. D. G. Lawrence 1968. Actually, the district had no residents as of this ruling.
16. Walt Disney Productions 1976, 21.
17. Ibid., 24–25.
18. Ibid., 20.
19. Economic Research Associates 1966.
20. Novak-Branch 1983, 6–7.
21. Ibid., 49.
22. Kunerth 1994.
23. *Business Week* 1971.
24. *Orlando Sentinel* 1990.
25. Doolittle 1994.
26. Tracy 1990.
27. Benedick 1990.
28. Lebowitz 1992b.
29. Roy 1994.
30. Lancaster 1996.
31. Roy 1995.
32. Kuhn 1990.
33. Walsh 1986.
34. Benedick 1990.
35. Lebowitz 1991a.
36. Ibid.
37. Lebowitz 1992a.
38. Vaughan 1994.
39. Taylor 1994.
40. Laws of Florida, 3775.
41. Walt Disney Productions 1967.
42. Knack 1996.
43. Foglesong 1994.
44. Blumfield 1989.
45. Fiore 1990.
46. Levenson 1990.
47. Fiore 1990.
48. Stone 1987a.

Robert E. Parker, "Las Vegas"

I wish to thank Joan Rozzi at the University of Nevada, Las Vegas, for her valuable research assistance on this chapter.

1. Moehring 1995, 118–19.
2. Ibid., 20.
3. Parker and Feagin 1992.
4. Moehring 1995, 119.
5. Steinhauer 1996b, 1.
6. Las Vegas no. 2 in hot travel spots, *Las Vegas Review-Journal* 1995, 10D.
7. H. Smith 1996, 7D.
8. Christiansen 1996, 70.
9. Ibid., 46.
10. Ibid., 62.
11. Palermo 1993, 9E.
12. Christiansen 1996, 70.
13. Major projects planned or under way in Las Vegas, 1995.
14. Collier 1996, 8.
15. Steinhauer 1996a, 1D.
16. *Book of Lists* 1996, 33.
17. Mattox 1995, 12.
18. Moore 1995, 15; Pledger 1995b, 1A.
19. Lawrenzi 1992, 30.
20. Ibid., 30–31.
21. Pledger 1994, 9C.
22. Havas 1993, 1.
23. Andersen 1994, 42.
24. Striesand 1994, 61.
25. Palermo 1994, 14E.
26. Pledger 1995a, 1A.
27. Ibid.
28. Ibid.
29. Christiansen 1996, 87.
30. Nevada no. 1 in job growth, 1996, 8D.
31. Douthat 1993, 3B.
32. Home, sweet home, gets more costly, 1995, 1M.
33. Berns 1996, 1A.
34. Yakubik 1995
35. Manning 1990, 7A.
36. State of Nevada 1994, 62.
37. State of Nevada 1996.
38. Ward 1994, 1B.
39. Cited in Moskowitz 1993, 19.
40. Burbank 1994, 7D.
41. Houses most affordable in the Midwest, 1995, 8E.
42. Collier 1995, 1.
43. Przbys 1996, 1E.
44. Edwards 1994, 5D.
45. Morrison 1996, 1B.

46. Caruso 1995, 5K.
47. Rogers 1996, 1A.
48. Davis 1995, 38.

Daniel Hiernaux-Nicolas, "Cancún Bliss"

1. In 1995, Cancún had 18,859 hotel rooms, or 11.6 percent of the rooms in Mexico, and Acapulco 17,647, or 10.9 percent.

2. At the moment, changes to the law on gambling have been proposed to the Parliament, with a negative result: even within the majority of the official party, there is strong opposition to this project, which is supported by the Ministry of Tourism and some entrepreneurs.

3. The annual growth rate for world tourism was 11 percent in 1950–60; 9 percent in 1960–70; 6 percent in 1970–80; and 3 percent in 1980–85 (Cazes 1989, 9).

4. Particularly in 1976, when President Echeverría promoted and approved a United Nations vote against Zionism; also after bank nationalization in 1982; and as a result of the earthquakes and disastrous economic situation of 1985–86. In brief, the internal situation in Mexico has been interpreted dramatically by tourists, principally from the United States.

5. Miguel Alemán was a leader in promoting tourism after he left office in 1952. Founder of the Continental Hotel chain, he also had decisive roles in the international marketing of travel to Mexico and the creation of new educational projects for tourism. A clear reflection of the ideas of his time, his tourism philosophy was oriented toward peace and international friendship. Those arguments were important in the development of Mexican tourism in the 1950s and 1960s (see Alemán 1983).

6. Lozato 1988; Cazes 1994.

7. Ramírez 1986, 6.

8. Cazes 1994, 77. The 1950s and 1960s in Europe were marked by the diffusion of this image of Mexico through movies, music, and operettas. The images projected an exotic version of Mexican culture but also of Brazil and the Latin culture in general.

9. Veracruz is the main Mexican port of the Gulf as well as the traditional contact with the rest of the world. Tourism developed there in the 1950s, but climatic conditions are not favorable, and the expected growth was never realized because of competition from Acapulco.

10. Jiménez 1984, 102.

11. Planning for Acapulco began in the 1960s: a main road was constructed along the coast, infrastructure was greatly improved, and housing programs were initiated for the urban poor. Nevertheless, housing, infrastructure, and services were inadequate to meet the large demands of the resort.

12. The World Bank and Inter-American Development Bank supported some large regional ventures in Mexico in the 1970s, particularly the Lázaro Cárdenas City project, which included a steel plant and new port projects.

13. Hiernaux 1989b.

14. In another paper, I have argued that landscape induces a sort of rent, not for the use of the space per se but for the privilege of viewing another space. Therefore, rent results not from the physical conditions of a piece of land but from the quality of surrounding space to be viewed (Hiernaux 1989a).

15. Hiernaux 1984.

16. Gay-Para 1985; de Ventós 1976.

17. Augé 1992. An interesting concept of space can also be found in Shields 1991.

18. Urry 1990, 10–11.

19. Nevertheless, Acapulco has a large number of rooms not included in the official statistics, mainly because they are in apartments and houses. A recent estimate includes 11,434 rooms in various categories (Hernández 1996, 87). Of course, Cancún also has a large number of rooms in apartments, condominiums, time-shares, etc., though fewer than Acapulco. If we use these statistics, Acapulco is still the largest resort, but with a greater distribution of rooms in varied categories.

20. Martí 1985.

21. In 1994 FONATUR estimated the population of Cancún (which started from scratch in 1975) to be around 240,000.

22. Instability was higher in Cancún in 1986 than in the rest of the tourist resorts of Mexico (Secretaría de Turismo 1986).

23. When working in FONATUR in 1983–84, I developed this comparison regarding the way of life of this new social group, which is interested not only in self-employment or high positions in the corporate structures but also in exploring new issues in Cancún, such as the environment (still a new concept in the early 1980s in Mexico). This peculiar lifestyle, a mix of late-American hippie and neo-Mexican hippie, had very different patterns from previous modes of living; it was oriented more toward a Californian, rather than a Mexican, way of life.

24. Acuña and de la Garza 1989.

25. The figures included in the table refer not only to Cancún but to all resorts in the state territory, including Cozumel, Bacalar, and the coast between Belize and Cancún.

26. We use the neologism that Lanfant used to describe a social process, but we assume it can also be appropriated for spaces (Lanfant 1994).

27. Urry 1990.

28. The Mexican press regularly offers information about houses, hotels, and other tourist facilities confiscated from drug dealers. Cancún, Puerto Vallarta, and the main tourist resorts in Mexico are plagued by the problems associated with drug money (see the newspaper *El Financiero* [Mexico City] 1994–96, inter alia).

Saskia Sassen and Frank Roost, "The City"

1. The Internet and, more generally, electronic space—whether public (like the Internet) or private—is too large a topic to address in this brief chapter. But it is important both as a space for entertainment (e.g., on-line chat clubs); a space for the consumption of entertainment products; and a space that has engendered a whole new set of relations with actual urban space. See, e.g., Rotzer 1995; Sassen 1997; Graham and Marvin 1996; *Futur Antérieur* 1995.

2. Scott 1995.

3. A. Smith 1991.

4. This is supported and made possible through a range of innovations and technical developments: digitalization, optical fibers, compression, navigation software, the new capacities of PCs, networks such as the Internet, and other internets.

Further, global corporations need seamless worldwide networking technologies that can support applications such as electronic data interchange, computer-integrated manufacturing, databases for information management, video conferencing, etc. This will require enormous investment and expertise and will favor global players.

5. Sassen 1998, 187–88.

6. New York City Economic Policy and Marketing Group 1993; Slatin 1995.

7. An important issue, and one that we do deal with here, is the transformation of the labor markets associated with these industries. Movie and television production has become more flexible, which has led to an extreme polarization in incomes: a few at the top earn enormous salaries at the same time that deunionization has resulted in lower wages for technical and craft workers. Paul and Kleingartner (1994) report that despite significant concessions by the unions, about half of Hollywood's craft and technical employment had become nonunion by 1988.

8. Columbia University 1995; Roche 1997.

9. Sassen 1997.

10. Roche 1997.

11. Bertelsmann tries to reduce its visibility by having subsidiaries with different names. In 1986 it acquired Bantam Doubleday and RCA Records, and in 1998 Random House.

12. Liedtke 1991.

13. Sassen 1994, chap. 4.

14. Zukin 1991.

15. Braun 1995.

16. A different development, though one that strengthens the attractiveness of the urban scene, is the rapid growth in the numbers of movies being filmed in major cities such as New York or London, where the city itself, or some legendary neighborhood, becomes an important ingredient of the film.

17. See, e.g., Warren 1994.

18. Fader 1995.

19. Sedaris 1994.

20. Roost (forthcoming).

21. Richards 1994.

22. Hammack 1991.

23. This area comprised one small and two large blocks between Eighth Avenue, Forty-Third Street, and Broadway as well as parts of two adjacent blocks (at Forty-First Street and Eighth Avenue and at Forty-Second Street and Broadway).

24. For a detailed account, see Fainstein 1994, chap. 6.

25. Dunlap 1992.

26. New York State Urban Development Corporation 1993.

27. Pulley 1995a.

28. Goldberger 1995.

29. Pulley 1995c.

30. Ibid.

31. Merkel 1995.

32. Kennedy 1995.

Bruce Ehrlich and Peter Dreier, "The New Boston Discovers the Old"

The authors are grateful to Judith McDonough for sharing her extensive knowledge of Boston's planning and preservation history and for her thoughtful comments on an earlier draft of this chapter. Much of this chapter is based on the following interviews with public officials and individuals involved in Boston's tourism industry, to whom we are indebted.

Bok, J. 1996. Former general counsel, Boston Redevelopment Authority, author of historic preservation legislation.

Bozzotto, D. 1996. President, Hotel Employees Restaurant Employees International Union, Local 26.

Canter, A. 1996. Executive director, Massachusetts Lodging Association.

Hyde, J. 1996. Director of North American Tourism and Marketing, Massachusetts Office of Travel and Tourism.

McDonough, J. 1996. Director, Massachusetts Historical Commission; former director, Boston Landmarks Commission.

Meehan, L. 1996. Director of Public Relations and Tourism, Greater Boston Convention and Visitors Bureau.

Park, S. 1996. President, Boston Preservation Alliance; director, Boston Harborfest.

Pollak, A. 1996. Former executive director, Boston Preservation Alliance.

Ryan, R. 1987. Former director, Boston Redevelopment Authority.

Salony, P. 1996. Director of Government Affairs, Massachusetts Lodging Association.

Saunders, R. 1996. Managing partner, Saunders Hotel Group.

Sidman, E. 1996. Chairman of the Board, Beacon Properties Corporation.

Thompson, J. 1996. Principal, Thompson and Wood.

1. The first annual world's best awards, 1996; Readers Choice Awards 1996.

2. See Meyerson and Banfield (1966), who did not even mention tourism in their treatise on Boston's renewal program.

3. Gans 1962; Mollenkopf 1983; Boston Urban Study Group 1984; Ehrlich 1987; Kennedy 1992; O'Connor 1993.

4. Completions of new office space averaged over 800,000 square feet annually between 1965 and 1974 and reached a high of 5.2 million square feet in 1975. Economic growth and new construction continued through the 1980s. Between 1960 and 1985, more than 20 million square feet of office space was added to Boston, almost doubling the amount of space available. Between 1950 and 1990, employment in Boston increased by 13 percent, from 550,719 to 622,433; employment in FIRE and services grew by 150 percent, from 140,921 to 352,963; and employment in all other sectors dropped by 39 percent, from 409,798 to 251,134.

5. See Cohen 1981; Stanback 1985.

6. Massachusetts ranks fourteenth among states in domestic travel expenditures and sixth among states visited by foreign tourists (Massachusetts Office of Travel and Tourism 1996).

7. Greater Boston Convention and Visitors Bureau 1995, 5; 1997.

8. Room rates make for hospitable hotel market, 1976.

9. Greater Boston Convention and Visitors Bureau 1995, 12.

10. Memo from J. Avault to Mariso Lago, June 6, 1996, in the files of the Boston Redevelopment Authority.

11. Ryan 1987.

12. Campbell 1995.

13. Thompson 1994; see also Sorkin 1992.

14. Northeastern University 1967, 211.

15. Massachusetts Office of Travel and Tourism 1996.

16. McPhee 1996. One nightclub catering to foreign students even banned domestic patrons.

17. Wilson 1996.

18. Boston National Historical Park 1994.

19. Whitehill 1968; O'Connor 1993.

20. Boston National Historic Sites Commission 1960.

21. Northeastern University 1967.

22. United States Bicentennial World Exposition Corporation 1969, vii–14.

23. Mayor's Office of the Boston Bicentennial 1973.

24. Boston National Historical Park 1974.

25. Dixon and Clancy 1995, 7.

26. Gans 1962.

27. O'Connor 1993.

28. Seifel 1979, 38. Back Bay and Beacon Hill also lost thousands of lodging units to private-market conversion during this time: in all, more than 90 percent of Boston's single-room units, or approximately 25,000 units, were lost between 1960 and 1985.

29. McDonough 1996; Bok 1996.

30. Quoted in Historic Boston 1992, 42.

31. Lupo et al. 1971; Kennedy 1992.

32. See Dreier 1996.

33. Sorkin 1992, xv.

34. Frieden and Sagalyn 1989, 107.

35. Boston Redevelopment Authority 1964.

36. Brown 1987.

37. O'Connor 1993.

38. Sagalyn 1989.

39. Thompson 1979.

40. Boston Redevelopment Authority 1992, 14.

41. Clements 1996.

42. Hall 1988.

43. Dreier 1983a; Kahn 1988, 1989.

44. Glickman et al. 1996; Osterman 1991.

45. See Dreier 1996.

46. Avault 1985.

47. Southworth 1984, x–xi.

48. Schauppner 1987.

49. In stunning contradiction to the central themes presented here—the public and authentic nature of Boston's tourist attractions—a lavish banquet held for the American Society of Association Executives (who select convention locations) during their 1996 convention in Boston led to the temporary enclosure of a street and

public park in Copley Square. The park was set as a miniaturized re-creation of the Public Garden, pond and swans included, though the original was just three blocks away. The people of the city were denied entrance to this private party in the "Public Garden."

50. Dixon and Clancy 1995.

51. Ackerman 1996; Greater Boston Convention and Visitors Bureau 1997.

52. Frommer 1988, 10.

Lily M. Hoffman and Jiří Musil, "Culture Meets Commerce"

1. Konrad and Szelenyi 1979; Stark 1992.

2. We apply Bourdieu's concept of cultural value (1972), which is typically used for individual or collective status, to the cultural resources of cities.

3. Humphreys, *Rough Guide* 1991, 39.

4. *Fodor's Czechoslovakia* 1992, xvi–xvii. On January 1, 1993, Czechoslovakia was divided into the Czech Republic and the Slovak Republic.

5. For a historical overview of Prague's urban development, see Hrůza 1994.

6. Hoffman 1994.

7. Musil 1968, 1980.

8. This and similar statements appearing in this chapter were obtained in confidential interviews.

9. In 1965, the official statistics began to include data on foreign visitors. "Visitor" refers to any person crossing the border. Traffic in border regions, such as shopping trips, inflates the numbers. The volatility of the yearly figures also reflects official reactions to such events as the Polish Solidarity Movement, an outbreak of foot-and-mouth disease in Hungary, or relaxed travel restrictions by the East Germans (Carter 1991).

10. Musil and Pohoryles 1993, 189–90.

11. Zukal 1993.

12. Masák et al. 1995.

13. Private lodgings existed before 1989, but the government did not encourage their use. Westerners could use these lodgings only in major cities and for no more than three nights. A 1990 law on private businesses made it possible to supplement incomes by renting registered rooms in private dwellings.

14. Ministry of Economy of the Czech Republic 1995, 26.

15. Tourism a major source of revenue all year round, 1995, 18. Including unregistered beds, we estimate a total of forty thousand to fifty thousand beds.

16. Neighboring Austria dominates both the hotel and construction industry (Levy 1995, 20a).

17. Fischer Reisen (founded by a Czech immigrant) moved its headquarters from Hamburg, Germany, to Prague and is now counted as a Czech firm.

18. Volkman 1995, 8.

19. Holub 1994.

20. International organizations that promote tourism development include trade associations such as the World Travel and Tourism Council and the Organization of Economic Cooperation and Development; European Union–related organizations such as the European Investment Bank; United Nations–related organizations and programs such as the World Tourism Organization, the United Nations

Development Program, and the United Nations Monuments Fund; and development banks such as the World Bank and International Monetary Fund (IMF).

21. There are recent indications that this attitude is beginning to change and that tourism is seen as less of a zero-sum game.

22. The Ministry of Economy publication *Tourism in the Czech Republic: 1993–1994* (1995) listed sixteen nongovernmental professional associations, but more exist.

23. Sýkora 1994, 1156.

24. Sýkora 1993.

25. The New Bohemians, *Economist*, October 22, 1994, 23.

26. Competition for nonhousing space is actually less than might be expected, because under socialism at least half of Prague 1 was used primarily for storage.

27. For a broader discussion of Prague's changing economic base, see Dostál and Hampl 1994. For a discussion of the new economic elite, see Fauci 1995–96.

28. Musil 1993.

29. Hoffman 1994.

30. Kratochvílová and Kovářová 1996, 4.

31. Blažek 1994; Blažek, Hampl, and Sýkora 1995.

32. For the global cities hypothesis, see Sassen 1994.

Arie Shachar and Noam Shoval, "Tourism in Jerusalem"

Epigraph: Wiesel, quoted in *Frommer's Israel* 1996, 141.

1. On the nature of pilgrimage, see Eliade 1969; Turner 1973; Turner and Turner 1978; Cohen 1992.

2. Towner 1985; Ben-Arieh 1979.

3. Brendon 1991, 120–23.

4. Brendon 1991.

5. Rinschede 1992.

6. Urry 1995, 24.

7. Bowman 1991, 98–99.

8. R. Smith 1992.

9. For an interesting example of the segmentation of tourist spaces in Paris, see Jules-Rosette 1993.

10. Jansen-Verbeke 1985.

11. Burtenshaw et al. 1981, 172.

12. Jerusalem was chosen as the capital of the Latin East, and the Crusader kingdom was named after the city: the Latin Kingdom of Jerusalem (see Prawer 1972).

13. Nolan and Nolan 1992.

14. MacCannell 1990.

15. Municipality of Jerusalem et al. 1996, 9.

16. All the data presented in this and the other tables in this chapter were gathered after the unification of Jerusalem in 1967.

17. Midgam 1996.

18. Ministry of Tourism and Israel Airport Authority 1988, 13.

19. Midgam 1996, 66.

20. The discussion that follows is based on Cohen 1971; Hoade 1971; Cohen et

al. 1988; *Israel* 1992; Baedecker 1995; Fodor's 1996; *Frommer's Israel* 1996; Fischer 1996a, 1996b.

21. The exceptions are Protestant denominations that regard the return of the Jewish people to its land and the establishment of the State of Israel as the beginning of the Jews' redemption, at the end of which will be the Second Coming of Jesus. These denominations are represented by such bodies as the International Christian Embassy, Jerusalem. The tour itineraries of these denominations would differ from those of traditional Protestants in that they would include national and Israeli sites in Jerusalem. Some of these denominations call themselves Christian Zionists.

22. Central Bureau of Statistics and Ministry of Tourism 1996, 28–29.

23. During the Mamluk period, a bitter dispute broke out between Christians and Jews over the control of the building that contained the room of the Last Supper and King David's tomb. As result of this dispute, the control of the building passed into the hands of the Muslims.

Charles Euchner, "Tourism and Sports"

1. Quoted in Euchner 1993, 55.

2. Meyers 1996.

3. This and other statements by sports figures and civic officials were made in a series of interviews conducted in early 1996. Because some of these interviews were confidential, the sources of some statements quoted in this chapter are not cited.

4. These figures come from SportsCorp, a consulting firm based in Chicago.

5. To an extent, such cooperation is necessary; as NFL lawyers argued in one antitrust case, sports is a kind of "natural monopoly." The league needs to maintain a stable setting for teams to compete with one another fairly. Early leagues faltered when wealthy clubs overwhelmed their competition. Leagues do not need to control all aspects of their operations, however; they should be able to cooperate when necessary to produce their product—teams with a reasonable balance of talent competing for a championship—but not on all matters. It is reasonable for franchises to cooperate on setting rules for drafting players, setting minimum salaries, and actually playing games. But it is unreasonable standards for stadiums that create the kind of financial disparities within the industry that force small-market franchises to seek public subsidies. Yet that is just what the NFL and MLB have done in recent years. See Weistart 1986.

6. Zimbalist 1992, 146; emphasis added.

7. Verducci, e.g., demonstrates that the fielding abilities of modern players are far superior to players from previous eras.

8. See also Whitford 1993, chap. 2.

9. For an important analysis of why urban elites are so cohesive when the rest of the population remains poorly organized, see Crenson 1982.

10. Lever 1983, 16.

11. Phares 1996, 19–20.

12. For an analysis of the danger of overbuilding, see Hilsenrath 1996.

13. Euchner 1991.

14. Euchner 1993, 43–45.

15. Ibid., 247.

16. Ibid., 245.

17. For an analysis of the design of the multipurpose Georgia Dome, see Harriman 1992.

18. Johnson 1993.

19. Ibid., 244.

20. These figures are from Zipp 1996.

21. Friedman 1996, 100.

22. Readers' poll results 1995, 139.

23. U.S. Department of Commerce 1994b.

24. For information about player residences, see the annual "Redbooks" published by the National and American Leagues. Teams that have the most members living nearby, predictably, are located in the warm-weather locations favored by players. The California Angels, e.g., have five players living near Anaheim—still a small number.

25. The majority of the jobs created by the downtown development of Baltimore went to outside communities. See Levine 1987, 13.

26. For an analysis of the importance of webs of activity in the service sector, see Schnieder and Fernandez 1989, 537–55.

27. See Northern Economic Planners 1995.

28. See Zipp 1996.

29. Brewers important but . . . , 1995.

30. Baade 1996.

31. Ibid.

32. See Noll 1974.

33. Owen 1993, 67.

34. Ibid., 64.

35. Hudnut 1995, 100–101.

36. Swindell, Rosentraub, Mullins, and Przybyklski 1995, 148, 150.

37. Rosentraub, Swindell, Przybyklski, and Mullins 1994, 233.

38. MacLeod 1996. The decline is probably greater than the official numbers suggest. Because the American League releases figures for the number of tickets sold rather than for the number of people who show up at games, actual attendance is lower by several thousand.

39. Hanson and Gauthier 1989, 15–19.

40. Lubove 1995.

41. See Quirk and Fort 1992, chap. 4.

42. See Bagli 1996.

43. Matheson 1996.

44. Hudnut 1995, 35.

Sabina Deitrick, Robert A. Beauregard, and Cheryl Zarlenga Kerchis,
"Riverboat Gambling, Tourism and Economic Development"

1. Goodman 1995; Harris 1994; Hirshey 1994; Popkin 1994; Urban League of Pittsburgh 1994, 4–5.

2. Stansfield 1978; Myerson 1996b.

3. Law 1994, 1–16, 27–38.

4. Britton 1991; Ioannides 1995

5. Barnes 1997, B1.

6. Harrah's Casinos 1994, 4, 13, Mandel and Landler 1994, 59–60; U.S. Department of Commerce 1994a, 453.

7. Eadington 1993.

8. Leiper 1989.

9. Law 1994; Zukin 1991.

10. Porter 1995.

11. Hine 1995, M5.

12. Browning 1995; Standard & Poor's 1995, 44.

13. Eadington 1993, 14.

14. Johnson 1996; Peterson 1995.

15. Goodman 1995, 57–85; Rich 1990.

16. Hunter and Bleinberger 1995.

17. DeBoer 1996, 2.

18. Kilborn 1996b.

19. Elliott 1994.

20. Braykovich and Henterly 1995.

21. Barnes 1995.

22. Beyard 1993; DeBoer et al. 1996, 15.

23. Pileggi 1995, 14–15.

24. Standard & Poor's 1995, 36.

25. DeBoer et al. 1996, 1.

26. Goodman 1995, 68 80.

27. DeBoer et al. 1996, 22.

28. Promus 1995.

29. Kilborn 1996a.

30. Grinols 1994, 1995; Nickerson 1994; Pizam and Pokela 1985; Urban League of Pittsburgh 1994, 21–22.

31. Grinols 1995, 9.

32. DeBoer et al. 1996, 11.

33. Kilborn 1996a, 1996b.

34. Standard & Poor's 1995.

35. Perniciaro 1995.

36. Deller and Chen 1994.

37. Hamer 1995, table 10; Perniciaro 1995.

38. DeBoer et al. 1996, 15; Kilborn 1996a.

39. Deller and Chen 1994.

40. See Parker, this vol.

41. Sterngold 1995.

42. Goodman 1995, 47–52; Urban League of Pittsburgh 1994, 24–30.

43. Johnson 1995; Volberg 1995.

44. Grinols 1994.

Patrick Mullins, "International Tourism and the Cities of Southeast Asia"

Earlier versions of this paper were presented at the New Urban Forms, New Housing Forms Conference, University of Queensland, July 2–4, 1996; and at the Urban Dynamics Symposium, University College, London, August 26–28, 1996.

1. On economic development, see Dixon 1991; Jones et al. 1993. On tourism,

see, e.g., Harrison 1992a; Hitchcock et al. 1993. On urbanization, see, e.g., Douglas 1989; Forbes 1996.

2. R. Smith 1992.

3. See Bianchini and Parkinson 1993; Hannigan 1995; Harvey 1990; Law 1992, 1993; Judd 1995; Zukin 1995.

4. Mullins 1991; Rimmer 1992.

5. The eighteenth and nineteenth centuries did witness the development of spa towns and resort communities, but on nothing like the present scale.

6. Brohman 1996; Harrison 1992a,b; Hitchcock et al. 1993.

7. EIU 1994c.

8. See EPAC 1993.

9. Harrison 1992a; Latham 1994; WTO 1995.

10. WTO 1995.

11. EIU 1994b; Richter 1989, 1992.

12. Jansen-Verbeke and Go 1995.

13. EIU 1991, 1993, 1994a,b,c, 1995.

14. EIU 1994a,b,c, 1995.

15. McCormack 1991; Mackie 1992.

16. Prime Minister's Office, Japan, 1990.

17. EIU 1991, 1994a,b,c, 1995; Fairclough 1995; Hall 1992b; Harrison 1992b; Hitchcock et al. 1993; Leheny 1995; Mackie 1992; Sherry et al. 1995; Varikiotis et al. 1995.

18. McGee 1991; see also Douglas 1991.

19. EIU 1994c.

20. Eng 1994; Kong and Yeoh 1994.

21. Forbes 1996.

22. Hamilton 1994; R. Smith 1992; Thaitakoo 1994.

23. EIU 1995; Cohen 1995.

24. Enloe 1990; Mackie 1992; Richter 1989.

25. Hall 1992b; Leheny 1995.

26. Leheny 1995, 373.

27. EIU 1994a.

28. Hussey 1982; Townsend 1994.

29. EIU 1991.

30. EIU 1994b; Richter 1989.

31. EIU 1993; Jansen-Verbeke and Go 1995.

32. Sklair 1991, 1996.

33. Sklair 1991, 1994a; Fine and Leopold 1993; Glennie and Thrift 1992.

34. Sklair 1991; Bocock 1993; Tiger 1992.

35. Sklair 1991; Allcock 1993.

36. Savage et al. 1992.

37. Britton 1982, 1983, 1991; Brohman 1996.

38. Ibid.

39. Ioannides 1995; Brohman 1996.

40. La Croix and Wolff 1995.

41. Ibid.

42. Hussey 1982.

43. EIU 1991; Debbage 1992.

44. Ioannides 1995.

45. Ibid.

46. Mullins 1991, 1994.

47. Jacob 1994; Wright 1985.

48. Jansen-Verbeke and Go 1995.

49. EIU 1991, 1994b; Jansen-Verbeke and Go 1995.

50. EIU 1991, 1993, 1994a,b,c, 1995.

51. Elliott 1983; Harrison 1992b; Jenkins and Henry 1982.

52. EIU 1993; Jansen-Verbeke and Go 1995.

53. Harrison 1992b; McKean 1978; Wall 1996; Wood 1993.

54. Hitchcock et al. 1993; Wall 1996.

55. Walton 1993; see also Sinclair and Vokes 1993.

56. Walton 1993.

57. Murray 1991.

58. Cohen 1986; Crick 1994; Pruitt and LaFont 1995.

59. Norris and Wall 1994.

60. Wolf 1992.

61. Ibid.

62. Castells 1995.

63. EIU 1995.

64. Richter 1989, 1992.

65. Chon and Singh 1994; Parnwell 1993.

66. Smith and Eadington 1992; R. Smith 1992; Long and Wall 1996.

67. Crick 1989; Hall 1992b; Leheny 1995; Mackie 1992.

68. Norris and Wall 1994.

69. The mall, the merrier 1994, 332.

70. Emerson 1995; Judd 1995.

71. Mackie 1992; McCormack 1991; Rimmer 1992, 1994; Traisawasdichai 1995.

72. EIU 1991, 1994a,b,c, 1995; Norris and Wall 1994.

Susan S. Fainstein and Dennis R. Judd, "Cities as Places to Play"

1. See also Mullins 1994.

2. See Ashforth and Tunbridge 1990.

3. See Fainstein and Fainstein 1982.

4. Ashforth and Tunbridge 1990.

5. Chaucer, in his *Canterbury Tales*, long ago pointed to the tourist functions of the pilgrimage.

6. The enclave phenomenon has also been avoided in huge cities like London or New York, where there are interesting sites dispersed throughout the metropolis.

7. Giddens 1990.

8. Cf. Lash and Urry 1994.

9. Giddens would use the term *radical modernity*, while many other theorists would call the present period *postmodern*.

10. See Sorkin 1992.

11. There are, of course, exceptions. South Africa is featuring tours of major locations in the struggle against apartheid, prisons being prime attractions. Tourists who value authenticity seek out facilities that have not been transformed into fan-

tasy creations, and many travelers try to partake of the ordinary life of the places they visit.

12. See, esp., Zukin 1991.
13. Sassen 1991.
14. See Fainstein and Fainstein 1989.
15. Bluestone and Harrison 1982, 53.

References

Ackerman, J. 1995a. Crowds no problem on Freedom Trail. *Boston Globe,* May 21.

———. 1995b. 1996 expected to be strong year for tourism. *Boston Globe,* August 24.

———. 1995c. Waterfront World. *Boston Globe,* September 24.

———. 1996. Tourist, business travel up 1% in Mass. *Boston Globe,* April 5.

Acuña, C., and M. de la Garza. 1989. La dimensión territorial del proyecto Cancún, Estado de Quintana Roo. In D. Hiernaux, comp. *Teoría y praxis del espacio turístico.* Mexico City, Mexico: Universidad Autónoma Metropolitana Xochimilco.

Adler, J. 1989. Origins of sightseeing. *Annals of Tourism Research* 16: 7–29.

Aguilar, M., and A. Reid. 1994. Psicología social del turismo. *Ciudades* 23 (July–September): 19–23.

Alemán, M. 1983. *Quince lecciones de turismo.* Mexico City, Mexico: Diana.

Allcock, J. 1993. Tourism, consumption, development: A sociological realignment. Paper presented at the Seventh General Conference of the European Association of Development Research and Training Institutes, Berlin.

Anderer, C. 1995. North American gaming report 1995. *International Gaming and Wagering Business,* July (special issue).

Andersen, K. 1994. Las Vegas, U.S.A. *Time,* January 10, 42–51.

Appledome, P. 1993. Atlanta: The city without a slogan. *New York Times,* October 6, A18.

———. 1996a. Despite flawed form Atlanta claims a victory. *New York Times,* August 5, 1,4.

———. 1996b. So, you want to hold an Olympics. *New York Times,* August 4, 4.

Arendt, H. 1978. *The life of the mind.* New York: Harcourt Brace Jovanovich.

Ashworth, G. J., and J. E. Tunbridge. 1990. *The tourist-historic city*. London: Belhaven Press.

Augé, M. 1992. Los "no lugares," espacios del anonimato (una antropología de la sobremodernidad). *Gedisa Editorial*. Barcelona.

Avault, J. 1985. *Economic and fiscal aspects of historic preservation development in Boston*. Boston: Boston Redevelopment Authority.

Baade, R. A., and R. E. Dye. 1996. Professional sports and economic development. *Journal of Urban Affairs* 18 (1): 1-18.

Baedeker. 1995. *Israel*. New York: Macmillan.

Bagli, C. V. 1996. The people's Yankees? Yes, city can steal Steinbrenner's team. *New York Times*, April 29.

Barboza, D. 1995. Conspiracy museum draws visitors who consider the plot the thing. *New York Times*, May 28, 22.

Barnes, T. 1997. "Gaming" vs. "gambling": It's anybody's guess. *Pittsburgh Post-Gazette*, January 26, B1.

———. 1995. Study sees millions for region in casinos. *Pittsburgh Post-Gazette*, March 15, 1.

Barry, A. 1995. Reporting and visualising. In C. Jenks, ed., *Visual culture*. London: Sage.

Barthes, R. 1979. *The Eiffel Tower and other mythologies*. New York: Hill and Wang.

———. 1981. *Camera Lucida*. New York: Hill and Wang.

Baudrillard, J. 1981. *For a critique of the economy of the sign*. St. Louis: Telos.

———. 1984. The procession of simulacra. In B. Wallis, ed., *Art after modernism: Rethinking representation*. New York: Museum of Contemporary Art.

Bauman, Z. 1993. *Postmodern ethics*. Oxford: Blackwell.

Beauregard, R. A. 1993. *Voices of decline: The postwar fate of U.S. cities*. New York: Blackwell.

Ben-Arieh, Y. 1979. *The rediscovery of the Holy Land in the nineteenth century*. Jerusalem: Magnes Press.

Benedick, R. 1990. Growth may force Disney to deal with the real world. *Orlando Sentinel*, January 22.

Berman, M. 1983. *All that is solid melts into air*. London: Verso.

Bermingham, A. 1994. Redesigning nature: John Constable and the landscape of enclosure. In R. Friedland and D. Boden, eds., *Nowhere*. Berkeley: University of California Press.

Berns, D. 1996. A place to play. *Las Vegas Review-Journal and Las Vegas Sun*, February 18, 1A.

Beyard, M. D. 1993. *Dollars and cents of shopping centers: 1993*. Washington, D.C.: Urban Land Institute.

Bhabha, R., ed. 1990. *Nation and narration*. London: Routledge.

Bianchini, F. 1993. *Remaking European cities: The role of cultural policies*. Manchester: Manchester University Press.

Bianchini, F., and M. Parkinson, eds., 1993. *Cultural policy and urban regeneration*. Manchester: Manchester University Press.

Blažek, J. 1994. Changing local finances in the Czech Republic—half way over? *GeoJournal* 32: 3, 261–67.

Blažek, J., M. Hampl, and L. Sýkora. 1994. Administrative system and development of Prague. In M. Barlow, P. Dostál, and M. Hampl, eds., *Development and administration of Prague*. Amsterdam: Institute for Social Geography, University of Amsterdam.

Blumfield, M. 1989. Orange County okays road deal with Disney. *Orlando Sentinel*, July 24.

Bocock, R. 1993. *Consumption*. London: Routledge.

Bohlen, C. 1996. Overrun by tourists, "David" puts his foot down. *New York Times*, May 27.

Boissevain, J. Forthcoming. "But we live here!": Perspectives on cultural tourism in Malta. In L. Briguglio et al., eds., *Sustainable tourism*. London: Cassell.

Book of Lists. 1996. Las Vegas: Las Vegas Business Press.

Boorstin, D. J. 1992. *The image: A guide to pseudo events in America*. New York: Vintage.

Boston National Historic Park. 1994. *The Broadside* (Autumn). Boston: Boston National Historic Park.

Boston National Historic Sites Commission. 1960. *Final report of the Boston National Historic Sites Commission to the Congress of the United States*. Washington, D.C.: U.S. Department of the Interior.

Boston Redevelopment Authority. 1964. *Downtown waterfront: Faneuil Hall urban renewal plan*. Boston: Boston Redevelopment Authority.

———. 1990. *Boston's hotel and tourism market*. Boston: Boston Redevelopment Authority.

———. 1992. *The hotel market in Boston and ten other cities*. Boston: Boston Redevelopment Authority.

———. 1993. *Boston's hotel market*. Boston: Boston Redevelopment Authority.

———. 1996. Unpublished employment data. Boston: Boston Redevelopment Authority.

Boston Urban Study Group. 1984. *Who rules Boston?* Boston: Institute for Democratic Socialism.

Bottoms, A., and P. Wiles. 1995. Crime and insecurity in the city. Unpublished paper. Sheffield, U.K.: University of Sheffield.

Bourdieu, P. 1972. *Outline of a theory of practice*. Trans. R. Nice. Cambridge: Cambridge University Press.

————. 1984. *Distinction: A social critique of the judgement of taste.* Cambridge: Cambridge University Press.

Bowman, G. 1991. Christian ideology and the image of a Holy Land: The place of Jerusalem pilgrimage in the various Christianities. In J. Eade and M. J. Sallnow, eds., *Contesting the sacred: The anthropology of Christian pilgrimage.* London: Routledge.

Boyer, M. C. 1992. Cities for sale: Merchandising history at South Street Seaport. In Michael Sorkin, ed., *Variations on a theme park: The new American city and the end of public space.* New York: Hill and Wang.

Boyle, R. 1990. Regeneration in Glasgow: Stability, collaboration, and inequity. In D. Judd and M. Parkinson, eds., *Leadership and urban regeneration: Cities in North America and Europe.* Newbury Park, Calif.: Sage.

Bramham, P., I. Henry, H. Mommass, and H. van der Poel, eds. 1989. *Leisure and urban processes: Critical studies of leisure policy in West European cities.* London: Routledge.

Bramwell, B., and L. Rawding. 1994. Tourism marketing organizations in industrial cities: Organizations, objectives and urban governance. *Tourism Management* 15(6): 425–34.

Braun, R. E. 1995. Exploring the urban entertainment center universe. *Urban Land,* Supplement 54(8) (August): 11-17.

Braykovich, M., and M. Henterly. 1995. Indiana gambling: Jackpot or joker? Riverboat casinos bet on favoritism, influence. *Cincinnati Enquirer,* June 25, A1.

Brendon, P. 1991. *Thomas Cook: 150 years of popular tourism.* London: Secker and Warburg.

Brewers important but business owners mad survey says. 1995. *Wisconsin Independent Businesses,* May 10.

Bringas, N., and J. Carrillo, eds. 1989. *Grupos de visitantes y actividades turísticas en Tijuana.* Tijuana: Cuadernos, COLEFF.

Britton, S. 1982. The political economy of tourism. *Third World Annals of Tourism Research* 9: 331–58.

————. 1983. Tourism and underdevelopment in Fiji. *Development Studies Centre Monograph, No. 31.* Canberra: Development Studies Centre, Australian National University.

————. 1991. Tourism, capital, and place: Towards a critical geography of tourism. *Environment and Planning C: Society and Space* 9: 451–78.

Brohman, J. 1996. New directions in tourism. *Third World Development Annals of Tourism Research* 23: 48–70.

Brown, J. 1987. Boston. In R. Levitt, ed., *Cities reborn.* Washington, D.C.: Urban Land Institute.

Browning, M. 1995. New Orleans reels as casino folds. *Pittsburgh Post-Gazette,* December 10.

Bryson, N. 1983. *Vision and painting*. London: Macmillan.

Burbank, J. 1994. Nevada ranks second in pay gains. *Las Vegas Review-Journal*, January 4, 7D.

Burd, G. 1977. The selling of the Sunbelt. In D. C. Perry and A. J. Watkins, eds., *The rise of the Sunbelt cities*. Beverly Hills: Sage.

Burtenshaw, D., M. Bateman, and G. J. Ashworth. 1981. *The city in West Europe*. Chichester: John Wiley and Sons.

Buzard, J. 1993. *The beaten track*. Oxford: Clarendon.

Campbell, R. 1985. Europe on the Charles. *Boston Globe Magazine*, September 10.

Campbell, R., and P. Vanderwarker. 1992. *Cityscapes of Boston*. Boston: Houghton Mifflin.

Carter, E., J. Donald, and J. Squires, eds. 1993. *Space and place*. London: Lawrence and Wishart.

Carter, F. 1991. Czechoslovakia. In D. R. Hall, ed., *Tourism and economic development in Eastern Europe and the Soviet Union*. London: Belhaven Press.

Castells, M. 1995. Interview with A. Cuthbert. *Polis* 3: 22–29.

Castells, M., ed. 1985. *High technology, space, and society*. Beverly Hills: Sage.

Cazes, G. 1989a. *Le tourisme international (mirage ou stratégie d'avenir)*. Paris: Hatier.

———. 1989b. *Les nouvelles colonies de vacances? (le tourisme international à la conquête du Tiers-Monde)*, vol. 1. Paris: L'Harmattan.

———. 1992. Le tourisme dans le monde. In A. Bailly et al., eds., *Encyclopédie de la géographie*. Paris: Economica.

———. 1994. *Fondements pour une géographie du tourisme et des loisirs*. Paris: Bréal

Central Bureau of Statistics, Israel. 1995. *Tourism 1994*. Jerusalem: Central Bureau of Statistics.

Central Bureau of Statistics and Ministry of Tourism, Israel. 1996. *Tourism and Hotel Services Statistics Quarterly* 24(1). Jerusalem: Central Bureau of Statistics.

Chalmers, D. 1976. *Neither socialism nor monopoly*. Philadelphia: Lippincott.

Chen, X. 1995. Chicago as a global city. *Chicago Office* 5: 15–20.

Chon, K., and A. Singh. 1994. Environmental challenges and influences on tourism: The case of Thailand's tourism industry. In C. P. Cooper and A. Lockwood, eds., *Progress in tourism, recreation, and hospitality management*. Chichester: John Wiley.

Choshen, M., and N. Shahar. 1996. *Statistical yearbook of Jerusalem 1994/5*. Jerusalem: Jerusalem Institute for Israel Studies.

Christiansen, M. 1996. The United States 95 gross annual wager. *International Gaming and Wagering Business* (August 1): 58. New York: GEM Communications, Inc.

City of Orlando Planning Department. 1989. Traffic count, March 20, 1989. Staff report.

Clements, J. 1996. At 20, marketplace showing its age. *Banker and Tradesman,* August 5.

Clines, F. X. 1994. The Pequots. *New York Times Magazine,* February 27, 51.

Cohen, E. 1992. Pilgrimage and tourism: Convergence and divergence. In S. A. Morinis, ed., *Sacred journeys: The anthropology of pilgrimage.* Westport: Greenwood Press.

———. 1995. Touristic craft ribbon development. *Thailand Tourism Management* 16(3): 225–35.

Cohen, M. 1971. *The holy places in Eretz-Israel* (in Hebrew). Jerusalem: Israeli Ministry of Religious Affairs.

Cohen, M., D. Darom, and C. Shulman, eds. 1988. *Jewish Israel: A guide for Jews to the land of their fathers.* Jerusalem: Nima.

Cohen, R. B. 1981. The new international division of labor, multinational corporations and urban hierarchy. In M. Dear and A. J. Scott, eds., *Urbanization and urban planning in capitalist society.* London: Metheun.

Collier, L. 1995. Paychecks aren't growing as fast as the work force. *Las Vegas Business Press,* October 9, 1.

———. 1996. How big will the next boom be? *Las Vegas Business Press,* January 15, 8.

Collins, C. 1993. Reservation roulette: Indian gaming. Documentary. Las Vegas: KLVX-TV.

Columbia University. 1995. *Lower Manhattan: Economic development at the core.* New York: Department of Urban Planning, Columbia University.

Conlin, J. 1993. Time to rally: We must resist the proposed cut in business meal deductions. *Successful Meetings,* April.

Convention centers spark civic wars. 1986. *U.S. News and World Report,* February 1, 7.

Cosco, J. 1986. Miami advice. *Public Relations Journal,* May, 17–22.

Crary, J. 1990. *Techniques of the observer.* Cambridge: MIT Press.

Crawshaw, C., and J. Urry. 1997. Tourism and the photographic eye. In C. Rojek and J. Urry, eds., *Touring cultures.* London: Routledge.

Crenson, M. A. 1982. Urban bureaucracy in urban politics: Notes toward a developmental theory. In J. D. Greenstone, ed., *Public values and private power in American politics,* 209–45. Chicago: University of Chicago Press.

Crick, M. 1989. Representations of international tourism in the social sciences: Sun, sex, sights, savings, and servility. *Annual Review of Anthropology* 18: 307–44.

———. 1994. *Resplendent sites, discordant voices.* Chur, Switzerland: Harwood Academic.

Cronkite, W. 1994. Legal gambling, the dice are loaded. Documentary, Cronkite Report Series. The Discovery Network.

Davies, L. 1987. If you've got it, flaunt it: Making the most of city tourism. *Employment Gazette*, April, 167–71.

Davis, M. 1990. *City of quartz*. New York: Vintage.

———. 1992. Fortress Los Angeles: The militarization of urban space. In M. Sorkin, ed., *Variations on a theme park: The new American city and the end of space*. New York: Hill and Wang.

———. 1994. Local 226 vs. MGM Grand: Armageddon at the Emerald City. *The Nation* 252 (July 11): 46.

———. 1995. House of cards. *Sierra* 80 (November/December): 36–41.

Dear, M., and A. J. Scott, eds. 1981. *Urbanization and urban planning in capitalist society*. London: Metheun.

Debbage, K. 1992. Tourism oligopoly is at work. *Annals of Tourism Research* 19: 355–59.

DeBoer, L., C. V. Oster, B. Rubin, and C. K. Zorn. 1996. The urban economic development impacts of riverboat gaming. Paper presented at the annual meeting of the Urban Affairs Association, New York, March.

Debord, G. 1994. *The society of the spectacle*. New York: Zone.

De Kadt, E. C. 1979. *Tourisme: Passeport pour le développement? (Regards sur les effets culturels et sociaux du tourisme dans les pays en développement)*. The World Bank and UNESCO. Paris: Economica.

Deller, S. C., and S. Chen. 1994. The impact of Native American gaming on rural areas. Paper presented at the annual meeting of the American Agricultural Economics Association, San Diego, August.

de Ventós, Rupert X. 1976. *Ensayos sobre el desorden*. Barcelona: Kairós.

Dial, B. 1990. Interviewed by R. Foglesong.

Disney maps $100 plan. 1965. *Orlando Sentinel-Star*, November 15.

Dixon, C. 1991. *Southeast Asia in the world economy*. Cambridge: Cambridge University Press.

Dixon, D., and G. Clancy. 1995. *The Freedom Trail*. Boston: Boston National Historical Park.

Doolittle, L. 1994. Pow wow crowd sans crime. *Central Florida Business*, May 30–June 5.

Dostál, P., and M. Hampl. 1994. Changing economic base of Prague: Towards new organizational dominance. In M. Barlowk, P. Dostál, and M. Hampl, eds., *Development and administration of Prague*. Amsterdam: Institute for Social Geography, University of Amsterdam.

Douglas, M. 1989. The future of cities on the Pacific Rim. In M. P. Smith, ed., *Pacific Rim cities in the world economy: Comparative urban and community research*, vol. 2. New Brunswick: Transaction.

————. 1991. Planning for environmental sustainability in the extended Jakarta metropolitan region. In N. Ginsburg, B. Koppel, and T. G. McGee, eds., *The extended metropolis: Settlement transition in Asia*. Honolulu: University of Hawaii Press.

Douthat, S. 1993. Nationwide shift toward gaming draws out problem gamblers. *Las Vegas Review-Journal*, February 1, 3B.

Dreier, P. 1983a. In Boston, a union grows up. *In These Times*, January 26.

————. 1983b. The vault comes out of the darkness. *Boston Business Journal*, October 10.

————. 1989. *Economic growth and economic justice: Populist housing and jobs policies in Boston*. In G. D. Squires, ed., *Unequal partnerships: The political economy of urban redevelopment in post war America*. New Brunswick: Rutgers University Press.

————. 1993. Ray Flynn's legacy: American cities and the progressive agenda. *National Civic Review* (Fall): 380–403.

————. 1996. Urban politics and progressive housing policy: Ray Flynn and Boston's neighborhood agenda. In W. D. Keating, N. Krumholz, and P. Star, eds., *Urban neighborhoods*. Lawrence: University Press of Kansas.

Dreier, P., and B. Ehrlich. 1991. Downtown development and urban reform: The politics of Boston's linkage policy. *Urban Affairs Quarterly* 26(3): 354–75.

Drott, J. 1986. Big gamble in Atlantic City. Documentary produced and directed by J. Drott. CBS News.

Drummond, T. 1995. Not in Kansas anymore. *Time*, September 25, 54–55.

Dunlap, D. W. 1992. Long delay likely in rebuilding plan for Times Square. *New York Times*, August 3.

Dye, T. 1992. Temporary workers are helping Las Vegas. *Las Vegas Review-Journal*, April 5, 13E.

Eadington, W. R. 1995. The emergence of casino gaming as a major factor in tourism markets: Policy issues and considerations. In R. Butler and D. Pearce, eds., *Change in tourism: People, places, processes*. London: Routledge.

Eco, U. 1986. *Travels in hyperreality*. New York: Harcourt Brace.

Economic Research Associates. 1966. Experimental prototype city of tomorrow: Outline of presentation to the Department of Housing and Urban Development, August 15. Los Angeles: Disney Company Archives.

Edensor, T. 1996. Touring the Taj. Ph.D. diss., Department of Sociology, Lancaster University, Lancaster, U.K.

Edsall, T. B., and M. D. Edsall. 1991. *Chain reaction: The impact of race, rights, and taxes on American politics*. New York: W. W. Norton.

Edwards, J. G. 1994. Nevadans face IRS audits more often than other Americans. *Las Vegas Review-Journal*, July 26, 5D.

————. 1996a. Electronics show draws 80,000. *Las Vegas Review-Journal*, January 4, 9D.

———. 1996b. 93,000 attend CES. *Las Vegas Review-Journal*, January 9, 6D.

Ehrlich, B. 1987. The politics of economic development planning: Boston in the 1980s. Master's thesis, Massachusetts Institute of Technology.

EIU (Economist Intelligence Unit). 1991. *Indonesia international tourism reports* 3: 23–40. London: Economist Intelligence Unit.

———. 1993. *Indochina-Vietnam, Cambodia and Laos International Tourism Reports* 2: 59–82. London: Economist Intelligence Unit.

———. 1994a. *Malaysia International Tourism Reports* 2: 41–61. London: Economist Intelligence Unit.

———. 1994b. *Philippines International Tourism Reports* 3: 47–68. London: Economist Intelligence Unit.

———. 1994c. *Singapore International Tourism Reports* 1: 65–86. London: Economist Intelligence Unit.

———. 1995. *Thailand International Tourism Reports* 3: 67–81. London: Economist Intelligence Unit.

Eliade, M. 1969. *Images and symbols*. New York: Sheed and Ward.

Elliott, J. 1983. Politics, power, and tourism in Thailand. *Annals of Tourism Research* 10: 377–93.

Elliott, S. 1994. HFS point man courts gambling-shy Pittsburgers. *Pittsburgh Business Times* 14 (November 21–27): 9.

Emerson, T. 1995. Gambling. Fool's gold. *Bulletin-Newsweek* 10 (October).

Eng, K. K. 1994. Bugis Street in Singapore: Development, conservation, and the reinvention of cultural landscape. In M. Askew, and W. Logan, eds., *Cultural identity and urban change in Southeast Asia*. Geelong, Australia: Deakin University Press.

Enloe, C. 1990. *Bananas, beaches, and bases*. Berkeley: University of California Press.

The entertainment economy. 1994. *Business Week*, March 14, 58–66.

EPAC (Economic and Social Commission for Asia and the Pacific). 1993. *State of urbanization in Asia and the Pacific*. New York: United Nations.

Euchner, C. C. 1993. *Playing the field: Why sports teams move and cities fight to keep them*. Baltimore: Johns Hopkins University Press.

Fader, S. 1995. Universal City Walk. *Urban Land* 54, Suppl. (August 1).

Fainstein, N. I., and S. S. Fainstein. 1982. Restoration and struggle: Urban policy and social forces. In N. I. Fainstein and S. S. Fainstein, eds., *Urban policy under capitalism*. Beverly Hills: Sage.

Fainstein, S. S. 1994. *The city builders: Property, politics, and planning in London and New York*. Cambridge, Mass.: Blackwell.

Fainstein, S. S., and N. I. Fainstein. 1989. Technology, the new international division of labor, and location: Continuities and disjunctures. In R. A. Beauregard, ed., *Economic restructuring and political response*. Newbury Park: Sage.

Fainstein, S. S., N. I. Fainstein, and P. J. Armistead. 1986. San Francisco: Urban transformation and the local state. In S. S. Fainstein et al., *Restructuring the city*. New York: Longman.

Fainstein, S. S., N. I. Fainstein, R. C. Hill, D. Judd, and M. P. Smith. 1986. *Restructuring the city*. Rev. ed. New York: Longman.

Fairclough, G. 1995. Doing the dirty work: Asia's brothels thrive on migrant labour. *Far Eastern Economic Review,* December 14, 27–28.

Fauci, C. 1995–96. Praha si zvyká na luxus (Prague goes upscale). *Prague Tribune,* no. 15, December 27–28.

Faust, F. 1994. It wasn't in the cards. *St. Louis Post-Dispatch,* April 10, 1E–5E.

Feagin, J. R., and R. E. Parker. 1990. *Building American cities*. Englewood Cliffs, N.J.: Prentice-Hall

Feifer, M. 1985. *Going places*. London: Macmillan.

Fenich, G. 1992a. Convention center development: Pros, cons and unanswered questions. *International Journal of Hospitality Management* 11(3): 183–96.

———. 1992b. The dollars and sense of convention centers. Ph.D. diss., Rutgers University.

Fernandez, F. 1989. The emerging suburban service economy. *Urban Affairs Quarterly* 24 (June): 537–55.

Fine, B., and E. Leopold. 1993. *The world of consumption*. London: Routledge.

Fiore, F. 1990. Disney's Florida cities warn of a greedy growth monster. *Los Angeles Times,* February 20.

The first annual world's best awards. 1996. *Travel and Leisure,* October.

Fischer, G. 1994. Espace de travail et appropiation. In M. Coster and F. Pichault, eds., *Traité de sociologie du travail*. Brussels: De Boeck.

Fischer, H. 1996a. *Muslim pilgrimages visitors handbook*. Jerusalem: Ministry of Tourism.

———. 1996b. *Pilgrims and Christian tourists: Promotion handbook*. Jerusalem: Ministry of Tourism.

Flint, A. 1997. The skyline's the limit in waterfront debate. *Boston Globe,* November 26.

Fodor's Exploring Israel. 1996. New York: Fodor's Travel Publications.

Fodor's Czechoslovakia. 1992. New York: Fodor's Travel Publications.

Foglesong, R. 1991. Baiting the mousetrap. *Orlando Magazine,* November, 36.

———. 1994. When Disney comes to town. *Washington Post Magazine,* May 15, 15–16.

Forbes, D. 1996. *Asian metropolis: Urbanisation and the Southeast Asian city*. Melbourne: Oxford University Press.

Foucault, M. 1970. *The order of things*. London: Tavistock.

———. 1977. *Discipline and punish*. London: Allen Lane.

Fowler, J. 1968. Interviewed by R. Hubler. Walt Disney Company Archives.

————. 1994. Interviewed by J. Horan. Walt Disney Company Archives.

Frieden, B. J., and L. B. Sagalyn. 1990. *Downtown, Inc.: How America builds cities*. Cambridge: MIT Press.

Friedman, D. 1996. The new civil war. *Inc.: The State of Small Business*, 18.

Frommer's, Israel: From $45 a day. 1996. New York: Macmillan.

Frommer, A. 1988. Historic preservation and tourism. *Preservation Forum* 2.

Futur Antérieur. 1995. *La ville-monde aujourd'hui: Entre virtualité et ancrage* (special issue), vols. 30–32. T. Pillon and A. Querrien, eds. Paris: L'Harmattan.

Gallant, J. 1992. Troubled Las Vegas teen-agers mired in rainbow of problems. *Las Vegas Review-Journal*, February 16, 4B.

Gans, H. 1962. *The urban villagers*. New York: Free Press.

————. 1993. Urban vitality and the fallacy of physical determinism. In H. Gans, ed., *People, plans, and policies*, 33–43. New York: Columbia University Press.

Garcia, L. 1995. The globalization of telecommunications and information. In W. J. Drake, ed., *The new information infrastructure: Strategies for U.S. policy*. New York: Twentieth Century Fund Press.

Garcia, S. 1994. Big events and urban politics: Barcelona and the Olympic games. Paper presented at the World Congress of Sociology, Bielefeld, Germany, July.

García de Fuentes, A. 1979. *Cancún: Turismo y subdesarrollo regional*. Mexico City: Universidad Nacional Autónoma de México.

Gay-Para, G. 1985. *La pratique du tourisme*. Paris: Economica.

Getz, D. 1993. Planning for tourism business districts. *Annals of Tourism Research* 20: 583–600.

Giddens, A. 1990. *The consequences of modernity*. Stanford: Stanford University Press.

Gilbert, D. C. 1989. Tourism marketing: Its emergence and establishment. In C. P. Cooper, ed., *Progress in tourism, recreation and hospitality management*, vol. 1. Chichester: John Wiley.

Glaab, C. N. 1967. Historical perspectives on urban development schemes. In L. Schnore, ed. *Social science and the city*. New York: Praeger.

Gladstone, D. 1998. Tourism urbanization in the United States. *Urban Affairs Review*, 34: 3–27.

Glennie, P., and N. Thrift. 1992. Modernity, urbanism, and modern consumption. *Society and Space* 10: 423–43.

Glickman, N., M. Lahr, and E. Wyly. 1996. *The state of the nation's cities*. New Brunswick: Center for Urban Policy Research, Rutgers University.

Goldberger, P. 1995. An old jewel of 42nd Street reopens, seeking to dazzle families. *New York Times*, December 11.

Goodman, R. 1994. *Legalized gambling as a strategy for economic development*. Northampton, Mass.: United States Gambling Study.

————. 1995. *The luck business*. New York: Free Press.

Goodrich, C. 1960. *Government promotion of American canals and railroads, 1800–1890*. New York: Columbia University Press.

Graburn, H. H., and R. S. Moore. 1994. Anthropological research in tourism. In J. R. Ritchie and C. R. Goeldner, eds., *Travel, tourism, and hospitality research: A handbook for managers and researchers*. 2d ed. New York: John Wiley and Sons.

Graham, S. and S. Marvin. 1996. *Telecommunications and the city: Electronic spaces, urban places*. London: Routledge.

Greater Boston Convention and Visitors Bureau. 1995. *1996 marketing plan*. City of Boston.

————. 1997. *1997 fact sheet*. Web site.

Green, N. 1990. *The spectacle of nature*. Manchester: Manchester University Press.

Greene, G. 1990. The man who stole the Eiffel Tower. In *The last word, and other stories*. London: Penguin.

Gregory, D. 1994. *Geographical imaginations*. Cambridge, Mass.: Blackwell.

Grimes, W. 1995. America realizes the arts attract tourists. *New York Times,* December 5, B1, B4.

Grinols, E. L. 1994. Bluff or winning hand: Riverboat gambling and regional employment and unemployment. *Illinois Business Review* 51: 8–11.

————. 1995. Gambling as economic policy: Enumerating why losses exceed gains. *Illinois Business Review* 52: 6–12.

Guskind, R. 1987. Bringing Madison Avenue to Main Street. *Planning* 53.

Guskind, R., and N. R. Peirce. 1988. Faltering festivals. *National Journal* 38 (September 17): 2301–11.

Hall, C. M. 1992a. *Hallmark tourist events: Impacts, management, and planning*. London: Belhaven Press.

————. 1992b. Sex tourism in Southeast Asia. In D. Harrison, ed., *Tourism and the less developed countries*. London: Belhaven Press.

————. 1994. *Tourism and politics: Policy, power and place*. Chichester: Wiley.

Hall, P. 1988. *Cities of tomorrow*. Oxford: Basil Blackwell.

Hamer, T. P. 1995. *Economic impact of the New Jersey casino industry*. Glassboro, N.J.: Management Institute, Rowan College,.

Hamilton, A. 1994. Dizzy development in Hua Hin: The effects of tourism on a Thai seaside town. In M. Askew, and W. Logan, eds., *Cultural identity and urban change in Southeast Asia,* 149–66. Geelong, Australia: Deakin University Press.

Hammack, D. C. 1991. Developing for commercial culture. In W. R. Taylor, ed., *Inventing Times Square*. Baltimore: Johns Hopkins University Press.

Hannigan, J. A. 1995. The postmodern city: A new urbanization? *Current Sociology* 43(1): 155–214.

Harrah's Casinos. 1994. *The Harrah's survey of U.S. casino entertainment*. Memphis: The Promus Companies.

Harrah's Entertainment, Inc. 1996. *Harrah's survey of casino entertainment*. Memphis, Tennessee: Harrah's Entertainment, Inc.

Harriman, M. S. 1992. High wire act. *Architecture* 81 (December).

Harris, T. R. 1994. Expansion of the gaming industry. Paper presented at the annual meeting of the American Agricultural Economics Association, San Diego, August.

Harrison, D. 1992a. International tourism and the less developed countries: The background. In D. Harrison, ed., *Tourism and the less developed countries*. London: Belhaven Press.

———. 1992b. Tourism to less developed countries: The social consequences. In D. Harrison, ed., *Tourism and the less developed countries*. London: Belhaven Press.

Harvey, D. 1987. *The urban experience*. Baltimore: Johns Hopkins University Press.

———. 1990. *The condition of postmodernity*. Oxford: Blackwell.

Havas, A. 1993. Grand Slam Canyon a hit with patrons, analysts. *Las Vegas Business Press*, August 30, 1.

Heidegger, M. 1977. *The question concerning technology and other essays*. New York: Harper Torchbooks.

Hiernaux, D. 1983. El papel de FONATUR en el desarrollo turístico de México. FONATUR internal report, Mexico, 71 pp. Mimeographed.

———. 1984. Inversiones en infrastructura y demanda turística en Cancún. FONATUR internal report, Mexico, 15 pp. Mimeographed.

———. 1989a. El espacio reticular del turismo. In *Geografía y desarrollo* 3, 31–39.

———. 1989b. Mitos y realidades del milagro turístico: Cancún. In D. Hiernaux, ed., *Teoría y praxis del espacio turístico*. Mexico: Universidad Autónoma Metropolitana Xochimilco.

———. 1994. En busca del Edén: Turismo y territorio en las sociedades modernas. *Ciudades* 23 (July–September): 24–30.

Hiernaux, D., and M. R. Woog. 1990. *Tourism and the absorption of labor force in Mexico*. Commission for the Study of International Migration and Cooperative Economic Development, paper no. 34. Washington, D.C.: United States Senate.

Hill, R. C. 1986. Crisis in Motor City: The politics of economic development in Detroit. In S. S. Fainstein, N. I. Fainstein, R. C. Hill, D. R. Judd, and M. P. Smith, *Restructuring the city: The political economy of urban redevelopment*. Rev. ed. New York: Longman.

Hillhouse, A. M. 1936. *Municipal bonds: A century of experience*. Englewood Cliffs, N.J.: Prentice-Hall.

Hilsenrath, J. E. 1996. The cost of luxury could blow sky-high. *New York Times*, April 7.

Hine, T. 1995. Entertaining the notion of new plans for the riverfront. *Philadelphia Inquirer*, May 5.

Hirshey, G. 1994. Gambling nation. *New York Times Magazine*, July 17, 34–44.

Historic Boston Inc. 1992. *Save our city.* Boston: Historic Boston Incorporated.

Hitchcock, M., V. King, and M. Parnell, eds. 1993. *Tourism in Southeast Asia.* London: Routledge.

Hoade, E. 1971. *Guide to the Holy Land.* Jerusalem: Franciscan Printing Press.

Hoffman, L. M. 1994. After the fall: Crisis and renewal in urban planning in the Czech Republic. *International Journal of Urban and Regional Research* 18: 691–702.

Holcomb, B. 1990. *Purveying places: Past and present.* Working paper no. 17. Piscataway, N.J.: Center for Urban Policy Research.

———. 1993. Revisioning place: De- and re-constructing the image of the industrial city. In G. Kearns and C. Philo, eds., *Selling places: The city as cultural capital, past and present*. New York: Pergamon Press.

Holcomb, B., and M. Luongo. 1996. Gay tourism in the U.S.A. *Annals of Tourism Research* 23(3): 711–13.

Holub, P. 1994. Nestrilejte na autokary. *RESPEKT* 32: 8–14.

Home, sweet home, gets more costly. 1995. *Las Vegas Review-Journal and Las Vegas Sun*, November 19.

Hoover, G., et al., eds. 1993. *Hoover's handbook of American business, 1994.* Austin, Tex.: Hoover's Inc.

Hornblower, M. 1996. No dice: The backlash against gambling. *Time*, April 1, 29–33.

Houses most affordable in the Midwest. 1995. *Las Vegas Review-Journal*, June 28.

Howden, S. 1990. Interviewed by R. Foglesong.

Hrůza, J. 1994. Historical development of Prague. In M. Barlow, P. Dostál, and M. Hampl, eds., *Development and administration of Prague*. Amsterdam: Institute for Social Geography, University of Amsterdam.

Hudnut, W. H. III. 1995. *The Hudnut years in Indianapolis, 1976–1992.* Bloomington: Indiana University Press.

Hula, R. C. The two Baltimores. In D. Judd and M. Parkinson, eds., *Leadership and urban regeneration: Cities in North America and Europe*. Newbury Park, Calif.: Sage.

Hummon, D. 1988. Tourist worlds: Tourist advertising, ritual, and American culture. *Sociology Quarterly* 29 (Summer): 179–202.

Humphreys, R. 1991. *Czechoslovakia: The rough guide.* London: Harrap Columbus.

Hunter, D. E., and E. E. Bleinberger. 1995. Gaming in America. *Economic Development Commentary* 19: 4–11.

Hussey, A. 1982. Tourist destination areas in Bali. *Contemporary Southeast Asia* 3 (March): 374–85.

Hynes, M. 1995. Extended strip a mixed blessing. *Las Vegas Review-Journal and Las Vegas Sun*, July 16, 10a.

Ihde, D. 1976. *Listening and voice*. Athens, Ohio: Ohio University Press.

Ioannides, D. 1995. Strengthening the ties between tourism and economic geography: A theoretical agenda. *Professional Geographer* 47(1): 49–60.

Irigaray, L. 1978. Interview with Luce Irigaray. In M. F. Hans and G. Lapouge, eds., *Les femmes, la pornographie et l'érotisme*. Paris: Minuit.

Israel: A travel survival kit. 1992. Hawthorn, Australia: Lonely Planet Publications.

Jakle, J. A. 1985 *The tourist: Travel in twentieth-century North America*. Lincoln: University of Nebraska Press.

Jacob, R. 1994. The big rise: Middle classes explode around the globe bringing new markets and prosperity. *Fortune*, May 30, 40–46.

Jacobs, J. 1969. *The economy of cities*. New York: Random House.

Jansen-Verbeke, M. 1985. Inner city leisure resources. *Leisure Studies* 4(2): 141–57.

———. 1990. Leisure + shopping = tourism product mix. In G. Ashworth and B. Goodall, eds., *Marketing tourism places*. London: Routledge.

Jansen-Verbeke, M., and F. Go. 1995. Tourist development in Vietnam. *Tourism Management* 16(4): 315–25.

Jay, M. 1986. In the empire of the gaze: Foucault and the denigration of vision in twentieth-century French thought. In D. Hoy, ed., *Foucault: A critical reader*. Oxford: Blackwell.

———. 1992. Scopic regimes of modernity. In S. Lash and J. Friedman, eds., *Modernity and identity*. Oxford: Blackwell.

———. 1993. *Downcast eyes*. Berkeley: University of California Press.

Jefferson, A. 1990. Marketing in national tourist offices. In C. P. Cooper, ed., *Progress in tourism, recreation and hospitality management*. Chichester: John Wiley.

Jenkins, C., and B. Henry. 1982. Government involvement in tourism in developing countries. *Annals of Tourism Research* 9: 499–521.

Jenks, C., ed. 1995. *Visual culture*. London: Routledge.

Jiménez, A., ed. 1992. *Turismo, estructura y desarrollo*. Mexico City: McGraw Hill.

John, M. 1995. Newcastle: Britain's good time town. *Times of Malta*, November 16, 42.

Johnson, A. T. 1985. The sports franchise relocation issue and public policy responses. In A. T. Johnson and J. H. Frey, eds., *Government and sport: The public policy issues*. Totowa, N.J.: Rowman and Allanheld.

———. 1986. Economic and policy implications of hosting sports franchises:

Some lessons from Baltimore. *Urban Affairs Quarterly* 21(3) March: 411–433.

———. 1993. *Minor league baseball and local economic development*. Urbana: University of Illinois Press.

Johnson, D. 1995. More casinos, more players who lose it all. *New York Times*, September 25, A1.

Johnson, K. 1996. With cash rolling in, Atlantic City raises stakes. *New York Times*, June 24, A1, B5.

Jones, E., L. Frost, and C. While. 1993. *Coming full circle: An economic history of the Pacific Rim*. Boulder: Westview Press.

Jones, H. M. 1946. The colonial impulse: An analysis of the promotion literature of colonization. *Proceedings of the American Philosophical Society* 90: 131–61.

Judd, D. 1995. Promoting tourism in U.S. cities. *Tourism Management* 16(3): 175–87.

Judd, D., and M. Parkinson. 1990. Leadership and urban regeneration: Cities in North America and Europe. *Urban Affairs Annual Reviews* 37. Newbury Park, Calif.: Sage.

Judd, D., and T. Swanstrom. 1998. *City politics: Private power and public policy*. New York: Longman.

Jules-Rosette, B. 1994. Black Paris: Touristic simulations. *Annals of Tourism Research* 21: 679–700.

Kahn, R. 1988. Make or break time. *Boston Sunday Herald*, November 20.

———. 1989. The heat's on. *Boston Sunday Herald*, December 10.

Katz, D. 1996. Atlanta brave. *Sports Illustrated*, January 8.

Keating, D., N. Krumholz, and P. Star, eds. 1996. *Urban neighborhoods: Growth, decline and revitalization*. Lawrence: University Press of Kansas.

Keith, M., and S. Pile. 1993. *Place and the politics of identity*. London: Routledge.

Kennedy, L. W. 1992. *Planning the city upon a hill*. Amherst: University of Massachusetts Press.

Kennedy, S. G. 1995. Disney and developer are chosen to build 42nd Street hotel complex. *New York Times*, May 12.

Kidd, B. 1995. Toronto's SkyDome: The world's greatest entertainment center. In J. Bale and O. Moen, eds., *The stadium and the city*. Keele, U.K.: Keele University Press.

Kilborn, P. T. 1996a. An Illinois city, once down and out, finds rebirth in riverboat gambling. *New York Times*, March 9, 6.

———. 1996b. Portrait from new era of nation's gambling. *New York Times*, February 28, A10.

King, J. 1989. Two sites' landmark status vetoed. *Boston Globe*, February 8.

King, M. 1981. *Chain of change*. Boston: South End Press.

Kinzer, S. 1993. For East German theme park: The bad old days. *New York Times*, November 9, A4.

Knack, R. E. 1996. Once upon a town. *Planning* (March): 10–13.

Knox, P., and P. J. Taylor, eds. 1996. *World cities in a world-system*. Cambridge: Cambridge University Press.

Kong, L., and B. Yeoh. 1994. Urban conservation in Singapore: A survey of state policies and popular attitudes. *Urban Studies* 31(2): 247–65.

Konrad, G., and I. Szelenyi. 1979. *Intellectuals on the road to class power*. New York: Harcourt Brace and Jovanovich.

Kratochvílová, K., and K. Kovářová. 1996. Prezident Havel kritizuje stavbu v proluce Myslbek. *Mladá Fronta Dnes*, September 3, 1–2.

Kuhn, B. 1990. Following the Mouse's tracks. Florida forecast '90. Special supplement to the *Orlando Sentinel*, March 4.

Kunerth, J. 1994. Orlando grows to number one. *Orlando Sentinel*, February 5.

La Croix, S. J., and D. J. Wolff. 1995. *The Asia Pacific airline industry: Economic boom and political conflict*. East-West Center Special Report 4. Honolulu: East-West Center.

Lancaster, C. 1996. Disney seeks deal on I-4 interchange. *Orlando Sentinel*, June 24.

Land speculators play Disney's money machine. 1971. *Business Week*, September 11.

Lanfant, M. 1972. *Les théories du loisir*. Paris: Presses Universitaires de France.

———. 1994. Identité, mémoire, patrimoine et "touristification" de nos sociétés. *Société* 46: 433–39.

Lanfant, M., and N. H. H. Graburn. 1994. International tourism reconsidered: The principle of an alternative. In V. H. Smith, and W. R. Eadington, eds., *Tourism alternatives, potentials and problems in the development of tourism*. Philadelphia: University of Pennsylvania Press.

Las Vegas no. 2 in hot travel spots. 1995. *Las Vegas Review-Journal*. May 11, 10D.

Lash, S., and J. Urry. 1994. *Economies of signs and space*. London: Sage.

Latham, J. 1994. Forecasts of international tourism. In C. D. Cooper and A. Lockwood, eds., *Progress in tourism, recreation, and hospitality management* 6: 273–82. Chichester: John Wiley.

Law, C. M. 1992. Urban tourism and its contribution to economic regeneration, *Urban Studies* 29(3/4): 599–618.

———. 1994. *Urban tourism: Attracting visitors to large cities*. London: Mansell.

Lawrence, D. G. 1968. Disney water bonds upheld by high court. *Orlando Evening Star*, November 28.

Lawrenzi, G. 1992. Las Vegas rolls out red carpet for families. *Las Vegas Business Press*, September 21, 30.

Laws of Florida. 1965. Chapter 67.

Lebowitz, L. 1991a. Critics pan Disney plan: Affordable housing at issue. *Orlando Sentinel*, November 16.

———. 1991b. Disney city idea sparks questions. *Orlando Sentinel*, July 6.

———. 1992a. Disney is building apartment complexes. *Orlando Sentinel*, February 8.

———. 1992b. Public-private partnership brings two toll roads to Osceola County. *Orlando Sentinel*, July 24.

Ledbetter, J. 1996. Merger overkill: When big media gets too big, what happens to open debate? *Village Voice*, January 16.

Lefebvre, H. 1991. *The production of space*. Oxford: Blackwell.

Leheny, D. 1995. A political economy of Asian sex tourism. *Annals of Tourism Research* 22(2): 367–84.

Leiper, N. 1989. Tourism and gambling. *GeoJournal* 19: 269–77.

Levenson, B. 1990. Disney bond coup has Orange County fuming. *Orlando Sentinel*, January 6.

Lever, Janet. 1983. *Soccer madness*. Chicago: University of Chicago Press.

Levin, D. 1993. *Modernity and the hegemony of vision*. Berkeley: University of California Press.

Levine, M. V. 1987. Downtown redevelopment as an urban growth strategy: A critical appraisal of the Baltimore renaissance. *Journal of Urban Affairs* 9(2): 103–24.

Levitt, R., ed. 1987. *Cities reborn*. Washington, D.C.: Urban Land Institute.

Levy, A. 1995. Antonin Brandejz: Hotel Pariz's "Last Mohican." *Prague Post*, September 27–October 3.

Lhotka, W. C. 1996. Gambling addict? State may let you deal yourself out. *St. Louis Post-Dispatch*, June 11, 8A.

Lietdke, R. 1991. *Wem gehoert die Republik? Die Konzerne und ihre Verflechtungen*. Frankfurt am Main: Eichborn.

Linsalata, P., and T. Ganey. 1994. Casinos prepare to throw the dice. *St. Louis Post-Dispatch*, April 27, 1, 12.

Logan, J. R., and H. M. Molotch. 1987. *Urban fortunes: The political economy of place*. Berkeley: University of California Press.

Long, V., and G. Wall. 1996. Successful tourism in Nusa Lembongan. *Indonesia Tourism Management* 17(1): 43–50.

Longman, J. 1995. A lot of optimism, but hurdles to leap. *New York Times*, July 19, B9, B12.

Lozato, J. 1988. *Géographie du tourisme*. Paris: Masson.

Lupo, A., F. Colcord, and E. P. Fowler. 1971. *Rites of way*. Boston: Little, Brown.

MacCannell, D. 1976. *The tourist: A new theory of the leisure class*. New York: Schocken.

———. 1990. *The tourist: A new theory of the leisure class*. 2d ed. New York: Shocken.

Mackie, V. 1992. Japan and Southeast Asia: The international division of labour and leisure. In D. Harrison, ed., *Tourism in the less developed countries*. London: Belhaven Press.

MacLeod, R. 1996. Jays' wings clipped by dwindling attendance. *Globe and Mail*, May 3.

Macnaghten, P., and J. Urry. 1997. *Contested natives*. London: Sage.

Major projects planned or under way in Las Vegas. 1995. *Las Vegas Business Press*, December 4, 17.

The mall, the merrier. 1994. *Economist* 332 (August 27): 55.

Malta Hotels and Restaurants Association. 1995. Seminar on product development. Leaflet. Malta: Malta Hotels and Restaurants Association.

Mannies, J., and M. Schlinkmann. 1994. Gambling's allure: Is it fiscal fuel or fool's gold? *St. Louis Post-Dispatch*, March 20, 1, 7A.

Manning, M. 1990. Sewer woes clog growth. *Las Vegas Sun*, September 19, 9A.

March, R. 1994. Tourism marketing myopia. *Tourism Management* 15(6): 411–15.

Martí, F. 1985. Cancún: Un utópico proyecto de banqueros convertido en realidad. A series of 14 articles. *Uno más Uno*, Mexico City, March 21–April 4.

Masák, M., R. Švácha, and J. Vybíral. 1995. *The trade fair palace in Prague*. Trans. A. Buchlerova. Prague: National Gallery in Prague.

Massachusetts General Laws. 1997. An act relative to the construction and financing of convention and exhibition centers in the Commonwealth. Chapter 152 of the Acts of 1997.

Massachusetts Office of Travel and Tourism. 1996. Tourism stats and facts. Boston: Massachusetts Office of Travel and Tourism.

Mathesian, C. 1996. If you can't bribe the owner, maybe you can buy the team. *Governing* (March): 42–45.

Mattox, J. 1995. Conventions rarely translate into big bucks for gaming. *Las Vegas Business Press*, December 18, 12.

Mayor's Office of the Boston Bicentennial. 1973. *Boston 200 Master Plan*. Boston: Mayor's Office of the Boston Bicentennial.

McCarthy, M. 1963. *Venice observed*. New York: Harcourt Brace.

McClintock, A. 1995. *Imperial leather*. New York: Routledge.

McCormack, G. 1991. The price of affluence: The political economy of Japanese leisure. *New Left Review* 188: 121–34.

McGee, T. G. 1991. The emergence of Desakota regions in Asia: Expanding a hypothesis. In N. Ginsburg, B. Koppel, and T. G. McGee, eds., *The extended metropolis: Settlement transition in Asia*, 3–25. Honolulu: University of Hawaii Press.

McKean, P. 1978. Towards a theoretical analysis of tourism: Economic dualism and cultural involution in Bali. In V. Smith, ed., *Hosts and guests*. Oxford: Basil Blackwell.

McPhee, M. R. 1996. International incident flares. *Boston Globe,* March 19.

McRee, B. R. 1994. Unity or division? The social meaning of guild ceremony in urban communities. In B. A. Hanawalt and K. L. Reyerson, eds., *City and spectacle in medieval Europe.* Minneapolis: University of Minnesota Press.

Meeting Manager. 1993. *Meeting Planners International.* September.

Meeting News. 1993. Vol. 17(12) (December): Riverton, N.J.: Miller Freeman.

Mehrhoff, A. W. 1992. *The gateway arch: Fact and symbol.* Bowling Green, Ohio: Bowling Green State University Popular Press.

Merkel, J. 1995. Fireworks on 42nd Street: Too much about economics, too little about architecture. *Competitions* 5(3) (May): 44–49.

Mervyn Jones, T. S. 1994. Theme parks in Japan. In C. P. Cooper and A. Lockwood, eds., *Progress in tourism, recreation and hospitality management.* Chichester: Wiley.

Meyers, S. L. 1996. Recalling Dodgers' flight, mayor makes his pitch for new stadium. *New York Times,* April 4.

Meyerson, M., and E. Banfield. 1966. *Boston: The job ahead.* Cambridge: Harvard University Press.

Midgam Consulting and Research Ltd. 1996. *Tourist's survey: March 1995–February 1996.* Jerusalem: Ministry of Tourism.

Ministry of Economy of the Czech Republic. 1995. *Tourism in the Czech Republic: 1993–1994.* Prague: Ministry of Economy.

———. 1996. *Incoming and outgoing tourism in the Czech Republic in 1995.* Prague: Ministry of Economy.

Ministry of Regional Development of the Czech Republic. 1996. *Tourism in the Czech Republic: 1996.* Prague: Ministry of Regional Development.

Ministry of Tourism and Israel Airport Authority. 1988. *Survey of tourists and residents departing by air 1986/7.* Jerusalem: Dahaf Research Institute.

Mishra, U. 1996. Room boom approaches as hotel market surges. *Boston Business Journal,* July 26.

Mitchell, M. 1996. Manufacturing in New York City: Design-oriented woodproducts. Master's thesis, Columbia University.

Mittelman, J., ed. 1996. Globalization: Critical reflections. *International Political Economy Yearbook* 9. Boulder, Colo.: Lynne Rienner.

Moehring, E. 1995. *Resort city in the Sunbelt: Las Vegas, 1930–1970.* 2d ed. Reno: University of Nevada Press.

Molina, S., M. R. Woog, and F. Cuamea. 1986. Turismo alternativo (Un acercamiento crítico y conceptual). *Nuevo Tiempo Libre México.*

Mommass, H., and H. Van der Poel. 1989. Changes in economy, politics and lifestyles: An essay on the restructuring of urban leisure. In P. Bramham, I. Henry, H. Mommass, and H. Van der Poel, eds., *Leisure and urban processes: Critical studies of leisure policy in West European cities.* London: Routledge.

Monthly Casino Review. 1993. Prudential Securities Incorporated. June.

Moore, T. 1995. Servicing conventions means cash for many. *Las Vegas Business Press,* December 18, 15.

Morrison, J. A. 1996. LV not pocketing tourist taxes. *Las Vegas Review-Journal,* January 22, 1B.

Moskowitz, D. K. 1993. "Vast underemployment" clogs LV job market. *Las Vegas Business Press,* March 8, 3.

Mullins, P. 1991. Tourism urbanization. *International Journal of Urban and Regional Research* 15(3): 326–42.

———. 1994. Class relations and tourism urbanization: The regeneration of the petite bourgeoisie and the emergence of a new urban form. *International Journal of Urban and Regional Research* 18(4): 591–608.

Mulvey, I. 1989. *Visual and other pleasures.* London: Macmillan.

Municipality of Jerusalem and the Israeli Ministry of Tourism and East Jerusalem Development Ltd. 1996. *Development of tourism infrastructure in Jerusalem, 1996–2000* (in Hebrew). Jerusalem: Municipality of Jerusalem.

Murray, A. 1991. No money, no honey: A study of street traders and prostitutes in Jakarta. Singapore: Oxford University Press.

Musil, J. 1968. The development of Prague's ecological structure. In R. E. Pahl, ed., *Readings in urban sociology.* Oxford: Pergamon Press.

———. 1980. *Urbanization in socialist countries.* White Plains, N.Y.: Sharpe.

———. 1993. Changing urban systems in post-communist societies in Central Europe. *Urban Studies* 30(6): 899–905.

Musil, J., and R. J. Pohoryles. 1993. *The role of the cities in Central Europe in the process of reconstruction.* Vienna: ICCR-Project AS-CEC.

Mutchler, T. 1992. Atlantic City employment numbers aren't adding up. *Las Vegas Review-Journal,* October 30, 10.

Myerson, A. R. 1996a. Forging an Olympic legacy. *New York Times,* August 2, D1, D5.

———. 1996b. A wave of casinos hits Mississippi Gulf Coast. *New York Times,* July 9, D1, D5.

Neill, W. J. V. 1993. Physical planning and image enhancement: Recent developments in Belfast. *International Journal of Urban and Regional Research* 17(4): 595–609.

Nevada no. 1 in job growth. 1996. *Las Vegas Review-Journal,* February 13: 8D.

The new bohemians. 1994. *Economist* (October 22): 23.

New York City Convention and Visitors Bureau. 1996. *New York City visitor statistics.* New York: New York City Convention and Visitors Bureau.

New York City Economic Policy and Marketing Group. 1993. *Film and televi-*

sion production in New York City. New York: New York City Economic Policy and Marketing Group.

New York State Urban Development Corporation. 1993. *42nd Street now!* New York: New York State Urban Development Corporation.

Nickerson, N. P. 1994. Tourism and gambling: Content analysis. *Annals of Tourism Research* 22: 53–66.

Nolan, M. L., and S. Nolan. 1992. Religious sites as tourism attractions in Europe. *Annals of Tourism Research* 19(1): 68–78.

Norris, J., and G. Wall. 1994. Gender and tourism. In C. P. Cooper and A. Lockwood, eds., *Progress in tourism, recreation, and hospitality management*: 57–78. Chichester: John Wiley.

Northeastern University. 1967. *Inventory and analysis of recreation, tourism and vacationing in Eastern Massachusetts.* Boston: Massachusetts Department of Commerce and Development.

Northern Economic Planners. 1995. The Appalachian Mountain Club's hut system and its contribution to the White Mountains regional economy, 1994–95. Gorham, N.H.: Appalachian Mountain Club.

Novak-Branch, F. 1983. The Disney World effect. Senior honors thesis, Rollins College.

No. 1 in sight with Disney help. 1990. Editorial. *Orlando Sentinel,* March 4.

O'Connor, T. H. 1984. *Bibles, brahmins, and bosses: A short history of Boston.* 2d ed. Boston: Trustees of the Public Library of the City of Boston.

———. 1993. *Building a new Boston.* Boston: Northeastern University Press.

Organization for Economic Cooperation and Development. 1993. *Tourism policy and international tourism in OECD Countries, 1990–1991.* Paris: O.E.C.D.

Osterman, P. 1991. Gains from growth? The impact of full employment on poverty in Boston. In C. Jencks and P. Peterson, eds., *The Urban Underclass.* Washington: The Brookings Institute.

Ousby, I. 1990. *The Englishman's England.* Cambridge: Cambridge University Press.

Owen, C. 1992. Building a relationship between government and tourism. *Tourism Management* 13(4): 358–62.

Owen, J. C. 1993. Indianapolis, Indiana. In A. T. Johnson, ed., *Minor league baseball and local economic development.* Urbana: University of Illinois Press.

Pagano, M. A., and A. O'M. Bowman. 1995. *Markets and images: Development policy in America's cities.* Baltimore: Johns Hopkins University Press.

Page, S. 1995. *Urban tourism.* London: Routledge.

Palermo, D. 1993. Corporations dominate Nevada gaming. *Las Vegas Review-Journal,* June 30, 9E.

———. 1994. New properties will be geared more toward adults. *Las Vegas Review-Journal/Sun,* February 6, 14E.

Parker, R. E., and J. R. Feagin. 1992. Military spending in free enterprise cities: The military-industrial complex in Houston and Las Vegas. In A. Kirby, ed., The Pentagon and the cities, *Urban Affairs Annual Reviews* 40: 100–25. Newbury Park, Calif.: Sage.

Parnwell, M. 1993. Environmental issues and tourism in Thailand. In M. Hitchcock, V. King, and M. Parnell, eds., *Tourism in Southeast Asia*. London: Routledge.

Parr, M. 1995. *Small world*. Stockport: Dewi Lewis.

Paul, A., and A. Kleingartner. 1994. Flexible production and the transformation of industrial relations in the motion picture and television industry. In *Industrial and Labor Relations Review* 47(4) (July): 663–78.

Pearce, D. 1987. Tourism today (a geographical analysis). London: Longman, Scientifical and Technical.

Perlman, E. 1996. The gambling glut. *Governing* 9(8): 49–56.

Perniciaro, R. C. 1995. Casino gambling in Atlantic City: Lessons for economic developers. *Economic Development Review* 13: 47–50.

Peterson, I. 1995. After 20 years, Atlantic City starts to reap casinos' benefits. *New York Times*, December 26, A1, B5.

Peterson, P. 1981. *City limits*. Chicago: University of Chicago.

Phares, D., and M. S. Rosentraub. 1997. Reviving the glory of days past: St. Louis's blitz to save its image, identity, and teams. In M. S. Rosentraub, *Major league losers: The real cost of sports and who's paying for it*. New York: Basic.

Pileggi, N. 1995. *Casino*. New York: Simon and Schuster.

Pizam, A., and J. Pokela. 1985. The perceived impacts of casino gambling on a community. *Annals of Tourism Research* 12: 147–65.

PKF Consulting. 1996. *Trends in the Hotel Industry* 15 (January): 1.

Pledger, M. 1994. Las Vegas sets pace for resorts. *Las Vegas Review-Journal*, June 2, 9C.

———. 1995a. Courting families no more. *Las Vegas Review-Journal*, October 29, 1A.

———. 1995b. Huge computer show brings people, traffic. *Las Vegas Review-Journal*, November 13, 1A.

Popkin, J. 1994. America's gambling craze. *U.S. News and World Report*, March 14, 42–44.

Port Authority of New York and New Jersey. 1994. *Destination New York–New Jersey: Tourism and travel to the metropolitan region*, pt. 2 of *Tourism and the arts in the New York–New Jersey Region*. New York: Port Authority.

Porteous, J. 1985. Smellscape. *Progress in Human Geography* 9: 356–78.

———. 1990. *Landscapes of the mind: Worlds of sense and metaphor*. Toronto: Toronto University Press.

Porter, M. E. 1995. The competitive advantage of the inner city. *Harvard Business Review* 73: 55–71.

Pratt, M. 1992. *Imperial eyes*. London: Routledge.

Prawer, J. 1972. *The Latin kingdom of Jerusalem: European colonialism in the Middle Ages*. London: Weidenfeld and Nicolson.

Pretes, M. 1995. Postmodern tourism: The Santa Claus industry. *Annals of Tourism Research* 22(1): 1–15.

Prime Minister's Office, Japan, 1990. *Kankoo haksho* (Tourism white paper). Tokyo: Ministry of Finance Press.

Promus Companies, Inc. 1995. *Economic impact of excursion riverboat casino entertainment*. Memphis: The Promus Companies, Inc.

Pronovost, G. 1994. Loisir et travail. In M. De Coster and F. Pichault, eds., *Traité de sociologie du travail*. Paris: De Boeck Université.

Pruitt, D., and S. LaFont. 1995. For love and money: Romance tourism in Jamaica. *Annals of Tourism Research* 22: 422–40.

Przybys, J. 1996. Tip city: Las Vegans' generosity touches all types of workers. *Las Vegas Review-Journal*, August 6, 1E.

Pulley, B. 1995a. A mix of glamour and hardball won Disney a piece of 42nd Street. *New York Times*, July 29.

———. 1995b. A restoration is announced for 42nd Street. *New York Times*, July 20.

———. 1995c. Tussaud's and movie chain join Disney in 42nd Street project. *New York Times*, July 16.

Quirk, J., and R. D. Fort. 1992. *Paydirt: The business of professional team sports*. Princeton: Princeton University Press.

Raban, J. 1986. *Coasting*. London: Picador.

Ramírez Saiz, J. M. 1986. *Turismo y medio ambiente: El caso de Acapulco*. Mexico City, Mexico: Universidad Autónoma Metropolitana Xochimilco.

Rapp, L. 1995. Toward French electronic highways. The new legal status of data transmissions in France. In L. Rapp, ed., *Telecommunications and Space Journal* 2: 231–46.

Readers Choice Awards. 1996. *Condé Nast Traveler*, October.

Readers' poll results. 1995. *Money*. September, 139.

Reedy Creek Improvement District. 1990. *Public review draft comprehensive plan*. City of Lake Buena Vista and City of Bay Lake, Fla.: Reedy Creek Improvement District.

Rich, W. C. 1990. The politics of casino gambling. *Urban Affairs Quarterly* 26: 274–98.

Richards, D. 1994. Disney does Broadway, dancing spoons and all. *New York Times*, April 19.

Richter, L. 1989. *The politics of tourism in Asia*. Honolulu: University of Hawaii Press.

————. 1992. Political instability and tourism in the Third World. In D. Harrison, ed., *Tourism in the less developed countries*. London: Routledge.

————. 1993. Tourism policy-making in Southeast Asia. In M. Hitchcock, V. King, and M. Parnell, eds., *Tourism in Southeast Asia*. London: Routledge.

————. 1994. The political dimensions of tourism. In J. R. Ritchie and C. R. Goeldner, eds., *Travel, tourism and hospitality research: A handbook for managers and researchers*. 2d ed. New York: Wiley.

Rimmer, P. 1992. Japan's "resort archipelago": Creating regions of fun, pleasure, relaxation, and recreation. *Society and Space* 24: 1599–1625.

————. 1994. Japanese investment in golf course development: Australia-Japan links. *International Journal of Urban and Regional Research* 18: 234–55.

Rinschede, G. 1992. Forms of religious tourism. *Annals of Tourism Research* 19(1): 51–67.

Ritchie, J. R. B. 1984. Assessing the impact of hallmark events: Conceptual and research issues. *Journal of Travel Research* 23(1): 2–11.

Ritchie, J. R. B., and B. H. Smith. 1991. The impact of a mega-event on host region awareness: A longitudinal study. *Journal of Travel Research* 30(1): 3–10.

Roche, E. M. 1997. "Cyberopolis": The cybernetic city faces the global economy. In M. Crahan and A. Vervoulias-Bush, eds., *The city and foreign policy*. New York: Council on Foreign Relations.

Roche, M. 1994. Mega events and urban policy. *Annals of Tourism Research* 21(1): 1–19.

Rodaway, P. 1994. *Sensuous geographies*. London: Routledge.

Rogers, K. 1996. EPA faults county on air quality. *Las Vegas Review-Journal*, August 7, 1.

Rojek, C. 1997. Indexing, dragging and the social construction of tourist sights. In C. Rojek and J. Urry, eds., *Touring cultures*. London: Routledge.

Room rates make for hospitable hotel market. 1996. *Banker and Tradesman*, July 29.

Roost, F. (forthcoming). Recreating the city as entertainment center: The media industry's role in the transformation of Times Square and Potsdamer Platz. *Journal of Urban Technology*.

Rorty, R. 1980. Philosophy and the mirror of nature. Oxford: Blackwell.

Rosentraub, M. S., D. W. Swindell, M. Przybylski, and D. R. Mullins. 1994. Sports and downtown development strategy: If you build it, will jobs come? *Journal of Urban Affairs* 16 (3): 221–39.

Rotzer, F. 1995. *Die Telepolis: Urbanitat im digitalen Zeitalter*. Mannheim: Bollmann.

Roy, R. 1994. Six miles of beltway call for new map. *Orlando Sentinel*, July 27.

————. 1995. Hood favors support group to promote I-4. *Orlando Sentinel*, September 15.

Russell, D. 1990. Clark County high school dropout rate ranks highest. *Las Vegas Review-Journal*, August 17, 6B.

Sagalyn, L. B. 1989. Measuring financial returns when the city acts as an investor: Boston and Faneuil Hall Marketplace. *Real Estate Issues* (Fall/Winter): 7–15.

Sanders, H. T. 1992. Building the convention city: Politics, finance and public investment in urban America. *Journal of Urban Affairs* 14: 135–59.

Sassen, S. 1991. *The global city*. Princeton: Princeton University Press.

———. 1994. *Cities in a world economy*. Thousand Oaks, Calif.: Pine Forge, Sage Press.

———. 1997. Electronic space and power. *Journal of Urban Technology*. 4(1): 1–18.

———. 1998. Globalization and its discontents. New York: Free Press.

Sassen, S., and M. Mitchell. 1996. Urban manufacturing. In C. Loomis, ed., *Manufacturing in cities*. Princeton: Princeton Architectural Press.

Savage, M., J. Barlow, A. Dicken, and T. Fielding. 1992. *Property, bureaucracy and culture*. London: Routledge.

Schauppner, S. 1987. An interview with Bill Rawn. *Boston Preservation Alliance Letter* 8(3): 4–5.

Schmalz, J. 1987. Sun sets on show that redefined a city. *New York Times*, May 18, A1, A14.

Scott, M. S. 1995. Entertainment in cyberspace. *Black Enterprise* 47(4) (December): 66-72.

Secretaría de Turismo. 1986. Mercado de trabajo en centros turísticos. Internal report. Mexico City: FONATUR.

Sedaris, D. 1994. Too much fun on 57th Street: The new New York that only tourists see. *New York Magazine*, September 5, 30–39.

Seifel, E. M. 1979. Displacement: The negative environmental impact of urban renewal in the south end of Boston. Master's thesis, Massachusetts Institute of Technology.

Sennett, R. 1990. *The conscience of the eye*. New York: Knopf.

Sharratt, B. 1989. Communications and image studies: Notes after Raymond Williams. *Comparative Criticism* 11: 29–50

Shaw, G., and A. M. Williams. 1994. *Critical issues in tourism: A geographical perspective*. Oxford: Blackwell.

Sherry, A., M. Lee, and M. Varikiotis. 1995. For lust or money. *Far Eastern Economic Review*, December 14, 22–23.

Shields, R. 1991. *Places on the margin (alternative geographies of modernity)*. London: Routledge.

Sinclair, M., and R. Vokes. 1993. The economics of tourism in Asia and the Pacific. In M. Hitchcock, V. King, and M. Parnell, eds., *Tourism in Southeast Asia*. London: Routledge.

Sklair, L. 1991. *Sociology of the global system*. London: Harvester Wheatsheaf.

————. 1994a. The culture-ideology of consumerism in urban China: Some findings from a survey in Shanghai. *Research in Consumer Behavior* 7: 259–62.

————. 1994b. Global sociology and global environmental change. In M. Redclift and T. Benton, eds., *Social theory and the global environment*. London: Routledge.

————. 1996. Globalization and society. In M. Warner, ed., *International encyclopedia of business and management*. London: Routledge.

Slater, D. 1995. Photography and modern vision: The spectacle of "natural magic." In C. Jenks, ed., *Visual culture*. London: Routledge.

Slatin, P. 1994. Wanted: Studios for TV productions. *New York Times*, April 2.

Smith, A. 1991. *The age of behemoths: The globalization of mass media firms*. New York: Priority Press.

Smith, D. 1980. New to Britain: A study of some new developments in tourist attractions. London: English Tourist Board; as cited in G. Shaw and A. M. Williams, *Critical issues in tourism*, Cambridge, Mass.: Blackwell.

Smith, H. 1996. Tourism boomed in 1995. *Las Vegas Review-Journal*, February 13, 7D.

Smith, N., B. Duncan, and L. Reid. 1994. From disinvestment to reinvestment: Mapping the urban "frontier" in the Lower East Side. In J. Abu-Lughod, ed., *From urban village to East Village*. Cambridge, Mass.: Blackwell.

Smith, R. 1992. Coastal urbanization: Tourist development in the Asia Pacific. *Built Environment* 18(1): 27–40.

Smith, V. 1992. Boracay, Philippines: A case study in "alternative" tourism. In V. Smith and W. Eadington, eds., *Tourism alternatives*. Philadelphia: University of Pennsylvania Press.

Smith, V. L. 1992. The quest in guest. *Annals of Tourism Research* 19: 1–17.

Smothers, R. 1991. No hits, no runs, one error: The dome. *New York Times*, June 15.

Sontag, S. 1979. *On photography*. Harmondsworth: Penguin.

Sorkin, M., ed. 1992. *Variations on a theme park: The new American city and the end of public space*. New York: Hill and Wang.

Southworth, S., and M. Southworth. 1984. *A.I.A. guide to Boston*. Chester, Mass.: Globe Pequot Press.

Spitz, J. J. 1996. Airport survey ranks Orlando 4th in the world. *Orlando Sentinel*, March 26.

Squires, G. D., ed. 1989. *Unequal partnerships: The political economy of urban redevelopment in postwar America*. New Brunswick: Rutgers University Press.

Stallybrass, P., and A. White. 1986. *The politics and poetics of transgression*. London: Methuen.

Stanback, T. 1985. The changing fortunes of metropolitan economies. In M. Castells, ed., *High techonology, space, and society*. Beverly Hills: Sage.

Standard and Poor. 1995. *Industry Surveys* 1: 36–47.

Stansfield, C. 1978. Atlantic City and the resort cycle: Background to the legalization of gambling. *Annals of Tourism Research* 5: 238–51.

Stansfield, C. A., and J. E. Rickert. 1970. The recreational business district. *Journal of Leisure Research* 2(2): 213–25.

Stark, D. 1992. The great transformation? Social change in Eastern Europe. *Contemporary Sociology* 21(2): 229–304.

State of Nevada. 1994. *Nevada statistical abstract, 1994*. Department of Administration. Carson City: State of Nevada.

State of Nevada. 1996. Fax, Department of Employment, Training and Rehabilitation, Information Development and Processing. Carson City: State of Nevada, February 29.

Steinhauer, A. 1996a. Conventional wisdom. *Las Vegas Review-Journal*, August 12, 1D.

———. 1996b. LV best spot for travel. *Las Vegas Review-Journal* and *Las Vegas Sun*, May 25, 1A.

Stepick, A. 1989. Miami's two informal sectors. In A. Portes, M. Castells, and L. Benton, eds., *The informal economy*. Baltimore: Johns Hopkins University Press.

Sterngold, J. 1995. Federal study would weigh costs of gambling's spread. *New York Times*, November 24, A1.

Sternlieb, G., and J. W. Hughes. 1983. *The Atlantic City gamble*. Cambridge: Harvard University Press.

Stone, C. N. 1987a. The study of the politics of urban development. In C. N. Stone and H. T. Sanders, eds., *The politics of urban development*, 3–24. Lawrence: University Press of Kansas.

———. 1987b. Summing up: Urban regimes, development policy, and political arrangements. In C. N. Stone and H. T. Sanders, eds., *The politics of urban development*. Lawrence: University Press of Kansas.

———. 1989. *Regime politics: Governing Atlanta, 1946–1988*. Lawrence: University Press of Kansas.

Storper, M., and R. Walker. 1989. *The capitalist imperative: Territory, technology, and industrial growth*. New York: Basil Blackwell.

Strauss, A. L. 1961. *Images of the American city*. Glencoe, Ill.: Free Press of Glencoe.

Striesand, B. 1994. Las Vegas gamboling. *U.S. News and World Report*, January 31, 61.

Successful Meetings. 1983. *Convention and exhibit market profile.* November. New York: Bill Communications, Inc.

Successful Meetings. 1993. *State of the industry, 1993.* July. New York: Bill Communications, Inc.

Sullivan, N. J. 1987. *The Dodgers move west.* New York: Oxford University Press.

Suttles, G. D. 1985. The cumulative textures of local urban culture. *American Journal of Sociology* 90(2): 282–304.

Swanstrom, T. 1985. *The crisis of growth politics: Cleveland, Kucinich, and the challenge of urban populism.* Philadelphia: Temple University Press.

Sýkora, L. 1993. City in transition: The role of rent gaps in Prague's revitalization. *Tijdschrift voor Economische en Sociale Geografie* 84(4): 281–93.

———. 1994. Local urban restructuring as a mirror of globalization processes: Prague in the 1990s. *Urban Studies* 31:7

Tabak, L. 1993. How much do we want their money? *Ingram's,* February, 30.

———. 1994. Wild about convention centers. *Atlantic,* April, 28–34.

Taskir Survey and Research Ltd. 1995. *Survey of tourists departing from Israel, 1994.* Jerusalem: Ministry of Tourism.

Taylor, G. 1994. Unions say no to offer by Disney. *Orlando Sentinel,* November 2.

Taylor, J. 1994. *A dream of England.* Manchester: Manchester University Press.

Teaford, J. C. 1990. *The rough road to renaissance: Urban revitalization in America, 1940–1985.* Baltimore: Johns Hopkins University Press.

Teibel, A. 1994. The pros and cons of second-tier cities. *Convene* 9(1): 32–37. Birmingham, Ala.: Professional Convention Management Association.

Tester, K., ed. 1995. *The flâneur.* London: Routledge.

Thaitakoo, D. 1994. Phuket: Urban conservation versus tourism. In M. Askew and W. Logan, eds., *Cultural identity and urban change in Southeast Asia.* Geelong, Australia: Deakin University Press.

Theroux, P. 1995. *The pillars of Hercules: A grand tour of the Mediterranean.* New York: G. P. Putnam's Sons.

Thomas, B. 1976. *Walt Disney: An American original.* New York: Simon and Schuster.

Thompson, J. M. 1979. Boston's Faneuil Hall. *Urban Design International* 1.

———. 1994. Three essays: The city and the millennium. Unpublished lecture notes.

Tiger, L. 1992. *The pursuit of pleasure.* Boston: Little, Brown.

Tighe, A. J. 1985. Cultural tourism in the U.S.A. *Tourism Management* 6(4): 234–51.

Tipton, V. 1993. Travel agents: A visit here removes a few bad impressions. *St. Louis Post-Dispatch,* September 22.

Tourism a major revenue source all year round. 1995. Sponsored section on the Czech Republic, *International Herald Tribune,* June 26, 18.

Towner, J. 1985. The grand tour: A key phase in the history of tourism. *Annals of Tourism Research* 12(3): 297–333.

Townsend, D. 1994. Denpasar, Bali: Triumph of the profane. In M. Askew and W. Logan, eds., *Cultural identity and urban change in Southeast Asia*. Geelong, Australia: Deakin University Press.

Tracy, D. 1990. Road overload. *Orlando Sentinel*, March 4.

Traisawasdichai, M. 1995. Chasing the little white ball. *New Internationalist* 263 (January): 16–17.

Turner, V. 1973. The center out there: Pilgrim's goal. *History of Religions* 12: 191–230.

Turner, V., and E. Turner. 1978. *Image and pilgrimage in Christian culture: Anthropological perspectives*. Oxford: Basil Blackwell.

U.S. Department of Commerce. 1994a. *Statistical abstract of the United States, 1994*. Washington, D.C.: U.S. Government Printing Office.

U.S. Department of Commerce. 1994b. *U.S. Industrial Outlook 1994*. Washington, D.C.: U.S. Government Printing Office.

U.S. Department of Housing and Urban Development. 1982. *The president's national urban policy report*. Washington, D.C.: U.S. Government Printing Office.

United States Bicentennial World Exposition Corporation. 1969. *United States Bicentennial Exposition, Boston, 1976*. Technical report. Boston: United States Bicentennial World Exposition Corporation.

Urban League of Pittsburgh. 1994. Riverboat gambling in Pittsburgh. Pittsburgh: The Urban League of Pittsburgh.

Urry, J. 1990. *The tourist gaze: Leisure and travel in contemporary societies*. London: Sage.

———. 1992. The tourist gaze revisited. *American Behavioral Scientist* 36: 172–86.

———. 1994. Time, leisure and social identity. *Time and Society* 3: 131–49.

———. 1995. *Consuming places*. New York: Routledge.

———. 1996. How societies remember the past. In S. Macdonald and G. Fyfe, eds., *Sociological review monograph: Theorizing museums*. Oxford: Blackwell.

Varikiotis, M., S. Sakamaki, and G. Silverman. 1995. On the margin: Organised crime profits from the flesh trade. *Far Eastern Economic Review*, December 14, 26–27.

Vaughan, V. 1994. Disney workers vote to reject contract offer. *Orlando Sentinel*, December 2.

Venturi, R., D. Scott Brown, and S. Izenour. 1972. *Learning from Las Vegas*. Cambridge: MIT Press.

———. 1977. *Learning from Las Vegas*. Rev. ed. Cambridge: MIT Press.

Verducci, T. Good hands people. *Sports Illustrated*, April 1, 52–66.

Virilio, P. 1977. *Speed and politics*. New York: Semiotext(e).

————. 1988. The work of art in the age of electronic reproduction. *Block* 14: 4–7.

————. 1991. *Lost dimension*. New York: Semiotext(e).

Vogel, E. 1994. Nevada has top ranking in dropouts. *Las Vegas Review-Journal*, March 8, 1–2A.

Volberg, R. A. 1995. *Gambling and problem gambling in Iowa*. Des Moines, Iowa: Iowa Department of Human Services.

Volkman, E. 1995. Travel agents bank on Czechs' wandering feet. *Prague Post*, October 11–17, 8

Waddell, L. 1994. Teenage gambling. *Las Vegas Review-Journal*, February 27, D2.

Wade, R. C. 1959. *The urban frontier: Pioneer life in early Pittsburgh, Cincinnati, Lexington, Louisville, and St. Louis*. Chicago: University of Chicago Press.

Wall, G. 1996. Perspectives on tourism in selected Balinese villages. *Annals of Tourism Research* 23(1): 123–37.

Walsh, M. 1986: It's not easy living with the Mouse. *Florida Trend*, December, 74–75.

Walt Disney Productions. 1967. Disney executive outlines legislative proposals (press release). Orlando: Disney World Depository, Orlando Public Library.

————. 1976. The first 20 years . . . from Disneyland to Walt Disney World (press release). Orlando: Disney World Depository, Orlando Public Library.

————. 1981. Florida's Disney decade. Film. Los Angeles: Walt Disney Company Archives.

Walton, J. 1993. Tourism and economic development in ASEAN. In M. Hitchcock, V. King, and M. Parnell, eds., *Tourism in Southeast Asia*, 214–23. London: Routledge.

Warren, S. 1994. Disneyfication of the metropolis: Popular resistance in Seattle. *Journal of Urban Affairs* 16(2): 89–107.

Watson, G. L., and J. P. Kopachevsky. 1994. Interpretations of tourism as commodity. *Annals of Tourism Research* 21(3): 643–60.

WEFA Group. 1994. *The direct impact of the casino industry: Purchase and employment effects in the major supply industries*. Bala-Cynwyd, Pa.: The WEFA Group.

Weistart, J. C. 1986. League control of market opportunities: A perspective on competition and cooperation in the sports industry. *Duke Law Journal* (December).

Wheeler, M. 1993. Tourism marketers in local government. *Annals of Tourism Research* 20: 354–83.

Whelan, R. K. 1989. New Orleans: Public-private partnerships and uneven development. In G. D. Squires, ed., *Unequal partnerships*. New Brunswick: Rutgers University Press.

Whitehill, W. M. 1968. *Boston: A topographical history*. 2d ed. Cambridge: Belknap Press of Harvard University Press.

Whitford, D. 1993. *Playing hardball: The business of professional team sports*. Princeton: Princeton University Press.

Wilson, A. 1992. *Culture of nature*. Oxford: Blackwell.

Wilson, S. 1996. Marking history's path in Boston. *Boston Sunday Globe,* April 21.

Wolf, D. L. 1992. *Factory daughters: Gender, household dynamics, and rural industrialisation in Java*. Berkeley: University of California Press.

Wood, R. L. 1993. Tourism, culture and the sociology of development. In M. Hitchcock, V. King, and M. Parnell, eds., *Tourism in Southeast Asia*. London: Routledge.

World Tourism Organization. 1995a. *Compendium of tourism statistics, 1989–1993*. Madrid: World Tourism Organization.

———. 1995b. *Global tourism forecasts to the year 2000 and beyond: The world*. Vol. 1. Madrid: World Tourism Organization.

———. 1995c. *Yearbook of tourism statistics*. Vol. 1, 47th ed. Madrid: World Tourism Organization.

———. 1996. *Compendium of tourism statistics*. Madrid: World Tourism Organization.

Wren, C. 1992. Will apartheid's prison become a tourist mecca? *New York Times,* February 28, A-4.

Wright, E. O. 1985. *Classes*. London: Verso.

Wright, P. 1985. *On living in an old country*. London: Verso.

Yakubik, P. 1995. Mom 'n pop shops squeezed off the Strip. *Las Vegas Business Press,* May 29, 1–20.

Zelinsky, W. 1973. *The cultural geography of the United States*. Englewood Cliffs, N.J.: Prentice-Hall.

Zimbalist, A. 1992 Baseball and billions: A probing look inside the big business of our nation. New York: Basic.

Zukal, J. 1993 Podnikani v Europe. *Lidové noviny,* April 12.

Zukin, S. 1989. *Loft living*. 2d ed. New Brunswick: Rutgers University Press.

———. 1991. *Landscapes of power: From Detroit to Disney World*. Berkeley: University of California Press.

———. 1995. *The cultures of cities*. Cambridge, Mass.: Blackwell.

Index